Eight Hateful Miles

*A sideline pass
to Tennessee's fiercest rivalry*

Eight Hateful Miles

*A sideline pass
to Tennessee's fiercest rivalry*

Stephen Hargis

Fresh Ink Group
Guntersville

Eight Hateful Miles:
A sideline pass
to Tennessee's fiercest rivalry

Copyright © 2018
by Stephen Hargis
All rights reserved

Fresh Ink Group
An Imprint of:
The Fresh Ink Group, LLC
Box 931
Guntersville, AL 35976
Email: info@FreshInkGroup.com
www.FreshInkGroup.com

Edition 1.0   2018

Cover by Matt McClane
Photo editorial by Geez/FIG
Book design by Amit Dey

Photo images used with permission from:
Chattanooga Times Free Press
University of Tennessee
Cindy Dodson Desrosier
Gene Fuller
Marion County High School
South Pittsburg High School

Except as permitted under the U.S. Copyright Act of 1976, no part of this publication may be reproduced, distributed, or transmitted in any form or by any means, or stored in a database or retrieval system, without prior written permission of the publisher.

Cataloging-in-Publication Recommendations:
SPO015000   SPORTS & RECREATION / Football
SPO019000   SPORTS & RECREATION / History
SPO000000   SPORTS & RECREATION / General

Library of Congress Control Number: 2018954292

ISBN-13: 978-1-936442-73-7 Papercover
ISBN-13: 978-1-936442-79-9 Hardcover
ISBN-13: 978-1-936442-74-4 Ebooks

For Riley and Lauren

My favorite moments in life
have all come from being your dad.

Acknowledgements

I would like to sincerely thank everyone who gave their valuable time to help bring so much of the insight you'll find in the pages ahead. This book began as an idea, then sat in a corner of my home office for several years, disguised as unorganized random notes or thoughts that I had scribbled down since I began working as a sports writer in Chattanooga in 1990. Much of what you'll read are things I witnessed personally — either walking the sidelines or by being allowed in the team locker rooms before, during and after big games through the years. The rest was filled in through a great deal of research and interviewing those willing to share their memories.

The book finally came to life through a lot of weekends and late nights of writing into the wee hours. I wanted it to be a true and honest depiction of the sights, sounds and feelings that give the rivalry life so the biggest change from the countless newspaper stories I've written was that I took away the filter and allowed each story to be told as real and raw as real life. As crazy as some of the antics you're about to read may seem, just know this — it all actually happened. And that's part of what made this project so much fun to write and what makes this rivalry unequaled throughout Tennessee.

There are far too many folks for me to thank individually, but a few I would like to recognize for their help in answering my endless questions are Marion County's Johnny Grimes and David Moore who not only read over the chapters involving their team but also pointed me in the right direction for others to speak with. Also Ken Colquette, who was extremely patient with a young reporter's ignorant questions when I began my career. As intimidating as he could be to interview back then, he was far more gracious in taking time to explain the ins and outs of his program and over time I came to understand why so many of his players respect and appreciate him.

I also have to thank South Pittsburg's Vic Grider and Danny Wilson, who read over the chapters involving the Pirates and helped make sure nothing was overlooked in putting this project together. Also to my friend and neighbor Boochie Moore and Mrs. Gladys Wooten for connecting me with so many resources from the McReynolds High School community.

To Mark Griffith and Pam Griffith, thank you for trusting me to tell Kennedy's story.

Special thanks to Chuck Thurmond — Marion County Class of 1984 — for your time and keen eye in taking the photos for the cover and to Matt McClane for your talent in creating the cover design.

I'd like each of these folks to know I appreciate your help and your friendship.

Finally, a special thank you to Amanda, who was incredibly supportive throughout the entire process. For all the nights I spent writing instead of having dinner together, words fail to express how much I appreciate your constant encouragement.

I would like to dedicate the portions of this book that focus on South Pittsburg to the memory of faithful Pirates Jim "Hoodie" Dunwoody and Bebe Fuqua. They and their families will always have a special place in my memories of growing up in the town I still call home. I would also like to dedicate the Marion County portions in memory of Rob Owens, who never missed a chance to support his Warriors.

At the beginning of each chapter I have listed a tone-setter — either a song lyric, famous quote or inspirational words to set up the overall theme of the corresponding chapter. If I had a quote to describe my own feelings after completing this project it would be the words of American author Dorothy Parker who said, "I often hate writing. But I love having written."

Despite my frustration with bouts of writer's block and being my own worst critic, as well as the struggle to find time to dedicate toward completing this book, I am very proud of the finished product. I hope you, my friend, enjoy it as well.

Stephen is a 1989 South Pittsburg graduate and has covered sports in the tri-state area since the spring of 1990. He was promoted to Sports Editor of the Chattanooga Times Free Press in February of 2015 and was inducted into the Chattanooga Sports Hall of Fame in the spring of 2017.

Stephen is one of the most decorated writers in the TFP newsroom, having won more than 60 awards at the state, regional and national level ranging from investigative to feature to news writing. He was named one of the top 10 sports writers in the nation at the Associated Press Sports Editors' conference in Kissimmee Fla. and has twice been recognized by the Society of Professional Journalists with Green Eyeshade awards, where his work was noted for its high standards of ethical journalism. He became the first writer from the TFP to be named the state's top overall sports writer by the Associated Press Media Editors, is the only writer from the staff to have won the prestigious Lawrenceburg Quarterback Club's Sports Writer of the Year and has been named the state's overall Writer of the Year three times. He was the recipient of an Associated Press national award, has been named the state's top prep writer 17 times and was recognized with the TSSAA's Sportsmanship Award for Contributor of the Year in the state twice.

Besides prep sports, Stephen has covered the NFL's Atlanta Falcons and Tennessee Titans, multiple NASCAR events including the Daytona 500, the Atlanta Braves, SEC football championship game, University of Tennessee football as well as Vols men's and women's basketball, UTC football and won a regional award for an opinion column he wrote from one of the numerous times he has covered The Masters golf tournament.

In 2013, Stephen co-authored a book about University of Tennessee football entitled "Game Of My Life".

Photo images used with permission from:
Chattanooga Times Free Press
University of Tennessee
Cindy Dodson Desrosier
Gene Fuller
Marion County High School
South Pittsburg High School

"As iron sharpens iron, so one man sharpens another."

— *Proverbs 27:17*

HATE

verb (hate): intense hostility and aversion usually deriving from fear, anger, or sense of injury; extreme dislike or disgust

RIVAL

noun (ri-val): two or more striving to reach or obtain something that only one can possess

— *Merriam-Webster*

Contents

Foreword by Phillip Fulmer....................... xv
Chapter 1: Unrivaled rivalry 1
Chapter 2: Irreconcilable differences 13
Chapter 3: 1963 Pirates 33
Chapter 4: Rusty Adcock 46
Chapter 5: McReynolds Dragons 52
Chapter 6: Bill Baker..................... 70
Chapter 7: 1969 Pirates/Warriors 80
Chapter 8: Eddie Brown..................... 100
Chapter 9: Jimmy Wigfall..................... 111
Chapter 10: Don Grider..................... 117
Chapter 11: Bill and Dave Baxter 135
Chapter 12: Ken Colquette 144
Chapter 13: 1990 Warriors 159
Chapter 14: 1992 Warriors 174
Chapter 15: 1994 – A game for the ages 199
Chapter 16: 1994 Warriors 207
Chapter 17: 1994 Pirates 226
Chapter 18: 1995 Warriors 250
Chapter 19: Eric Westmoreland 271

Chapter 20: Marion's train whistle 286

Chapter 21: Eddie Moore 291

Chapter 22: 1999 Pirates 311

Chapter 23: 2007 Pirates 339

Chapter 24: 2010 Pirates 369

Chapter 25: Vic Grider 393

Chapter 26: Kennedy Griffith 412

Chapter 27: That Brockman guy 425

Series history 427

Team, Individual Honors 429

About the Author 433

Foreword

Growing up and playing in Winchester, I have always considered myself to be part of the valley. We were just on the other side of the mountain, but the towns and the way of life are very similar, so I always identified with the people from Jasper and South Pittsburg.

When I was in high school, we actually came down and scrimmaged South Pittsburg one time and that single-wing they ran was really tough to stop. We were having a tough time so, me being an older player, I asked our coach if I could move over to where they were running it at us. They wound up blocking me out of the way and knocked me all the way off the field and over by the fence. I found out that day that you'd better respect how tough those guys were and it taught me a lesson about questioning a coach too.

I later recruited that area as a coach and have a lot of fond memories of coming to Jasper and South Pittsburg. We've had great success at the University of Tennessee in getting some of their talented players and each of them became not just great players for us, but also men of character and great leaders who were well liked and respected in the locker room. That's a reflection of their upbringing and the coaching they received in high school.

It really is quite amazing that so many great and talented players have come from that small area. It's a compliment to their coaches and the community support for the teams. The emphasis that's put on sports there is unique and it shows in the quality of the teams and the excitement in those towns on Friday nights.

— Phillip Fulmer
University of Tennessee athletic director and former national championship winning head coach, who played with Marion County's Bill Baker and Eddie Brown, then later recruited and coached Marion's Eric Westmoreland and South Pittsburg's Eddie Moore

Chapter 1
AN UNRIVALED RIVALRY

"Players, fans, mothers and daddies — they all know each other because they grew up together. They're all our friends, and nobody can hate you like your friends."

— John McKay, USC coach on rival UCLA

For many years the county where I grew up was known for two things: it was the epicenter for some of the best high school football in all of Tennessee and it routinely had the highest teen pregnancy rate in the state.

It's true. Google that second one if you don't believe me. Despite ranking 51st in total population of the Volunteer State's 95 counties, the young people in Marion County, about 25 miles west of Chattanooga, understood the farmland that surrounded us wasn't the only thing fertile.

And in the south, where boys are always looking for ways to prove their manhood, these two statistics were seen as indisputable evidence that from the time they could form-tackle or fornicate, nobody in our great state did either better.

Technically, there are three high schools in the county: Marion County in Jasper, South Pittsburg and Whitwell. But while I'm sure the boys in Whitwell were helping contribute to the number of teenage girls who found themselves in a delicate condition, more often than not the Tigers weren't scoring nearly as much on the field.

The towns of Jasper and South Pittsburg combine to cover less than 15 square miles, both with populations of around 3,200 souls and the two high schools in those map-dot towns sit just eight miles apart.

But while the schools and towns are geographically close, their residents believe they're a world apart in every way. For at least one week every fall the stretch of county Highway 72 separating them is paved by good old-fashioned unbridled hate. Think Hatfields and McCoys, or imagine a Mayberry setting where Sheriff Andy Taylor and Floyd the barber might, at any moment, begin feeding each other knuckle sandwiches.

In the heart of the Bible belt, only one thing could drive folks to set aside the good Lord's commandment to love thy neighbor and it isn't politics, religion or how to kick-start the local economy. Instead, in a county best known for being the Fireworks Capital of the South, it's one of the state's oldest high school football rivalries that keeps their fuse lit.

South Pittsburg and Marion County players shake hands before the 2017 game.

Despite having one of the smallest enrollments among all football-playing schools (fewer than 250 students in grades 9-12), South Pittsburg is the only program in the state to have played for a state championship in all six decades the Tennessee Secondary School Athletic Association has had a playoff format.

Meanwhile Marion County's Warriors won four state titles in six years in the early to mid-1990s, compiling an envious 56-1 record during that time.

Heading into the 2018 season, the Warriors and Pirates have claimed more state championships (9 combined), more title game appearances (20 total), more playoff wins (137) and more all-state players (109 combined) than any other programs among the 75-school radius of Chattanooga's tri-state area.

In a county with more pride than prosperity, that level of football achievement has fueled the rivalry's intensity for nearly a century. The residents, packed in tighter than gunpowder, are tenacious about guarding their team's tradition as if their identity depends on it.

The proximity and pride of the communities is what energizes the atmosphere of the games. Familiarity truly does breed contempt.

"I'm not sure anybody from outside this county really gets just how much these two teams and towns don't like each other," said South Pittsburg Hall of Fame coach Vic Grider, who along with his dad, the late Don Grider, are the winningest father-son coaching tandem in state history. "People that are born in these two towns are taught to hate the other. It's in your blood. I'm never going to like them and nothing will change that.

"The two towns have never gotten along and never will. The one word you keep coming back to, at the end of the day the reason both sides feel the way we do, is pride. They've got so much pride in their school and program and community and so do we. And we're both hell-bent on outdoing each other."

The two teams have played since 1924, taking breaks only during World War II and again in 1954 because of the threat of violence between the towns. Harriman and Rockwood have played since 1921 and every year consecutively since 1924, making the Marion/South Pittsburg match-up the second-oldest rivalry in the state, but by every account it is without question the most heated.

Pirates coach Vic Grider doesn't hide his feelings for his rival.

Or as former TSSAA executive director Ronnie Carter once said matter-of factly, "It is the rivalry without rival. There's nothing that even comes close."

Carter began working for the TSSAA, the governing body for all of the state's high school sports, in 1978 after more than a decade as a high school coach and administrator in the mid-state. Before his retirement in 2009, Carter had seen enough across the length and breadth of the state to know and understand the make-up of every small community and large city from Bristol to Memphis.

Spirit signs are displayed each week on storefront windows throughout both towns.

A tall man with salt and pepper hair and glasses, Carter is somewhat of a professor on the subject of prep sports throughout the nation, having also served as the president of the National Federation of High School Associations.

"People would ask me about rivalries all the time because everybody thinks theirs is the biggest or the best," Carter said. "But I always told them that the biggest rivalry in our state, by far, is Marion County and South Pittsburg football. People should see for themselves or else you just don't realize how much those two places don't like each other.

"It's not pretend either, they genuinely do not like each other. People from both towns hate hearing this, and they won't agree with it, but they're very much the same. The bulk of the people will end up living right there and working in that area. They don't get out, and they're so tightly packed in next to each other that it actually makes the rivalry more intense."

Talent comes in cycles in small towns but there are far fewer down years here than at most other small schools across the state.

Not only does South Pittsburg and Marion have the tradition of glory days gone by, they've also maintained a level of success that separates them from nearly every other program in the state. Through the first 50 years the TSSAA has had a playoff format there have been only four seasons in which either the Pirates or Warriors failed to reach the postseason.

When the 2017 season ended, either one or the other had played for a state championship in 8 of the previous 10 years. In the other two seasons, considered throw-aways by those programs, one of them reached at least the quarterfinals.

"There isn't an area in our state with more tradition," added Carter, who coached football and wrestling at Overton High School before joining the TSSAA staff. "Oh, there are schools that will be dominant for five or six years or a decade even, but nobody can match the sustained excellence of those two programs.

"It's amazing how you could have two small schools be so close together and for both to be so outstanding over such a long period of time."

Warriors coach Ken Colquette once guided the program to four state titles in six seasons.

DIVIDING LINES DRAWN

*"We'll fight 'em til hell freezes over.
Then we'll fight 'em on ice!"*

*— Dutch Meyer,
Texas Christian University coach*

Maybe football became the identity of the two towns because so many of the first settlers in the Appalachia area came from Irish and

Scottish descent, with their bloody-knuckled refusal to back down and internal need to conquer.

"Anytime you competed against your brother or best friend, you wanted to beat them so bad you couldn't stand it. And usually you'd wind up in a fight," said Marion's Hall of Fame former coach Ken Colquette.

Marion County supporters play on South Pittsburg's "little brother" complex by proudly reminding Pirates fans which team carries the county name on its helmets. Conversely, Pirates fans view that as an act of arrogance and refuse to use their rival's official name, calling them "Jasper" instead, and saying it with the same contempt normally reserved for referring to atheists and yankees.

Yard signs announce team allegiance in the county.

"Them calling themselves Marion County has never bothered me," said Vic Grider, who admits a good bit of the reason he dislikes his rival so much is that he never beat them as a player. That pent-up frustration from the jabs he took during his playing days comes boiling over now as a coach. "I won't call them that because I don't have enough respect for them. When I was growing up 'Jasper' is all I knew them as. Even today, if I said Marion County my mom would slap me.

"I just take a lot more pride in saying I'm from South Pittsburg than worrying whatever the hell they want to call themselves.

"The people who crack me up are the ones on both sides who say 'I want them to do good when we're not playing them.' No you don't. Bullshit. Even when it's not us playing them, I don't want them to win, and I know they want us to get beat, too. When they're wearing that purple uniform we all want them to lose every game."

The two communities mirror one another in many ways. Nestled against a backdrop of cornfields and mountains, there's a Norman Rockwell feel to driving the postcard streets, lined with evergreen trees and quaint mom-and-pop family-owned businesses.

Although the median income in Marion County is less than half that of the rest of the state, the cost of a home is also nearly half what it costs outside the county, and the slow pace is ideal for raising a family. Fathers like the area because real estate is affordable. Mothers like it because the towns were small enough that they feel safe letting their kids roam.

SOUTH PITTSBURG

Less than a decade after the Civil War ended, the residents of a small community hard against the Alabama state line and walled in by rolling mountains on one side and the Tennessee River on the other were widely spaced out. No attempts had been made to establish an organized town until a group of British investors formed the Southern States Coal, Iron and Land Company, hoping to establish a major industrial operation in the Sequatchie Valley. On May 23, 1876, the name of the Battle Creek Mines post office was changed to "South Pittsburg" in hopes that the city would one day grow to become a great iron manufacturing center like Pittsburgh, Pennsylvania, or the "Pittsburg of the South".

South Pittsburg was, without argument, the metropolis of the Sequatchie Valley with more than 4,000 residents.

But the iron ore played out and the steel mills planned for the town moved to Birmingham (Ala.) instead. The loss of employment for hundreds of men working in South Pittsburg's foundries brought about a dramatic decline in population for the city.

After failing to live up to expectations, those who stayed in the little town developed a stubborn belief that they could work to find a way to reclaim the town's identity. Two new businesses which were founded around the turn of the century would provide the shot in the arm needed to steady confidence in the town's financial future.

Lodge Manufacturing Company, which produces cast iron cookware, was founded in 1896 by Joseph Lodge and is still owned and managed by the descendants of the Lodge family. To this day the company maintains a steady workforce of local residents and ships products internationally.

Less than a decade after Lodge began manufacturing cast iron, the Dixie-Portland Cement Company (later known as Penn-Dixie) established a cement production center in an area just south of South Pittsburg. The company hired New York insurance executive Richard Hardy to oversee the development of a company town, which became known as "Richard City". The plant operated until 1980 and Richard City was eventually annexed by South Pittsburg in 1985.

Today South Pittsburg is made up of just under six square miles and maintains around 3,100 citizens, a population made up of 80-percent white residents, with about 21-percent of its total living under the national poverty line. It is best known outside the county as being the home of the National Cornbread Festival, which is held the last weekend each April and can bring in nearly 20,000 visitors over the two days of the event.

Pirates fans show up early to assure they get the best seats.

The first organized South Pittsburg football team played in 1923, the same year the Princess Theater, which rests along the front street and remains in operation, was built. In their first season of competition the Pirates finished unbeaten, outscoring opponents 196-32, and the standard was set.

The Pirate's football dynasty truly began with the late coach Phil Beene, a Marion County graduate who became the first in a long line of folks who would cross from one side to the other. Beene had played tackle at the University of Tennessee from 1927-31 under General Robert Neyland and took over South Pittsburg's program in 1934, going on to win 71-percent of the games he coached.

That included a win over Bradley Central in 1940 that was noted by the Chattanooga media for two reasons — it was one of the first high school games in the area to be played under lights and South Pittsburg upset a school with nearly triple its enrollment.

Pirates players warm up as the sun sets behind the stadium.

Days after the game, the front page of the South Pittsburg Hustler (the town's weekly newspaper) ran a story bragging on both the game's atmosphere and the results, writing: *"Everyone in this territory will be glad to know you have not seen the game at its best until you see this latest treat, one played on a Friday night. Bradley brought their large 35-piece band with four majorettes and four cheerleaders but the Pirates, with more than 1,200 in attendance, claimed a 7-0 upset."*

Beene would later become the school's principal and the stadium where the Pirates play is named in his honor.

"One thing that Coach Beene began that is still true today — this is a football town," said former Pirates offensive guard Don Elledge, who played for Beene in the early 1960s. "Everything still centers around football and the players are looked at differently in the community. They're admired. That aura started with Coach Beene."

JASPER

Formed in 1820 from lands acquired from Betsy Pack — the daughter of Cherokee Chief John Lowery — Jasper is named for William Jasper, a Revolutionary War hero from South Carolina. The town lies in the southwestern Sequatchie Valley in a relatively flat area surrounded by steep portions of the Cumberland Plateau on the north and west, low hills on the east, and part of the Tennessee River to the south.

The town's primary north-south street, which follows a section of Tennessee State Route 150 and passes the high school, was named in honor of Pack.

A billboard outside Marion's field proclaim the program's accomplishments.

Jasper serves as the county seat, with the courthouse built in the heart of the town square, and as such the town's high school — Pryor Institute, which had opened its doors in 1889 as the public high school for the county — was officially renamed Marion County High in 1910. Shortly thereafter the school fielded the county's first prep football team.

The town has about two hundred more citizens living on three more square miles of land than its rival neighbor to the south. It is made up of just over 90-percent white residents and has fewer families living under the poverty line than South Pittsburg.

Marion County and South Pittsburg played twice in both 1924 and 1925 and it didn't take long before the teams became bitter rivals.

In a story that appeared in The Hustler on December 3, 1936, the game recap read more like Shakespearian literature than a football game summary:

"The South Pittsburg Pirates and Marion County Warriors, the two feudal elevens, surged in on the football tide Thanksgiving Day to settle their ancient score of fifteen years. The Jasper field was filled with spectators for the event. When the smoke of battle had cleared away, the Pirates viewed a scoreboard that gave them a victory of 21 to 0. Thus the Pirates became Marion County's champions. Despite the bitter rivalry between the teams and student bodies, the game was played in conduct becoming gentlemen and sportsmen."

Of course, the conduct from both sides would not remain as cordial in the years that followed.

Less than two weeks before the bombing of Pearl Harbor, fliers were hung in store fronts throughout South Pittsburg with a headline that read: *"South Pittsburg Pirates vs. the Jasper Warriors – at South Pittsburg, Thursday, Nov. 27, 1941"*.

It was one of the earliest examples of Pirates supporters refusing to call their rival by their official name, a disrespecting practice that has continued through the generations that followed.

The first night game between the teams came on Sept. 10, 1943 at South Pittsburg, and according to the rosters neither team had a player who weighed more than 182 pounds. For many years the game was played on Thanksgiving Day and included parades through both towns, but that all changed after the 1953 "Thanksgiving Day massacre", when the Pirates walloped the Warriors 69-0. The next year's game was canceled because of an overwhelming threat of violence between the fans and when the series resumed it was never again played on Thanksgiving and did not include festive parades.

It was at that point that the relationship between the sides was clearly broken beyond repair.

"I was standing with Charles Knight, one of Jasper's better players back then, and we were congratulating each other on a good game," recalled Roy Ferrell, a Pirates end in the early 1960s. "All of a sudden one of our players gets jumped by somebody from Jasper and before you knew it everybody was fighting, including me and Charles.

"If you wear black and they wear purple and the fight breaks out, you fight."

Chapter 2
IRRECONCILABLE DIFFERENCES

"The hatred of relatives is the most violent."
— Tacitus, ancient Roman philosopher

This is a place where sons learn how to loft wobbly spirals to their dads and, years later, many of those same fathers leave work early to sit in their cars or unfold lawn chairs and watch their sons practice in the fading daylight of early evening.

There is no movie theater in Marion County. No putt-putt golf course. No mall or even a place for teens to just hang out. It's a place where kids are often so bored they have to work just to find trouble and much of who you are in life can be decided before high school graduation.

Few escape the gravitational pull of the small-town way of life.

Football stitches many of the residents of the two communities, past and present, and unites people in each town with a sense of belonging to something uniquely their own.

Ironically the thread that ties the towns together is the same one that often divides its people.

Joey Mathis, a native Georgian who was a stranger to the rivalry before becoming a Marion assistant in 2014, then taking over as head coach in 2016, admitted the burden placed on the outcome of one single rivalry game was a bit of a daunting adjustment at first.

As he pushed a mound of biscuits and gravy across his plate one morning, Mathis searched for the right words to describe the level of dislike he, as a transplanted outsider, was still struggling to understand.

"You really can feel hate coming at you from the other side," he said with a sigh. "I'm sure they feel the same way. The small town part is what separates it from any other rivalry I've known. Most people that grew up in one of these two towns never leave so they have to see the same people the rest of their life. They either work with them, go to church with them, live near them or see them in the same stores, so their identity, their whole self-worth is tied into which set of teenagers performs on one Friday out of every year."

It's always a bruising game when the Pirates and Warriors clash.

The values of both communities, what serves as the backbone for each, can be traced back along the hard wooden pews of the more than 50 churches that seem to spring up from every street corner. But these people would rather change the 10 commandments than their way of life so fortunately for them the great majority of those churches are Baptist, making it easier for so many to ask forgiveness rather than permission to hate their rival.

However the pulse of the towns, what keeps the energy flowing with youthful gusto, rises from the bleachers of the high school football stadiums on Friday nights each fall. When it comes to small-town devotion, nothing else is as revered as those fields.

The seating capacity at both stadiums is more than the population of either town. It's almost as if the builders of both structures understood that even the people who did move away would find themselves returning home in the fall, just to be part of the Friday night atmosphere, and so they made the stands large enough to welcome everyone back. Sort of a class reunion every week.

On the winter days when only a few stubborn remnants of autumn remain on the trees, the dominant colors throughout these towns remain the same as those worn by their beloved teams.

As she watched the locker room doors swing open and the team come marching single-file out into the evening light, the late Bebe Fuqua, South Pittsburg's long-time girls' basketball and volleyball coach once said, "When you see that black and orange coming out on the field, well, it's hard to explain if you're not from around here. But anybody who has been a part of the school will tell you it's a very special part of their life. And it always is."

Just as you enter the city limits of both towns, visitors are first greeted by large signs proclaiming the years state championships were won. There is no mention of the runner-up finishes, however. Those are as forgotten as the years when they didn't even reach a title game.

"We were getting on the bus before the '99 state game," recalled former Pirates defensive coordinator and principal Allen Pratt. "Coach (Dave) Baxter grabbed my hand, pulled me in and said 'Don't come back with the silver ball.'

"I said 'I know, Coach.' But he just squeezed tighter, pulled

Fans overflow from the stands onto the track to cheer on their Pirates.

me closer and said, 'No, you don't understand. You're not remembered if you come back with the silver ball. Bring the gold one back.' That stuck with me that whole day because I knew what he was saying was exactly how the entire town felt, too."

When the Family Dollar in Jasper caught fire in December of 2016, it burned to the ground because the entire fire department was in Cookeville to watch the Warriors play in the state title game.

The game is as essential as air conditioning here.

"I get chills just talking about what playing here meant to me," said Larry Richards, who joined the Warriors coaching staff in 1980 after his playing days ended. "This football program is the biggest thing we've got in this town. It's the one thing everybody here agrees on and supports unconditionally."

The orange and black flags with the Jolly Roger skull and crossbones that hang from downtown light posts along South Pittsburg's front street as well as the purple and white homemade spirit banners taped to windows along the short drive from Jasper's town square, along Betsy Pack Drive, to Bill Baxter Stadium all proudly proclaim each town's identity to anyone passing through.

"They were the only team that had the same grit and fight as us," assessed former Marion all-state player Anthony Martin. *"As soon as we stepped on the field I knew there was a difference between them and Whitwell or Sequatchie or any of the other teams we played. Those other teams would quit once we started pounding on them. South Pittsburg wouldn't quit. Ever. Even when we were up on them, they would keep coming, trying to punch us right back.*

Marion's Ridley Rowdies student section awaits kickoff.

"As much as we hate each other, we need each other."

TEMPORARY INSANITY

"The very existence of flamethrowers proves that some time, somewhere, someone said to themselves, 'You know, I want to set those people over there on fire, but I'm just not close enough to get the job done.'"

— George Carlin

Every season when the rivalry is renewed something dramatic seems to bubble up from beneath the surface and remind everyone — especially those outside the county — the level of magma-hot dislike just waiting to boil over.

Pirates Sawyer Kelley is up-ended by a big hit from a Marion defender.

Typically it amounts to nothing more than a tempest in a teacup, just small town shenanigans. But every so often it becomes much bigger news, and never was that more obvious — or more in the public eye — than in 2013. On Halloween, the night before Marion was set to host South Pittsburg with the region title on the line between two state-ranked rivals, then Warriors head coach Mac McCurry instructed three assistant coaches to vandalize the team's field house with orange and black spray paint to make it look like it had been done by South Pittsburg supporters.

That storyline marinated throughout the day but an hour before kick-off, standing in the end zone closest to the Marion field house, I was approached by Matt Blansett, a county investigator.

"The vandalism wasn't done by South Pittsburg people," Blansett said with certainty in his voice. "Be ready for a huge story to break real soon because I'm almost certain it was done by Jasper's coaches. I've just got to figure out for sure how many were in on it."

Blansett's instincts were proven true when, just days after the Pirates won the game, insult was added to injury as investigators discovered evidence that revealed it had been an inside job.

The details trickled out through local media and were even featured by several national outlets — including ESPN. Text messages between the coaches discussing how to pull off the caper were made public and Blansett even discovered video surveillance from a local

Wal-Mart of one of the assistants buying the orange and black spray paint while still wearing his purple and white Marion County coach's shirt and cap.

It all led to McCurry's dramatic resignation and the three assistants being forced to leave the team as well.

Weeks later, the remaining coaching staff continued guiding Marion's gritty players through an inspired playoff run, while South Pittsburg was also making its own push deep into the playoffs. South Pittsburg principal Danny Wilson instructed students from the school to checkout early and line the streets along the route where Marion's team bus would pass on the way to their quarterfinal game at powerhouse Trousdale County.

"After everything that had happened, I thought it would be a nice gesture to give their kids a send-off," Wilson said. "Their kids had nothing to do with what had happened and since we weren't going to be playing them again that season, I just figured it would be good to show some community support."

In the fireworks capital of the south, every Friday night is reason to light up the night sky.

But as they stood along the sidewalk, moments before the Warrior's bus came into view as it rolled out of Jasper, the South Pittsburg students, including Pirates football players in their game jerseys and jeans, began grumbling about being ordered to show support for their rivals.

As the buses passed and the South Pittsburg students, along with a few faculty and fans, gave a half-hearted wave, they were met by blank, confused stares from the Warriors inside their bus. Then one Marion player seated near a back window raised his hand, pressed it against the glass and gave the waving Pirates contingent the middle-finger salute.

Pirates players wave the Jolly Roger before running onto the field.

Several South Pittsburg students returned the favor, flipping off the bus as it steamed by and one football player yelled in Wilson's direction, "See, they don't want us here any more than we want to be here!"

That brief interaction, perhaps more than any other, summed up the antagonistic relationship between the two. Neither side wants to be the one standing on the curb watching as the parade passes.

"It's two programs with a lot of tradition and pride and two communities that want to prove they're better than the other," Wilson said. "There's so much competition and jealousy on both sides, it's not a stretch at all to say there's quite a bit of hatred."

In the same way the sustained success sets the two programs apart, the fact that the 2013 exchange is more commonplace than rare is what separates the rivalry as a whole from others, including Baylor/McCallie and Bradley Central/Cleveland in the Chattanooga area alone.

"I covered Bradley/Cleveland for several years when I worked for the (Cleveland) Daily Banner," said Chuck Thurmond, a 1984 Marion County graduate. "That's a pretty intense rivalry across the board, but when you look at just football and the way the people in Jasper and South Pittsburg feel about each other, nothing comes close to that. It's just completely different, kind of in a scary way, than anything else I've experienced."

Pirates family tradition: Matt, Jake, Wesley and Johnny Stone (left to right) show their state championship ringsright) show their state championship rings.

Three years after it had made national news, the rivalry's off-the-field antics again threatened to upstage the game. Shortly after the 2016 school year began Dylan McQueen, an all-star player who had been expelled from Scottsboro (Ala.) High School after an arrest on burglary charges, enrolled at South Pittsburg. The talented athlete — who had been Scottsboro's leading scorer the previous season — was cleared by the TSSAA prior to the third week of the season, just in time to make his debut against top-ranked Marion at Beene Stadium.

But less than two hours before kickoff his mother arrived at the field house, frantic after their attorney had informed her an Alabama judge had declared her son in contempt of court by crossing state lines to attend school. McQueen, who was already dressed and ready to take the field for pregame warmups, was instead taken home by his mother.

Just thirty minutes after that story was posted online by the Times Free Press and all three Chattanooga TV stations, the pregame dramatics became even more surreal when news broke that the TSSAA was placing

Marion County on two-years probation for recruiting violations that had taken place weeks before.

Suddenly, before the game had even kicked off, a circus atmosphere swirled around the stadium threatening to overshadow anything that could happen on the field.

As the teams began warming up, one curious dad of a Warriors player asked Marion assistant David Moore how he felt about the game.

"We're about to embarrass them in front of their girlfriends and their mamas," Moore joked.

Marion, which had drilled South Pittsburg the year before, was outscoring opponents by an average of 42 points and would go on to play in the 2A state title game later that season. But the Pirates used a stingy defense and several momentum-shifting plays by Cade Kennemore to set up one of the most dramatic finishes in series history.

After Marion had tied the game with a short field goal with one minute left, South Pittsburg answered with a long kickoff return by Kennemore, who then hauled in a 28-yard game-winning touchdown toss from Hogan Holland with just 11 seconds remaining.

Danny Wilson has guided both the Pirates football and baseball teams to state titles.

And just as it has so many times through the years, inexplicably the game itself eclipsed all the pre-game drama.

South Pittsburg fans poured, en masse, over the concrete wall onto the field to celebrate and the cannon which sits atop the Pirate ship in the north end zone fired round after ear-splitting round until the final Marion fan had exited the stadium.

"I've never been more miserable," former Marion all-state player Anthony Martin said. "I couldn't get out of there fast enough."

Because of the schools proximity to one another, there are numerous cases of people who have worn both team's colors. And paid the price for electing to do so.

"I've been cussed out at ball games before. I'm used to that," said Troy Boeck, who worked as an assistant at South Pittsburg before later becoming head coach at Marion. "But people I go to church with on Sunday were cussing at me during that game.

Superfan Harvey Allison is always the first to greet Pirates players as they make their way toward the field.

"With every other rivalry I've been around, it's more civil. You don't deal with the same level of animosity. The emotion of that game makes it the most intense rivalry in the state, bar none. You might fight at the 50 yard line on game night and then have breakfast in the same place the next morning."

Boeck, a former All America lineman at the University of Tennessee at Chattanooga, has also coached at Chattanooga's Baylor School and Soddy-Daisy as well as Rhodes College.

"When I was at those other places they would introduce each other by what they do now, whatever their profession is. At South Pitt and Marion they introduce each other by what they accomplished in high school. They'll say 'This is Billy, he was an all-state guard in the 70s.'"

Prior to the 1995 game, one year after the Warriors had shut out the Pirates to open a season in which both teams went on to win state championships, Marion students made T-shirts that read "Pirates football - No. 1 in the state, No. 2 in the county." That game

Marion often brings more fans to away games than the home team they play.

also marked the first time in Tennessee prep history that two defending state champions kicked off a season against each other.

"You hate Jasper even before you have a reason to," said former Pirates all-state receiver Mike Jackson. "And then you play them and they give you a reason to hate them."

During the first half of the 2016 game Pirates lineman Drew Daniels stopped on his way back to the huddle to bend down and check on an injured Marion player. As he did, a woman's raspy voice from the South Pittsburg sideline yelled, "Drew, don't you help that son of a bitch up!"

For several seasons in the 1990s, players from both sides would walk halfway onto the field for the pregame coin toss, then turn their backs toward each other, refusing to acknowledge the opposing side.

"With consolidation and the way things are now you just don't see rivals go back that far and be that bitter," said former Marion County coach Dale Pruitt, father of University of Tennessee coach Jeremy Pruitt.

Dale Pruitt has won nearly 300 games, most while coaching in Alabama, and was 2-0 in the rivalry in his two seasons as Warriors coach. "It don't matter if your daddy is a doctor or if you even have a daddy, you can make a name for yourself by what you do in that game. It's electrifying," he added. "I'm not kidding when I say you felt a little uneasy about what could happen from how those people feel about each other. If you put every police officer in the county out there and the riot did happen, they couldn't stop it."

In 2001 the game became so physical — a prison riot in cleats as described by one observer — that five players had to be taken away by ambulance.

"I've never been a part of a rivalry, at any level, that was as intense. Nothing compares to the emotion around that game," said former Marion County all-state running back and safety Eric Westmoreland, who went on to become an All SEC linebacker at Tennessee and played for six seasons in the NFL. Westmoreland has been an assistant coach at Baylor School for more than 10 years.

"The Baylor/McCallie game is pretty heated," he added. "But I don't think it's as scary as far as how the people feel about each other."

Some of the more petty exchanges between the two sides have been off-the-field gamesmanship. Pirates coaches once accused Marion's staff

When the Pirates are playing at home, it's the biggest show in town.

Pirates runner Joseph Lilly is surrounded by Marion tacklers.

of nailing the window in the visitor's coaches box shut and smearing grease over the glass to obstruct their view of the game.

In 2017, Pirates coaches were told there was no room for them to sit in the press box because the visiting coaches box had been reserved for Marion administrators. Instead South Pittsburg assistants were assigned a section at the top row of the visitor's bleachers, complete with a small canopy in case of rain.

"When we walked out on the field and looked up at their press box you could see through the windows that they had several empty rooms where our coaches could have sat," Vic Grider said. "It was obvious that they just wanted to be pricks about it and have our coaches sitting in the stands."

The following spring South Pittsburg's quarterback club and community supporters helped remodel Beene Stadium's two-story press box with around $20,000 of improvements that included enclosing the new climate-controlled structure and updating both the home and visiting coaches rooms.

However, Grider said he doesn't expect there to be room for Marion's staff when the Pirates host their rival.

There's never an empty seat in the house for Pirates home games.

"I'm sure we can find some space up in the visitor's stands for them to use," he said with a laugh.

The antics have carried over onto the field as well, most notably in the days leading up to the 1994 game when a group of South Pittsburg students used pick-up trucks to uproot Marion's goal posts. A couple of years after that, when Marion cheerleaders rode into the stadium on Harley Davidson motorcycles minutes before kickoff, a group of South Pittsburg fans unfurled a sign that read "Hogs on hawgs".

If either town were a person on trial, you could argue temporary insanity to define such behavior.

"We have people at our school that won't shop in South Pittsburg or even go to their Cornbread Festival because they don't want to give that town money. Now that is hatred," added David Moore, who also played for the Warriors from 1968-70.

"One year we beat them at their place and after the game a parent of one of our players came into our locker room," Moore recalled. "He was wearing a black hat with a 'P' on it so our coaches thought he was from

South Pitt and as they start carrying him out the door they're hitting him — I mean just really roughin' him up, punching him in the ribs and neck and face and wherever they can.

"Once the guy gets thrown out of the field house, one of our fans thinks he's fighting with our coaches so he hits him with a haymaker. Our people are fighting each other thinking it's South Pittsburg people.

Then, all of a sudden, the South Pittsburg people think one of their fans is getting ganged up on so some of them jump in and start punching.

"We had to get the police to escort us out and told our big kids to walk on the outside and form a protective wall around the little ones. By the time the last of us coaches left, my God we walked through a tunnel of hell with their fans yelling and trying to get to us."

Former South Pittsburg center Wesley Stone, who along with his father, younger brother and oldest son were all a part of state championship teams with the Pirates, has coached at Boyd-Buchanan and Madison Academy (Ala.) as well as South Pittsburg. He was once so willing to help his alma mater prepare to face Marion that he took a one-week hiatus from his job as an assistant coach at Madison Academy.

Stone, who had success stopping Marion as the defensive coordinator at Boyd-Buchanan before joining the Madison Academy staff, was asked by Pirates coaches if he had any insight he could share that might help as they prepared to play the Warriors.

"From my time at Boyd, I still had film on them from every game and every scrimmage over the previous three years," Stone recalled. "I had over 2,000 offensive plays loaded into my database. That's how badly I wanted to beat them.

"After I met with South Pittsburg's coaches, I wound up calling our coach at Madison Academy to tell him I wouldn't be at practice that week, or at their game on Friday because I had to help the Pirates beat Jasper.

"There's nothing I hate more in this world. I don't own anything purple and I've told my wife that our four boys are not allowed to ever have any purple on their body. Not even underwear or purple trim on a shoe. Nothing.

Cade Kennemore hauls in the game-winning TD catch in the final seconds of the 2016 match-up.

"I actually hate it that I hate something so bad because it's unhealthy. But I just can't help it. It's in my soul."

Just as unhealthy is the matching animosity former Marion County all-state linebacker T.J. Gentle feels for South Pittsburg, admitting the shared hatred is the only thing he has in common with Pirates supporters.

"I didn't know what hate was until South Pittsburg," said Gentle, now an attorney in Chattanooga. "I remember as a kid walking through a sea of orange, through all these horrible people, and not feeling safe again until we got to the purple side.

"We don't even live in Jasper now but our family won't buy orange jack-o-lanterns on Halloween because I can't stand the color. We get those plastic purple ones instead.

"I never understood that enjoyment of seeing another person fail until I saw one of my sons grin when the other struck out. In some ways it's more negative than hate. It's a begrudging respect that you don't want to give to them. If you're giving everything you've got every play and the other guy is giving everything he's got on every play, that's the essence of that game."

Chattanooga resident Sam Parfitt is the founder and Chief Executive Officer of The True Athlete Project, which works on an international level to teach athletes how to use sports to influence positive change in society. He once worked with a nonprofit organization that was able to convince the United Nations to declare a global day of peace in sports.

But Parfitt, a native of Norfolk, a rural town in the east of England, believes not even the UN could deliver peace to this rivalry.

Marion proudly displays its championship hardware outside the school's main office.

"As a bystander you could just feel the tension rising between the two sides," said Parfitt, whose proper King's English is not even elegant enough to lend an air of dignity in describing the rivalry.

Parfitt even jokingly compared the months when the two teams are not playing to the story of the one-day Christmas truce which was agreed upon between warring British and German soldiers during World War I. Those soldiers took a break from shooting at each other to exchange gifts, play soccer and even sing holiday carols before going back to the business of killing one another the next day.

"It can be insanely tough to get people on the same page when it comes to sports, and especially when they're located so close together. That just seems to build a natural 'us versus them' mentality," Parfitt concluded.

But Pirates coach Vic Grider doesn't see the animosity as a negative, believing instead it's part of what has pushed both programs to maintain their level of sustained excellence.

"If you hate failure, hate losing, hate anything that makes you feel vulnerable or weaker, how is that a bad thing?" Grider asked. "I feel very fortunate to have somebody so close to us constantly driving us to be better."

COMMON THREAD

"Educated in a small town
Taught the fear of Jesus in a small town...

I've seen it all in a small town
Had myself a ball in a small town...
Yeah, I can be myself here in this small town
And the people let me be just what I want to be."

— **John Mellencamp, Small Town**

For all the differences and dislike that separates the two towns and programs, it's the list of similarities and shared customs that have linked the Pirates and Warriors for decades and will continue to do so for generations to come.

It's the moment during warm-ups when the drum corps enters the stadium and puts a little extra bounce in everyone's step.

It's smoke drifting from the concessions stand, carrying the aroma of flame-kissed burgers across the stands.

It's South Pittsburg players reaching up to touch the horseshoe over their locker room door and Marion's line of players tapping the "I will give my all" sign on their way out to the field.

It's fans packed in tighter than a Pentecostal tent revival, yelling, cheering and ringing cowbells at the first sight of their team emerging from the locker room.

It's old-timers, some in frayed overalls or camouflage jackets, lining the fence by the field, wishing more than anything they could suit up just one more time, but instead settling for telling the players as they pass to, "Give 'em hell boys!"

It's cheerleaders from both sides holding up oversized, hand-painted paper spirit signs for players to come crashing through.

It's all heads bowed for the Lord's prayer in the locker room and hands over hearts in the bleachers for the national anthem.

It's grown men trying not to spill the splash of bourbon over icy Coke in their hand as they jump to their feet and celebrate when their team scores.

It's the South Pitt band playing "The Horse" after every touchdown and Marion's thunderous train whistle blaring over the crowd noise after a big play.

It's Harvey Allison's Pirate restaurant, where you're greeted at the door by the thick smell of fried food and loud conversation. Harvey's — with framed photos and newspaper clippings of past South Pittsburg teams — has fed Pirates players and cheerleaders free cheeseburgers after every win for more than four decades and closes up early on game nights so Harvey himself can greet the players before they run onto the field.

It's the entire police force from both towns patrolling the game because, hell, there's nobody left outside the stadium to get into mischief anyway.

It's the four gold ball trophies on display just inside Marion County's main entrance and the area outside South Pittsburg's dazzling new gym that serves as a Hall of Fame for all-state players and championship teams and a shrine for their own five gold trophies.

Pirates players slap the horseshoe over their locker room door on their way to the field.

Both schools have had random success in other sports, but football pays the bills and brings the spotlight to both towns. After all, as Colquette once surmised,

"Basketball can't even start at either place until our season is over. Neither school has a wrestling team, so football is king. It's all there is. That got started before us and will be going long after us."

It's Bob Sherrill, who once went door-to-door soliciting votes for mayor of South Pittsburg, only to have people greet him at the door by saying, "I know who you are. You're the guy who does the PA at Pirates games. You've got my vote since you're with the team." Sherrill's voice is unmistakeable, especially when he reminds a packed stadium that an opposing player was stopped "by a host of Pirate tacklers".

It's the Ridley Rowdies, faces painted, purple shakers rising in the air to join the rhythm of the Pride of the Valley band playing the war chant.

It's four fingers in the air at the end of the third quarter.

It's the point of the season when the chill in the air has turned the lush green Bermuda grass a golden brown, but the Pirates and Warriors are still making a playoff run.

It's making plans over Thanksgiving dinner for what time they'll meet friends and family at the stadium the next day to claim their usual spot in the stands or load up the car for a semifinal road trip.

It's the marquee outside South Pittsburg's Princess Theater, the one normally reserved for announcing local events, posted with the reminder, "Last person out of town turn off the lights" when the Pirates are making another trip to play for a state championship.

It's Marion County's team bus being met at the Jasper exit off I-24 by police cars and fire trucks, all with lights flashing and sirens wailing, to escort the team across the remaining three miles to the school after a state championship trip. And South Pittsburg's team bus, as it returns home after a state title has been added, stopping at first street and opening its doors to allow players to walk the remaining five blocks — through a corridor of adoring fans — to the field house as fireworks light up the late-night sky.

It's unstoppable. Grass grows, seasons change, waves pound the sand. And for one week of each year, the great majority of people from Jasper and South Pittsburg come together across eight hateful miles.

Chapter 3
1963 PIRATES

"The man who thinks he can and the man who thinks he can't are both right"

— **Confucius**

Just inside the entrance of the grand gymnasium stands an impressive 6-foot glass structure running the entire length of one wall leading inside the arena. It houses plaques, trophies and other assorted awards from more than seven decades of accomplishments by South Pittsburg High School teams and individual athletes.

Resting on a top shelf of the trophy case is a shiny gold reminder that the school's proud football history reaches back long before the state's playoff format began deciding championship teams. On a nearby wall, a photo of the group which earned that hardware — the program's first significant state-wide recognition — appropriately hangs next to other championship Pirate teams.

Forever frozen as flat-topped teenagers, with determined looks of confidence on their faces, the boys who made up the 1963 Pirates are remembered as the team who laid the foundation for numerous championships that would follow. At the time they were simply trying to live up to the standard of toughness set before them, a cycle that has been carried on for generations that have followed.

"When we first got to the high school some of us boys would go to the old Hall of Fame area and look at all those pictures of great players and teams before us," said Don Elledge, a senior guard and team captain on the 1963 team. "I would look at all the storied history and the scores and wanted to be a part of it.

"Those pictures had an effect on me. I think it did on a lot of us who wanted to leave our mark too."

A decade earlier — long before the TSSAA began having playoffs, and when bowl games were the only postseason honor — South Pittsburg's football team had earned a spot on the front page of the Chattanooga Times sports section under the headline "Unbeaten, Untied, but Uninvited" after failing to be given the chance to play in any of the state's bowl games despite finishing the regular season with the only unblemished record in the Chattanooga area.

In that story from 1953, Soddy-Daisy coach Harland Burnette, whose team had been steamrolled by the Pirates, called them "the best single-wing high school team in these parts I can recall seeing."

The snub placed a boulder-sized chip on the shoulder of everyone involved with the program and added extra motivation to earn the respect Pirates coaches and players felt they had been denied.

South Pittsburg's massive trophy case includes the 1963 Civitan Bowl hardware.

Having just lived through the Cuban missile crisis a year earlier, 1963 began with a volatile first eight months in what would become the defining year of the civil rights movement. During his inaugural address in mid-January, Alabama governor George Wallace made it clear there was still a broad gap dividing many blacks and whites by defiantly declaring "segregation now, segregation tomorrow, and segregation forever!"

Wallace would later stand in the doorway leading to the University of Alabama's admissions office, blocking the entrance of two black students. But those were mild demonstrations by a bigoted politician compared with the violence that was to come that year, beginning in May when Alabama authorities unleashed police dogs and sprayed water cannons — with enough pressure to rip bark off trees — on thousands of African American demonstrators who were protesting segregation in Birmingham.

Weeks later civil rights activist Medgar Evers was assassinated in Jackson, Mississippi.

"We would hear of things that happened around the south but it seemed like a whole different world for most of us," said Roy Ferrell, a senior co-captain that season who played wingback and defensive end.

"There was racism in parts of town but nothing like what was going on outside of our community. South Pittsburg was a mostly working-class town where many of the whites and blacks worked next to each other. I don't think most of us felt like we were any better than anybody else."

It would be two years before students from McReynolds — the all black school in town — would integrate into SPHS and aside from breaking Coach Phil Beene's rule against dating girls during the season, most of the buzz-cut boys walking the halls of the school would be considered as square as a game of checkers by today's standards.

The Pirates had been stout defensively the season before, allowing the fewest points in the state — only 28 points, including 14 in one game — to finish 8-0-1. The 55 players who made up the football team, who as seventh-graders were the last group to wear leather helmets with no face mask, made sure to shine their black high-top cleats before each game.

"That was just how much pride we had in wearing that uniform," Elledge said. "You wanted to look your Sunday best when you jogged out on the field for games.

Assistant Sam Brooks presents Rusty Adcock with the state Player of the Week award.

"We were taught to gang tackle on every play. It was a failure in our eyes when the other team got a first down. Rusty Adcock was a really good leader for us. He had a good personality and got along with everybody and Coach Beene thought so highly of him that he allowed Rusty to call plays, which was very unusual in those days. We knew Rusty and the other backs were going to get the exposure but we as linemen didn't get caught up in that. We were happy whoever scored. It was a very unselfish group."

The season kicked off one week after Martin Luther King Jr. delivered his "I have a dream" speech on the steps of the Lincoln Memorial to an audience of 250,000 for the March on Washington protest. On Labor Day weekend, a day before the Pro Football Hall of Fame opened in Canton, Ohio with 17 charter members, South Pittsburg easily handled Rockwood 26-0.

A week later, for the second time in as many games, Ferrell was knocked so silly that he walked toward the wrong huddle before clearing the cobwebs and helping the Pirates to a 24-6 win over Fayetteville.

After cruising past cross-county rival Whitwell 48-7, the Pirates finally hit a speed bump in week four at Manchester, where referees called back three touchdowns for penalties.

"Coach Beene never yelled," Ferrell said. "He didn't have to. But I've never seen him so frustrated and upset as when those touchdowns kept getting called back. It was ridiculous really. Coach (Don) Grider kept having to push him back onto the sideline because Coach Beene was going after those referees."

Late in the game, with the Pirates clinging to a 7-0 lead, Manchester converted a fourth-and-21 with a 39-yard pass, then scored on a short run to tie the game at 7-all. Despite finishing with fewer than 50 total yards, the Red Raiders had managed to walk off the field with a 7-7 tie.

"When the game was over we were crying because we had let them tie us. It felt like a loss," Elledge said. "Still to this day I hate that tie. It's hard to talk about even now."

Still frustrated from the previous week, South Pittsburg rebounded with a resounding 26-0 win over Bridgeport (Ala.), an outcome that came with the Pirates running just four different plays.

"Coach Beene said we had played sandlot football the week before," said Ferrell, who led a defense that allowed just 41 total yards. "So we basically ran the same two plays — 46 and 319 (a sweep) over and over, with two others every now and then.

"He told us before the game that we were going to run those base plays until we got it right. Once Bridgeport figured out that we were running the same plays over and over they stacked all 11 defenders

South Pittsburg co-captain Roy Ferrell.

up around the line and we took a beating because they knew what was coming.

"The only way we were going to gain any yards was to just be more physical than them. I don't care what the score said, that was a brutal game."

By now the Pirates were the must-see team of the Sequatchie Valley, drawing enormous crowds at each stadium they visited. After playing in front of more than 4,500 at Bridgeport, the Chattanooga Times estimated another standing room only crowd of better than 4,000 packed into Tracy City to watch South Pittsburg face Grundy County in a battle of unbeaten teams.

After trailing 7-0 at halftime, Adcock led an offensive avalanche in the second half that buried the Yellow Jackets under a pile of points. The 150-pound Adcock earned state Back of the Week honors from the Associated Press after rushing for 157 yards, much of that running behind the blocks of fullback Donnie Phipps, and throwing for another 94 in the 33-7 win.

That would become the start of a dominating run in which South Pittsburg outscored its next three opponents by a combined 192-8. It began with an 86-2 annihilation of Sequatchie County, setting a program record for points scored in a game that still stands. Eight players scored for the Pirates, who out-gained the Indians 532-63 in total yards.

"There was one point late in the game where Rusty Adcock looked around the huddle and asked 'who hasn't scored yet?'," Ferrell remembered. "In the fourth quarter the referees came over to use our towels and wipe sweat. We had ran those refs ragged keeping up with us running up and down the field and they needed a break."

"They weren't the only ones," added Elledge with a laugh. "I've never been so tired just from running down on kickoffs. It was long runs for scores and then sprinting down the field on kickoffs again. All 55 players played in that game."

After the game, Coach Beene was unapologetic about the score, explaining that he could not teach his players to hit hard in practice and then ask them to ease up during a game.

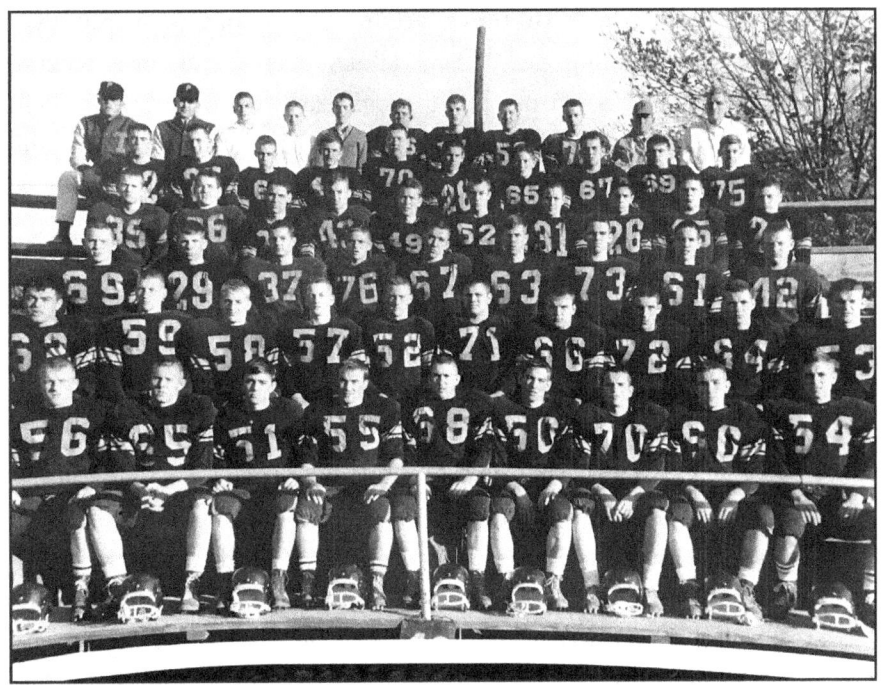

The undefeated 1963 Pirates.

"That's not how we teach our boys to play," Beene told the Chattanooga Times. "We played our varsity in the first half and our younger boys in the second. Sequatchie was just weaker than we thought."

For the next few weeks the Pirates continued lighting the scoreboard up like a pinball machine, following up the Sequatchie game with a 66-6 win over St. Andrews-Sewanee and a 40-0 thumping of Bledsoe County.

"The St. Andrews coach had said in the paper before the game that we may run it but we will not be able to pass it," Ferrell recalled. "Coach Beene put in a weak-end fly and Rusty threw it to me on the first play of the game for a big gain. We had never opened a game with a pass before, so that was just to make a point."

In the regular-season finale, South Pittsburg traveled to Jasper for a parade at 3 p.m., followed by the game at rival Marion County, which was led by star tailback Bill Baker who would go on to play at the University of Tennessee.

"There were a couple of times we thought we had them put away but they just kept coming back because Baker was so shifty and hard to catch," Adcock said. "If Jasper had a good player we would run it right at him, send two guys to block him on every play to wear him out and demoralize the rest of their team. We'd beat the guy to death."

Eventually the Pirates finally did wear down the Warriors to take a 39-20 decision to finish off an unbeaten season with another win over their rival.

"Our class can say we never lost to Jasper and that means a lot," Elledge said with a proud nod. "I've become friends with a lot of guys from Jasper and played softball with them, and I respect them but that don't mean when we play that it's ok to lose to them.

"With the other teams there wasn't a lot of mouthing but with Jasper there was. You wanted to beat their eyeballs in. We didn't hate them, but we had to prove a point."

Having built a reputation for being an elite program with a strong fan following, and that season's gaudy victory margin — the Pirates had outscored opponents 356-35 — they were selected to play in the second annual Civitan Bowl at Tennessee Tech University against Knoxville Powell. In the years before the TSSAA would implement a playoff system (1969) the Civitan Bowl became one of the most prestigious postseason games a team could be invited to.

South Pittsburg sold out its allotment of more than 2,000 tickets in the first two days after the game was announced.

"It was a huge deal," Ferrell said. "There wasn't a state championship game back then, but this had that type of atmosphere around it. The whole town was charged up when word got out that we were going to play in that game."

Because it was also years before classification would be introduced, not much thought was given to the fact that South Pittsburg — which had the state's longest unbeaten streak — would be facing an opponent with more than double its enrollment. Powell, led by senior quarterback Jim Courtney, had upset Sevierville, the No. 3-ranked team in the state, to earn its spot.

Besides the 6-2, 200-pound Courtney, and his brother Jeff who played halfback, the Panthers had six starters who weighed over 200 pounds — four of whom went on to sign college scholarships — while the Pirates had just three players on their entire roster who weighed more than 180.

"When we came out on the field we honestly thought Tennessee Tech was finishing up their practice," Adcock said. "We had never seen a team so big. They all sort of had this smirk on their faces when we walked past, like they just knew they were going to beat us into the ground.

Powell's Jim Courtney (left) congratulates Pirates captain Don Elledge after the Civitan Bowl.

"It was also bitterly cold. I put my hand down on the ground during warmups and jumped back up because the field was so cold."

Led by the passing ability of Courtney, who would go on to play football and baseball at Mississippi State, the Panthers jumped out to a 14-0 lead in the first quarter, looking as if they would in fact beat the Pirates into the cold ground.

"After they scored the second touchdown we got together and said we're putting the stake in the ground right now. They are not going to score again," said Ferrell, who was such an optimist that if he had gotten a stocking full of manure for Christmas he would've believed he had a pony around somewhere.

"It was never in our mind that we could lose a ballgame. That was just the second time all year we had been behind but there was no negativity. We were going to fight back right then."

The Pirates brought the majority of the more than 6,200 in attendance to life when Adcock tossed a 24-yard touchdown pass to David

Hudson, who made a juggling catch that is still marveled over by those who saw it.

"He tipped the ball into the air with his fingertips and then brought it in for the catch," Adcock said. "It was an unbelievable catch for a big play that we really needed. It definitely gave us some momentum.

"Coach Beene came into the locker room and said, 'I'm sorry we brought you boys up here to get embarrassed. I should've known these big-city boys would whip you.' That really pissed us off for the second half."

Adcock continued the momentum swing with his second TD toss of the game, this time to Ferrell on a down-and-out pattern. Ferrell stiff-armed one final Powell defender to the ground and raced 45 yards for the score.

"Roger Allison would run the extra points for us because he was short, had great leverage and was always good to get 3-4 yards," said Elledge, who would clear a path to the end zone from his right guard spot. "Roger would put his hand on my belt and follow me into the end zone.

"Powell could shuttle in subs from their bench and we would see a different face line up against us on about every play. But when Roy scored that TD it pumped so much life into the team that we were a different bunch than we had been to start the game. We weren't in awe of them anymore."

Having fought back to even the score, the Pirates traded punts before continuing their second-half surge with a huge fourth-quarter play when Ferrell drilled Courtney from behind, forcing a fumble that was recovered by Pirates defender Charles "Good-boy" Allen. That set up the go-ahead two-yard TD run by Adcock, completing the unlikely comeback.

"I think they were over-confident from jumping on us quick," Elledge said. "Then we started getting physical right back with them and once we did things started going our way. We put two of their better defensive players out of the game on back-to-back plays. That had to sting them.

"They got tired and the game got easier as it went."

After Adcock intercepted a Courtney pass and returned it to the Powell 13, the Pirates drove to the 2 and players begged Coach Beene to run another play and try to score again. But Beene opted to run out the clock, and the 21-14 win not only polished off a 10-0-1 season but put the program on the map statewide.

As the Pirates walked off the field junior fullback Donnie Phipps, who also played linebacker and never came off the field, dropped to his knees, unable to move for a few minutes because of sheer exhaustion.

"That was the most outmanned team I ever saw," said Bobby Carter, who played at South Pittsburg in the late 1940s and later coached at Marion County. "By the end of the game South Pittsburg just manhandled them."

Looking back on the game years later Courtney agreed.

"We didn't know anything about them and evidently our coach didn't either," Courtney said. "We were big for a high school team and thought we should be able to beat them pretty easily, especially after we scored as quick as we did.

"But they were a different team in the second half and we had a bad time of it from then on. We didn't make changes at halftime and their coaches did a good job of adjusting. They had a really good team, a lot better than we thought and they were a lot faster than we expected. They basically just whipped us in the second half."

Both teams attended a banquet on the Cookeville campus later that evening, but Courtney admitted he and his Powell teammates weren't thrilled with having to be there.

"The organizers of the game presented us the trophy and Coach Beene made a speech to both teams," Elledge said. "He kept it simple and was very humble about it but you knew he was proud of us.

"There's a certain level of being tough and living up to the past that must play on us. We would hear it over the years and just believe we were tougher than anybody else we played, no matter how big they were."

A convoy of supporters had been arranged in the days leading up to the game, including two state troopers leading the team bus and a parade of cars from South Pittsburg to Cookeville before the game. On the return trip the patrol cars would open up their siren through each town, announcing to everyone that something important was passing through.

Just one week after the celebration of the Civitan Bowl victory, President John F. Kennedy was assassinated in Dallas and South Pittsburg's residents joined the rest of the nation in mourning before life eventually began moving forward again.

"When news broke that JFK had been assassinated, that stopped all the celebrating the town had been doing in the days after the bowl game," Ferrell said. "All anybody had on their mind was the president being shot and it took a while before anybody felt like having a good time again."

The souvenir program from the 1963 Civitan Bowl.

In late December a mop-top foursome from Liverpool, England released their U.S. single — "I want to hold your hand" — and Beatlemania swept through the country.

Around that same time word began circulating through South Pittsburg that one of their football heroes had received the state's top honor.

"Coach Beene called an assembly, stood in front of the student body with a very serious look on his face and said, 'Well scholars, we're going to have a hanging today.'," recalled Adcock, who had 2,014 total yards and scored 130 points that season. "We were all scared because we thought somebody must really be in big trouble. But then he said 'Russ Adcock is going to have his picture hung as our first All-State player.'

"When my kids got a little older I took them to the school to show them my picture. It's something I'm really proud of."

Adcock's total yardage was 436 more than Pirates opponents had mustered for the entire season and he was the first in what has become a long line of Pirates to earn All-State recognition. Joining him on the All Sequatchie Valley Conference team were Elledge, David Hudson, John Layne and Goodboy Allen.

As change continued to sweep through the country the members of the 1963 Pirates used the lessons they learned on the field to become admired fathers and community leaders in their hometown. Elledge, Ferrell and several others would have sons, and even grandsons, who carried on the family tradition of wearing the orange and black Pirate uniform.

"Phil Beene and South Pittsburg football had a tremendous impact on my life," Elledge explained. "I came from a poor family but Coach Beene had a profound influence in making us want to excel, not only on the football field but in life and better ourselves.

"The trophy cases and Hall of Fame area in the new gym are really impressive and it makes me feel proud to see our accomplishments in there as part of so much history. When I look at that picture of our team, I see guys that love one another. It's hard to put it into words the camaraderie on that team but it was something very special to be a part of."

Chapter 4
RUSTY ADCOCK

*"We make a living by what we get.
We make a life by what we give"*
— Winston Churchill

So much of what separates South Pittsburg's football program from its contemporaries is its link to the past. Sturdy roots of tradition, running enviously deep, have assured the down cycles that every program eventually faces are short-lived for the Pirates.

One of the sturdiest links helping maintain the long-term health of the program is Rusty Adcock, who first helped the Pirates earn state-wide respect as a pigeon-toed senior tailback in 1963 and has been the team's doctor for more than four decades, tending to everything from broken bones to bruised egos.

As identifiable as the Pirates solid black uniforms is the little black bag, and the man who carries it on the sideline.

"We'll be at some of the most God-forsaken places on earth and he'll just come walking up carrying his little bag, ready to look after any of the kids who might need him," Pirates coach Vic Grider said. "Way before most teams had a doctor on the sideline, he was there looking after our kids. It's another one of those things that makes this program and this community special."

The program's first all-state player — when he out-gained all 11 opponents in total yards by himself — Adcock understands the team's importance to his home town, and the town appreciates his importance to the team.

"When you talk about South Pittsburg football, he's a part of it all. The history and what separates it from the majority of places in the whole state," said former Pirates coach and principal Danny Wilson. "The thing about Rusty is he's the same humble, giving guy the day I met him years ago as he is now."

The youngest of three siblings, Rusty watched as his mother, Clarice, worked at the local post office for 37 years to support her family after the death of her husband.

By the time his senior season rolled around — a year when the U.S. Postal Service first launched the ZIP Code System to make mail delivery more efficient, Alcatraz Penitentiary closed its iron-bar doors for good and The Flintstones debuted — Adcock's combination of athleticism and outgoing personality made him an easy choice for classmates to vote him Mr. SPHS, Most Popular and Best All-Around.

Pirates long-time team doctor Rusty Adcock (left).

On the heels of an unbeaten season capped by an upset of powerhouse Powell in the Civitan Bowl, Adcock earned a chance to continue his playing career at the University of Tennessee. But at 5-foot-9, 155 pounds, he quickly realized he was over-matched.

"I was out of my league playing quarterback there," Rusty recalled. "I was small with about average speed so I had learned to cut and bounce around on the field to avoid contact in high school, just trying to save myself from getting hurt.

"But I wasn't going to make it at UT and I knew it. Sam Brooks was really good to me when he coached me in high school and luckily he mentioned me to Sewanee's Shirley Majors one day while they were playing golf. Coach Majors ran the single-wing and Coach Brooks knew I would fit right in as a tailback at that level."

Unsure of what he wanted to do for a living, Rusty took nuclear engineering at UT for a year then switched his major to math for a semester, before settling on a degree in political science.

With the Vietnam War raging, Rusty drove to Nashville intent on joining the Air Force. But after spending the night out on the town with some buddies he had to change that plan.

"The morning I went to sign up I was very hung over and sick as a dog," Rusty said with a laugh. "The line for the Air Force was really long and it was hot outside, which was making me feel even sicker. So I saw around the corner that the line was shorter for the Navy but the shortest line of all was for the Marine Corps. I was feeling worse by the minute standing out in that heat so I signed up with the Marines just to get back home and lay down for a while."

While Rusty was going through the officer's training program, his college course experience opened the door for two jobs that would keep him out of

Rusty Adcock became the Pirates first all-state player.

combat. First was working as a legal officer, then with the Marine Air Support Squadron, where he was in charge of night bomb drops.

"Working in that confined space, sending out coordinates for where to drop bombs, I became claustrophobic," Rusty said. "And it's the reason I still don't use computers because it triggers flashbacks from Vietnam.

"But I never had to fire my rifle the whole time I was there."

Once he returned from the war he again faced the question of what profession to pursue. He enrolled in medical school and after studying in Mexico and a one-year internship in Chattanooga, came back to begin a family medical practice in South Pittsburg.

It wasn't long after settling back in at home before Rusty returned to the sideline to help his alma mater the best way he knew how.

"I was going to go to the games anyway, so I figured I might as well be down on the field looking after the kids when they got hurt," Rusty explained. "It means so much to me just to get to be a part of the team again. Being on the sideline you still feel the energy from the crowd and I get a kick out of being in the locker room at halftime listening to the coaches talk about the game.

"Once I started going to home games, I decided I might as well just tag along with them wherever they went to play and now I haven't missed many games over the years."

While he was serious about his work, he found ways to have fun with the kids along the way. He once had a player come off the field with what coaches worried was a concussion. After asking a few simple questions to gauge how clear-minded the kid was, Rusty offered $5 for the player to go to the concession stand to get both of them a Coke and a hotdog.

"He was going to take the money and stagger off toward the concession stand and that's when I knew this kid had no damn idea where the hell he was at," Rusty recalled with a laugh. "I told the coaches he wouldn't be allowed to go back in that night."

The four Pirates head coaches over the past 30 years knew they not only had a team doctor that would be on the sideline for every game, but also one who would give the entire team preseason physicals — all at no cost to the school.

"You couldn't put a price on what he's meant to our program," Vic Grider said. "Through the course of a season, whether it's a kid with the flu or an injury you know you're putting them in the hands of someone who has a vested interest in the program. He's been there. He played the game in high school and college and knows that fine line between being hurt and being injured.

Rusty Adcock.

"He would never put a kid in jeopardy. He's the only doctor, other than a specialist, I've ever been to in my life. That's how much I trust him."

But his inclination to give back to his school didn't end on game nights. Rusty has been instrumental in helping the athletic program and school by opening his checkbook or using his influence among community leaders to do the same.

When a new $5.2 million gym was built in 2008, Rusty was part of a group of supporters who raised more than $115,000 to purchase extra items for the new arena — including a custom built trophy case, having every Hall of Fame photo framed so that they would match, locker room upgrades, stadium chair seating and numerous orange and black Pirate logos throughout the building.

He was also one of the donors who helped get a new field house built and his family established the Adcock Academic award, with a scholarship going to the football player with the highest grade-point average.

"Wherever I go, if you mention South Pittsburg people ask about the football team," Rusty said. "It just seems like it's part of our city heritage. We grew up with Pirates football. It's our legacy. When the lights come on, everybody wants to be a part of it in some way and I guess I'm not different than anyone else.

"I just love the program and I was glad to find a way of giving back to my school."

Chapter 5
McREYNOLDS DRAGONS

"You have within you the strength, the patience and the passion to reach for the stars, to change the world."
— Harriett Tubman

It was an unmistakable sound, and one that became an identifiable opening act to the game night production that was McReynolds High School's football show. The team could be heard approaching before they were visible to fans in Hancock Stadium, the click, clack, click, clack of metal spikes on asphalt as players crossed the four-lane highway from their locker room to the field.

"South Pittsburg games are like a show with the Pirate ship blowing flames in the air and the music blaring over the speakers and the whole atmosphere, but McReynolds was the original show in town," said Boochie Moore, who played at the all-black school in the mid-1960s. "The team would dress in the gym locker room and then when they'd make their way to the stadium the police would stop traffic going both ways to let them cross. You'd hear them coming across the street, then down those concrete steps and they'd always have the biggest guys out front for intimidation. It worked. Every head in the stadium would turn and watch them coming down to the field."

Moore played quarterback for the Dragons, but as a middle school kid who just wanted to be part of the program, he volunteered to work as a ball boy, and at the first sound of the Dragons approaching the stadium, he'd look at the opposing team and announce what was coming.

"Ohhh, you boys messed up now," Moore would say, spinning a football in his hand. "You had your chance to get off this field but now them Dragons are here and you've gotta take an ass whippin'!

"You hear that? That's some gladiators coming for you!"

Before integration McReynolds High — the only educational option for African American children in South Pittsburg and the surrounding area — produced some of the most talented prep football players in the Sequatchie Valley from its inaugural team in 1930 until the final season in 1964.

For a four-year span between 1960-63, the Dragons were one of the most consistent programs in the state, compiling a 35-3-2 overall record and winning four consecutive Region 1 conference championships.

Professor M.M. Burnett was the long-time principal at McReynolds.

In 1963 — the same year that South Pittsburg's Pirates, their white counterparts across town, went unbeaten and won the Civitan Bowl — McReynolds finished undefeated for the first time in program history. At a time when defense and smash-mouth football reigned, the Dragons used a wide-open passing offense that was years ahead of its time to light up the scoreboard and average nearly five touchdowns per game.

"It was two schools less than two miles apart, in the same little town, that had probably the best teams in the whole state," Moore said. "There were always rumors that the Pirates and Dragons would play one day, or at least scrimmage, but it never happened. That was always the debate, who was better.

"We would go watch their games on Friday nights and we'd see their players standing on the hill to watch us when we played and there was a lot of mutual respect between the players.

"The kids at McReynolds had the same attitude as the South Pittsburg kids. We were both small, rural schools with a chip on our shoulder wanting to prove how tough we were. We took a lot of pride in that maroon and gold uniform and when people excelled from our school the whole community was proud."

HUMBLE BEGINNING

According to county records, besides the Cherokee Indians, among the first settlers in South Pittsburg were a community of free African Americans, who had escaped slavery in South Carolina. By the turn of the century, the black community numbers grew, along with the rest of the town's population during the industrial boom.

But with educational opportunities lagging, on May 3, 1919, a committee appointed to represent the black community as a whole went before the Marion County Board of Education to propose building an all-black elementary and high school in South Pittsburg.

The presentation by the committee — composed of Dr. W.J. Astrapp, Dennis Martin, Arthur Haywood and Brown McReynolds — was approved by the board, as was the recommendation by Dr. Astrapp that the new school be named in honor of McReynolds, who had worked tirelessly to establish the school for the community.

McReynolds High School, located in front of the old City Cemetery on the northern edge of the downtown area and later called the "Soul of Marion County", was completed in 1921 and students from South Pittsburg, Jasper, Whitwell and even Bridgeport (Ala.) were bused in to attend.

A wide brick staircase led to the grand front entrance, where three large photos hung in the hall leading into the school — Abraham Lincoln,

Booker T. Washington, Dr. Mary Bethune, creator of the United Negro College Fund. The two-story building had large windows along the wall facing town and the downstairs rooms served as the elementary school while the upstairs was reserved for high school classes.

Among the school's early students who went on to become prominent members of the community were Ken Jordan and Hiram B. Moore. Jordan graduated from the University of Tennessee law school and Moore went on to Nashville's Meharry medical school before returning to set up a general practitioner's office in South Pittsburg. Dr. Moore, and his longtime nurse Patsy Williams, offered free walk-in medical assistance to Dragons players every Monday after games and he became one of the most respected doctors in the area, tending to generations of patients from both the black and white communities.

More than 30 years after the school opened, the inequality in the nation's separate but equal segregation beliefs came into focus and the needed change, which had been as slow as December molasses in coming, was finally set in motion.

Black schools, as a whole, were underfunded and ill-equipped, particularly in comparison to white schools, leading to the unanimous 1954 decision in Brown v. Board of Education, which ruled segregation in public schools unconstitutional.

That decision opened the door for black students to begin attending previously all-white schools, although it took two years before Clinton High School became the first public school in Tennessee and the south to integrate. The threat of violence from white supremacists prompted National Guard troops to be called in to protect Clinton High for more than two months once school began, and two years after it had been integrated, a series of dynamite explosions severely damaged the school.

The message was clear — not enough progress had yet been made for much of the Jim Crow south to accept the high court's ruling that all races should be treated equally. The importance of educational opportunities, and the rapid progress that could be made by them, was seen through a completely opposite spectrum by those white southerners who agreed with one politician who was quoted as saying "A negro with a book is more dangerous than one with a gun."

"Looking back on it, I never had a book in school that didn't come from one of the other white schools in the county," Moore said. "We rarely had anything new at our school, so separate but equal may have sounded good, but there was no way it was true."

Although integration had not made its way to Marion County yet, the towns of Jasper and South Pittsburg had at least managed to avoid, for the most part, the violent resistance that rang through much of the surrounding southern neighbors.

After attending McReynolds, David Hale went on to become an all-state player at South Pittsburg.

"Maybe it's because it's such a blue-collar town, where black and white folks worked side by side, but we really didn't have the fear in South Pittsburg that other places in the south dealt with," Moore said. "My family moved to Cleveland, Ohio for a year when I was a freshman and honestly that was my first taste of racism. Back home, we lived in the same neighborhood with white kids and we would play together and even go to each other's house to eat.

"We would all walk to school together, but the difference was once we reached the front street, my white friends would turn left to go to SPHS and the black kids would take a right down the sidewalk to go to McReynolds. We didn't think anything about it at the time. It's just the way things were.

"The biggest difference in town wasn't based on race, it was whether you were rich or poor."

There were certainly pockets of racism — both the hushed, beneath the surface kind as well as those who were more overtly open about their bigoted views — in and around South Pittsburg and Jasper, although the more outlying areas of the Sequatchie Valley seemed to care less about hiding their ignorance and hate.

Gladys Wooten, a 1949 McReynolds graduate and overseer of the county's African American Historical Association, grew up in the shadow of the school, where neighborhood kids would zip past her family's house at the bottom of the hill.

Her father, Charlie Streeter, worked at Lodge and was greatly admired as a pillar of the community, while her mother Margaret worked from home as a seamstress and her younger brother James played for and later coached the Dragons.

"South Pittsburg really was an integrated town," Mrs. Wooten said. "It was a true community with working class people of both races living next to each other and working together. You read about or heard what life was like for black people outside our little community, but at home we never were told to use the back door at a business or have to use separate water fountains or bathrooms.

"The only real trouble between the two races came in the late 50s and early 60s when talk of integration picked up. That's when we found out who the people in town were that had kept their racism hidden."

With integration on the horizon, the fear that change was becoming a reality eventually revealed the ugly true feelings some harbored. Just before the calendar turned to begin 1960, and what would become a tumultuous new decade, a rumor of an interracial relationship between a black boy and white girl began circulating around town and led to the first public show of intimidation by the Ku Klux Klan, which burned a cross on the hill next to McReynolds.

The next day word spread through the black community that the KKK — members from Marion County joined by others from outside the area — intended to drive a convoy of cars through town, wearing their white hoods, as a show of force.

"My father was a very educated and proud man," Wooten said. "He instructed my mother to have all the kids join him on the front porch, with the lights on, and spread word through the community for our neighbors to do the same.

"When the KKK drove their parade through town, he wanted to show them that we were not afraid. They drove down the front street, turned around and came back through town, but we were all standing on our porch, with the lights on, watching them.

"Days later, several people from the white community started telling my father and other black leaders who the local KKK members were. Some of them were business owners and one of them was with the police, but they were all outed by other whites who didn't approve."

SHOWTIME

The first football team at McReynolds High was organized in 1930 and took bus trips to play against other all-black schools in Chattanooga, Cleveland, Knoxville, Murfreesboro, Tullahoma, Winchester and north Alabama. In their first season the Dragons won a conference championship and the program remained competitive against larger schools through its first three decades of competition.

The school's gym was built in 1949 and nine years later Dorsey Sims was hired to coach basketball and football. Sims coached for two years before taking over the basketball program at Chattanooga Riverside, which he guided to two state championships before later leading Memphis Melrose to a pair of state titles, then joining the Memphis State University staff.

After using Marion County and South Pittsburg football stadiums as a borrowed home for several seasons, the Dragons finally got a field of their own in 1960. That was also the season when Harold Smith was brought in as head coach and his no-nonsense attitude turned the program from being simply competitive to dominant.

The 6-foot-5 Smith, who had played briefly as a lineman with the Baltimore Colts, brought the mindset of "look good, play good" to the Dragons. After looking at the program's hand-me-down helmets, shoulder pads, game uniforms and mismatched practice jerseys, he knew things had to change so he approached the Marion County school board asking for the money to buy new equipment and uniforms — maroon home jerseys and gold road jerseys as well as matching practice uniforms.

"We're going to look like a champion and then play like a champion," he told the team during his introduction. "We're going to be big-timey. No more thinking small-timey."

"We went from about 20 players to more than 40 on the team because every able-bodied kid wanted to be a part of it," said Anthony Murphy, who worked as the team manager throughout Smith's coaching tenure. "Coach Smith put that pride in the program that had been lacking a little. He wanted everything from practice to the game to have a winning feel to it and that's why, for those years in the early 60s, there wasn't many schools in our division that could beat us.

"Coach Smith was like our Bear Bryant. He was so tough that games were a relief because they felt easier than his practices."

Whether it was stalking through the rows of players as they stretched before practice or watched closely as they circled the field running endless conditioning laps, Smith would repeatedly yell his trademark reminder of what he expected, "You can't be mediocre! You have to pay the price in order to win!"

Led by Robert Tipton, Milt Cobb, Charlie Cook, Robert Collier and Dave "Hoss" Robinson the Dragons became known for ferocious hits. Robinson, a freshman who had two sons that became college athletes — Tyrone played football at the University of Tennessee and Vincent played basketball at UTC, as well as three grandsons who played college football — was also a star running back. He and quarterback Dallas "Baby Boy" Moore and Dave Martin highlighted an offense that featured a pro-style set instead of the single-wing that most other teams — black and white — utilized at the time. Smith even allowed his quarterbacks to call audibles at the line if they saw something that would work against a particular defense.

"They used their speed on sweeps and passes to get into open space and run but they could also line up and just pound it right at people," Moore said. "It was different than just about every other team around; exciting and the crowds really packed the place to watch them."

In Smith's debut as coach the Dragons defeated Chattanooga's Booker T. Washington 6-0 in the rain. BTW had previously had its way with McReynolds, but the opener announced a new era and the Dragons went on to shut out three of their first four opponents, then blasted Winchester Townsend 55-7 and Cleveland's College Hill 65-0 on the way to a 7-1-1 record and the Region 1 Southeast Conference championship, not allowing more than 14 points in any game that season.

With the foundation for their coach's expectations set, the Dragons followed by opening the 1961 season with a 7-6 win over North Alabama region champ Fort Payne. The next week, the bus ride to Chattanooga to take on rival BTW took nearly an hour, which made Smith's rule of no talking on the way to games even more of a challenge, especially since the cheerleaders were allowed to ride at the front of the bus.

A talented sophomore class, led by new quarterback Luther "Stinger" Wilkerson and the backfield of Kelly McBride, Dave Martin and Greg "Tricks" Gurley gave a glimpse of just how good they would be in the years to come with a 12-6 win that ran the program's winning streak to nine. The loss infuriated BTW's fans so much that they began throwing rocks at the McReynolds players, coaches and even fans as they left the stadium.

The scary exit was quickly forgotten when Smith not only lifted the ban on talking, but allowed players to sit with cheerleaders on the ride home.

As they did throughout the years, when the Dragons team bus rolled back into South Pittsburg, the driver slowed through town and honked the horn to announce they had returned. People seated inside local restaurants came out on the sidewalk to wave, clap and cheer as the team passed.

"That was one of the really neat things about riding with the team," recalled Wooten, who was a cheerleader and later would ride a pep bus to follow the team when her brother played. "There would be black and white people in town all coming out to greet the team and cheer for them and that would tickle the kids.

"It was something else that reminded you that everyone in town was proud when either school accomplished something."

McReynolds had its win streak snapped the next week at home against Hartsville's Ward High — a sign of things to come as teams from South Pittsburg would go on to struggle against Trousdale County opponents years later.

The Dragons, who outscored opponents 25-3, finished a 10-1 season, and their second straight conference championship, with a 34-0 win over Lewisburg's Jones Training School in the Liberty Bowl.

McReynolds High was built in 1922 and burned in 1966.

McReynolds sat high on a hill overlooking South Pittsburg.

Coach Smith called Howard coach Chubby James to extend a challenge that McReynolds would play Chattanooga's powerhouse Hustlin' Tigers "any place, any time. Winner take all the bragging rights."

James refused the offer, but McReynolds did manage a bit of bragging rights later by claiming basketball wins over both Howard and Riverside.

With the majority of starters returning for the 1962 season, McReynolds fans openly expected the program's first unbeaten season. That talk heated up after Wilkerson connected with Dave Martin on an 80-yard touchdown pass on the first play of a 25-7 thumping of BTW to kick off the season.

The next week McReynolds destroyed Athens' Cook High 58-7 for the 10th win in its last 11 games but a 7-7 tie at Hatcher High, in Centre (Ala.) followed, putting an end to the talk of an unblemished season.

Late in the season, Wilkerson quit the team after an argument with Smith and, without their starting quarterback the Dragons lost at

Pikeville's State Training Facility. On the silent bus ride home — players were not allowed to talk after a loss — the ultra competitive Smith, sick over the loss, instructed the bus driver to pull over so he could throw up on the side of the road.

McReynolds rebounded with a 46-0 win over College Hill of Cleveland for its third consecutive conference title and an 8-1-1 record.

One of the most popular pages of the student newspaper — The Maroon and Gold — was "The Snooper", a section where kids would expose each other's secret crushes and rumors. But not even the school's gossip column knew ahead of time that Smith would announce his resignation late in the spring to take a job back in his home state of Florida.

Suddenly the promise of another championship that fall — the final season together for a loaded senior class that had transformed the program — looked to be in jeopardy. When Shannon Jolly, a McReynolds alum who had gone on to play at Knox College, was named the new coach, senior leaders had just one request — keep the same offensive and defensive systems that had been so successful the previous three years.

As the new season was set to kick off, folks in Marion County, like many others across the nation, were still trying to wrap their mind around the shock after the bombing of the 16th Street Baptist Church in Birmingham by the Ku Klux Klan, which killed four children and injured 22.

"It was just a real scary time," Moore said. "You would hear or read about horrible things happening all around us, throughout the south, and none of it made sense. You did feel safer in our little town, but you also knew there was a section of ignorant people who didn't like you just based on the color of your skin and so you knew who to steer clear of."

Having built a reputation for being a must-see team, McReynolds opened the 1963 season against rival BTW with a packed house at Engel Stadium that included most of Howard's players watching and sizing up the Dragons.

With a new staff in place, Wilkerson returned at quarterback and threw a touchdown pass to Gurley to help claim a 13-12 win.

The confidence from that win catapulted the Dragons to blowout wins over Dayton's Carver High, Winchester's Townsend High, Ft. Payne (41-0), Athens (33-0) and Sweetwater (31-7).

Their success through the years had created an issue for the Dragons that both South Pittsburg and Marion County would experience later — few potential opponents were willing to schedule McReynolds if they didn't have to.

That left coaches to search out established programs further away and in week seven the Dragons would visit one of those — Norris High in Attalla (Ala.), which had not lost a game in more than three seasons and had a roster twice the size of McReynolds.

After a two-hour bus ride to Attalla, located just outside of Gadsden, the Dragons barely drew a second glance from the overflow home crowd as they stepped onto the field.

"They didn't know anything about us and their team and fans were so used to beating everybody they played that you could tell they assumed this little school from across the state line was going to be just another easy victim," said Murphy. "Our guys were used to going into hostile environments, so nothing really fazed them. They just got ready to go to work."

Those expecting to see another Norris blowout got exactly the kind of start they were used to as the hosts connected on a flea-flicker pass that went for a 65-yard touchdown on the first snap, which helped them to a 12-6 halftime lead. By the fourth quarter McReynolds' deficit had swelled to 12 points before a long scoring drive cut it to 18-13.

A defensive stand gave the ball back to the Dragons at their 25 with 2:40 remaining. A Hoss Robinson run off right tackle went for 15 yards and James Battle followed with a 20-yard run, taking the ball across midfield and exposing a tired Norris defense.

Facing third and eight with just 52 seconds to go, Coach Jolly called for a short pass hoping to gain just enough to gain another first down. But since he had kept the exact same offense that Smith had installed, including the ability for the quarterback to audible any call, Jolly was as surprised as everyone else in the stadium when Wilkerson changed the play to a deep post to the speedy Gurley, who outran the secondary and made an over the shoulder catch for the go-ahead touchdown.

After Terry Ware intercepted a desperation Norris pass near midfield, McReynolds was able to run out the clock on a shocking 20-18 upset.

"We had beaten rival schools when they were really good and had even won a bowl game and several conference championships, but that was the biggest win in program history," Murphy explained.

When the Dragons returned to the visitor's dressing room, the glass doors of the school had been shattered by a water cooler, which was still lying on the floor, and there were loud shouts being hurled toward the players from the home fans.

Coach Jolly instructed the players to grab their clothes without showering or changing and keep their helmets on as they rushed back to their bus. With an agitated crowd gathering in the parking lot, the Norris principal stood near the Dragons bus with a pistol under his coat and asked the town's police to escort the team to the city limits.

"I'll never forget that scene," Murphy said. "It was scary trying to get out of there, but that long bus ride back was a lot of fun once we got out of Attalla."

Two more lopsided wins followed, setting up the chance to finally finish off an unbeaten season with a finale against Fayetteville West End.

The familiar sound of the Dragons warm-up music — "Green Onions" by Booker T and the MG's — met the team as they entered their home stadium on a Saturday evening. The funky instrumental — with electric guitar and organ riffs and heavy beat — made the McReynolds cheerleaders shake their skirts in such a way that even the white boys standing on the hill stopped watching the teams to check them out.

"We had some beautiful cheerleaders," Murphy said with a laugh. "And not even the white boys could resist taking a peek."

With a chance to make history hanging in the air, the Dragons jumped out to a commanding 28-0 halftime lead and continued to pour it on in a 47-7 win that secured a fourth straight conference championship and, more importantly, the program's first unblemished season.

One week later their white counterparts at SPHS capped an unbeaten season of their own by winning the Civitan Bowl over heavily favored Knoxville Powell.

"When I watched them, what impressed me was the style they played," said Roy Ferrell, a senior captain that season on South Pittsburg's Civitan Bowl championship team. "They were very creative and could score a lot of points, which led to a lot of gambling going on in the stands and out on the hill where we stood and watched.

"We knew all of their players so we were happy for what they were doing. Obviously there was division by us going to separate schools but we were all representing our hometown so we were very proud of the success McReynolds had and it helped create the reputation for how good football was around here."

"A SAD DAY FOR US ALL"

The ominous mixture of black and charcoal gray smoke rose high into the warm summer sky and could be seen for miles. The sound of wailing sirens broke the mid-morning quiet as firetrucks raced to the scene near the northern edge of South Pittsburg's city limits.

McReynolds High School had stood proudly on the hill overlooking the town's business district for more than 40 years. But on July 28, 1965 at around 9:30 on what had began as a peaceful Wednesday morning, the first call came into the town's fire department that smoke was rising from inside the building.

Minutes later the somber news was already spreading through town and as firemen began battling the blaze, nearly 100 students and curious onlookers stood at the bottom of the hill and watched helplessly as flames jutted from the large windows to lick the roof and eventually cause the interior of the two-story structure to collapse in on itself.

Two firemen were injured battling the blaze, which consumed all of the main school, leaving only the gym — which was a separate building.

As the reality that their school was being engulfed began to sink in, tears streamed down the faces of teenagers and adults alike who had walked several blocks from the nearby black community.

"I heard the commotion and when I came out of our house you could hear people running down the street yelling that the school was on fire," said Anthony Murphy, who attended McReynolds through the eleventh grade, then was part of the first integrated class to graduate from South Pittsburg High in 1966. "It was already hot that day but when you got to the bottom of the hill you could feel the heat from the fire. It was an inferno. I kept hoping they could salvage something, but there was no way they were going to put that fire out before it completely destroyed the building.

"I was looking forward to our prom, homecoming, going to Washington D.C. for our school trip. It was all gone. When we integrated things were a little weird at a new school so it was like those of us from McReynolds lost out on our senior year.

"That was a sad day for us and we hurt over it for a long time. McReynolds is still in my bloodlines. It nurtured me and shaped who I am. I loved it. We all did. When we get together we still talk about McReynolds and the games and growing up together there.

"Whenever I come back home to visit, I still look up on that hill where the school stood and shake my head because it's gone. It's a memory, but it's still a very special place for a lot of us."

Less than two months before the fire the Marion County Department of Education had been given a directive from the state to submit a plan for the desegregation of all its public schools by the start of the 1966-67 school year.

The fire had been set by an arsonist who was never identified. There had been discussion that once the state mandated integration was complete, McReynolds would serve as a junior high for both black and white students in town. That led to speculation that the likely culprits were racists who opposed having their kids attend the historically black school.

"It was already a done deal that the schools would integrate," Moore said. "The black community loved McReynolds and we were very proud of it, so nobody other than a racist redneck would've had any reason to burn that school."

Regardless of who lit the match the events of that morning had a demoralizing affect that was felt throughout the Sequatchie Valley's black community.

"Me and my three siblings had all graduated from McReynolds," Wooten said. "Our family would go watch my baby brother play football there and those game nights were a big deal for everyone involved.

"The teachers there cared so much, not only about our education but about how we should carry ourselves. The school was the source of a lot of pride. When I heard the sirens blow, I ran outside to see what was happening and as soon as I looked up and saw the building on fire I began to cry. I cried the whole time it burned and so did many others who had to stand there and watch."

The fire had been front-page news in South Pittsburg's weekly newspaper the weekend after the incident, but the following week there was not even a follow-up mention of it or an investigation, although there was a front-page story announcing the start of the Pirates fall football practice.

The rubble smoldered for several weeks and when the new school year arrived the black students who had been part of a close-knit community were scattered. Some elementary classes gathered at a local community center and church, while most of the high school kids attended class in the gym.

The seniors and junior high students were integrated into South Pittsburg High. On the first day of the new school year, SPHS principal Phil Beene, who was also the Pirates legendary football coach and had the reputation for being a strict disciplinarian, called an assembly of the entire student body.

"We were seated in the auditorium, the white kids looking at us, wondering what we were all about, and us feeling pretty out of place," Murphy said. "We were still in our home town, but we were strangers at that school. Coach Beene stood on the stage and said, "Scholars, we've got new students joining us, and I don't want anybody messing with them. If you have a problem with them you'll have to come see me.'

"Everybody knew you didn't mess with Coach Beene and his message resonated with them. After that nothing nasty was said to us, at least not directly to our faces. The black kids stuck together and we really didn't mingle at first, until basketball season when we all played on the same team.

"Sports helped bring us together and eventually everybody realized we were just teammates and not really any different from one another."

Because black students were given the choice of which school they would integrate into, Moore followed two of his best friends who already lived in Jasper and attended Marion County, where he played basketball but gave up football because, as a strong-armed quarterback, he felt he didn't fit into the single-wing system.

One young player who certainly would fit into the run-oriented offense was Jimmy Wigfall, who came to South Pittsburg from McReynolds and would later lead the Pirates to the program's first state championship with a school-record rushing season in 1969.

"We were dirt poor growing up so I couldn't afford to get into the games at either place, but a lot of us would stand outside the stadium at South Pittsburg and watch them play and then go watch McReynolds.

"Both schools had a hell of a team and you could learn how the game was suppose to be played just by watching them. They had different styles, but they were both tough and well-coached and I couldn't wait to get to be a part of it."

As the first in what became a continuous line of talented black athletes who have helped the Pirates maintain their status as one of the premier programs in the state, Wigfall also coaxed David Hale — a tough as nails underclassman who would become a star lineman and later an influential coach — to join the team prior to the 1969 season.

"Jimmy knew which buttons to push to get me to come out," Hale said with a chuckle. "I had told him I didn't want to play so he said 'Get your big ass out there. Or are you scared?' I went out that spring just to prove to him that I wasn't scared to hit anybody and by that summer I realized I could be pretty good.

"I had been a mean kid; kind of a bully growing up, so football was a way to get to prove how tough I was."

Hale was the only freshman starter on the state title team and was named to the All Sequatchie Valley Conference team his next three seasons before eventually earning a scholarship to play at Vanderbilt, where he became a team captain.

"Wigfall and David Hale set that early standard for all the kids that followed them from the black community," said Moore, who had three sons that played for the Pirates, including one that led the tri-state area in scoring, one who was named all-state and another who was part of a state championship. "I chose to go to Marion when the schools integrated because that's where my best friends were going, and I'm proud of the success both schools have had through the years.

"My sons played at South Pittsburg and my diploma says Marion County, and I will always support both those schools, but like everybody who ever went there, my heart will always be a McReynolds Dragon."

Chapter 6

BILL BAKER

"Success is when preparation and opportunity meet."
— **Bobby Unser**

As a player, coach and professional scout Bill Baker's football career spanned more than six decades — covering seven college programs, five NFL franchises and three high schools teams across 10 states.

But it all began on a simple homemade obstacle course his dad built in a field near their house, which was surrounded by 30 acres of farmland in Jasper.

"I loved football from the first time daddy threw me passes in our yard," Baker explained. "But I got really serious about it around my freshman year in high school. He bush hogged an area so we could build a training course — with bales of hay for me to jump over, barrels to run around and old tires for me to step through to practice my footwork. It was just a way for me to train and get better and I was out there every day running around."

Baker had been so anxious to begin his football career that he lied about his age to join Jasper Elementary School's seventh grade team as a fourth-grader. It wasn't until an elbow injury — more than a week into summer practice — sent him to a local doctor that coaches realized he was too young to play with the junior high Warriors.

"I had already earned a spot as a starting tailback before I got hurt," Baker recalled. "The one thing I could always do was run fast. Daddy was eager for me to get to play and we were disappointed when I was told I would have to wait a couple of years before I could play."

Once he was finally old enough to rejoin the Warriors, Baker quickly earned a reputation as one of the best young players in the Sequatchie Valley and announced his arrival on the big stage as a sophomore for Marion County, scoring three touchdowns, including a 55-yard punt return, against Grundy County.

By the time his senior year began Baker had worked his way into becoming one of the top college recruits in Tennessee. In that 1964 season, with the eyes of college scouts and opposing defenses focused on him, Baker ignored the added attention as the team's workhorse to rush for more than 1,400 yards — averaging 7 yards per carry — and threw for another 500 to lead Marion County to an 8-2 record, the most wins for the program in seven years.

"Growing up working on a farm, we didn't have much, but mama and daddy taught us about hard work," said Baker, who grew up with two older sisters and a younger brother. "No matter what we did, we knew we were expected to work hard and never quit until the job was done."

In an early-season match-up against county rival Whitwell he set the tone for big things to come by running for 202 yards and four touchdowns. The following week, on the Friday morning before Marion played Sequatchie County, Baker received a Western Union telegram from University of Georgia assistant Doc Ayers that read, "Good luck to you and your teammates in your game tonight."

That night Baker threw for three touchdowns and ran for another in a blowout win. Later that fall he helped rally Marion from a 19-0 halftime deficit against Chattanooga Valley, throwing for a 15-yard score and breaking loose for a 47-yard TD run to spark a 21-19 come-from-behind win.

The Warriors earned an invitation to the Civitan Bowl in Cookeville, and again it was Baker who played a key role in the 7-0 win over Grundy County that also secured the Sequatchie Valley Conference championship. Baker, who had led the SVC in rushing and scoring to earn all-state and SVC Most Outstanding Back honors, ran the ball on nine of the 10 plays on Marion's opening possession, including a one-yard dive into the end zone.

The Warriors defense, highlighted by Johnny Grimes' late goal line stop, made the lead stand for their second win over the Yellow Jackets that year.

Bill Baker with UT coach Doug Dickey.

Weeks later, a letter from University of Tennessee president Andy Holt arrived in the mail for Baker and began "Coach Doug Dickey has informed me that you are one of the top athletes in our entire state and his staff will tender you a scholarship application on Dec. 12. I would like to congratulate you on this great honor!"

Although he also had offers from Alabama, Georgia, Vanderbilt, Memphis State, Florida State and Colorado, there was no question where Baker would sign to continue his football career.

"If I had gone anywhere but Tennessee it would've killed my dad," he said. "I was heavily recruited, but we had grown up listening to UT games on the radio and that was a big deal for both of us that I was going to get to play there."

Doug Dickey was hired to take over at UT at a time when the program was struggling, having failed to win more than six games in a season or reach a bowl game in seven straight years. The only way the no-nonsense Dickey knew to rejuvenate the program was to recruit better players, then put them through a grueling series of workouts designed to reveal the most resilient and tenacious competitors.

Those would be identified in what was later referred to by the players simply as Section X. In the bowels of Neyland Stadium, a large cinderblock area with concrete floors beneath Section X housed what Dickey and his staff used as a makeshift offseason workout area that would reconstruct the program and weed-out those who couldn't hack the grind of becoming the toughest team in the Southeastern Conference.

The UT staff put together what they called the "county fair", an assortment of grinding physical tests much more demanding than any weight room workout the players had experienced.

"There was steam coming up from grates in the floor and the room was dark, and dingy," Baker said. "It had a very gloomy feel to it as soon as you walked it, like it should've been condemned. As soon as you walked into the room you were hit with the smell of mildew and sweat. You wanted to throw up just from walking in there.

"They had pegboards on the wall and a wrestling mat on the floor and they would put us through absolute hell. We did barrel rolls, agility drills and all sorts of physical training in there. The coaches set large trash cans all around the room for us to throw up into and I think everybody on the team used them.

"Coach Dickey would put us young guys on the mat and yell 'Who wants him?' and the biggest son of a buck senior would come walking out and just pin us and beat us to a pulp. You'd be on the ground and the coaches would get down there and yell in your face 'Are you quittin'? Are you a quitter?'

"After the first day of that we lost about 10 guys who just couldn't take it. For a while, there would be a couple more who would sneak out at night and never come back, but I knew I couldn't quit. My daddy would've killed me if I had come home. Growing up on the farm and playing for Coach Bill and Dave Baxter at Marion prepared me to be tough.

"Section X was far different than anything I had ever experienced. Everybody there was considered to be a star athlete so you were constantly competing against the best, but not everybody could take it. There were fights in the dorm after practice almost every day. It was the younger guys who were competitive and not willing to put up with getting beat. We developed a camaraderie and those of us that stayed, that's the reason we turned the program around and won."

At the time freshmen weren't eligible to play with the varsity, but the freshman team lost only once in the fall of 1965 and the next season, with the hardened freshman class added to a saltier group of upperclassmen, the Vols finished 8-1-2 and Dickey was named SEC Coach of the Year.

The following season UT traveled to the west coast in its opener, losing narrowly to UCLA, but rebounded to claim nine straight wins and the SEC title, earning a trip to the Orange Bowl and were named national champions by Litkenhous.

Not only was Baker a part of the group that helped reclaim past glory at Tennessee, but those first teams under Dickey also began traditions that still carry on — the "Power T" on the sides of the helmets, the checkerboard end zones and running out onto the field through the 'T' formed by the Pride of the Southland Band.

"Coach Dickey brought hard-core discipline back to the program," Baker said. "Tennessee had been good, then hit a down cycle and he wanted to get it back and make us winners again. I'm very proud to be a part of the group that helped the program turn the corner.

"For a Tennessee boy to run out on the field and have 52,000 people — which is what Neyland Stadium held back then — cheering for you, that was a very emotional experience."

Baker became so emotional before his first varsity competition, in the spring Orange and White scrimmage, that his nerves made him sick at his stomach.

"I said then that if he could get himself that worked up over a spring game, then we had a ball player on our hands," Dickey said later.

What Baker became best known for during his UT career was his versatility. The 6-foot-1, 200-pounder played in both the offensive and defensive backfields and returned punts and kicks throughout his three-year varsity career, even leading the SEC with a 10.5-yard punt return average his senior season.

"Bill Baker is typical of the type athlete we like to have here at the University of Tennessee," Dickey told the Chattanooga News-Free Press during Baker's senior season. "He is a great competitor and always ready to give it everything he had. He reminded me of the old saying about giving a good, honest day's work because he not only was ready to play at top speed when the ballgame rolled around, but went at it in practice that way every day.

"Such boys don't come along very often."

The Vols compiled a 25-7-1 overall record during his three years, playing in the Gator, Orange and Cotton Bowls to set a standard of toughness for others to follow.

"Bill was one of those guys I looked up to because he was already an established player and with me coming from Winchester and him being from Jasper, we had similar backgrounds," said Tennessee athletic director Phillip Fulmer, who was a freshman offensive lineman during Baker's senior season. "He was older but was a great teammate, a really good player and leader and just a super nice guy."

During his junior year Baker married his high school sweetheart, Paula Anne Brown. Her brother, Eddie was an all-state tailback at Marion County at the time and would later become an All America punt returner and defensive back for the Vols.

Bill Baker during his playing days at Tennessee.

"When he was at Tennessee I got to go there quite a bit and be around the atmosphere and get to know some of the players, so I knew what to expect once my time came to go there," Eddie Brown said. "It also eased my mind to see a guy from the same home town and same school doing so well because it let me know that I really could do it too."

After his playing career ended, just before he graduated from UT, his hometown proclaimed May 3, 1969 as "Bill Baker Day". He and Coach Dickey flew from Knoxville to the airport in Jasper, where a motorcade carried them to Marion County High School for a banquet and the key to the city was given to the former Warriors star in front of a crowded cafeteria.

Although he wasn't sure how just yet, Baker knew that he would pursue a career that kept him involved in the sport which had broken his nose three times, dislocated his shoulder numerous others and broken his collar bone among other injuries.

The winding journey began at Sandy Springs (Ga.) High School, where Baker worked as an assistant for just one season before getting a call from Tullahoma High with an offer to take over the program as a 23-year old.

"Paula and I had a lot of fun there and loved it," Baker said. "We went 5-5 that first year and thought we were going to settle down there."

Instead another former Vol, Wayne Grubb who had been a part of the defense that stopped LSU running back Billy Cannon short on a two-point conversion to seal an upset of the top-ranked Tigers, called with an offer to join his staff at Samford University.

By his second year there Baker's secondary led the nation in interceptions, which opened the door for an offer to take the same job title at Austin Peay University, where he stayed only a year before another promotion was offered, this time the chance to join Jim Wright, Phillip Fulmer, John Stuckey and Frank Emanuel on the staff at Wichita State.

Baker was promoted to defensive coordinator his second year with the Shockers.

"I had a chance years later to work on the same staff with him at Wichita State when I was beginning my coaching career and quickly understood that he was an incredibly smart football coach," Fulmer added. "With me being a young, single guy, he took me under his wing and he and his wife Paula let me stay with them and I had many meals with them. We developed a great friendship that has carried through the years."

Having established himself in the coaching community, Baker received a call from his alma mater, which had begun to struggle under Bill Battle. The Vols had two open assistants positions — receivers and secondary — and Baker interviewed for both before taking the offer to coach his former position.

Unfortunately he joined Battle's staff in the final year of what had been a steady decline in performance for the Vols, who had gone from a 10-win team in 1972 to 8 wins the following year, followed by two seven win seasons and finally a 6-5 finish in Baker's only season on staff. Battle was fired after that 1976 season and new head coach Johnny Majors did not retain Baker on staff.

Old friend Wayne Grubb, who was now the head coach at the University of North Alabama, hired Baker to be his offensive coordinator and he remained there for two years before the coaching carousel spun him to Louisville for four seasons, where he worked as secondary coach and defensive coordinator before leaving for his final coaching job at the University of Richmond, where he remained for six seasons, longer than he had at any previous stop.

The Spiders had gone winless in the season before Baker arrived, but won five games in his first season as defensive coordinator and reached the I-AA playoffs each year that followed, advancing as far as the semifinals.

"There had been a few times when I wanted to be a head coach," Baker admitted. "I interviewed four times — at Nicholls State, which I turned down, then at East Tennessee State, James Madison and Richmond. I never got another head coaching offer after Nicholls State.

"I finally decided we had drug my daughter (Jennifer) around the country enough and it was time to get out of coaching and find something where my family could put down roots."

Among the network of friends he had made in the NFL was Atlanta Falcons general manager Ken Herock, who hired Baker to become a roving scout. During his nine seasons with the Falcons in the 1990s, Baker helped scout and recommend the team draft a pair of future Hall of Fame players — cornerback Deion Sanders from Florida State and quarterback Brett Favre from Southern Mississippi, who the Falcons eventually traded to Green Bay.

Bill Baker was a three-sport athlete at Marion.

"Brett was wild and he would go out with all his offensive linemen at night and then come to practice the next morning with beer still on his breath from partying the night before," Baker said. "June Jones was the offensive coordinator at the time and as a devout Christian wouldn't tolerate that, so we wound up trading away a guy who became one of the all time great quarterbacks.

"Deion was just as flashy off the field as people thought, but when he stepped on the field he was all business. He knew how to play and he had a world of ability. He showed up for the combine in a limo, got out and when he ran the 40-yard dash for all the scouts and coaches and front office people there, he just kept right on going out a tunnel and back to his limo to fly home.

"He had ran an unbelievable 4.27 and didn't even bother to stay and do any interviews or any other workouts. He said later he had shown all we needed to see, so he just kept running right out of the building and flew home. That was something we had never seen."

Similar to his circuitous college coaching career, Baker's 22-year resume' as an NFL scout also kept him on the move, although his wife and daughter were at least able to remain in Richmond, where the family lived for 24 years.

After nine seasons with the Falcons, he spent three with the Seahawks as their national scout, then three years as scouting director for the Steelers, six with the Dolphins and two with the Redskins before deciding to retire and move back to Knoxville.

"The travel and hotels and being away from home got old," Baker admitted. "Mama was 91 then and having health issues too, so I needed to be closer to her.

"Retirement didn't last long because when I first got back to Knoxville Derek Dooley was taking over UT's program and he asked me to come on as their NFL coordinator, to help seniors get ready for the draft and show pro scouts around and talk to them about our players who were draft eligible. I had recruited Derek when I was at Richmond, so we knew each other. He trusted me and I loved being back at UT and helping the program."

Baker remained with the Vols through Dooley's three seasons and worked on the Butch Jones staff for only three months before finally deciding to retire from the game completely.

"The game opened so many doors for me. I don't know where I'd be today if not for football," Baker said. "I never would've had the opportunity to be more than I was, a poor boy from a small town, but the game gave me and my family everything we were able to have and become a success in my career.

"Of all the places I've gone, it was my hometown and my coaches at Marion that shaped me and developed me into who I've always been. That's where I first saw how football can unite an entire community and of everything I've ever done, some of my favorite memories are my high school days and my college days at UT. Those are the times that go by way too fast, but you will always remember fondest."

Chapter 7
1969 – SEASON OF CHANGE

"Insecurity is at the heart of every rivalry."
— Beth Moore

Less than two months after man first set foot on the moon's surface and Neil Armstrong's memorable words "That's one small step for man, one giant leap for mankind," crackled through the television static, the winds of change barely seemed to rustle the leaves in the Sequatchie Valley.

The TV news each evening detailed chilling events — racial tension, Vietnam War protests by angry young people with long hair wearing green military jackets decorated with peace signs and a drug culture that seemed to spread through an entire generation. But all of that felt so far removed from life in Marion County that it might as well have also been happening on the moon.

After all, most of the folks who enjoyed living right and being free around Jasper and South Pittsburg believed the lyrics to Merle Haggard's 'Okie from Muskogee' were based on their way of life, where they "still waved old glory down at the courthouse, and white lightnin's still the biggest thrill of all".

The surrounding mountains seemed to shelter the area from the counter-culture scene sweeping much of the nation.

"I think I remember knowing one guy who had smoked pot, and he was kind of a loner," recalled Eddie Brown, a Warriors senior in 1969 with a mop of brown hair that made the girls giggle. "We still said 'yes sir' and 'no ma'am' like we'd been taught so we were pretty far behind on all that wild stuff that was going on around the rest of the country."

The year began with newly elected President Richard Nixon taking office and the New York Jets, led by cocky quarterback Joe Namath, upsetting the heavily favored Baltimore Colts in Super Bowl III. By early summer the first withdrawal of U.S. troops from Vietnam had begun.

While folks in South Pittsburg were rummaging across the creaky wooden floors of Kuhn's Variety Store for back-to-school specials that included ladies' wide-leg slacks for $1.94 and men's long sleeve collared shirts for $1.77,

Jimmy Wigfall, principal Phil Beene and Steve Smith admire the state championship trophy.

members of a California cult led by Charles Manson murdered seven people over two days, including actress Sharon Tate, who was eight-months pregnant.

Weeks later, on the same weekend that nearly half a million free-spirited music fans, better known across the south simply as hippies, landed on a muddy upstate New York farm to hear the biggest rock bands of the day — Jimi Hendrix, The Who, and Crosby Stills Nash and Young — play live at Woodstock, the big event in the Sequatchie Valley was the annual football jamboree, hosted by South Pittsburg.

Summer was beginning to give way when a new TSSAA rule was announced, allowing for two points to be scored if a team ran or threw the ball across the goal line following a touchdown. Of course one point would still be rewarded for kicking the ball through the uprights.

But it was another new addition being introduced by the state's high school sports governing body that would become much bigger news as a playoff format would produce an unquestioned state champion. Previously bowl games had been the only postseason offered, leaving the question of who truly was the best team in the state up for debate. The new playoff system would finally settle that argument on the field.

There was significant on-the-field change too at South Pittsburg, where after seven years as an assistant, Don Grider was taking over for legendary head coach Phil Beene. Remaining on the assistants staff were W.T. "Hoot" Gibson and Sam Brooks, who would eventually become known throughout Tennessee as one of the fathers of classification. Brooks would win more than 300 games as the boys' basketball coach, even guiding them to the program's first and only state tournament appearance in the mid-1980s, but was known throughout the state's coaching ranks for being instrumental in convincing the TSSAA to classify athletic programs based on the size of enrollment.

The new small and large school classification system, which was also introduced in 1969, would be the first of many ways the state would use to divide teams over the coming decades.

Season expectations for the Pirates were tempered by the fact the 34-player roster was made up mostly of juniors and sophomores, and even some freshmen who would have to start.

What became apparent only months later was that despite their inexperience, this would be an unflinching group blessed with playmaking backs and undersized linemen who refused to back down.

The only thing faster than senior tailback Jimmy Wigfall was barbershop gossip, but at just 5-foot-7, 140-pounds, he wasn't expected to be able to handle the beating to carry a team through the Sequatchie Valley Conference, which was recognized as one of the most physically grueling leagues statewide.

With the majority of starters returning, and its sheer size advantage up front, Whitwell was thought to be the team to beat in the SVC, along with Marion County.

Bill Baxter had averaged seven wins a season heading into his seventh year coaching Marion, including two SVC championships, and the

Warriors were coming off a 9-0 season. They had all-conference talent in tackles Byron Kelly and Ronnie Parker, safety Donald Payne, linebacker Jimmy Holtzclaw, and Brown, who starred on both sides of the ball as well as on special teams.

The year before Brown had been a two-way star at tailback and defensive back, and was now projected to be the top college prospect in the area.

Because teams in the Sequatchie Valley played in the Central time zone, they had agreed to a preseason request from the Chattanooga Times to move kickoffs up 30 minutes, beginning at 7 p.m., so that their games could be better covered in each Saturday's sports section, which worked on an Eastern time zone deadline.

In small print along the front page of the August 21 edition of South Pittsburg's weekly paper, The Hustler, was news that Marion County teachers were delaying the signing of their contracts because they were dissatisfied with announced budget cuts that would mean less pay.

But despite the potential educator's work stoppage, the dominant photo and story on The Hustler's front page was the Pirates team picture and the announcement of the jamboree, along with large bold letters encouraging the entire town to support the team as the season approached.

BETTER THAN EXPECTED

The season began on Labor Day weekend, and South Pittsburg opened against Sequatchie County in one of only three home games it would have.

In what would develop into a trend for the season, the Pirates wasted no time in jumping out to an early lead. In just six plays Wigfall found the end zone from 18 yards out for the first of his two touchdowns as the Pirates raced out to a 22-0 lead by halftime.

Wigfall would finish with 134 rushing yards, threw for another 55 and sophomore fullback Donald Blansett established himself for what would become a breakout season by scoring twice. Bobby Joe Ford recovered a fumble and Booster Case and Charles Garner each intercepted passes as the Pirates cruised to a 28-8 win.

"It usually only took one block to spring Wigfall," Blansett remembered. "A lot of times, I would make a block and then catch myself standing there watching him run. He was something else."

Meanwhile on the opposite end of the valley, Marion County got off to a roaring start to its season by beating Bledsoe County 26-13 in its opener. Eddie Brown was even more impressive, running for 169 yards on 31 tough carries and completing 7 of 17 passes for 115 yards. He accounted for all but 21 of Marion's total yards and three of its four touchdowns.

Marion out-gained Bledsoe 178-15 in total yards in the first half and were jump-started in the second half when Dwayne Chastain caused a fumble which Byron Kelly recovered at the Bledsoe 3, and two plays later Brown scored a TD that put Marion ahead to stay.

A week later the only thing that could stir emotions more than South Pittsburg's devotion to its football team was the frightening possibility presented by a proposal to sell liquor in town. A local minister wrote an opinion column that appeared on the front page of The Hustler, challenging the

The 1969 state champion Pirates.

town's men to "show backbone" and vote against the referendum, warning that should the city allow liquor to be sold, the citizens could expect its sons to become alcoholics and daughters to find "unwanted trouble". The minister summed up his letter by adding, "What a price to pay". The edition included three full pages of signatures from townsfolk on a petition to vote against "legal whiskey". Besides the signatures, the only artwork on the pages was a skeleton hand holding a martini glass. The not-so-subtle insinuation being that should South Pittsburg suddenly succumb to the selling of booze, death would certainly follow soon behind.

The sober citizens eventually won out, voting down the liquor referendum with nearly twice as many votes, meaning that for at least a while longer the best way to tell the difference between the town's Baptists and Methodists was that at least the Methodists would speak to you in the liquor stores outside city limits.

While Marion had a chance to breathe easy in week two with a mismatch against Grundy County, the Pirates would be tested at Whitwell, the SVC preseason favorite. Or so it was thought.

On the the third play from scrimmage Wigfall cut off left tackle and sprinted 67 yards for a TD. He then connected with Bobby Joe Ford for the two-point conversion and the tone was set.

After Whitwell's Cliff Pickett returned the second half kickoff 85 yards for a score, Wigfall was again the answer for the Pirates. This time he broke free for a 27-yard TD, then added the two-point pass to Billy Berryhill for a 16-6 win.

"Early in that game Coach Beene was yelling for Coach Grider from behind the fence," Blansett said. "He had seen something that he wanted to point out, but Coach Grider never turned around to see what he wanted. I asked Coach Grider about that years later and he said he didn't turn around because it was his butt on the line as the head coach and he was going to do what he thought was best to help us win."

The Warriors had a much easier time that night, as Brown, with a University of Georgia scout watching from the stands, ran for three TDs, threw to Jackie Sharp for one and returned a punt 75 yards for another in a 34-6 whipping. Brown finished with 150 rushing yards, 140 more on two punt returns and the defense held Grundy County to 87 total yards.

As September came to a close, the first episodes of Scooby-Doo, The Brady Bunch and Sesame Street made their debut, to the delight of kids for years to come. That same month The Beatles released their Abbey Road album and made their last public performance together, on the roof of Apple Records.

With slightly less fanfare, South Pittsburg remained unbeaten with a shutout win over Stevenson in the rain and a hard-fought 20-8 decision at Spring City, led by Blansett, Wigfall, Ford and freshman lineman David Hale, who caused a fumble in each of those games by blasting ballcarriers.

The Warriors matched South Pittsburg win for win, shutting out Bridgeport for their 12th straight victory, and in the process rolling up 239 rushing yards, most of that from Brown and Tim Martin. Meanwhile the defense, led by Byron Kelly, Nathan Hargis and Bishop Chastain, held the Tigers to just 21 total yards.

That win streak came to an end the following week however as the Warriors failed to score despite driving inside the Whitwell 5 three times. Steve Daffron intercepted Marion passes at the 1 and later at the 2 and linemen Dexter Dodson and Johnny Carr helped the Tigers defense stop the Warriors on four downs from the 4-yard line just before halftime.

While the Tigers defense held Marion scoreless for the first time in 24 games — limiting Brown to a season-low 79 total yards — Cliff Pickett, known more as a bruising fullback, was the offensive hero. He returned the opening kickoff 86 yards for a TD and ran for 148 yards and another score in the 12-0 upset.

That same night, on Monteagle Mountain, South Pittsburg took out the frustration of a grueling week of practice on Grundy County. Unhappy with how his team had played the previous week, Don Grider had put the team through a hellish week of practice to get their attention. It clearly worked as the Pirates easily drove for a score on their first possession, intercepted four first-half passes, two by linebacker Steve Blevins, one by Grey Smith and another by Wigfall, who also threw for two scores and ran for another.

The Pirates got their third shutout win in four games the next week at Bridgeport, rolling up 377 total yards and holding the Tigers to 38.

As the season wound down, Marion shut out Stevenson then hammered Copper Basin and Polk County, behind nine rushing TDs from Brown in those two games, helping the team gain steam heading toward the finale.

Over the last two weeks of October, South Pittsburg clinched the SVC title with a Blansett-led win over Bledsoe County that included two rushing TDs and an interception by the sophomore. Wigfall returned a kickoff 80 yards for a score and connected with Ford on another.

The week before the cross-county showdown with the Warriors, the Pirates traveled to Sweetwater to square off against another unbeaten team in a game that would eliminate one from playoff contention.

Jimmy Wigfall, head coach Don Grider, and Steve Smith are all smiles after the semifinal win.

The Wildcats drove to the Pirates 11 in the first quarter, but on third down David Hale broke through the line for a huge 8 yard sack and on the next play, Ford intercepted a pass at the goal line and returned it 37 yards.

On the ensuing drive Wigfall avoided a defender and found Ford for a 37-yard TD, giving the Pirates the early lead and some much-needed confidence.

The Wildcats began the second half by driving to the Pirates 6 before being stopped on downs, but after recovering a Pirates fumble, drove inside the 10 again. A third down pass into the end zone was tipped away by Wigfall and a desperation fourth-down pass was batted down as the Pirates continued to avoid disaster.

Two plays after having a 73-yard scoring run called back by penalty, Wigfall broke free for a 66-yard TD to put the game out of reach.

In the days leading up to South Pittsburg's trip to Jasper, the TSSAA announced it would notify 12 schools — four in each of the three classes – that they would be selected for the playoffs after the final week of games. Teams were selected from four regions on a points system (10 points for each win) and the Pirates' next closest foe was Charleston which had one loss but played a 10-game schedule. Because the Pirates played just 9 regular-season games, if both teams won their last game they would each finish with 90 points and the TSSAA would decide who got invited to the playoffs.

A day before the biggest game in the history of Tennessee's best prep football rivalry, all of the talk on the national sports stage revolved around New York's Miracle Mets rallying from last-place laughingstock to become World Series champions.

LAST MAN STANDING

Whether their car radio blared Creedence Clearwater Revival's 'Bad Moon Rising', Sly and the Family Stone's 'Everyday people' or Elvis's 'Suspicious Minds' — all of which dominated the airwaves that fall — on the short ride into Jasper to fill the stands, fans from both towns passed Ayers Used Cars, which teased a 1968 6-cylinder Ford Mustang for $1,895. They also passed Hale's Super Market, with paper signs plastered across storefront windows advertising "premium steaks for 59-cents a pound!" Most of the other signs taped to the town's businesses were in support of the Warriors.

"There were signs everywhere in the buildup around both towns the week of the game," Marion's Brown said. "I can still remember the feeling of so much excitement every year for that game.

"I've played in a Super Bowl and I've never played in a bigger rivalry game than against South Pittsburg. It's two strong-willed communities who take a lot of pride and bragging rights for a whole year, all centered around that one game. It wasn't just the students or players, it was the whole communities."

A swirling wind added a chill to the early-November evening as the two teams reached the season finale with more than just bragging rights riding on the outcome. The SVC championship would be decided, and adding to the pregame electricity was the knowledge that only the winner stood a chance to earn a spot in the playoffs. The teams boasted two of the state's most dynamic playmakers.

But the baddest man in the valley was not either of the two prep stars for the Pirates or Warriors. On that same evening, about the time the game was kicking off, Earl Allison of Stevenson (Ala.) would make front-page news when he killed a bobcat with a carjack on Russell Pike Bridge overlooking Crow Creek.

Marion sent the dynamic Brown back deep to return the opening kickoff, a feat itself since he had missed school on Wednesday and Thursday with the flu, and was still in bed sick the morning of the game.

"I finally stopped throwing up that morning, so I decided to go to school so I could play that night," Brown said. "I knew everybody was depending on me. This was the biggest game of my life and I had to play well for us to win. I always had the ability to play through pain and I just thought that's what you did. All I ever saw from my daddy was when there's work still to be done, you tough it out and fight through it."

Brown showed no ill-effects from the sickness when he brought back the opening kick 47 yards to the Pirates 40, and likely would have gone all the way had Wigfall not caught him.

Both teams ran the single-wing offense, and ran it well.

"My senior year, Coach Bill (Baxter) let me call most of our offensive plays," Brown said. "Jesse Dalton was as good a single-wing center as there ever was. In three years he never had a bad snap. Depending on the play he could put the ball on your right knee or left knee, whichever way we were going."

The Warriors set out on an eight-play drive toward the goal line, ending when Brown connected with Jackie Sharp on a 20-yard touchdown pass, and Brown added the point-after kick.

It marked only the second time all season the Pirates had trailed in a game, but it was a short-lived deficit as they put together an eight-play drive of their own, with Wigfall scoring on a five-yard run and adding the two-point conversion as well.

Fans on the visitors' side had barely had time to settle back into their seats when Brown took his turn to electrify the home side, sending everyone in purple leaping to their feet when he brought back the ensuing kickoff 96 yards to put the Warriors back out in front. Brown also hit Sharp in the end zone for the two-point conversion and the back-and-forth tone was set as the teams continued to trade haymakers like a pair of heavyweight boxers for the rest of the night.

Brown nearly added what could have been a back-breaking score to his first-half total when he tucked the ball under his right arm, cut up inside the block of the fullback and raced 75 yards, reaching the Pirates five-yard line before Wigfall again caught him from behind.

"I didn't think I would catch him. I just made a desperation dive and I caught his feet," Wigfall said.

Two runs gained two yards and on third down South Pittsburg dodged a bullet when Charles Garner intercepted a Brown pass near the goal line.

"That play still haunts me to this day," Brown admitted. "More than 30 years after that game, I was at Coach Bill's house talking about it and he said he

Eddie Brown was an all-state tailback at Marion in 1969.

wished he hadn't called that pass play. It was obvious that it still haunted him too."

But the Pirates returned the favor on a drive deep into Marion territory when a Wigfall pass was intercepted, keeping the Warriors narrowly ahead at the half.

"I remember sitting in the locker room and Coach Grider going over what we needed to do in the second half," Wigfall recalled. "He finished his speech and then all eyes turned to the door as Coach (Phil) Beene walked in.

"He was this big, intimidating man who had coached us up until that year and he an aura about him that you could just feel when he walked in the room. He stepped in the room with that hat pulled down so low you could barely see his eyes and his hands in the pockets of his trench coat. He never said a word. He just kind of stared at everyone. Nothing else needed to be said or done, we knew then we had to take care of business."

Inside Marion's locker room, coaches were looking for a way to refuel their star.

"By then my legs felt like they weighed 10 pounds each," Brown remembered. "Our coaches gave me two chocolate bars to try and give me some energy. Back then that's what people thought you had to do when you were tired.

"But there's only so much adrenaline and chocolate can do and I found that out."

After the Pirates fumbled to begin the third quarter, Brown — still jacked up from his halftime sugar rush — scored on a 16-yard fourth-down run up the middle and then added the point-after kick for a surprising 22-8 lead.

Marion also recovered the onside kick, but was held on downs and punted the Pirates back to their 10.

"We were in the huddle and Terry Everett, who played middle linebacker and offensive guard, looked at us and said 'If they're going to beat us we're at least going to knock their ass off for the rest of the game.',"

Blansett remembered. "Just because it was Jasper none of us were going to give up without a fight."

Two runs went for minus-five yards, but on third down the stage was set for more Wigfall heroics.

Coach Grider had called for the Pirates bread-and-butter play — 46, an off-tackle run to the right side — but after taking the direct snap and drifting back into the end zone to avoid two tacklers, Wigfall found no daylight off the right side. He planted his right foot in the ground, cut back to his left and found a wall of black-jersey blockers.

"I can still see that play as it happened," Blansett said. "We had a line of guys just cutting people down like trees to clear a path for Jimmy."

Wigfall evaded one last tackle and, like a whisper of smoke, disappeared from his pursuers, racing 95 yards for a touchdown.

"The six hole was full of Warriors, so I just ran the other way," said Wigfall, who also connected with Ford for the conversion, cutting Marion's lead to 22-16.

"Wigfall could stop on a dime," Brown said. "He had a step that was quicker than a cat and he could stop and redirect better than about anybody I remember playing against.

"We were both just doing what we did, trying to make a play to help our team win. When he broke that long run at the end, there wasn't anything I could do about it."

When Marion was forced to punt on its next possession the momentum had clearly swung in South Pittsburg's favor. On the first snap of the fourth quarter Wigfall found Blansett on a short pass and as Blansett turned upfield he picked up blocks from Everett, Bobby Ambrester and Ford to go 68 yards for the TD. Wigfall's conversion run was stopped short, keeping the game tied at 22-all.

"I remember seeing the film on that one. Blansett was so slow everybody had a chance to throw a couple of blocks before he scored," Wigfall joked. "Bobby Jo cracked back on Brown and blindsided him — it was a highlight. Jasper probably could have run out the clock after that and the game would have ended in a tie. Of course if we had tied it would have been just as bad as a loss because someone else would have made the playoffs."

The teams traded punts before, with four minutes remaining, Ford intercepted a Brown pass at the Pirates 48, and on the ensuing possession Ford caught a 46-yard pass from Wigfall to move the ball deep into Marion territory. Wigfall then capped his incredible night by sprinting to his right, stopping suddenly to raise up and throw back to his left to a wide open Billy Berryhill for the go-ahead 21-yard touchdown with just under two minutes left on the clock.

The conversion pass failed, leaving the door cracked for Marion to still potentially rally for the win, but Ford added to a memorable night of his own by intercepting his second Warriors pass of the quarter, allowing South Pittsburg to run out the clock and hold on for as thrilling a win as can be remembered in the rivalry.

"The town was was pretty well lit after the game," Don Grider would say later. "That game ranks right up there with the best. Both boys lived up to their billing that night."

The Chattanooga News-Free Press reported that after the game Marion County tackle Charles Gamble was seen at the Pirates bus saying, "Y'all can do it. Y'all go all the way."

South Pittsburg ended the game with 408 total yards to Marion's 198 and the Pirates also intercepted four Warriors passes.

Brown finished with 125 rushing yards and a touchdown on 15 carries, a 96-yard kickoff return for a score and threw for 56 yards and another TD.

Wigfall was named Associated Press Back of the Week in the state for his stat line that included accounting for 192 of his team's 228 rushing yards, with two TDs, completing 7 of 11 passes for another 154 yards and another two scores, as well as rushing for one two-point conversion and throwing for another.

His 379 total yards set a school record that still stands.

"I think the two best teams in the state played that night," said Brown, who finished his senior season with 1,793 total yards. "South Pittsburg won the rest of their playoff games easily, so I believe that game was the state championship.

"I've always wished they had started the playoffs a year earlier. We went undefeated my junior year and I have no doubt we would've won the state then. We just weren't as good my senior year."

Ending all doubt about South Pittsburg claiming the final playoff spot, Charleston lost its final game to Tellico Plains 20-6. Sweetwater drilled Madisonville 78-0 to finish 9-1, but had lost head-to-head to the Pirates, so the four-team playoff bracket would be made up of South Pittsburg and Oneida in the east and Tennessee Preparatory School and Lake County in the west.

Elsewhere around the Sequatchie Valley, Whitwell would go on to finish 9-2 and beat Sweetwater 10-8 in the Jaycee Bowl at Rockwood.

Marion's Brown, Ronny Parker and Byron Kelly earned All-SVC honors, along with South Pittsburg's Everett, Billy Berryhill and Wigfall, who was named the league's Back of the Year.

But more than any individual awards, South Pittsburg's players were squarely focused on the playoffs, and the chance to earn a state championship.

FIRST STEP TOWARD A TITLE

Two weeks after the thrilling win over its biggest rival — and a week after other area teams had completed their season in bowl games — South Pittsburg set its sights on the debut of the playoffs, traveling to Dayton for a neutral site showdown with Oneida.

It took just four plays before the Pirates let it be known there would be no hangover from the emotional win over Marion as Wigfall broke loose off right tackle and sprinted 65 yards for a touchdown.

Oneida answered with a 39-yard scoring run from quarterback Curtis Thompson on a bootleg, but the Pirates began to wear on the Indians in the second quarter. It began with a seven-play, 61-yard drive — highlighted by Wigfall's 20-yard pass to Ford — and capped by Wigfall's nine-yard TD run.

The momentum shift continued on the next series when the Pirates defense stuffed Oneida and Steve Smith blocked a punt that was recovered at the 22. On the next play, Wigfall again connected with Ford, this time for a TD and a 20-6 halftime lead.

South Pittsburg wasted no time in breaking Oneida's spirit, beginning the second half with a seven-play, 77-yard drive that ended with Wigfall's four-yard touchdown run, putting the game away.

The Pirates ran for 314 yards, while Smith led the team in tackles and ran for 68 yards to go with his key special teams play just before halftime. Everett and Blansett each had interceptions.

Charles Garner (10) finds running room as Bobby Joe Ford (88) looks to block.

"We didn't even realize what we were doing," Blansett recalled. "We didn't really understand how big the playoffs were at the time. We were just country boys playing ball."

FEASTING ON A CHAMPIONSHIP

On the day after Thanksgiving, local businesses closed a half-day early as nearly the entire town filled up on .35 cents per gallon gas and made the two-hour trip to Nashville's Overton High School where the Pirates would face a TPS team that had completely dominated every opponent to that point.

The unbeaten Buckin' Broncos had shut out eight of their 10 opponents and were averaging 50 points per game, with margins that included

42-0, 40-6, 74-0, 42-0, 80-12 and 86-0. In its game-day edition, the Nashville Tennessean predicted TPS would win by two touchdowns, noting the size difference — 20-pounds heavier across the line — and the 22-game win streak the program was riding.

But one overlooked stat was that they had only played one team with a winning record, while half the Pirates opponents had finished with winning records.

When South Pittsburg arrived at the stadium, just hours before kickoff, coaches were informed that as the visiting team they would need to wear white jerseys. The problem with that was the Pirates owned just one set of uniforms — the black jerseys and pants.

The only solution was for host school Overton to loan out their white jerseys for the Pirates to wear for the game. But when they emerged from the locker room — in their borrowed white jerseys with red numerals — the Pirates were unrecognizable to their large contingent of supporters.

"Our fans didn't know who we were. They thought we were TPS coming out at first and some of them were hollering at us and booing," Blansett said. "A few other South Pittsburg people thought they had come to the wrong game. They didn't recognize us at first."

While it took a while for their own fans to identify them in their foreign colored jerseys, everyone across the state would have to recognize the Pirates as the best team in Class 1A after the performance they put on during the game.

On the first play of the game Wigfall took the direct snap and followed his blockers into open field for a 60-yard touchdown run. An official brought the ball back to the TPS 40, saying Wigfall had stepped out of bounds as he made his cut along the sideline.

Grider was animated protesting the call, reaching down to show the divot where Wigfall's cleat had clearly dug into the dirt inbounds. But all the commotion over the call was quickly forgotten when Wigfall again broke loose on the next snap, this time taking it for the score without any issues.

As easy as the first score was, however, it would stand as the only points of the first half as the Pirates had two drives halted by interceptions. But on the second possession of the second half, South Pittsburg scored again on an 11-yard run by Blansett, which was set up by a 29-yard pass from Wigfall to Berryhill.

TPS managed to cross midfield only once all game, on a 53-yard pass play that set up their lone TD, cutting the Pirates lead to 12-6.

South Pittsburg answered by using up more than seven minutes off the clock in going 64 yards in 11 plays before Wigfall capped the drive with a 13-yard scoring run off left tackle.

Wigfall then found Bobby Joe Ford for the two-point conversion, making it 20-6.

The Pirates put the game away after Charles Garner intercepted a pass and returned it to the 4, setting up a 3-yard scoring run from Blansett for the 26-6 win. And with that TD they had scored more points in one game than the Buckin' Broncos had allowed in every other game combined all season.

"A little place like South Pittsburg showed that it could go all the way," senior Steve Smith told a reporter as he walked off the field.

"A couple weeks ago that University of Tennessee computer predicted TPS to win this thing," said Pirates assistant Sam Brooks. "I say this, and you can quote me, 'To hell with that computer.'"

Wigfall, who ran for 168 yards and intercepted a pass, said, "They weren't as tough as everyone thought. I tell you right now, we were better than anybody tonight."

Wigfall set the school's single-season rushing record by finishing with 2,165 yards and averaged 196 total yards per game with 28 touchdowns. He would later sign with Austin Peay University.

"I don't know who picks those all-state teams but they sure missed one," Coach Grider told the News-Free Press after the game, adding that he couldn't understand how Wigfall had been snubbed of that honor. "Pound-for-pound, he's the best running back in the whole state and he's proved it every week.

Jimmy Wigfall (21) runs behind the blocks of Donald Blansett (35), Charles Garner (10) and Willis Mayfield (63) for a Pirates touchdown.

"It's a great feeling to know that South Pittsburg is a state champion."

On the way out of the stadium one Pirates fan asked the TPS crowd as they filed out dejectedly, "I thought TPS was the best team in the state?"

Another mid-state fan chimed in, "They were until y'all came over here."

Three decades later, four members of the 1969 team — Donald Blansett, Freddie Blevins, Gary Reames and Johnny Stone — had sons who helped the Pirates claim another state title.

"That was a great feeling," Blansett said. "To see your son accomplish something like that too is pretty rare. No matter how much time passes, whenever you see those guys you played with there's a brotherhood there.

"When we get together we'll ask about each other's family and then it doesn't take long before the conversation turns to reliving those games we played in together. It means more to me when I see one of my old teammates than just somebody else I went to school with. It's a fellowship you develop through a lot of hard work and accomplishing something not many people get to."

SOUTH PITTSBURG 1969 RESULTS

Sept. 5	Sequatchie County	28-8
Sept. 12	at Whitwell	16-6
Sept. 19	Stevenson	28-0
Sept. 26	at Spring City	20-8

Oct. 3	at Grundy County	32-0
Oct. 10	at Bridgeport	30-0
Oct. 24	Bledsoe County	36-25
Oct. 31	at Sweetwater	14-0
Nov. 7	at Marion County	28-22

Playoffs

Nov. 21	Oneida (at Dayton)	28-6

State championship

Nov. 28	TPS (at Overton)	26-6

1969 Pirates

Players: Jimmy Wigfall, Danny Durham, David Frame, Bobby Ambrester, Jackie Robinson, Ed Gray, Steve Smith, Carl Roberts, Terry Everett, Billy Berryhill, Steve Blevins, Charles Garner, Randall Vinson, Kenny Case, Gary Reames, Willis Mayfield, Donald Blansett, Jerry Holden, Bobby Joe Ford, Gray Smith, Johnny Stone, Mike Ridley, Rip Gibson, Donny Stone, Freddie Blevins, John Ladd, Harold Massey, David Hale, Ronald Mitchell, James Case, Mike Cardin, Jimmy King, Earl Gott, Gary Frame.

Coaches: Don Grider, Sam Brooks, W.T. "Hoot" Gibson

Chapter 8

EDDIE BROWN

"There are two great days in a person's life - the day we are born and the day we discover why."

— **William Barclay**

Wedged in among the tightly-packed capacity crowd of 45,682 at Shields-Watkins Field, Eddie Brown shrugged off the shivering 30-degree temperatures and craned his neck to get a better view of the action.

His dad, Paul, had bought tickets for the University of Tennessee's biggest game of the 1959 season and brought seven year old Eddie to watch the Vols take on No. 1-ranked LSU, led by All American running back Billy Cannon, who would go on to win the Heisman Trophy later that year.

The freezing weather had been such a surprise for LSU that coaches were forced to scramble and find extra layers for players to wear. But from the wind-blown top row of their seats in the corner of the south end zone the only concern for Paul and Eddie Brown was whether or not their beloved Vols could pull off an upset.

Tennessee had scored twice in the third quarter to take a 14-7 lead before LSU closed the gap to one point with a short touchdown run early in the fourth. The Tigers elected to try for the two-point conversion and the lead, but the Tennessee defense knew exactly which play was coming and when Cannon took a pitch to the right he was met by three defenders short of the goal line and the Vols held on for a one-point win that became famous after Sports Illustrated ran an article with the headline "The day the Cannon didn't fire".

By the time he followed his dad down the bleacher steps late in the afternoon, Brown knew he wanted to one day be a part of the action down on the field. That was the day that motivated Brown to become the most accomplished athlete the Sequatchie Valley has produced.

"I loved every second of being at that game with daddy," he recalled. "I can remember almost every play as if it just happened. Sitting there, watching those guys play the game and hearing the crowd react, from that day on — even at seven years old — I knew I was going to play football for Tennessee."

HARD WORK PAYS OFF

It took countless hours of hard work and gallons of sweat for Eddie Brown to earn the shot at realizing his dream.

Growing up just outside of Jasper, in the Haletown community, he was slightly built but oozed athleticism and simply out-worked everyone around him. He also seemed to have a knack for finding the open lane and avoiding tacklers.

"There was an older kid who lived near us and when we would all get together to play murder the man with the ball he would just lay into us. I figured out real fast that I didn't like to get hit like that so I learned to escape."

Having watched Bill Baker, who was five years older, star at Marion and earn a scholarship to Tennessee made Brown's own dream seem more attainable. He saw the blueprint laid out by Baker, who would later marry Brown's older sister, and followed in his brother in law's footsteps.

When he tried out for the varsity at Marion County the coaching tandem of Bill and Dave Baxter put Brown on defense and ran a series of plays right at him, just to see if he would wilt or be tough enough to stand the punishment. Once he had proven he wouldn't back down from any challenge, Brown was given one piece of advice from head coach Bill Baxter.

"You've got to put on some weight, son, or you're going to get killed."

Much as he always had for his three children, Paul Brown — who worked as a machinist — made sure his only son got the support needed to pursue his goal.

"We couldn't afford to buy a weight bench, so daddy built one and moved it into our living room," Eddie said. "He moved the couch and some other furniture around to make room for it so I could work out every day. Mama wasn't real happy about having that thing in her living room, but daddy won that one and the weight bench stayed."

Eddie Brown at Tennessee.

In the years that followed, whether it was a second helping at dinner or drinking protein shakes to gain weight, waking up early to run a mile to Hale's Bar Dam — while wearing ankle weights — any extra time was spent training his body for football and reaching the goal he had set for himself.

"He didn't joke or cut up about it, he was focused on going to Tennessee and playing football there," said his younger sister, Teresa Brown Rogers. "It really was amazing when you think back on it just how dedicated he was.

"He was a lot like my dad in that way, as far as being focused on accomplishing something and then being willing to work for what he wanted."

Prior to the 1969 season — Brown's senior year — the TSSAA introduced a new playoff format that would determine a state champion. Marion County, which had graduated several talented players off an unbeaten '68 team, would have to rely on Brown to carry the team more than he had previously. Knowing he would be the target of every opposing defense that season, as well as one of the top college prospects in the Chattanooga area, he spent much of the summer putting in even more time training than he had.

"The only thing most of us did back then to get stronger during the summer was to work on farms," said David Moore, who played on Marion's '69 team. "There was one hot day where a bunch of us had baled hay all day and we wanted to go swimming to cool off. We asked Eddie to go with us but he said he was going home to work out. We laughed and called him a big dummy for not going swimming and goofing off with us. We were telling him what he'd be missing, but that fall it was clear who had put in the work to be in the best shape.

"He was also the smartest guy on the team, so it was like having a coach on the field. Everything Eddie got was from him just outworking everybody else and that included studying the game. Nobody matched what he put into the game. He was the heart and soul of our team."

Marion coaches had decided before the season began to have a rotating group of captains for each game, but midway through the schedule players voted Brown team captain the rest of the way.

He set the tone for a monster season in the opener when he accounted for 284 yards, all but 21 of Marion's total, and scored three of the Warriors four touchdowns. The next week, with a University of Georgia scout watching from the stands, he ran for three TDs, threw for one and returned a punt 75 yards for another in totaling 290 yards.

By the time the fourth game of the season was complete Brown had already amassed more than 900 total yards.

"We hadn't seen anybody like him before," said Landon Pickett, who played at Whitwell and later coached at Marion. "He was quick, fast and just a very heady player. He really stood out as one of the most elite backs I ever saw."

Going into the season finale against South Pittsburg, Marion's offense was cruising, having scored 49 points in back-to-back blowout wins, and Brown was making spectacular plays seem routine, both as a running back and on special teams.

But he spent much of the week leading up to game day in bed with the flu, including a 101-degree fever for two days. When he woke up on Friday morning and was able to keep food down for the first time all week, he decided he would play that night.

"The doctor told him he shouldn't even try and mother and daddy didn't want him to either," Teresa said. "But he said he was going to suck it up and do everything he could. That was just the way he was.

"I had seen him go to the doctor to have fluid drained from his knee on the morning of a game and then play that night, and there was a game earlier where another player stepped on his hand with a metal cleat and it cut him so bad that his hand looked like hamburger meat. He just taped it up and kept right on playing, so I knew he was going to give it everything he had. Nothing was going to keep him from trying to play against South Pittsburg."

With the region championship on the line, Brown brought back the opening kickoff 47 yards, nearly breaking loose for a touchdown. Later in the half he returned a kickoff 96 yards for a score and went on to finish with 125 rushing yards, 56 more passing and nearly 200 yards in returns.

But his amazing effort, which gave him more than 1,800 yards for the season and earned All-State honors, fell just short after Pirates half-pint running back Jimmy Wigfall turned in a herculean night to lead his team to a six-point win that catapulted them into the playoffs.

"That gave me a lot of pride knowing as good as he was, I outplayed him that one night," Wigfall said later. "We never were friends but I always had a lot of respect for Eddie as a player and my wife went to Jasper and said he was a very nice guy.

"He went to Tennessee and I went to the Army, but I always kept up with him and was proud to know a guy from Marion County was doing so well. He did a great job at every step of his career."

Although he had several other colleges recruiting him, including Alabama, Georgia and Vanderbilt, there was never any drama over where he would sign once Tennessee made its scholarship offer. Brown, who was also the school's salutatorian, signed with UT on December 13. Less than a month later Doug Dickey resigned to take over the program at Florida, but UT's new head coach, Bill Battle, made sure Brown felt wanted, sending a telegram during his first week on the job that read, "It is with great anticipation that I look forward to working with you as your new head football coach at the University of Tennessee. I am planning to visit personally with you and your family in the very near future."

Once he arrived on campus in Knoxville, it didn't take Brown long to fully realize his boyhood dream of becoming one of those players in orange jerseys bringing the crowd to its feet. He intercepted three passes and recovered two fumbles as a sophomore but really established himself as a junior when he became a dual threat, similar to his days at Marion.

Eddie Brown at Marion County.

"The first thing I was impressed by was how fast he was," said former Vols running back Haskel Stanback, who set a school rushing record that stood for more than 10 years and later played for five seasons with the Atlanta Falcons. "You didn't have many fast white guys, but Eddie could run and he was very tough. Things seemed to come easy for him on the field because he was so athletic and just had another sense about how to move and where to go.

"We came to UT in the same class, at a time when not a lot of black athletes had played with white players, but we hit it off right away and a lot of that was because of his family. I hadn't had a lot of role models in my life but his dad told my mom he would look after me and he made me feel like a part of their family. The more I got to know him the more I realized he came from good stock."

During Brown's junior season, as the only non-senior to start in the Vols secondary, he was in on 64 tackles, intercepted two passes and averaged 10.2 yards per punt return and 21.5 on kickoff returns — all with his parents sitting in the same corner of the end zone where he and his father had watched his first game more than a decade earlier.

"The thing everybody respected was the way Eddie just went about his business without saying a whole lot," Stanback added. "He was a quiet leader, but if somebody wasn't doing what they should he didn't hesitate to get in their face and set them straight.

"He had one of those muscle cars, so we went cruising around campus one day with the windows down and I asked him to put some music on. He reaches down and puts in a tape of Tammy Wynette. I had no idea who she was, but there we were, two good looking young guys in a good looking car just blasting Tammy Wynette. I just figured that must be what guys did back where he came from."

As the only returning starter in the defensive backfield his senior season Brown, who was again voted a captain by his teammates, was the unquestioned leader and turned in an All America senior season. He intercepted five passes, returned two punts for touchdowns and averaged 19.7 yards on kickoff returns.

One of his most memorable games came against Kansas in Memphis, where he made plays all over the field to help rally the Vols. Midway through the second quarter he blocked a field goal attempt but got to the point where the ball was kicked so quickly that he got kicked in the face and had four teeth knocked out on impact.

"I only remember two plays in my entire career where I didn't have my mouthpiece in, and that was one of them," Brown said. "I came up spitting blood and my mouth felt numb and then I realized I had gotten my front four teeth knocked out.

"I took some Tylenol at halftime for the pain, but I wasn't leaving the game."

Once again showing the toughness he had become known for, Brown had two long punt returns, a fumble recovery and a 74-yard interception return to help the Vols take a 28-27 lead. He then topped the effort that earned him Sports Illustrated's national Back of the Week recognition by making the tackle that stopped the Jayhawks two-point attempt, similar to the play he had watched from the stands as a boy when the Vols defense had held off LSU.

That was one of five games the 1973 Vols won by six points or less, on their way to an 8-win campaign.

During his three-year career as a starter, Brown — who finished with 199 tackles, 10 interceptions and led the team in punt returns his final two seasons to earn All SEC honors — helped the Vols compile a 27-7-2 overall record and play in three holiday bowl games.

"You talk about a workaholic, that's Eddie," said Bill Baker. "When he asked me for advice as a high school player I told him to just work hard and he really took that to heart. He had a lot of natural ability already but his competitiveness and work ethic really made him special."

Brown assumed his career ended with a Gator Bowl loss to Texas Tech four days after Christmas, but just one month after his final college game, he was taken in the eighth round of the NFL Draft, by the Cleveland Browns with the 199th overall pick.

That late January draft later produced five Hall of Fame players, including four for the Steelers — receivers Lynn Swann and John Stallworth, linebacker Jack Lambert and center Mike Webster, as well as Cowboys defensive lineman Ed "Too Tall" Jones.

"I didn't even know I got drafted," Brown said. "I was planning to become a veterinarian after school, so I was sitting in class at the time.

"Somebody in my dorm told me after class and I called home to tell my dad and mom."

On the other end of the phone, back in Haletown, Paul Brown couldn't keep up a tough exterior when his son gave him the news.

"I seldom ever saw my dad cry, but he cried the day Eddie called him to say he'd been drafted," Teresa recalled. "A lifetime dream had come true. All those years of working so hard and being focused had paid off and he was so proud."

It was a dream shared by father and son and the moment has never been lost on Eddie, even years later.

"Our family was never well off," he said. "In fact we were poor. Daddy and mama would work overtime or take on odd jobs to earn the extra money to make sure me and my sisters had whatever we needed.

"The support I got from my parents was unbelievable. Daddy would have to get up at 4:30 the next morning for work but he never missed a single game that I played whether it was football, basketball or baseball. When you've been as lucky as I have, you didn't get there by yourself and I never forgot that."

Brown's first two seasons in the pros came and went without him finding his niche. But once he was traded to the Washington Redskins, where legendary coach George Allen recognized his toughness and elusive ability as a punt returner, his career took a dramatic turn for the better.

An injury to the Redskins kick return specialist opened the door for Brown and he made the most of the opportunity. He returned a punt 45 yards with two minutes remaining in the season opener that led to the game-winning touchdown against the Giants and two weeks later he intercepted an Eagles pass in overtime to set up a game-winning field goal.

Later, on the game's biggest stage — Monday Night Football — Brown wowed Howard Cosell and a national television audience by sloshing through the RFK Stadium mud and a downpour for a 71-yard punt return for a touchdown against the St. Louis Cardinals.

Just like he had done since the days of murder the man with the ball back home in the back yard, Brown found a clearing that put him past the initial wave of tacklers, then sprinted toward the right sideline, breaking a couple of tackle attempts before getting in the clear. He stumbled twice as he reached the 10 yard line, then collected his balance and scored a touchdown that helped the Redskins claim a 20-10 win that earned a playoff berth.

Brown went on to become a Pro Bowl selection, and earn All-Pro honors in both 1976 — when he led the NFL in punt return yards with a total that ranked second all-time — and 1977, when he was named the Redskins Most Valuable Player.

Eddie Brown gets a kiss from his mom, Nellie, after signing scholarship papers with UT. Vols assistant Ray Trail (left) and Brown's father Paul look on.

"One year I played with two cracked ribs in my sternum in the regular season," Brown said. "It was the worst pain you can imagine. There were times I literally didn't think I could get back up after getting tackled."

In 1978, he was traded to the Los Angeles Rams where, a year after arriving in LA, he was a key part of a stingy Rams defense that won the NFC title and played the juggernaut Steelers in Super Bowl XIV.

Brown intercepted a Terry Bradshaw pass in the third quarter, but the Steelers eventually pulled away for a 31-19 win to become the first franchise to claim four Super Bowl titles.

"I've got a nice ring that says NFC Champions," Brown said. "But it doesn't say World Champions. That still sticks with me."

He later played with the Chicago Blitz and Arizona Wranglers of the USFL in 1983-84 returning one of his eight interceptions for a TD before retiring from the game.

Once his playing days ended Brown began working as a sale rep for Jostens, where he helped championship teams and seniors choose rings and memorabilia of their own, even helping design the national championship rings for the Vols after their 1998 title.

"I had one of the fan's collection rings made for daddy and when I gave it to him he was so tickled he wore it everywhere," said Brown, who was inducted into the Tennessee Sports Hall of Fame in 2002. "I still love going to UT games now, just like I did with daddy all those years ago. Anytime we had guys from back home, Eric Westmoreland or Eddie Moore, at Tennessee I would reach out to them and let them know if they needed anything to let me know because I'm always glad to see a kid from back home make it to UT. It just made me proud to know those little schools are still producing that type player and student.

"I go to a lot of schools in my line of work but you don't see many where being a football player means more than it does back home. You're somebody special in those towns if you play football and playing in that atmosphere in high school teaches you how to handle yourself in big moments later on.

"I played at every level of the game and had some great rivalries, Tennessee and Alabama, Redskins and Cowboys, but I honestly never played in a game that was more intense or with more electricity or where you felt like more was riding on the outcome than in high school. Whoever wins that Marion County/South Pittsburg game has final say in the valley for a whole year and it doesn't get any bigger than that."

Chapter 9
JIMMY WIGFALL

"It's not how big you are, it's how big you play"
— **UCLA basketball coach John Wooden**

Outside of his community, Jimmy Wigfall's football heroics are relatively unknown. But spend any time at all around South Pittsburg and it quickly becomes obvious that he is revered like few other athletes. For that matter, there are few citizens more respected, and Wigfall is even more well-known than any local politician or business owner.

Since 1969 the pint-sized Pirate has been the measuring stick for what's expected of the program's players — first on the field, then making the transition from Friday night hero to pillar in the community.

In 1969 the TSSAA began classifying high school sports by enrollment. Along with the new classification system, a playoff format was implemented and that fall, Wigfall's senior season, as a 5-foot-7, 140-pound bantam-weight ballcarrier, he led the Pirates to a dramatic come-from-behind win over rival Marion County — where only the winner could advance to the new playoff — followed by two extraordinary efforts to lead the team to its first state championship.

"We were just kids and the playoffs were so new that we didn't even realize what we had done at the time," Wigfall said. "We just kept showing up every week to play whoever they put out there against us.

"Looking back on it, you start thinking we must have been pretty good to have so many people still talking about us after all this time. We didn't realize then that it was the start of a special tradition."

Because of the program's importance in the community, generations of fans have grown up hearing stories of the heroics of past teams. Wigfall's speed and toughness are traits that every runner who has followed have been gauged against.

"He was probably, pound-for-pound, the best back in the state his senior year," the late Don Grider once said.

Jimmy Wigfall remains a South Pittsburg legend.

"Dad coached a lot of good high school players, but he would always go on and on about Jimmy," said Vic Grider, who has coached at his alma mater since the early 1990s. "He coached guys who went on and played at a higher level but I don't know if he would've traded any of them for Jimmy.

"At every school there are two or three names that are synonymous with that program. At South Pittsburg everybody knows Jimmy Wigfall and Eddie Moore. Their reputation still speaks for itself and they give the kids coming up somebody to admire.

"Having people like them, who you're proud to associate with your program is tremendous."

Wigfall came to SPHS as an eighth-grader, having moved back home after his family spent one year in Dayton, Ohio. It was the year after McReynolds High — the all-black school in Marion County — had burned, forcing integration to finally arrive in South Pittsburg.

That fall was the first time Wigfall had played organized football and his talents quickly became obvious.

"It seemed like in practice and in games, every time I touched the ball I scored," Wigfall recalled. "I was always smaller, but I learned that speed was the great equalizer, and I had that. Despite my size, I didn't mind contact because I had grown up watching the great backs at McReynolds and I wanted to be a physical runner like those guys I had idolized. I guess that's why I always seemed to be banged up until my senior year. That's when I finally got the chance to be the feature back.

"Football made integrating smoother because those of us who played seemed to make friends easier. Sports builds relationships on the field and the thing about Coach (Phil) Beene was, he didn't care how big you were or what your skin color was. If you could play, you played, so I was determined to prove I was good and get on the field."

Wigfall had already proven he could play long before South Pittsburg made the short trip to Jasper to take on its bitter rival, with a spot in 1969's inaugural playoffs on the line. But the chance to go toe-to-toe with Marion's wonderfully talented Eddie Brown definitely stirred the ultra competitive Wigfall and when the yellow school

Jimmy Wigfall and Steve Smith ready to take the field.

bus pulled into the parking lot for the game, he couldn't wait to get on the field for the showdown.

"The first thing you noticed was the crowd," Wigfall remembered. "It was packed all around the stadium so you knew that was the place to be that night for pretty much everybody in the whole area. Our fans were there early and they were always rowdy. We had already had one road game earlier that year where one of the refs put his jacket on the fence before the game and our fans set it on fire with a lighter.

"We knew if we lost our season was either over or we'd be going to a bowl game that didn't mean much. There's never been any love lost in that rivalry. You respected them, but you really didn't like them. There wasn't a handshake before or after the game back then."

Wigfall — so shifty he would've been hard to tackle in a phone booth — matched each of Brown's big-plays with one of his own, and actually out-played the future University of Tennessee star to lift the Pirates to the win.

"Early in the game we were struggling a little bit on offense," said David Hale, a two-way lineman on the 1969 team. "Jimmy comes back to the huddle once and said 'if y'all ain't going to block just get out of my damn way and I'll do it myself.'

"The next play he cut back on a 46 and went for a touchdown. He was fast but the difference was how he could cut back and then accelerate again. He was a good leader and knew how to take care of business. It takes a certain mentality to play football and Jimmy had it."

Wigfall accounted for 192 of his team's 228 rushing yards, scoring twice, and completed 7 of 11 passes for another 154 yards and two more scores. He also ran for a two-point conversion, threw for another and chased down his counterpart, making a touchdown saving tackle of Brown that proved even bigger after the Pirates defense turned the Warriors away without points.

Wigfall's 379 total yards set a school record that still stands and earned Associated Press Back of the Week honors for the state.

Brown, who had been fighting the flu in the days leading up to the game, finished with just over 300 total yards as well.

"We had heard that Eddie was sick coming into the game," Wigfall admitted. "But I don't mind saying I was glad because he still gave us fits, even after the flu.

"That game usually has a way of making guys play at their best no matter what. That's the pride we all have for playing for our community."

The only blemish on an otherwise spectacular senior season came when Wigfall was snubbed from being named all-state.

Walk through the entrance to South Pittsburg's gymnasium and the first thing you'll notice are the trophies of past football success. Along the hall that runs behind the home side bleachers, hang framed photos of past legends — all-state players and state champion teams. The '69 Pirates team photo is there, the first in a row of state champions, but noticeably absent from the all-state section is Wigfall, along with any other Pirates players from that year.

"When they picked all-state back then I believe they looked at size more than stats," Wigfall reasoned. "At the time it didn't bother me, but as I've gotten older it does. I look at the pictures of Rusty Adcock and David Hale and it bothers me

Jimmy Wigfall during his senior season.

because I believe my picture should be hanging right between those two guys.

"I've wondered how we could be the best team in the state that year and not have anybody make all-state. And I don't mean this to be arrogant, but when you look at the stats and what we accomplished, I don't believe there was a better back in Tennessee than me that season."

When his high school career ended Wigfall signed to play with Austin Peay University, but wound up volunteering for the Army before ever setting foot on campus.

"I didn't have the money to go away to school, so I figured the Army was my best choice for an education," Wigfall said. "I wound up being stationed in Germany, which was fine with me because I love to travel.

"I love my town but I've also seen a lot of kids through the years who could've gone on to big things but were scared to leave. They make it as far as the Favorite Market on first street but get pulled back. This town is like a security blanket, which can be good and bad."

Once his two-year stint in the military was complete, he eventually began working as an electrician for TVA, where he stayed until his retirement in 2012.

Since then he has remained an active supporter of the Pirates as well as his community, even working as a city commissioner.

"I never dreamed I would get into politics or be in the public eye," Wigfall said. "But I saw some things that I thought could be improved in our town, so I decided to do something about it.

"I just always had it in me to want to try to do what's right. Not that I thought I was setting an example for anybody else, I've just tried to be who I am and maybe others will see that a black kid who played at South Pittsburg can do some positive things even after football is over.

"I feel like I've been pretty successful in life. I have a great wife and daughter. Something that always weighed on my mind was wanting to make sure I never did anything to embarrass my family, my team or my town. That's always been my motivation."

Chapter 10

DON GRIDER

"A good coach will make his players see what they can be rather than what they are."

— Ara Parseghian, former Notre Dame coach

The house sits barely more than the length of a football field off Highway 72. Between Kimball's swarm of chain restaurants and the peaceful streets of South Pittsburg, tucked in on a corner lot at the first narrow curve along Sweetens Cove Road, the modest red-brick ranch home with black shutters is almost hidden behind a row of thick trees.

Evergreen shrubs and yellow daffodils line the sidewalk leading to the front door, where a white porch swing sways in the breeze, creating a cozy picture straight from the pages of Southern Living magazine.

Through the years the house served not only as home to the first family of South Pittsburg football — head coach Don Grider, his wife Gaynelle and their sons Vic and Heath — but was also the headquarters for Friday night get-togethers.

And for the 25 years that Grider was head coach of the Pirates the surest way to tell how the team had played was to drive past the home. When South Pittsburg won the front driveway looked like a used car lot with trucks, sedans, jeeps and motorcycles wedged tightly along the concrete, some even parked in the grass or spilled over into a neighbor's yard.

Covered dishes spread across the kitchen counter and cold beer filled the fridge. Some of the men brought coolers with iced-down extras, just in case the night called for an overtime of celebration.

"After a while it was just something we all knew we were going to do. We didn't even talk about it, we all just showed up at Coach Grider's house," said Donald Blansett, who played fullback on Grider's 1969 state championship team and has been a life-long supporter of the program since. Blansett was one of the regulars who helped make the Grider home a bit more lively well into the wee hours, reliving every key play between long sips, while the kids chased lightning bugs or played tag in the yard.

Heath Grider followed in his dad's coaching footsteps.

"The thing I really liked about those nights was getting to see a different side of him," Blansett added. "We would go fishing together and our families would go on vacation together, but I never called him anything but 'Coach' because that's what he was to me. But those nights at their house, it was different. There were always a lot of good friends having fun and you just felt like part of a big family there."

There is likely no other family in the state whose name is more synonymous with a high school football program and town than the Griders and South Pittsburg.

Don Grider returned to his alma mater in 1962 after four years at Tennessee Tech to teach and join Phil Beene's assistant's staff. He spent seven seasons under Beene before taking over the program, winning a state championship in his first year as head coach and taking the Pirates back to the title game three more times. He won 192 games before retiring and either one or both of his sons have worked on the Pirates staff since 1991.

"It came as such a surprise to him to win a state championship his first year," said Gaynelle, who worked at the school as a book keeper for 43 years, always making sure to wear orange on game days. "That was so important to him because he had helped his school really accomplish something.

"This was home and Don never even thought of going somewhere else. It's such a special community with how they supported the program and our family. Those nights having so many people at our house after games, we were having the best time of our lives. Football was just a really big part of who we were as a family from the very start."

During his years as an assistant, Grider adopted not just Xs and Os ideas from Beene, but also learned the principles of how to run a disciplined program for the long haul.

Coach Beene had played at the University of Tennessee in the 1920s and brought the single-wing to South Pittsburg when he began coaching there. The Pirates tweaked it to the side-saddle style — with the quarterback turning sideways between the center and right guard so he could either handle the snap or let it go directly to the fullback or tailback — in 1950 under Alex Williams, who lost only one game in three years of using the offense. Phil Beene took over the program again in 1960 before handing it off to Grider for safe keeping.

"I remember the day he came to meet with Coach Beene," said former Pirates end Roy Ferrell, a 1964 graduate. "We were in the auditorium for study hall and we saw this guy walk in wearing a green jacket and cowboy boots. Every step he took echoed in that big room and somebody sitting next to me leaned over and asked, 'Who in the hell is that?' Don just had a presence about him.

"We found out later that Coach Beene had grilled him on his philosophy that day, to make sure it was a good fit. Don had been at Tech, which ran the T-formation, and Coach Beene wanted somebody who would teach the single-wing. As time would prove, Don had no trouble switching the offense he would teach and coach."

"46"

It is as basic a play as there is in football. As simplistic as grammar school math but somehow the Pirates made it tougher than trigonometry for opponents to figure out.

The bread-and-butter play from Grider's single-wing was known simply as "46" — a power run off right tackle that became the foundation for the program's identity.

"It was three yards and a cloud of dust," said Donald Blansett, who played fullback and later tailback in the offense. "Coach Grider told us that three things can happen when you throw the ball and two of them are bad. So we rarely ever threw it."

"We never had a whole lot of size on our line, so the single-wing was a way to use quick, tough guys and they'd double team the ends and tackles and make holes for us to run through. It was a system that worked pretty good here for a long time."

Grider ran it in practice to the point of exhaustion for players, making sure they understood their role for each snap. One legend surrounding the play is that he was so unhappy with the way his team ran it in a game that the following week he ran almost nothing else, determined to make sure his players got it right.

Dave Baxter, Don Grider, Danny Wilson and David Hale celebrate Grider's retirement.

"A mama asked me one time, what's good about football?" Grider once said. "I told her that at least for those two hours he's with me, he won't get into trouble.

"People don't always like a winner, but they respect a winner."

By the mid-1980s, however, the

single-wing had become a thing of the past and, like Latin, was thought to be dead. South Pittsburg remained the only team in the state, and one of the last in the nation, to continue running the old-school offense.

"It's been real good to us here and it doesn't make much sense to change for the sake of change," Grider said once. "It's a tribute to Phil Beene. He helped build it into such a tradition thing here and we've tried to carry it on."

Under Grider, the single-wing produced six all-state tailbacks, including Johnny Sisco, who in 1985 gained more than 1,500 yards and led the Pirates to the state championship game.

Former UT coach Johnny Majors, who had been a Heisman Trophy runner-up tailback running out of the single-wing for the Vols, sent Grider a letter after arriving too late to watch the Pirates play for the title. In the hand-written note, Majors wrote, *'I am sorry I couldn't be there to see your outstanding back, Johnny Sisco, run because you know I am a single-wing man! Give my regards to "The Sisco Kid" and your fine team.'*

But it was the star of his first team as head coach — Jimmy Wigfall — that Grider held as the standard for the program. He even took time from celebrating after the team had won the 1969 championship to voice his displeasure to the media after believing that Wigfall had been snubbed.

"I'm not sure who picks those all-state teams," Grider told the Chattanooga Times moments after Wigfall had become the school's single-season rushing leader with more than 2,100 yards and 28 touchdowns. "But they sure missed a great one by not having our guy on there. If there's a better back in the state, I don't know of him."

Through the years, even after Grider's retirement, Wigfall remained the example by which all other Pirates runners were measured.

As far as Wigfall is concerned, it was very much a mutual admiration.

"Coach Grider was easy to play for," Wigfall said. "He didn't holler or scream like some coaches. He'd make a point to let you know if something wasn't done the way it should be, or how he wanted it, but he did it in a way where he never belittled you. He was more into analyzing plays and teaching how to do it right."

One other special back that came as close as any to supplanting Wigfall was Bobby "Bo" Haden, a 1976 all-state runner who would go on to star at Louisville and was drafted by the Washington Redskins before finishing his playing career in the Canadian Football League with Montreal.

During one early-season practice the 6-foot, 190-pound Haden was handed the ball for a bull-in-the-ring session — a tackling drill in which coaches would call out a defender's number to try and bring down the ball carrier. The runner stayed in the ring until he was finally tackled. On this day, Pirates assistant Mickey Wilson called out number after number hoping to find a defender who could bring Haden to the ground. Finally, he ran out of players to call on and after getting no takers when he asked if anybody else wanted to take a shot, Haden tossed the ball to the frustrated Wilson.

Haden was such a vital part of the team's success that he did not play defense, a rarity for a small school not to have its best athlete playing on both sides of the ball. He was so quick to the hole that Grider moved him back two steps in his stance to avoid having him beat the pulling guard to the hole and when South Pittsburg visited Marion County in 1974, Haden was again a one-man wrecking crew. He rallied the Pirates from a late one-point deficit by taking the direct snap on another 46 play in the fourth quarter, breaking seven tackles near the line, then pulling away for the winning touchdown in a 13-7 decision.

When the Pirates returned to their field house, Grider stood in front of the team and said loudly, "I've never given a game ball in my life, but here's the game ball to Bo! He deserves it because the rest of you sons of bitches didn't help him."

As a player, assistant and head coach, Grider went a combined 16-16 against the rival Warriors, but win or lose he never once referred to them by their official name, instead simply calling them "Jasper". And when the Pirates snapped a dreadful eight-year skid to the Warriors in 1986 with a 14-13 win that came only after stopping a late two-point conversion attempt, the party at the Grider's home was more suited for celebrating a state championship.

"When I think of Don, the first thing that pops in my mind was that dang side-saddle single-wing offense he ran and how tough it was to stop," said former Marion County coach Ken Colquette. "He kept it simple — they'd run one play over and over and if you were going to beat them you had to stop that play. But he took boys with less size and talent than a lot of teams and beat them by just being tougher and making fewer mistakes.

"He was a little older and I thought if I studied him enough I could learn some things. He had a great impact on me, just with how he would handle both winning and losing with class. It meant so much to me that I made a point of doing that to younger coaches as I got older."

Colquette and Grider developed an unlikely friendship through the years, one based on mutual respect but not easily recognized by the divided communities who expected there should be as much animosity between coaches as there was between the supporters.

When a star running back in the late 1980s got upset over getting chewed out, and threatened to transfer to Marion, Grider called Colquette to tell him the kid might show up. Colquette — a master of psychology — took it upon himself to make sure the kid would want to make his way back to South Pittsburg.

"Sure enough, the kid shows up at our field house and all of our kids were excited because they knew he was a good player and they wanted him to transfer," said former Marion assistant Don Stewart. "Ken acted glad to have him but he had me take the kid into the room where our uniforms were and tell him the only jerseys we had available were number 52, 59, 73 and 77. The kid interrupts and says 'Coach I'm a running back, those are offensive linemen numbers.'

"I said 'You're too fat. You'll be a guard here. We've got plenty of running backs.' He looks at me and Ken for a second, kind of pissed off, then turns and walks out the door to get back in his car and takes off back to Pittsburg.

"Ken called Coach Grider to tell him the kid was headed back and that the next time he gets lazy during practice to just tell him 'Those Jasper coaches were right, you're too fat to run the ball.'"

TEACH MORE THAN THE GAME

Superstitious even by a coach's standards — Grider carried a buckeye in his pocket for luck and during construction of the new field and locker room in 1966, which sits across the street from the school's original field, when a worker uncovered a horseshoe in the dirt, Grider hung it above the team's locker room door. When the new field house was built in 1992, the team's good luck charm made the move as well and reaching up to touch the horseshoe on the way out remains a part of the pre-game ritual followed by Pirates players and coaches.

Marion's Ken Colquette and Don Grider respected one another as rivals.

But those rituals did little to ward off the bad luck that prevented Grider from winning another championship beyond 1969. His Pirates were state runners-up three times and suffered a heartbreaking 7-6 loss to Marion in 1980 — Colquette's first year — that prevented another potential run at a title. At the time only the district champion advanced to the playoffs and the one-point loss kept one of Grider's most talented teams from even reaching the playoffs.

"The losses always seem to stay with you more. They can eat at you and that one definitely stayed with him for a long time," said Grider's son Vic. "He really thought that team had the talent to get there and maybe win it all but only one team went to the playoffs back then and that loss kept him out of it."

Mack Moore was an all-state receiver and kick returner on that Pirates team and like so many former players he carried lessons his coach had taught him long after his playing days had ended.

"Even when things didn't go our way Coach Grider would do things the right way and he demanded his players do the same," said Moore, a retired training chief at the Chattanooga fire department. "When I played for him he had this look that let you know what he expected and you better live up to it. I would think about that later in life and how I wouldn't want to do anything to disappoint him.

"He wasn't touchy-feely but his players knew he cared about us. That's why I would always make it a point to stop by his house and see him whenever I would come home to visit family. Those visits would always bring a smile to his face, but I just wanted him to know he was one of the most influential men in my life."

Moore's words are a testament to Grider's coaching philosophy, which he shared once by saying, "If all a kid learns is football then you've done something wrong."

He believed his job was equal parts making sure the kids who played for him learned how to win like a man, and just as importantly how to handle losing like one too.

After that emotional 1980 game, with fans' tempers flaring on both sides, Colquette hurriedly led his team to the bus. But before the Warriors got out of the parking lot, Moore, the Pirates senior captain, stopped the team and asked to step on board.

"He got on the bus, stood in front of our team and congratulated us and wished us well in the playoffs," Colquette said. "I was stunned. I had never seen that happen in a rivalry that's so heated. But I knew right then that a kid who would do that after such a tough loss played for one heck of a classy coach."

An all-state lineman on the Pirates 1969 state title team, David Hale returned home after a solid career at Vanderbilt with no intention of coaching. But after just one conversation with his former coach, Hale was convinced the program needed him and joined Grider's staff in 1980, where the relationship morphed from coach and pupil to simply friends.

"I'd go to Coach Grider's house every Sunday to watch pro games before we would go to the field house for our meetings." Hale said. "The main thing he'd talk about was his kids and how important family was to him. I didn't realize it at the time, but just during those conversations he was molding me and guiding me in the direction of being a good man. Gaynelle and the kids were the most important thing in his life and even when the kids were off at college we'd talk about how they were doing.

"That was our time to talk about everything – politics, our families and football. He made it clear that after the Lord and his family, he cared more about teaching the kids who played for him to work hard and be good men instead of just winning games."

The closest the Pirates came to adding another title under Grider was in 1986 when they lost 21-20 in overtime on a controversial officials ruling. After scoring a TD to pull within one point in overtime, Grider opted to go for two, and the win, but one referee ruled that all-state tailback Carl Lehr had been stopped inches shy of crossing the goal line, giving Spring Hill the title.

Days later, however, the head of the officiating crew called Don at the school and said he had reviewed video of the game and the conversion should have been ruled good. He offered to come to the school and apologize personally.

"Does this mean you're changing the outcome of the game?" Don asked. When told no, that the Pirates would not be rewarded with the win, Grider fired back, "Then you can keep your apology in Nashville."

THE FAMILY BUSINESS

Both of Don's and Gaynelle's sons were born during football season — Vic on the day after a win, which led to his dad naming him Victory, and Heath the day before another win. Both boys also played for their dad and would go on to work as managers for the University of Tennessee football program.

But their outlook toward the game was very different. Heath was interested only in the strategy, while Vic was absorbed with every aspect of it. Nothing else captured his attention like the game, despite getting ran over at practice more times than he can remember, or having his dad yell for him to get out of the way, or even one night after begging to ride with the team on the bus back from a game at Alcoa.

Preoccupied by rehashing the game in his mind, it wasn't until the bus was halfway home that Don Grider blurted out, "Oh God, I left Vic in Alcoa!" But after turning on the interior light of the bus, he saw Vic slumped in a back seat, fast asleep.

"Dad didn't really talk a lot about the game at the house," Heath remembered. "He was a hard-nosed coach, but he was rational. I'll never forget one lesson he taught me was at halftime of a game at Grundy when I had gotten the hell beat out of me in the first half and I was crying in the locker room. He ripped my ass and told me to suck it up and not be a baby because sometimes you're going to get your teeth kicked in and you have to get up.

"That was about as mad as I ever saw him and it really wasn't anything about the game as much as it was just wanting me to toughen up."

Heath remembers another day when the Pirates were in a preseason scrimmage at Vonore and a fight broke out between the two teams. Don called his team together and got straight to the point, "Listen boys, we came over here to play football, but if y'all want to fight we can do that too. Just let me know which one y'all want to do and let's get to it."

Don Grider and his biggest supporter, wife Gaynelle.

"I'm more like dad as far as being more steady emotionally," Heath continued. "He never got too high or too low and I don't either. I honestly couldn't tell you the last time I cried about anything and that's how dad was. Vic wears his emotions on his sleeve a lot more. He doesn't hide how he feels. We're different that way and I'm not as consumed with the game either.

"Dad read a lot of military books, so we had that in common too. We both liked the strategy part of football. I honestly never thought I'd want to coach, but when Vic got the job and asked, I wanted to help my brother and I knew the program was very important to my family."

Heath spent several years in the corporate world before coming back home to join the family business when Vic was promoted to head coach.

In Vic's first year back he worked as the Pirates middle school coach in 1991. The next year, Don's last as head coach, Vic was an assistant on his dad's staff.

"Words can't describe what it meant to Don to have Vic and Heath follow his footsteps," Gaynelle explained. "He was really proud. Lots of evenings he would say to me, 'Take me to practice.' He just wanted to watch his boys."

And his boys understood how important the program was to their dad. In 1994, after the Pirates won their first state title since '69, the school surprised Don with a championship ring.

"They didn't get rings back when he won his so we all wanted him to have one," Vic said. "Boy was he ever proud of that."

Before the team left for the '99 title game, Don joked with the coaching staff that if they came back without the gold ball, "I'll lead the mob calling for the whole staff to be fired," he said with a smirk. "Starting with the head coach."

"Don was on dialysis the day of the 1999 game but went anyway," Gaynelle recalled. "The next day Vic and Heath and their families came out and stayed all day and relived the game. He was so proud that a Grider had won it again."

By the end of the 2017 season, Don and Vic Grider had more combined wins (387) than any father-son tandem in state history.

"The biggest thing I took from my dad is the structure and discipline," Vic explained. "I heard him say a thousand times, kids are starved for discipline, especially the ones who don't get it at home. That's something Heath and I both inherited from him.

"We've got something special here. You either carry it on or you drop it. That's a lot of pressure, but it's a good kind of pressure. You have to do things the right way because you know people are watching."

A TOWN MOURNS

Grider was diagnosed with diabetes as a 19-year old college freshman. But rather than complain about his failing health he dealt with it much the same way he taught his players to handle adversity saying, "Life throws you tough times. Learn to deal with it and keep fighting."

Complications from the disease caused him to spend two weeks in the hospital in 1985, and for the first time in his career he missed coaching the Pirates. Long-time assistant Dave Baxter filled in with an 18-3 win at Copper Basin that sealed the district championship and earned a spot in the playoffs.

His health continued to decline in the latter years of his coaching career with failing eyesight leading him to lean on assistants for input about down and distance situations on the sideline. That's when he knew it was time to step away from the game he loved and he retired after the 1992 season.

Eventually the disease affected his ability to walk and caused him to become legally blind, but still he remained a fixture at games. Even after Grider had undergone several hours of dialysis on Friday afternoons, he would ask Gaynelle to drive him to the stadium, where she would park their car in the end zone closest to the field house that bears his name. Once they had found their usual spot, Grider would roll down the window and take in every drop of Friday night atmosphere as he listened to the game on the radio.

As fans from both sides passed on their way into the stadium, many would stop to say hello and wish him well, a testament to the respect he had earned.

"I really can't see what's going on, but I listen for the crowd and when they're loud I know something good is happening for us," Grider once said. "As long as I'm able, I'll be at their games on Friday nights. I just love high school football, and there's no other place I'd rather be when they're playing."

Don Grider gives a play to Pirates receiver Robert McClain.

The adrenaline rush from game nights and the thrill of having former players and assistants stop by for visits kept Grider energized and feeling like he was never too far from the program he cared so much about.

But on a muggy spring morning in 2007 diabetes had finally taken too much of a toll and Grider passed away at the age of 67.

News swept quickly through the tightly knit community and the town, which has hung its helmet on football for more so long, felt an emptiness over the loss of its coach. Regardless of school ties — from the mountain of Grundy County through Jasper and into Bridgeport (Ala.) — the Sequatchie Valley mourned.

"Despite all the animosity between Jasper and South Pittsburg, he was one of my best friends," Colquette said. "I can't think of anybody I've coached against that I respected more.

"It really hurt me when he died."

The ripple effect of his influence even reached outside the valley, far beyond the boys who played for him.

"You always heard about what a great football coach he was, but those of us who really knew him talk more about the person," former TSSAA executive director Ronnie Carter said. "He's in a very select group in my mind because he was class in everything he did. Don Grider was South Pittsburg."

When the funeral ended, knowing how much the program meant to him, the family had the hearse circle the football field one more time before he was buried on the hill overlooking Beene Stadium.

"He always said that's where he wanted to be so he could watch over practice," Vic said.

HONORING THEIR LEGEND

In the months that followed Don's death, every player and coach involved with the program knew the best way they could honor him was to focus squarely on winning every game and bringing back another state title.

"Nobody reveled in us being successful more than him," Vic said. "There's a lot of pride to be coaching in the same place as your dad. He was South Pittsburg football. We're just a byproduct."

So each Friday, moments before leaving the locker room for kickoff, South Pittsburg's '07 team would huddle together to pray for safety as well as a special blessing on the Grider family.

"It really made us a lot closer as a team," said Robert Robinson, a senior all-state fullback that season. "We had never seen our coaches hurt like before we all went to the funeral. You could see how much they were missing their daddy, so it gave us something extra to play for."

When South Pittsburg hosted Lookout Valley in week three, the Pirates' first home game of the year, both sons said there was an empty feeling without having their dad there. He had been such a security blanket for them, just by sitting in his car in the end zone to watch previous games. Seeing their mom standing alone affected both of them.

"I know how much she misses him, so that was probably worse in my mind," Vic said. "People think our family is all about football, and during the season we are. But what I miss most is seeing him play with the grandkids. It was neat to see him be a completely different person with them."

The Pirates were tested only once during the 2007 regular season, holding off Tyner 25-21, and winning every other game by at least four touchdowns. Once they reached the playoffs the foot never came off the accelerator and the focus never wavered, not even during practice.

Don Grider before another state championship game.

"Knowing dad is up there watching makes you work harder," Heath said. "I'm sure we both look up there and think about him quite a bit. You better be doing things the right way or Daddy Don will be down there to straighten it out."

The Pirates continued putting on a show in the title game against McKenzie, building such a commanding lead in the second half that the running clock mercy rule was invoked.

Following a touchdown early in the fourth quarter of what would be a 52-20 thumping, Vic found a way for one final tribute by calling the play that his father had run thousands of times. Rather than kick a meaningless extra point, he had quarterback Cody Robinson turn sideways and the snap go directly to Montrell Mitchell. The 46 play was stopped inside the McKenzie 1, just short on the two-point conversion attempt, but the play had served its purpose.

"We put that in the day before the game and I told the kids I didn't care if they gained a yard," Vic said. "I just wanted to run it as a tribute to my dad. We didn't score on it, but it sent the message I wanted."

Some former players admitted they had goosebumps or even got choked up when the Pirates ran the play.

"Before and during the game you're worried about taking care of business," Heath said. "But once it got out of hand, I started thinking about dad and what he meant to this program and to me personally."

As the final seconds dripped off the MTSU stadium scoreboard Gaynelle stood near midfield watching her sons hug their wives and children. For so many years she had celebrated victories with her husband. Moments later she made her way to her sons, hugged both boys and wiped tears from her cheeks as she walked away.

"I told Vic his daddy is responsible for this," she said, watching the team rush toward midfield to accept their gold ball trophy. "He brought us here and I could feel his presence all night. We've been at our lowest point, and now we're at our highest.

"Football and our community have been very good to our family. Don was a special man, and he's looking down smiling on this team and his boys tonight."

Grider's sons took the Pirates back to the championship game three times after that night, adding another title and finishing runners-up twice before Vic stepped away from the game in 2012 to spend more time with his family.

But after just two years away, the program began seeing a drastic decline and it was an old family friend, David Hale, who convinced Vic he needed to return and rebuild the program that has been so much a part of his family's history.

Remembering those Sunday conversations in the Grider family's den, and the advice from his mentor, Hale reminded Vic just what the program meant to his father, his family and the community.

"That day when he came to talk to me, David got right to the point," said Vic, who helped guide the team to the quarterfinals in his first year back, followed by two trips to the semifinals — using the principles of tireless work he learned from his dad. "It kind of reminded me how my dad was. He just said that my dad had helped build this program and that it was hurting real bad and I knew what needed to be done.

"As soon as he left the room I got pretty emotional just thinking about how right he was. This program means so much to so many people in our town. But I knew there was nobody who cared more about the program than our family and it was time to get to work.

"Dad was usually right and he knew even better than I did that me and Heath being out there on that field together is just where we're suppose to be."

Chapter 11

BILL AND DAVE BAXTER

"A brother is the only enemy that you can't live without."

— Unknown

When Bill Baxter agreed to take the head coaching job at Marion County his only stipulation was that his younger brother Dave would be offered an assistant's position to come with him. Aside from the fact that he knew Dave understood the physical style the program would teach, Bill had also promised their mother that he would look after his brother, and besides, he couldn't move without bringing his best fishing and coon hunting buddy.

In other words, Bill knew he needed a big dose of home to come with him if he was going to be successful and put down roots in a new community.

"For as far back as I can remember they've been inseparable," said Bill's son Tim. "Dad and Uncle Dave were always the best of friends, whether it was hunting or fishing or football, they just liked doing things together.

"They probably listened to each other when they wouldn't listen to anybody else."

The Baxter boys had learned to be tougher than a pine knot growing up on their family's Polk County farm and football was their ticket out.

Both were stars at Polk County High School and Bill, five years older, went on to play at Tennessee, where he blocked for Johnny Majors for two seasons before transferring to Tennessee Tech to get married and finish out his playing career.

He returned to Polk County to take a job as an assistant football and head girls' basketball coach and was content to be back home for five years before the offer to take over the Marion County program was extended.

Dave Baxter.

While he was cutting his coaching teeth back home, younger brother Dave was making a name for himself as a two-time All America at Tennessee Tech. He had been an all-state running back at Polk County but all those years of getting whipped by Bill growing up finally paid off when his grit helped him make the move to become an undersized two-way lineman.

"If it hadn't been for Bill I'd still be in Polk County, probably broke," Dave once said with a wink. "He kept an eye on me to make sure I didn't screw up. When I was still in high school I was going to quit football but mama called him while he was at Tech and he came home that weekend to set me straight.

"He took me up there for the spring game one year and that's when I decided I wanted to go to college.

"My sophomore year I had never played in a game, and then our starting tackle got hurt. I heard my name being called but I couldn't even find my helmet because I hadn't expected to get to play. Once I got in I never left the starting lineup again and played both sides of the ball."

It was also while at Tech that he formed a life-long friendship with roommate Don Grider, another small-town kid who was devoted to football. Dave even had to learn to give Grider, who had just been diagnosed as diabetic, his insulin shots.

"The first time he did it Don jumped and told him he nearly killed him because he poked him with the needle in the wrong spot," said Dave's daughter Lynn. "That was a friendship that wound up meaning a lot to daddy and they stayed really close from then on."

When his college career ended, Dave was drafted by the Dallas Cowboys but the 215-pound defensive end wound up being the final player cut before the 1962 season began. Buffalo called a week later to offer a tryout for their AFL squad but he decided his playing days were through and instead he joined his brother's staff at Marion, to coach offensive and defensive linemen.

"When the job was offered they told me there was one assistant's job open and I said I wanted to bring my brother," Bill said. "They asked me if he could teach and I told them I didn't know about that, but at least he had his degree and how hard could it be to learn to teach.

Marion coaches Dave Baxter, Bill Baxter and Johnny Grimes.

"I already knew he would be a good coach for us."

Together the Baxter brothers turned Marion into one of the premier programs in the Sequatchie Valley Conference, finishing unbeaten twice, including in 1968 when a one-point win over South Pittsburg punctuated a 9-0 finish.

The formula for the Warriors' success was simple — hours of hard work until the players were as tough as sandpaper. Their single-wing offense featured cat-quick tailbacks running behind the same type of physical farm boys they had been themselves.

"Coach Bill believed in doing every drill, every play as many times as it took until you got it right. And you'd better go full speed on every snap," said former Warriors all-state tailback Eddie Brown. "He would tell us 'Once you make a decision, don't if, and or but about it, just go. Even if it's wrong you might be able to work it out if you're hustling.'

"He had a way of just looking at you or talking to you and, without even raising voice, letting you know if you had messed up. If he rubbed his head and walked away for a minute, you knew you were in trouble."

Brown's teammate, David Moore, was so impacted by the lessons he learned while playing for the Baxters that he dedicated his life to following in their substantial footsteps, becoming a teacher and coach.

"I loved those two men," Moore said. "No matter what, you just didn't want to do anything to let them down. Coach Bill came up to me after the football banquet one year and told me how proud he was of me and how he thought I had done a good job coaching. My heart about exploded. It was the greatest compliment I ever received.

"I told him everything I had learned, I learned from him and Coach Dave, and that the one thing he taught me more than football was how to be a good dad."

Before Brown was sprinting past opposing defenses, his future brother in law Bill Baker was an all-state running back for the Warriors and admitted that even five decades after his high school playing days had ended he could still close his eyes and see Coach Bill squatting in the huddle during practice, tugging at grass as he thought about which play to call next.

"He was like a second dad to a lot of us because we respected him so much," Baker recalled. "He coached you aggressively and got onto you hard but he always loved you and put his arm around you at the end of practice or a game to make sure you knew he still cared about you.

"He coached you like he would his own son. He pushed you hard to be your best but if you played for him it was like being in his family."

When Bill gave up coaching, after 15 seasons, to become Marion's principal, he turned the program over to Dave who guided the Warriors for the next three years. Despite a 20-13 record during that time, Dave decided he wasn't cut out for all the added responsibilities that come with being the head coach and was ready to step down, believing he would just teach and go to games as a fan for a while.

Dave and Bill Baxter always carried a close bond as brothers.

That idea was short-lived once his old college roommate called and asked if he wanted to make the move eight miles to the south and join the staff at South Pittsburg.

It was the equivalent of a Civil War soldier swapping his Union uniform to join the Confederacy.

"I figured I could go back to just being an assistant but the people at South Pittsburg didn't take to me at first because I had been at Jasper for so long," Dave said. "It took a while for them to trust me but eventually I became just one of them."

When he made the announcement to the family, Dave let his two daughters — Lynn and Dee — decide whether they would stay at Marion or transfer to South Pittsburg. His son, Bob, was never given the choice — he would come to South Pittsburg so his dad wouldn't have to worry about coaching against him.

"Lord, me and my sister cried and pitched a fit because we didn't want him going to South Pittsburg," Lynn said. "But then we saw how the people there made him feel welcome and it's like anybody who changes sides in the rivalry, once you find out the other people aren't as bad as you thought and that they're actually really good people, you adjust.

"We would cheer for Marion County every week except when they played South Pittsburg and then, even though we went to school in Jasper, we cheered for the Pirates because of daddy. He actually grew to develop a real dislike for the Warriors and like everybody else in South Pittsburg, eventually he would just call them Jasper."

After spending 18 years at Marion, Dave coached South Pittsburg for the next 20 years and earned a reputation for squeezing every ounce of ability and toughness from a kid who other coaches had given up on. More than once he took a player who was as slow as the last day of school and turned him into a key part of championship teams. He produced eight all-state linemen for the Pirates.

"There's nobody I ever worked with that I put more stock in than him," said Pirates coach Vic Grider, Don's son. "Any advice he gave or if he said something positive about us would mean the world to me. He was very opinionated but he was spot-on right so you'd better listen to whatever he said if you wanted to win.

"My first year as an assistant on my dad's staff Dave wanted to run a screen and kept telling me to convince my dad to call it. He'd say 'You're his son, he'll listen to you. He never listens to me.' Well, I convince dad to run it right before halftime of a close game and it gets intercepted.

"We could hear my dad cussing at us on the sideline, so me and Dave sprinted for the locker room and hid out the whole halftime. We could hear him cussing and saying 'where the hell are those two dumbasses who told me to call the screen?' We tried to stay real quiet until it was time to go back out for the second half but Dave kept giggling and I was sure my dad would find us and yell at us."

For nearly all of the two decades that Dave coached at South Pittsburg, Bill was the principal at Marion and eventually the two ultra competitors, who lived just a mile apart, agreed they would simply not discuss the game for the week that rivalry was renewed each season.

"We would get together to hunt and fish a lot during the year," Bill said. "But it could get pretty heated for that game and we didn't want to wind up making the other mad, so we just wouldn't call or go see each other until the next week.

"We would root for each other the rest of the year and call each other after the games to see how each other's team played, but that week we just left each other alone."

Years after his retirement, Dave was coaxed into coming back out to coach for one more year by Vic and helped mold a group of linemen that led the Pirates to the 2007 state title.

"Coach Dave was a huge reason why we won it all that year," said Pirates two-way lineman Matt Wayne. "He gave us an edge, a toughness we didn't have before and we played at a different level that season because of him."

In the seasons that followed that championship, Coach Dave would find his spot in the stands to sit and monitor the games, quietly critiquing every little detail of the program he had grown to call home.

Before he passed away in 2017 Dave

Bill Baxter before a Marion state title game.

instructed his family to set up a vocational scholarship fund in his name for South Pittsburg students, and although his family's home had been in Polk County, he also requested to be laid to rest in Marion County.

"They both believed in a very hard-nosed, physical style of coaching and playing the game," said former Warriors defensive coordinator Landon Pickett. "I enjoyed getting to know them because they were such good people.

"The morning before we played in our second state championship Coach Dave called me and said 'good luck to y'all'. I had a lot of respect for him, so that was really big for me."

The surest sign of respect for both Baxters was the fact that former players from both sides of the rivalry addressed them simply as Coach Bill and Coach Dave.

The stadium at Marion County High is named in Coach Bill's honor and, similar to his younger brother, once he retired from the school he remained a fixture in the stands cheering on the team he adopted as his own.

"Both of their lives revolved around the game," Tim Baxter said. "Dad loved the passion for football that the folks in the valley have and Friday nights were always his favorite thing in the world to do.

"When he would see those boys walk out there on the field before the game his face would just light up."

On the eve of the 1994 season opener, when Marion County would travel to South Pittsburg, Warriors senior defensive lineman Jason Dykes was so worked up before his first career start that he finally decided to get out of the house and go coon hunting, just to get his mind off the enormity of the game.

When he pulled up in the woods to his usual spot where he would turn his dogs loose, Dykes found two other hunters had beat him there.

"Coach Bill and Coach Dave were there about to go hunting," Dykes said. "Coach Bill asked what I was doing out so late on the night before a game and I told him my nerves were tore up and I had to get out for a while.

"They asked me to go with them and after we treed the first coon Coach Bill took me back to my truck and told me to go home and get

Bill Baxter celebrates the Warriors championship with several players.

some rest. Just being out there with them talking about other stuff besides football really helped get my mind off the game and calmed me down."

As Dykes climbed back into his truck, it was Coach Dave who brought up the impending game for the first time all evening, saying simply, "Good luck, son."

Bill turned and joked, "I can't believe you wished a Warrior luck against the Pirates."

"We're going to whip y'all's ass anyway so what's it matter if I wish him luck?" Dave shot back.

Dykes watched as the brothers drove away, their pickup truck fading into the night.

"You could just tell how much they loved each other," Dykes said. "Anybody who has a brother would understand and wouldn't trade that kind of relationship for anything.

"Getting to experience that time with them, just watching and listening to them is something I'll always remember. You wouldn't be able to find any better fellas than those two."

Chapter 12
KEN COLQUETTE

"Pretend inferiority to encourage others' arrogance."
— Sun Tzu, *The Art of War*

Standing in front of a large green chalkboard, a nubby stick of white chalk in his right hand, Ken Colquette began quizzing his defensive coordinator on worst-case scenarios. With an opponent's formation already drawn on the board, Colquette diagrammed potential plays that might be thrown at Marion County's defense.

"What if they motion here and run to the wide side out of this set?" Colquette asked worriedly.

"Then we'll slide our linebacker over here and take it away like this," Johnny Grimes answered, pointing out how he would defend Colquette's problem. Grimes, a 1965 Marion graduate who played defensive back and had been an assistant since 1969, called every defensive play for the first 12 years of Colquette's head coaching tenure with the Warriors. It was his job to have a solution ready for every possible scenario, and few did it better.

Colquette believed so strongly in defense being the cornerstone of a championship team that he began every practice with that side of the ball, and like every other part of the game, he fretted constantly over being prepared, beginning with the Sunday afternoon chalkboard sessions when the Warriors staff would meet to begin putting together their game plan for the next opponent.

"Okay," Colquette would counter Grimes' first solution, "But what if they line up like this and run play-action?"

"They've never ran that before," Grimes assured.

"But what if they do?" Colquette repeated.

After a long pause, glancing at the diagram, then back at Colquette, Grimes threw his chalk against the board in frustration and replied, "Damnit, Ken! Then I guess they'll just beat us!"

This was the way Colquette approached almost every game of his storied head coaching career, which began at Bridgeport (Ala.), followed by Marion — where he won four state championships and finished runner-up twice in 17 seasons — and continued through three other programs. By the time he retired, Colquette had a staggering 257-94 overall record, with 181 of those wins coming at Marion, where he won 82-percent of the games he coached.

Ken Colquette walks the sideline.

By the end of his run at Marion, an atheist in Jasper meant someone who didn't believe in Ken Colquette.

But while his teams typically created headaches for opponents on game night, none of those wins came without first giving Colquette a few ulcers of his own. He was such a perfectionist that if he had married a supermodel he would've expected her to cook too.

For all the wins and all the championships he brought back to Jasper, he was just as well known for being a professional worrier and poor-mouther.

Some species of whales will sleep near the surface of the ocean and can go undetected until it's too late for a ship to change course and miss the collision. There are stories of certain ship captains who would worry themselves into a tizzy over the possibility of crashing into one of the sleeping giants.

That is Colquette, a captain who fretted over what may be lying just below the surface, always certain there was some unknown, unseen catastrophe lurking to wreck his team's season.

"Coach Colquette made everybody who played for him a student of the game," said Chip Lockhart, an all-state lineman on Marion's 1992 state championship team. "He was such a perfectionist that he could see if just one guy took a half step in the wrong direction on a play in practice and he would stop us and make us line up and run it again.

"That's something I still carry with me, even now at work. I will slow down and assess a situation and remember how I was taught to solve any problem and make sure a job gets done exactly right. If you played for him you were always prepared and knew what to do in every situation.

"The biggest compliment I can pay him is that all these years later, you could line us up right now, and even though we'd be a few steps slower, we'd still run anything from our playing days to perfection. That's how well we were taught."

A COACHING SPONGE

The oldest of two sons born to working-class parents — Kenneth Sr. worked for the Sequatchie Valley Electrical Co-op and Anna Louise was an elementary school teacher and librarian — young Ken played fullback and linebacker at Grundy County High School, and tried playing basketball.

"I was the worst basketball player God ever created," Colquette said with a laugh. "So I stuck to football until I tore my knee up."

After graduating from Grundy County in 1965, he went on to a short-lived career at Tennessee Tech before a knee injury made him confront his future, and what career path he would pursue.

"Most of the guys around me in school were taking engineering classes but that wasn't appealing to me so I decided I would give up ever making much money and teach and coach instead," he said.

Colquette's first coaching job was at the junior high level in Sumpter (S.C.), where he also met on Saturdays with the high school staff to help put together the plan for their next game. It was there that he was introduced to the split-back veer offense.

"I saw the team go from struggling to win a game to being really tough to stop," Colquette recalled. "That's when I decided I was taking the veer with me wherever I went. I also picked up another trick there because I noticed how the coaches would build up the team they were about play to be better than they actually were. I saw how that would get the players' attention, so I decided I would take that with me too.

"I was like a sponge, just soaking up whatever I could from the older coaches. I was suppose to scout the team the varsity would play next, but on my first trip I looked down at my notepad at halftime and realized I had just been watching the game. I hadn't written down any names or numbers or taken any notes. That taught me to be disciplined to the details of whatever my job was."

His first varsity job would also provide plenty more chances to soak up wisdom as he joined Luther Welsh at Dougherty High in Albany (Ga.). Welsh was already an established veteran coach and would go on to win more than 330 games and earn induction into the Georgia Sports Hall of Fame.

On the day Colquette arrived at his new house in Albany, Welsh met his young assistant to help unload his belongings from the truck. The conversation quickly moved to football and despite being worn out from the long drive and longer hours spent moving in, Colquette stayed up past 2 a.m. explaining what he liked about the veer offense.

"He was asking a lot of questions, but I didn't think anything about it until two days later when I walked in for our first staff meeting and he announced we were switching from the I-formation, which they had always ran, to the split-back veer," Colquette said.

"He put me in charge of the defense but I had never even heard of the 50-slant, which is what he'd always ran, so I had to call the guy who used to be their defensive coordinator and get him to explain it to me. I kept him on the phone for hours trying to figure out how to run it.

"At our first practice, I was so nervous that I just froze. I didn't know what to do. One of the kids finally asked if I wanted them to hit the sled and I snapped out of it and said 'That's a dang good idea.' I finally loosened up and I've ran the 50-slant and split-back veer at every place I've coached since."

After a three-year stay in Albany, Colquette coached at Cleveland for one year, where he reached a crossroads. With a young family to support, he knew it was time to either find a head coaching job or to leave coaching for good and pursue another career.

Ken Colquette celebrates with his players.

"I looked into TVA and even thought about selling used cars," Colquette said. "I interviewed at Bridgeport, which was going to be my last shot before finding something else to do. My daughter (Tracy) was two and my son (Corey) was a newborn and I had to find something that would pay better than being an assistant.

"Bridgeport's administration kept delaying making a decision, so I finally called the principal and told him I'd been offered a job in Gatlinburg but didn't want to go that far away. I was bluffing. There wasn't any other job offer. But Bridgeport called back the next day and offered me their job."

While Colquette was trying to build Bridgeport into a contender, neighboring rival Stevenson was already there. Under polarizing coach Kenneth McKinney, Stevenson won Alabama state titles in two of the three years (1977, 79) Colquette was at Bridgeport. He was so successful that when Colquette's second Bridgeport team pulled off an upset, a rumor began circulating among Stevenson fans that Colquette had paid McKinney — who was already known for some shady decisions — to agree to take a dive and lose on purpose.

"It was about the stupidest thing I'd ever heard but there were a lot of people who believed it and kept it going," Colquette said. "Me and my wife were literally living paycheck to paycheck, with two small kids and one car that was broke down and people thought I had extra money to pay off a rival coach to let us win.

"So a few weeks later when our two schools played each other in basketball I took an empty envelope, handed it to some Stevenson fans and asked them to pass it up to the top of the bleachers to Coach McKinney. I made sure everybody in the gym saw me hand that envelope over and point toward McKinney and boy did that ever get people talking about what could've been in that envelope.

"I actually got along well enough with McKinney that he asked me to help coach from the press box during a couple of their playoff runs. That didn't sit too well with our folks in Bridgeport, but I was just trying to learn as much as I could from a guy who was having a lot of success."

Although Colquette went 21-10 in his three seasons with the Tigers, including 9-1 in his final year, he never got along with school administrators, so as soon as the offer was made to take over Marion County's program, he brought the veer and 50-slant 15 miles across the state line and began laying the foundation for one of Tennessee's top prep programs.

"The principal at Bridgeport didn't have the sense God gave a grape," Colquette said. "We had the worst facilities in the state and he refused to help us improve anything. We couldn't even host playoff games because our stands and field were in such bad shape.

"I got sick of fighting about it, and I knew (Marion principal) Bill Baxter was a former coach and wanted to run a top-notch program, so I wanted to work for him. That was the best career decision I ever made."

NEW SHERIFF IN THE VALLEY

As the disco decade came to an end it was clear that the 80s would be a time for big news — and later big hair — from the get-go. Historical events came fast and furious as the new decade dawned, beginning with the United States Olympic hockey team — comprised of college-level players — knocking off the four-time gold medal winning Soviet Union in arguably the greatest upset in sports history. Aside from the "Miracle on Ice" the biggest sports story was the Pittsburgh Steelers becoming the first NFL franchise to win 4 Super Bowls, defeating the Los Angeles Rams in Super Bowl XIV, also preventing former Marion County great Eddie Brown from earning a championship ring.

Recognizing the need for round-the-clock news updates, Ted Turner's Cable News Network (CNN) began broadcasting that summer as the first 24-hour news source, the first rap song to receive radio air play — Sugar Hill Gang's "Rapper's Delight" — debuted and quirky new inventions — Rubik's cube, Pacman video game and the Magnavox VHS Recorder — entertained us and took our money.

Millions tuned in to find out who shot J.R. Ewing on the wildly popular weekly soap opera Dallas, but sadly it was an actual shooting that broke the world's heart when former Beatles member John Lennon was killed outside his Manhattan apartment.

Back home in Marion County, the news that had everyone buzzing was the announcement of a new shopping center to be built at the state line. It would include a K-Mart, Red Food Store, Revco Drug Store, Pic-N-Pay shoes and an arcade (Electric Circus).

Shortly after that announcement, news spread that Marion County had hired Colquette. For his first two seasons, Colquette ran the program with only one assistant (Grimes).

"Johnny ran the defense and I coached the offense," Colquette recalled. "But it wasn't long before we realized we needed some help if we were going to compete with some of the teams we'd be playing every year."

Within a few seasons Marion had one of the most envied staffs in the state with assistants Donnie Stewart, Jerry Tate and Landon Pickett joining Grimes and Colquette to give the Warriors more than 100 years of coaching experience.

Colquette made his Warriors debut on Labor Day weekend with the Warriors traveling to Jackson County and rolling 43-0. The next week, in their home opener — led by quarterback Troy Womack who ran for one touchdown and threw for another to Gary McCallie — Marion beat Bledsoe County 22-6.

An easy 39-8 win over Grundy County followed and the next week, in a match-up at his former school, Marion rallied for a 22-21 overtime win over Bridgeport. After trailing 7-0 at halftime, the Warriors tied the game with an eight-play, 66-yard scoring drive to begin the third quarter, capped by Will Wooten's 1-yard scoring run. Wooten then added a 37-yard punt return for the go-ahead TD and also ran for the 2-point conversion for a 15-7 lead. Tigers quarterback Tyrone Robinson, who later played at Tennessee, threw for a TD then added the game-tying two-point run with four seconds remaining to force overtime. Womack hit Leroy Garner on a 24-yard scoring pass that put Marion ahead in overtime, and Robinson countered by tossing a 15-yard TD. But on the conversion pass, the Tigers receiver was ruled to have come down out of the back of the end zone, giving Marion the dramatic win.

Marion's roll continued by shutting out Northwest Georgia, thumping Whitwell and holding off McKinney's Stevenson team 13-7. Against Sequatchie County, the Warriors fell behind 13-12 going in to the fourth quarter before Womack connected with Donnie Keef for a TD pass and Will Wooten ran for a 44-yard TD to lead another come-from-behind win.

The following week, while the county voted in favor of Jimmy Carter, the nation elected Republican Ronald Reagan President and days later an overflow crowd showed up on the first Friday of November to watch as the District 6-A title was on the line at South Pittsburg.

Despite Marion being unbeaten and South Pittsburg having just two losses, only the winner would qualify for the playoffs.

The Pirates quadrupled Marion in first-half rushing yards, but led only 6-0 at halftime after losing two turnovers in Warriors territory. The only score had been set up when Mark Allison connected with Mack Moore on a 37-yard gain, followed by a 14-yard scoring pass from Allison to Dale Dennis with less than two minutes left before halftime.

The teams continued to miss scoring chances — the Pirates lost a fumble at the Marion 10 and the Warriors were held on downs at the South Pitt five — until Womack completed 3 of 5 passes to spark a late drive. With 5:23 remaining, Womack kept the ball on an outside veer to the right and raced 24 yards, diving into the end zone. Leroy Garner added the extra point that would prove to be the game-winner as the Warriors claimed their third straight win in the series, 7-6.

"Troy never wanted to play quarterback," Colquette said. "I had told him earlier in the season that if we could find somebody else to do it he wouldn't have to. We never did and he turned out to be a really good player for us.

"After that season, Don Grider talked to me about moving the rivalry away from the last game. His point was you put so much into that game, then it's hard to get back up emotionally for the next game in the playoffs. He was right, so we moved it and never played it on the last week again."

In his first season Colquette had set the bar extremely high, guiding the Warriors to the first 10-0 season in program history, a huge rivalry win over South Pittsburg and a trip to the playoffs.

The first-round playoff loss that followed the next week against Meigs County, although disappointing, did nothing to dampen optimism for the direction the program was headed.

"When I got hired everybody I met said I'd be ok so long as we beat Pittsburg," Colquette recalled. "I ignored it at first, but as I grew into the job I realized if you could beat Pittsburg you probably wouldn't lose many because they were always going to be one of the top teams.

"I always used it as motivation to our kids that you knew Pittsburg was going to be good so you don't want them to show you up. My goal was to catch the series back up, which we eventually did."

Not only was Colquette 14-3 against the Pirates while at Marion, but there was even a 10-year period, from 1987-96, when the Warriors never trailed at any point against their rival.

For his career — at Bridgeport, Marion, Sequatchie and Grundy — Colquette finished with a 19-7-1 record against South Pittsburg.

He frustrated Pirates fans so much that as he made the short walk from the visitor's locker room to

Johnny Grimes ran Marion's defense for 12 seasons.

the field before a game at South Pittsburg in the early 90s, a man wearing a black hat with an orange 'P' yelled from the sideline, "Hey Colquette, remember God loves you. But the rest of us think you're an asshole!"

BUILDING A MACHINE

By the mid-80s, possibly the only thing more synonymous with one another than Marion County and the split-back veer were Burt and Loni. The difference, of course, was Marion's marriage to its old-school, physical brand of offense never soured.

By design, the veer rewards patience and persistence. To stop it every defensive player must be in position on every snap. If even one defender misses an assignment, so long as the quarterback makes the correct read, the veer will deliver a big-play punch to the nose.

Or as legendary T.C. Williams coach Herman Boone famously said in 'Remember the Titans', "The split-back veer is like novocaine, just give it time and it always works."

"You knew exactly what you were going to get when you played Marion," former South Pittsburg coach Danny Wilson said. "You didn't worry about what kind of offense you'd have to plan for because you knew it was the split-back veer, and they were going to be dang good because they were very well coached at it."

By the end of his first decade in Jasper, Colquette had made the Warriors perennial playoff fixtures, winning 10 or more games six times and reaching the state title game twice. But Marion hadn't yet won a championship.

That changed in 1990 with the program's first title and the Warriors would claim three more over the next five years. Despite the runaway success, Colquette maintained the same poor-mouthing technique he had learned as a first-year assistant in South Carolina.

"The things Coach Colquette said in the paper, about us being underdogs and not very good, were the same things he preached to us every day at practice," said Shane Thomasson, who quarterbacked Marion to the '90 state title. "After listening to him, even I felt sorry for us for having me play quarterback.

"He knew which buttons to push to make you play harder and better. My first year of playing for him, I went home and complained to my dad about how Coach Colquette was getting onto me. My dad just shook his head and said 'then do it right.' That taught me to keep my mouth shut, work harder to get things right and after that Coach kept riding me because he knew I could take it."

By the time the Warriors hit their stride in the 90s, Colquette was considered to be the Yoda of the split-back veer, a master at teaching quarterbacks how to make the right read against any defense. Regardless of the subject, few teachers have understood their subject more thoroughly.

Known for reading psychology books in his football office — with a plastic McDonald's spit cup nearby — Colquette reserved some of his toughest nitpicking for the team's most talented players.

"When I was a freshman I had a good game against Tyner," recalled Eric Westmoreland, who went on to become a two-time all-state player. "I returned a punt for a touchdown and had an interception and was feeling pretty good about myself. He came to me after I messed up at practice the next Monday and said 'You may be a star in everybody else's mind but you're still just a screw-up freshman to me.' That brought me back to reality real quick.

"You could have a great run for a touchdown and when you'd come off the field he'd pat you on the back and say 'Good run. For a minute I thought you were going to fumble it.' You either rose to your best ability under him or you melted under the pressure."

His demanding demeanor also gave players something every kid needs — somebody they didn't want to disappoint.

"About halfway through my sophomore year I made the mistake of telling my uncle that it felt like Coach Colquette had given up on me because he wasn't chewing me out as hard in practice as he did some other guys," said T.J. Gentle, who played linebacker for the Warriors in the early 90s. "That next Monday, from the time school started until practice ended he was on me about something all day. I teared up in practice and he looked over at me and said 'I guess you'll keep your mouth shut from now on won't you?'

"You wanted to earn his respect so bad because it didn't come easily. You never wanted to be the guy who let him down. All the guys who played for him are grown men, with kids of our own now, but we all still call him 'Coach' when we see him because of the respect we have for him."

Colquette once informed Rodney Rankin, a sophomore linebacker, that he had been voted onto an all-star team the afternoon before a playoff game. Before walking away, he added, "I don't know how. Lord knows I didn't vote for you."

Just as certain as the plastic water bottle stuffed in the back pocket of his bike coaching shorts, or calling either inside-veer or quarterback keeper near the goal line was the fact that every back-handed compliment or tongue-lashing at practice was calculated.

"Everything he said or did was about psychology," said longtime assistant Don Stewart. "He would always tell us that we had to have a bad guy and a good guy at practice every day. He'd remind us that there were 11 kids on the field and he could find one of them who did something wrong. After he'd chew on the kid for a while he wanted one of us to go pat the kid on the back and tell them they did a hell of a job. We played that game every day at practice.

"Sometimes before we went out he'd say 'I'm tired being the bad guy.' And then he'd designate one of us to be the guy who chewed on the kids that day. One day he told (secondary coach) Jerry Tate that it was his turn to be the bad guy. Jerry was the nicest man on the planet and never cussed. Ken made him be the bad guy that day and about the worst thing Jerry could think of was to tell his defensive backs they weren't playing worth a shit. You should've seen those kids' expression. They were heart-broken the rest of the day because they had made Coach Tate cuss. Ken never made him be the bad guy again."

As wildly successful as the program was under him, it would have been futile to question Colquette's tactics. He understood he could work the players like a rented mule because the majority of them came from blue collar families — tough-as-nails country boys who worked on farms and spent their spare time in a tree stand deer hunting or on a creek bank fishing.

He averaged 11 wins per season — 12 of his 17 years the Warriors finished with at least 10 wins — and had one four-year stretch from 1992-95 where Marion compiled an extraordinary 56-1 overall record. During Marion's back-to-back titles in 1994-95 Westmoreland was the only Division I signee.

"We had kids who were either too slow or too little or too dumb to get into college, but they sure could play high school ball," Colquette explained. "A huge part of the success was because of the buy-in for the town and how much it meant. It's a little extra burden when the whole town is so engaged, but at the same time it's what really drives the success of the program. The kids accepted that. They knew that was the price it took to win because they had seen it pay off for all those teams before them.

State titles became a routine thing for Marion under Ken Colquette.

"I'd go around the halls to the girls and tell them 'do not break up with your boyfriend until after the playoffs. No matter how sorry he is, you better put up with him.' That would tickle those girls, but I meant it.

"The kids had seen us win for so long that they just believed they were suppose to be good, even when we weren't the best team. We won some games just because our kids expected to win and the other team was more worried about our tradition, which made them doubt they could beat us. That was all the edge we needed."

At the rate Colquette's teams won he was approached almost on a yearly basis by other programs hoping to lure him away. Two of the better offers from larger schools that he flirted with but eventually turned down were from Bradley Central and Scottsboro, but one he could not ignore came from Vidalia (Ga.), which offered the chance to earn nearly $30,000 more than his salary at Marion.

The financial boost was simply too good to pass up.

"Seeing how much more the Georgia schools paid got my attention," Colquette admitted. "But that was a mistake. I never should've left. It wasn't home, it wasn't the same. This place felt more like home than anywhere, including where I grew up."

After resigning from Marion in 1996 — which was also the only season he finished with a losing record — Colquette stayed briefly at Vidalia, then came back to Grundy County before later migrating as an assistant between Soddy-Daisy and Ooltewah. He even returned to Marion County as an assistant for one season before ending his career as the head coach at Sequatchie County, where he stayed for two years before deciding it was time to walk away from the game for good.

But he never wandered too far from the game, or the team, that he's been identified with for so long.

Twenty years after his last game as Marion's head coach Colquette returned to watch and support the team as it made a run toward the state title game. Standing with several former players on a frozen semifinal Friday night, he leaned against the chainlink fence behind the home bench and watched as the Warriors took a commanding halftime lead.

Grimes, who continues to chart plays and help the staff coach from the sideline, glanced over at the Colquette contingent as he set an assistant's headset on the bench.

"The kids are locked in," Grimes said. "Playing well right now."

As Colquette watched the Warriors trot off the field toward their locker room, he nodded in agreement. Seconds later the worrywart coach inside him crept back to the surface as he turned to a friend and countered.

"Yeah, but them suckers over there have got a lot more speed. What if they come out throwing it all over the field in the second half?"

Chapter 13
1990 WARRIORS

"It's hard to beat a person who never gives up."
— **Babe Ruth**

Something was most definitely wrong. The pain in Shane Thomasson's back was unlike anything he had felt; to the point that even taking a deep breath felt like shards of jagged glass slicing down his left side. As teammates — in their all-white uniforms with purple numbers and WARRIORS emblazoned across the front of their jerseys — sat at their lockers awaiting their coaches to file into the room and begin instructing them on second-half adjustments, Thomasson slogged to the bathroom.

Standing at a urinal inside the visitor's locker room at Vanderbilt Stadium, Thomasson looked down and fought back the instinct to gasp as he realized he was pissing blood.

Somehow among the whirring thoughts racing through his mind Thomasson remembered the last thing his coach had said earlier that evening, just moments before sending the team onto the field.

Scouring the room, Ken Colquette had warned his anxious players, "I want no excuses. I don't want to hear it if somebody gets injured, if it snows or rains or the sun gets in your eyes. No excuses."

Thomasson remembered feeling that Colquette had paused to lock eyes with him, as if to use that momentary silent glare to remind his quarterback that much of the game's outcome rested squarely on his shoulders.

On the first play of that Class AA state championship game, Colquette called for an outside veer and Johnny Morrison fired off a step late, causing Thomasson to trip over his lineman's foot and begin to fall forward. Just as he was able to reach his arm out and hand the ball to halfback Brian Janeway, Thomasson was hit by a defender, the collision causing his body to bend backward in a way that drew groans from most of the 12,000 in the stands. On his way to the turf another tackler drilled him in the back with his helmet and Thomasson lay on the frigid carpet for what seemed an eternity.

The game had just begun and already the one player the Warriors couldn't afford to be without was writhing in pain. The first words to escape Colquette's mouth were the same ones most of the huge contingent of Warriors fans filling the visitor's side were thinking.

"Oh shit," Colquette said, stepping from the sideline toward the field. "Come on Shane, get up boy."

Marion players celebrate the program's first state title.

Thomasson had been injured weeks earlier, in the first quarter of the last game of the regular season, and without him there to make the right reads operating their veer offense Marion had been hammered by Alabama power Etowah, 47-14.

"We couldn't win without Shane. We all knew that," said Rodney Rankin, who played linebacker and fullback. "We had some guys who were really good at their job, but we knew we had to have Shane running the offense or we were in trouble."

Once he limped to the sideline Thomasson spent the rest of that first series as well as Marion's first defensive stand getting looked at by the medical staff. What wouldn't be discovered for another two days, when he finally broke down and confessed the pain was too much to take and agreed to see a doctor, was that the hit had broken two ribs and bruised Thomasson's kidney.

"I thought I'd broke my back," Thomasson said. "The pain was really bad. It sucked. The coaches knew something was wrong so they told my dad I had hurt my back and they needed his permission for me to keep playing.

"We had played our whole lives for that moment. You'd have to kill me to keep me out of that game and my dad knew it so he told the coaches that if I wanted to play to let me. There was no other option. There was no way I wasn't playing."

"THERE WAS A MEAN STREAK ON THAT TEAM"

In the year between his sophomore and junior seasons Thomasson had grown five inches, gained more than 20 pounds and earned the right to take over as Marion County's quarterback. That put him at the controls of a group that would intimidate every team they lined up against because of their size, speed and flat-out willingness, at any moment, to turn a game into a barroom brawl if that's what it took to win.

"That group of guys, you could've probably called us bullies or you could just say we knew we weren't gonna take shit off anybody," said Rankin. "I think the eye-opener for us and our coaches that we would be a different kind of group came during our freshman year. We were at a camp at Carson-Newman and a fight broke out on the field and some of the older guys were going after a freshman. I figured if they were going to fight one of us they'd have to fight us all, so I jumped in and a bunch of the other freshmen jumped in right behind me.

"We were younger and we might take an ass whippin', but we weren't going to just sit back and take it. I think the coaches really liked that about us right off," added Rankin, who along with fellow inside linebacker Johnny Morrison were the team's enforcers. At 6-foot, 195 pounds, Rankin had a grown man's mustache by the time he was 17 and the rebel's attitude to go with it, routinely drawing warnings from officials for shoving an opponent's face into the dirt as he got up or for giving an extra forearm to their neck.

"There was a mean streak on that team," Thomasson recalled. "Guys like Rodney and Johnny Morrison held everybody else accountable. We weren't going to lose because they wouldn't tolerate it."

Soon after taking over the quarterback job, what Thomasson quickly realized was that once he crouched under center it also put him squarely in the crosshairs of a perfectionist head coach. As the team ran through plays each afternoon at practice, if Colquette detected even one piston firing out of sync in his well-oiled machine he would order Thomasson and the other 10 offensive players to line up and run it again.

"It wasn't easy at all being the quarterback for Coach Colquette," Thomasson said. "He expected you to get every read right. I remember I whined and complained to my dad after one of my early practices but all he said was 'Well, get it right then.'

"There were times I just wanted to go play defense, but then he knew how competitive I was and that I didn't want anybody else to play quarterback so he'd keep pushing my buttons, just to piss me off and make me determined to show him I could do it.

"I can still hear Ken's voice in my head now saying 'Do it again! Do it right this time!' no matter what I'm doing. Doesn't matter if I'm at work or around the house, I'm always looking for ways to do things better because of him."

Warriors quarterback Shane Thomasson fights for yards.

MAKING A PROMISE

Before they had even joined the varsity, the core group that would make up the 1990 Warriors already had big ideas. And the confidence to back them up. Their eighth-grade year, as they returned home from Grundy County to polish off only the second unbeaten season in the middle school program's history, the players were joined by Colquette and Johnny Grimes, the varsity's defensive coordinator, as the bus pulled into the school parking lot.

After being congratulated by their future coaches, several of the young Warriors made a vow to both Colquette and Grimes.

"We told them that we would be the first team to win the state championship for the school," Rankin said. "We just had that air about us, maybe it was cocky, but we really believed we were that good as a group."

Thomasson and Rankin had come to Jasper from neighboring towns while they were still in elementary school and several years later Brian Janeway would transfer in from Alabama to give Marion's offense the final piece it needed to line up a backfield that could pound opposing defenses into submission with brute force or simply run past them with elite speed.

To outsiders, the shy Thomasson appeared as quiet as December snow, but taking what Colquette dished out each day at practice to fuel himself, he proved to be as competitive as anyone. Meanwhile Rankin and fellow linebacker Morrison were piss-and-vinegar tush hogs, who loved football because it allowed them to throw an occasional punch, talk trash and generally bully anyone else on the field.

Janeway was pure silk with a football tucked under his arm and once that group joined the likes of linemen Jon Calhoun, Jonathan Caldwell and Ruben Prince as well as fleet receiver Mark Moreland the foundation was laid for something special.

"That backfield put a lot of pressure on defenses because there was no way to stop all three of those guys running behind that line," said long time Marion offensive line coach Don Stewart.

Marion had knocked on the door several times in the 1980s, including title game losses in '82 and '84, followed by runs to the quarterfinals or semifinals each of the five years before the 1990 season. The '84 team allowed just 44 points in winning its first 13 games before falling and the '88 bunch lost to Alcoa by one point after a late two-point pass attempt failed.

The close calls had taken a toll and that frustration was the motivation for players to run extra sprints or put in an extra rep in the weight room during offseason workouts. There were enough internal issues to cost them two early-season losses, including a one-point defeat at rival Sequatchie County where three turnovers in Indians territory had resulted in a players-only meeting to address the problems once they returned home.

"We basically committed to each other that we were not going to let anything else prevent us from living up to what we'd said we were going to do when we were eighth graders," Rankin said. "I think we finally realized that our careers were coming to an end and we had to start practicing and playing together like we all knew we could. We were a different team from then on."

HITTING ANOTHER GEAR

While the rest of the world celebrated the demolition of the Berlin Wall, allowing East and West Germans to be reunited, back in Jasper there had been a renewed sense of coming together as well. Once the playoffs began it was clear that by airing out whatever internal issues the Warriors had during the regular season, all was forgotten and they were locked in and ready to live up to what had just been flashes of potential to that point.

There was no question a state title was the ultimate goal, but the more immediate target most of the players zeroed in on was avenging the one-point loss to Sequatchie in the regular season. To have that chance both teams would have to win their first three playoff games, which would set up a rematch in the semifinals, with a spot in the championship on the line.

Brian Janeway turns the corner for a big gain.

"My mentality in the playoffs was I wanted to play Sequatchie again," Thomasson said. "We all wanted them so bad. Anybody that lined up in front of us was in our way to getting back to Dunlap because we knew we were better than them. As soon as our game was over after those first couple of weeks we would check their scores to make sure they had won too."

Not even heavy rains throughout the week of the opening round of the playoffs could dampen Marion's focus. With standing water on the field, the Warriors practiced on the concrete and gravel surface in the school parking lot, a move that caught the eye of local news and was an example of the team's toughness.

Marion blistered its first three playoff opponents — Smith County, Howard and Alcoa — by an average of 46-9, but Sequatchie County stumbled and was knocked off in the quarterfinals by Gatlinburg-Pittman. The Warriors quickly brushed aside the disappointment of not having a shot at revenge and instead unloaded on visiting Gatlinburg-Pittman from start to finish.

The defense intercepted six G-P passes, the offense ran for 277 yards — Thomasson ran for three touchdowns, threw for two more, both to Janeway — as Marion built a 42-0 lead late in the third quarter in a statement win.

With just one game remaining, Thomasson, Janeway, Rankin and receiver Mark Moreland had combined for more than 6,000 all-purpose yards. But even those video game numbers weren't enough to gain the respect of Memphis University School, which awaited Marion in the championship. The Owls were unbeaten and unimpressed and were about to let the entire state know that they viewed the Warriors as nothing more than a bug on their windshield as they motored toward a possible second state title.

"THEY ONLY RUN FOUR PLAYS"

Six days before they would meet at Vanderbilt to settle the Class AA state championship, four Marion players and three seniors from MUS, were part of media day at Vanderbilt's Stadium Club in downtown Nashville. The event brought representatives from all six teams playing for state titles in the TSSAA's three classifications to one location for lunch and to allow the state's media to pepper players and coaches with enough questions to help provide a week's worth of preview stories leading up to the games.

Marion's contingent quickly noticed an air of superiority coming from their opponents, and to put it bluntly, it ticked them off to no end.

"The first thing that got our attention right off the bat was they didn't offer to shake our hand," Thomasson said. "They sat off in a corner of the room, away from everybody else and were just the cockiest bunch I've ever seen. I grew up in a cove in Jasper so I'd never been around anybody that acted like that.

"We were just small-town country boys so they weren't anything like us. I wouldn't have wanted to hang around them."

As players from the two teams were asked to stand near each other for pictures, MUS' Trevor Benitone sized up the Warriors and said "I don't know if you're really good or really lucky. Maybe you just haven't played anybody yet."

Rankin glanced at Janeway and said, "We ought to tackle one of them now and see how tough they are."

The smugness came from MUS having ran through the season with barely a hint of being tested. The Owls headed to the title game with a perfect 14-0 record that included wins over Germantown, which was playing for the AAA championship, as well as perennial power Brentwood Academy.

Junior quarterback Marc MacMillan, who would go on to sign a baseball scholarship with Mississippi State, had thrown for more than 2,000 yards, ran for nearly 500 more and accounted for 30 touchdowns.

The Owls defense was allowing an average of just 105 rushing yards to that point and they clearly didn't think much of Marion's old-school attack. Among the disparaging comments that appeared in newspaper stories across the state that week came one from MUS defender Tom Hutton, who when asked about the Warriors vaunted veer offense replied, "It's a lot easier to defense than the wishbone. There's less for us to worry about. They only run four different plays."

BRIDESMAID NO MORE

As game day approached the Warrior seniors, to a man a superstitious group, made it clear they wanted no part of following the same schedule of the previous two Marion teams that had played for a title. Rather than staying overnight in Nashville, as the '82 and '84 teams had done, the team voted to make the two-hour drive to Vanderbilt the Saturday morning of the game.

By mid afternoon the December sky was already gray and the lights shined brightly down on Dudley Field as both teams stepped onto the artificial turf to decide who was the best high school football team in Tennessee.

Like any good prize fight the early moments were mostly a feeling-out process. Thomasson's gutsy return from getting blasted on the opening play had re-energized the team and on their third series the Warriors drove the length of the field to the MUS 6 yard line before a fumble kept them from denting the scoreboard.

"Even though we didn't score, I knew then we could drive and score on them," Thomasson said. "We ran it right down their throats on that drive and hadn't even started throwing it yet. Defensively, from my spot at free safety, when I saw our line was getting penetration into their backfield early I knew they were in trouble."

Shane Thomasson waits for instruction from his coach.

Knowing the key to stopping Marion's offense was taking out the quarterback, the MUS coaches sent defenders off the edge to plant Thomasson in the turf on every snap. Each time he was laid out on the cold ground he wondered how he would get back up, only to glance up and see a teammate's hand reaching down.

Finally, after more than a quarter of scoreless back-and-forth, Thomasson rolled to his right and lofted a long spiral that dropped into Mark Moreland's arms on a post route at the MUS 40. After shaking one defender Moreland sprinted into the end zone.

"Boom! Stick that up y'all's ass!" Rankin yelled as he ran past stunned Owls defenders.

Earlier in the week MUS players had degraded the Marion offense for being too simple and running just four plays. But the 80-yard touchdown pass served notice that it's not the number of plays you have in a playbook that matters, just how you execute the ones you do have.

On the ensuing drive Moreland stepped in front of a MacMillan pass at the Marion 6 to not only prevent a potential game-tying score just before the half, but give the Warriors a chance to add to their lead.

With just 1:26 to go before halftime Thomasson went back to work, completing two quick passes to move the ball inside MUS territory. After Janeway raced 20 yards to the 1, Rankin bulldozed his way across the goal line with 17 seconds left in the first half, handing the ball to an MUS defender who batted it to the ground in disgust.

Marion's players were beginning to realize that despite all their talk, amazingly, MUS couldn't slow them down any more than the previous playoff teams they'd whipped the past four weeks.

With his team nursing a surprising two-score lead, Thomasson made sure not to tell a soul, not even teammates, about the fact he was pissing blood, or to let on that it felt like he was being stabbed in the back with an ice pick any time he turned or twisted or bent or even breathed.

Only 24 minutes of game clock separated Marion's 14 seniors from fulfilling the promise they had made four years earlier to Colquette and Grimes, and Thomasson believed he could gut it out that long if it meant helping bring the gold ball back to a championship-starved community.

"I wasn't about to tell anybody how bad I was hurting," said Thomasson, who would later play professional baseball in the Mariners organization. "I was afraid if I did they'd take me out and I knew I had to keep playing."

It didn't take long for the Warriors to bring their side of the stadium back to its feet as the second half began. On the second snap of the third quarter Rankin took a hand-off on an inside veer and broke through the right side of the line before changing direction, his black hightop Nikes carrying him 78 yards for the score that broke the Owls' spirit.

"After I scored I turned around and yelled at the guys chasing me, 'We just put the nail in the coffin!'," Rankin recalled. "I knew we had it right then and after all their talk before the game I was going to let them know it."

For all its bluster from earlier in the week, there was simply no way MUS was going to come back from a three-score deficit. Not on this Marion defense. Not on this night.

Gene West put an exclamation on the night for Marion's defense by returning a MacMillan interception 24 yards for a score, making the final 26-7 and setting off bedlam on the Marion sideline and in the stands as fans threw purple shakers into the air and hugged anyone they could find.

That was one of five turnovers forced by a head-hunting defense led by Jon Calhoun's seven tackles. Morrison and Thomasson each had five tackles, and Thomasson added 162 passing yards.

Rodney Rankin accepts the state title game's MVP plaque.

Grimes, who taught the 50-slant with the same passion and understanding that chemistry professors preach the periodic table, punched his fist into the cold night air as the final seconds dripped from the clock. Against his unit, the arrogant Owls managed just 61 rushing yards and although MacMillan threw for 150 yards, on 13 of 26 attempts, he was intercepted three times and limited to minus-7 rushing yards on 14 carries.

"You know what won this game? Defense!" Colquette spat over the roar of his team's yelps and the tractor whistle blowing long and loud from a nearby parking garage.

Pausing to collect his thoughts, Colquette wiped his face with a towel and added, "The one that would've really liked this bunch most would have been my dad. This was a gritty, tough and mean bunch and "Pop" would have liked that. The boys played their guts out and we won't have to hear about being the bridesmaid anymore."

Rankin, who came into the game hobbled with a bruised right foot he had injured punting a ball before Marion's final walk-through practice the day before, was named the game's Most Valuable Player after carrying the ball 10 times for 118 yards and two TDs.

"The dream has come true. It doesn't seem like it's over, but I'm glad it ended like this," said Janeway, who ran for 81 yards and couldn't hold back tears of joy streaming down his cheeks as he lifted his index finger high above his head. "We're number one baby!"

Colquette gave players the option of staying in Nashville to celebrate that night, as long as their parents gave permission, and quite a few decided to take advantage and stay downtown.

"Some of us got a hotel room and that was the first time my dad ever bought me a beer," Thomasson said with a chuckle. "He said I had earned it that night."

By the time the rest of the team returned to Jasper, a sign was already hanging over the field house declaring it "Home of the 1990 state football champions".

"I have never felt another kinship like that the rest of my life," Rankin said. "Every Friday when we would walk out on that field I knew I never wanted any of those coaches or any of my teammates to come to me

Shane Thomasson brings his team to the line.

and say it was my fault we lost. We played for each other and I'm proud of the foundation we laid for the guys that came after us and all they accomplished.

"I could cry right now thinking about winning that first championship for our school."

MARION COUNTY 1990 RESULTS

Aug. 31	South Pittsburg	32-14
Sept. 7	Bledsoe County	54-6
Sept. 14	Murphy (N.C.)	40-13
Sept. 21	Whitwell	28-0
Sept. 28	McCallie	6-20
Oct. 5	Sequatchie County	6-7
Oct. 12	Ooltewah	34-6
Oct. 19	Grundy County	28-0

| Oct. 26 | Notre Dame | 63-21 |
| Nov. 2 | Etowah (Ala.) | 14-47 |

Playoffs

Nov. 9	Smith County	50-0
Nov. 16	Howard	47-14
Nov. 23	Alcoa	42-14
Nov. 30	Gatlinburg-Pittman	42-20

State championship

| Dec. 6 | Memphis University School | 26-7 |

1990 Warriors

Players: Brian Janeway, Scott Barton, Shane Thomasson, Jason Lawhorn, Brian White, Donnie Pemberton, Scott Stephens, Stephen Bourque, Jamie Thomas, David Donahue, Randy Graham, David West, Kenny Matthews, Mark Moreland, Scott Davis, David Dame, Jason Evans, Rodney Rankin, Kevin Tipton, T.J. Gentle, Bodine Willis, William Griffith, Keith McGrew, Tim Newsom, Rodney Anderson, Jamie Wells, Brad Bradford, Reuben Prince, Keith Walden, Billy Poe, Jason Caldwell, Tim Rash, J. Privett, Chad Rollins, Patrick Moon, R. Lewis, David Wells, Dale Underwood, Patrick Evans, Brian Hargis, J. Thomas, Johnny Morrison, Jon Calhoun, Chip Lockhart, Billy Skinner, David Brewer, Davey Graham, Michael Kirk, Jerry Pittman, Jacob Dawson, Matt Renfro, Michael Hogwood, Kevin Anderson, Gene West, Andy Koger, Scottie Howard, Paul Roberson, Joseph Colley.

Coaches: Ken Colquette, Johnny Grimes, Don Stewart, Jerry Tate, Larry Richards, Eddie Reed, Waymon Mosley, Steve Williams, Bob Winston.

Chapter 14
1992 WARRIORS

"Then David took for himself five smooth stones from the stream and put them in the pouch of his shepherd's bag. With his sling in hand, he approached the Philistine."

— I Samuel 17:40.

It sits noticeably out of place among the brown accordion folders filled with legal documents and sterile white notebooks. On the top shelf of a wooden bookcase in his office, resting proudly beside a cup filled with pens, sits T.J. Gentle's gold state championship ring.

He's past the age of wearing it, but the symbolism serves as a reminder that nothing — whether it's a stack of paperwork for a new business merger he's been assigned to read over or a hurdle in his personal life — should be considered unattainable.

"I look at it every day," said Gentle, an attorney in Chattanooga. "When I think the impossible can't be done, that ring is a reminder that yes it can, but not by yourself.

"When you do what we did, when you come from behind to accomplish something that everybody, including the people who support you, think you couldn't achieve, it puts you on a path of 'don't tell me I can't do something'. If you're determined, there's nothing you can't accomplish."

There was no reason for anyone, not the most loyal Marion fan or even the players' parents, to truly believe the 1992 Warriors would bring back a state championship.

Aside from the fact it was suppose to be a rebuilding year, awaiting the Warriors in the championship game would be nationally-ranked Brentwood Academy, a team looking to defend its title from the season before with a roster loaded with future college talent.

Warriors offensive line coach Don Stewart assessed the match-up matter-of-factly, "They had guys going to SEC programs and we had kids who were going to pay to get in and watch those guys on Saturdays."

HOGS TO THE TROUGH

The memory of how the previous playoff run had ended — dejectedly walking off a cold, soggy field at Rockwood on the short end of a six-point decision in the second round — still weighed heavily on the mind of every Marion coach and player in the summer months leading to the 1992 season.

Frankly, it pissed them off every time they were reminded of it.

"We won 10 games but we had a real bad taste lingering from that 91 season," said Chip Lockhart, who would be a senior two-way tackle on the 1992 team. "There was no team chemistry in '91. There were even arguments in the huddle over who would get to carry the ball, but there was no way we were going to let that happen again.

"We had a group of unselfish guys who liked playing together and even went fishing or camping together when we weren't at school. We also had people around town telling us that we weren't going to be very good and that ticked us off and drove us during summer workouts too."

Lockhart had transferred to Marion from cross county rival Whitwell after his freshman season and became a three-year starter who earned all-state honors as a 6-foot-3, 292-pound anchor along the line as a senior.

"Kids are drawn to the team that's winning and that was Marion," Lockhart recalled.

Coach Stewart certainly remembered the day he was introduced to Lockhart.

"Our principal called me in and said there was a freshman they wanted to put in my class," Stewart said. "I told them I didn't want a freshman in my class, but then they told me the kid was 6-2, 245 and could play tackle. I said 'Okay, we'll find a place for him in class.'

"You could see that Chip was going to be special. He was strong as hell and had a mean streak that would fit right in with the rest of that group we had."

During the miserably humid summer days leading up to the start of fall practice, the group that would make up Marion's line rotation — Lockhart (right tackle) and fellow seniors Timmy Rash (center), Cheyney Graham (guard/tackle) and Keith Walden (guard), along with juniors Davy Graham (left tackle) and Patrick Moon (left guard), sophomore Adam Billingsley (right guard), as well as tight ends Jamie Wells, Andy Koger, Gentle and Scotty Howard — would meet to pull bulky tractor tires up and down the practice field.

"Only their coaches and their mamas and daddies knew what they did," Warriors coach Ken Colquette would say later. "It's a special breed that plays on the line."

As long hair was to Sampson, the offensive line became the strength of the '92 Marion team, which would go on to average 300 rushing yards

David Donahue finds plenty of room to run.

per game. That season the Warriors didn't have a 1,000-yard rusher or 1,500-yard passer, but the sum parts of the machine worked together to bulldoze over any weaknesses.

And the foreman who saw to it that the team's heavy equipment continued paving the way toward a state title was a slightly-built man with a salt-and-pepper beard, a jaw full of Beechnut tobacco and a knack for never mincing words.

Don Stewart became Marion's offensive line coach in 1984, joining Colquette four years after he had taken over the program. The two had played together at Grundy County and Stewart came back to the Sequatchie Valley after stints at Houston County and Red Boiling Springs, where he remains that program's winningest head coach.

His relationship with Colquette was the reason he chose the offer to join the Marion staff over a similar assistant's opportunity at rival South Pittsburg.

"Coach Stewart never had to yell for you to know he was tough," said Rash, an undersized center on the '92 team. "You were like a student of the game and if you wanted to be the best, then you had to do it a certain way, his way. If you didn't, he didn't want you in his top five.

"I'm proof that it wasn't always the biggest guy who would start for Coach Stewart, it was whoever would do things the right way. Every single play had to be perfect."

Unlike Colquette, whose motivational tactic was to hammer even the slightest mistake, Stewart would shout positive reinforcement every time one of his pupils would drive a defender off the ball, giving the linemen reason to want to hear their name called out.

"I had a personalized license plate that said 'Hogs 90' on it and that group decided it would be a big deal if they could be good enough to make me have to get a new one that said 'Hogs 92'," said Stewart, who coached Warriors linemen for 17 seasons. "They knew the only way to do that was to win it all.

"The thing about that group was they would do whatever you asked them to. Their technique was really good because all of them boys had worked with me, other than Chip, for four years. You could tell from the time we started lifting weights in January that the year before had been put in the rearview mirror. They were determined to leave their mark and prove they could play with anybody."

LEARNING TO BE GREAT

Marion opened the season on Labor Day weekend by holding off stubborn South Pittsburg 14-7 on the road. Just a week before the game there had been a fight between players from the two teams at a party, which only added to the bad blood on both sides.

"When the fight broke out I remember one of their linemen, Kevin Denney, was on crutches and wound up hitting me over the head with them," Lockhart recalled. "The crutches shattered and the metal wing nut gashed me and I wound up having to get 14 stitches.

"It just so happened that I lined up opposite Kevin during the game and we went at it pretty good for a while. But he didn't finish the game.

"I never liked those guys. It was all about whose town is better and to be honest, it was as heated in the stands as it was on the field. We pretty much hated each other."

The Warriors won their next six games by an average of 36 points before narrowly escaping City High 7-0 with an unenthused effort.

"We really took them lightly but that turned out to be one of the defining moments of that season," Lockhart added. "We were not a real talented team athletically and that game proved to us that if we didn't prepare and play together then we could lose to any team on our schedule.

"The Monday after that game, Coach Colquette told us if we weren't going to take the game serious, then why were we wasting our time and his. He slammed his water bottle down, walked off the practice field, went to his truck and left.

"That woke us up. From then on we were the best pure team, as far as playing together, that I ever played on."

The team responded by rolling through their last two regular-season games, then blistered the first two playoff opponents by a total of 109-12.

The first true roadblock that stood in the way of the Warriors quest to become special came the day after Thanksgiving, with a quarterfinal trip to Knoxville to face South Doyle, a team making its first playoff appearance.

"The whole team had battled the flu that week and I woke up with it on game day," Lockhart said. "I was throwing up and it was really the sickest I ever remember feeling. That bus ride to the game was not fun. We all felt awful and the nerves before the game didn't help because we knew they were big and well-coached.

"For us seniors, we were afraid of losing and having it all end like it had the year before. We had a job to do and our goal was to finish undefeated, so we had to find a way to tough it out."

South Doyle's administration had also prohibited Marion's infamous train whistle from being allowed inside the stadium, or anywhere near the school grounds.

The Warriors found alternate ways to make noise, however, bringing the large contingent of fans from Jasper to their feet time and again with gutsy third-down plays — converting 11 of 14 third downs, including two on their final possession when they ran 10 plays to take the final minutes off the clock for a 29-22 win.

Those muggy summer days of pulling tractor tires paid off as Marion leaned heavily on the strength of its offensive line, running the ball on 52 of 58 offensive snaps for 278 yards.

Freshman running back Eric Westmoreland proved what type clutch player he would become by rushing for two second-half touchdowns, including a 54-yard sprint on his first carry of the third quarter. He would finish with 120 rushing yards and also recovered an onside kick with just over four minutes remaining which allowed Marion to hang on for its 13th win of the season, tying the school record for most in a season.

The following week, in the semifinals, Marion hosted a Knox Powell team that had played for the state title the season before, finishing runners-up to Brentwood Academy.

The Panthers had one of the largest rosters in Class AA and when they trotted out onto the field in a downpour for pregame warmups, their line of players stretched from goal line to goal line.

"It didn't intimidate our kids, but it scared the heck out of me," Colquette said.

After a scoreless first half, a bad punt snap on Marion's first possession of the third quarter gave Powell the ball at the Warriors 7. Panthers quarterback Matt Lowe scored from the 5 two plays later on a rollout, but the point-after try failed.

Powell's 6-0 lead held into the fourth quarter, but with 10:22 remaining Marion took advantage of a short punt to begin at the Panthers 38. After two runs by David Donahue netted just three yards, quarterback Scott Stephens hit tight end Jamie Wells slanting across the middle for a 29-yard gain to the 6, and a face mask penalty moved the ball to the 3.

Donnie Pemberton covered those final three yards to tie the game, leaving Marion's coaches to decide whether they should try to kick the extra point in horrible weather conditions or rely on the offensive line once more to pave the way on a two-point attempt.

"We had taken a timeout and I was on the sideline when Coach Colquette asked if we should kick it or go for two," Lockhart recalled. "As a lineman I wanted to go for two, but I knew they had given us fits all night just trying to make a yard, so I said 'Let's kick it. He can do it.'"

The decision left the potential fate of the game, and the season, resting on the leg of sophomore Lenny Cookston, who made good on the call to kick the extra point, giving Marion a nervous 7-6 lead with 8:09 to go.

The Warriors defense, which held Powell to 17 total yards and no first downs in the second half, made the lead stand over those final minutes, earning a trip to the state championship game.

"That was one of the toughest games, physically, that I can remember us ever playing in," Coach Stewart said. "The conditions were terrible, but those big ol' hogs didn't seem to mind getting down in the mud. That's where we won it again, up front on both sides of the ball."

"AIN'T GOT A SNOWBALLS CHANCE IN HELL"

Helping to settle down the locker room celebration, and frankly bring a concerned hush over the room, was the news that Marion's opponent in the championship game would be Brentwood Academy, which had clobbered Humboldt 21-0 in its semifinal to earn the chance at defending its title from the year before when it had destroyed Powell.

"They might as well have told us we had to play the Dallas Cowboys," Stewart said. "Brentwood Academy had the reputation as being more than a great high school team. They were this thing out there that just sort of scared everybody they played. Just the name was intimidating."

Coaches from both teams met early Saturday morning to exchange film and Marion's staff gathered later inside the field house to begin watching this "thing" they were about to line up against, hoping to find even the slightest weakness they could exploit.

With the lights off, and only the flickering images from the large TV screen lighting the room, it might as well have been a horror movie the Warriors staff watched. One by one each coach's face dropped as they saw what equaled to a college team demolishing every opponent with scary precision.

Colquette's voice was the first to break the silence.

"We ain't got a snowball's chance in hell," he said.

Several seconds of awed silence followed. No one in the room could disagree. Just then Stewart squinted his eyes, spat tobacco juice into a cup and said, "Bullshit!" The other coaches broke from watching the film to glance over at Stewart, wondering what the old man had seen.

"Maybe we don't. And if we don't execute they will kick our ass and embarrass us in front of the whole damn state. But if we tell those kids they ain't got a chance, then we might as well not even bother showing up. They're the only ones that count. We've got to make them believe we can play with that bunch."

The next afternoon after the players trickled into the field house — some from Sunday church service, others straight from bed after sleeping in — Colquette and his staff had their own come-to-Jesus meeting with the players.

"Boys, everybody outside of these walls is going to tell you this game is a mismatch. They'll say we ain't got a snowball's chance in hell. They'll talk about all these college players Brentwood Academy has and how they never lose. So if you want me to I'll go in my office and pick up the phone and call Ronnie Carter at the TSSAA and tell him we're just going to forfeit."

Several players looked at each other and a few nervously laughed at Colquette's words. But after a few seconds the room was eerily quiet once again and all eyes were focused back on their coach standing in front of them.

"Alright then. We've got a plan on how we're going to beat them suckers because I think y'all are just mean enough and tough enough to do it."

Marion's offensive line celebrates after paving the way to a state title.

Former Warriors all-state linebacker Rodney Rankin, who had helped bring the program's first state championship in 1990, had come to the meeting and was standing with a couple of assistant coaches when Colquette asked him if he had anything he wanted to say to the team.

Rankin was short and to the point.

"The two proudest days of my life were earlier this year when my son was born healthy," Rankin said, holding up his right index finger. He then held up a second finger and added, "And the other was walking off that field as state champs.

"I can't even put in words what that feels like. Y'all will just have to go get it done and experience for yourselves."

Both teams met in a sprawling hotel conference room in downtown Nashville on the Monday morning before the game for the annual media day. It was a chance for reporters from other parts of the state to get to interview players and coaches from teams outside their coverage area.

But the only reporters who stopped at Marion's table to speak with its contingent were the same familiar faces from the two Chattanooga newspapers.

Meanwhile BA's players chose not to sit at the table marked "Class AA teams" and instead found an empty table near the back corner of the room. They barely had time to sit before several writers and TV cameras surrounded them and began asking questions, most of which revolved around their run of dominance and which college teams they were thinking of signing with.

After all the Eagles were coming into the championship having won 26 straight games and already owned seven state titles in 12 appearances. They were nationally ranked by USA Today and their starting lineup included more than a half-dozen that would go on to sign college scholarships.

"You grew up knowing BA was a factory," Rash said. "But to not have any of the media come over and want to ask us about the game, and then for the BA players to act the way they did, not shaking our hands or wanting to sit at the table with us, it all made us feel very disrespected.

"We were undefeated too and we had earned our way to that game just like them. You could just tell their players and all of the media, everybody in that room looked at us like sacrificial lambs."

Once the media day event ended, on the two-hour drive back to school for practice, Colquette noticed the mood of his players had changed fiercely.

"They weren't nervous anymore. They were pretty pissed off," Colquette said. "Brentwood Academy had players who had come there from all over the country. They had four quarterbacks and none of them were from Tennessee. Their best lineman was from Texas. And they were real dang good. But it meant more to our kids because they were wearing that same purple and white jersey that their daddy or their uncle or their brother had worn. Our kids were representing their family and our community."

As it turned out, the grand plan the coaches had come up with was rinse-and-repeat simple — they went back to the fundamentals: base blocking, leverage, make the right read and hold on to the dang ball on offense, wrap up and hit them suckers as hard as you can on defense.

It was basically another round of the brutal early-August practices with lots of contact. The only difference was the staff had agreed that, for once, everything they said and did all week would be with a positive tone toward the players.

"We were pumping sunshine all week," Stewart said with a loud laugh. "Except for Ken. He couldn't help himself. He'd still raise hell about nothing."

Nit picking had been Colquette's style for as long as he had stalked a practice field with a water bottle tucked into his back pocket. He wasn't about to change a motivational tactic that had worked well to that point.

"Ken came up to me on the first day of practice that week and said, 'Son, I don't know what to do. I can't hide you this week. If I had anybody else who could snap the ball and block, you'd be in the stands with the cheerleaders.'," said Rash. "He knew how to piss you off just enough to make you focus and play harder than you ever thought you could.

"While I was standing there, that first day of practice, it also dawned on me that this would be my last go. My last week of practice. My last time to wear a football uniform. I knew I would never play the game again after that week, so all of that just kind of pushed me."

Rash, all 5-foot-8, 184 pounds of him, would draw the unenviable task of having to line up opposite, and somehow block, Brentwood Academy all-state noseguard Reggie Williams (6-2, 287), AKA "The Mountain".

The idea was to put the Warriors biggest back-up lineman, Kelvin Spears (6-4, 350), over Rash during practice that week so he could learn to not only avoid being mauled, but to use his quickness to take the big man's legs out from under him.

After watching the first couple of days of practice that week, one old-timer, sitting at a table sipping coffee with a group of armchair coaches, told the group, "I'm tellin' y'all, ain't no horse can't be rode and no cowboy can't be throw'd."

The players weren't the only ones buying into the sunshine the staff had been pumping.

On the final day before the game, Coach Stewart's linemen — the group that had been most responsible for getting the Warriors to this point — gathered for one more round of sled work. Any lingering doubts about their focus, intentions or level of confidence were quickly erased when the starters fired off in unison at the chirp of the Stewart's whistle, extended their arms and lifted the padded metal contraption off the ground.

"All five of them hit that sled at the same time, lifted it and turned it over. I thought they had broke it," Stewart said. "They were the first ones I ever remember turning that thing over. I kind of thought to myself, 'Damn! I don't know about the rest of us, but by-God that bunch is ready!'"

"YOU'VE GOT TONIGHT"

When the Marion players emerged from their locker room and trotted onto the cold, hard artificial turf at Vanderbilt's Dudley Field, they passed a group of Brentwood Academy linemen who were stretching near the sideline.

One of the mammoth Eagles players called out toward the Marion players, "Where's your varsity? Or are all of y'all pee-wee sized?"

As they saw it, there was simply no way a little podunk town like Jasper — which probably sat so far back in the woods they had to pipe in sunshine — could put together a team to compete against them.

Once the teams finished warming up and returned to their locker rooms for last-minute instructions, Colquette waited for the Warriors to settle in before he spoke. The room, filled with players, coaches and a few nervous supporters, was church-prayer quiet and all eyes focused on Colquette as he began to speak in his slow drawl.

"Boys, you know what we've got to deal with. Pretty much their whole team is going to play college ball somewhere — Tennessee, Alabama, Georgia, Texas, MTSU. Somewhere. Most of y'all ain't going anywhere except back to Jasper to work on a farm or in some factory. That's it. They've got all these Saturdays coming up where they'll still be playing and you'll be watching or riding some tractor.

"But you've got tonight. You've got tonight to show them suckers something about us. You can make them remember you for as long as they live with what you do tonight. So think about that for a minute and then let's get after their ass on every snap."

Had the metal doors been locked every one in the room would've made a hole through the concrete walls to get out onto the field after Colquette's speech. With all the adrenaline running through their bodies, the Warriors now believed that maybe, just maybe they were about to show big, bad Brentwood Academy a thing or two about football.

WEATHERING THE STORM

A record crowd for a state championship game — nearly 17,000 — filled all but the endzone stands. Just before kickoff the first faint sound of Marion's infamous tractor whistle blew from the top level of a concrete parking structure across the street from the stadium. After a warming up, the whistle's operator let loose with a loud blast that lasted for several seconds and brought the Warriors fans to their feet.

Brentwood Academy, decked out in its scarlet red jerseys with matching helmets and gray pants looked like a college team as it jogged confidently onto the field. Marion players, in their all white uniforms, with white "Marion County" in script lettering across purple helmets, turned toward their fans and began waving their arms up and down to coax more noise.

But it took just one snap for the passion and pride that Colquette had stirred in his team to wear off. That first play, when the gap in individual talent and strength was on full display, was a stern reminder that there had been a lot of emotion at the Alamo too, and nobody survived.

"After the first play I remember Chip looked around the huddle and said, 'Holy hell y'all, we've got hold of some grown-ass men now.'," Rash recalled. "You see it on film, but to be on the other side of it, was unreal how good they were. They were a machine."

The Eagles came into the game averaging a balanced 174 rushing and 166 passing yards per game and were very business-like in taking their opening drive 79 yards in 11 plays. They were slowed briefly along the way, but on fourth-and-two from the Warriors five, Nick Peoples took the pitch on an option left and raced for the corner of the end zone.

Marion could not respond, getting stuffed on three plays before BA returned the punt 30 yards to the Warriors 21. Peoples went 17 yards on the next play before quarterback Paul Murray, who had thrown for more than 1,400 yards that season, ran in a four-yard TD off left tackle to give the Eagles a commanding 13-0 lead late in the first quarter.

"They got up on us so quick it was like a blur," Rash said. "One minute we were jumping around, all excited at the start of the game and then we blinked and looked up and they were up two touchdowns and just kicking our ass.

"Their players weren't even excited. They acted like it was no big deal. Just ho-hum, business as usual for them."

The Warriors remained on the business end of the early battering for the next two series, first when they were forced to punt and then unable to stop another BA march toward the goal line.

But what could have been the back-breaking 26-yard touchdown pass on second down was dropped in the end zone by a wide-open Lyle Husband. On the next play the Eagles tried a reverse and Gentle stuffed it for a four-yard loss.

Marion defenders swarm a Brentwood Academy runner.

BA lined up for a 47-yard field goal attempt, but another miscue, this time a delay of game penalty, pushed them out of range and Marion had dodged a howitzer-sized bullet.

Riding the wave of good fortune, Marion's offense finally found its footing, sort of. The first two plays netted minus-six yards, but on third and 16 from their own 16, quarterback Scott Stephens pitched to Donnie Pemberton on an option right and after two shuffling steps, Pemberton launched a 35-yard pass to Lenny Cookston, who was finally tackled at the Eagles 41.

Two more runs gained just three yards, before Stephens hit tight end Jamie Wells across the middle for a 30-yard gain, setting up first-and-goal at the eight yard line. Two more plays gained just two yards and on third down, an option to the right by Westmoreland was stuffed for no gain. But a face mask penalty moved the ball inside the three and gave the Warriors another third down snap. This time, Pemberton followed a wall of blockers on the right side, led by Lockhart, into the end zone with 3:42 left before halftime, making it 13-6 after the point-after attempt was partially blocked.

"We blew that whole side of their line back into the end zone," Lockhart said. "Donnie was laying on top of the linemen when he fell into the end zone, which tells you how far we had driven them back.

"We were pretty pissed at how we had played up until that drive. I had been getting recruited by some SEC schools but Alabama told me a few days before the game that they were taking BA's Josh Swords instead of me. That was my motivation. I lined up over him every snap and there was lots of trash talk between us, mostly from me. I told him 'I hope you do well at Alabama because I'm going to kick your ass tonight.'"

A large section of Marion fans were still waving their shakers when BA's Lennie Harris returned the ensuing kickoff 97 yards for a TD that would have sucked a lot of life out of the Warriors had the play not been called back by a holding penalty on the Eagles.

The frustration from its first-half missed opportunities and not putting the Warriors away when they were reeling was magnified when Murray's left leg gave way and he crumpled to the turf with a torn ACL after trying to change directions as he chased Pemberton on an interception return on the final play of the first half.

Having somehow weathered several first-half haymakers, Colquette burst into his team's locker room and announced, "They screwed up boys. They left y'all in it. They don't know how tough you are. You won't ever quit. Just keep playing and let's see what happens."

The fact that the Eagles had more than doubled Marion in total yards in the first half didn't matter. All that did was that the Warriors were still just one big play from evening the score and gaining the momentum they would need to somehow pull off a major upset.

"We had all kinds of trick plays ready to use in the second half," Stewart said. "But when the coaches met to talk about what we were going to do Ken said to throw them all away. "We don't need them," Colquette told his staff. "We can beat them straight up now."

SECOND HALF SURGE

The damning mistake the Warriors needed to avoid to continue whittling away at BA bit them on the opening series of the second half when they lost a fumble and the Eagles quickly capitalized to take a 20-6 lead when sophomore backup quarterback Kirk Johnson threw an 11-yard TD pass to Lenny Harris with 6:23 left in the third quarter.

If there was even a hint of desperation about falling behind by two scores, after fighting so hard for so long to get back in the game, it never showed on the Marion sideline. Instead the Warriors answered with a physical 14-play, 75-yard scoring drive of their own, converting four third downs, including a 24-yard run on third and six by Pemberton. The crucial drive was capped when Stephens scored on a six-yard run off the right side, leaping over one of his blockers before crossing the goal line with :35 showing on the third quarter clock. Stephens then found Pemberton for the two-point pass, pulling the Warriors within 20-14.

"As the game wore on things started to turn our way a little," Rash said. "We had all played long enough and knew football enough to realize we could play with them. We started forgetting that it was Brentwood Academy and we just started doing our job the way we'd been taught.

"And you could sort of sense that maybe these guys weren't used to being in a game where somebody kept fighting back instead of just rolling over for them."

As the fourth quarter began, BA looked to answer with a drive that could finally put the stubborn Warriors away. But kicker Matt Young, who had been reliable throughout his career with the Eagles, pulled a 20-yard field goal attempt wide left, and with 8:09 to go Marion suddenly had the game's outcome in its hands.

Facing fourth-and-one from their own 29, Warriors coaches called timeout and discussed whether they should go for it or punt the ball back to BA.

"I intended to punt the ball and try to stop them to get the ball back," Colquette admitted. "But some of our other coaches were warning me that if we punted it we probably wouldn't get the ball back because we really hadn't stopped them.

"Pemberton spoke up and said, 'Coach, I'll get the first down.' That pretty much made my mind up about what to do."

The call was for Pemberton to take the ball on an outside veer and, true to his word, he earned the first down with just over six minutes remaining.

Moments later, however, the Warriors faced another fourth-and-short, this time needing two yards to keep the drive going at their 40. Without hesitating, Colquette again called for Pemberton to carry the ball on an outside veer and the senior sprinted through the left side of the line for a six-yard gain that only continued the momentum surging through the team's huddle.

"That's when we started to believe we weren't going to lose that ball game," Rash said. "We had played against superior talent all year but I've never seen a high school coach who could dissect a team like Ken could. He just out-coached BA. He would say I'll put you in the right position, then it's up to you to make the play."

> *"Reaching into his bag and taking out a stone, he hurled it with his sling and hit the Philistine in the forehead. And Goliath stumbled and fell face down on the ground."*
>
> *— I Samuel 17:49*

A roughing the passer penalty moved the ball to BA's 39 and on the next play, Stephens hit Guy Hansard on a seam route that was taken to the end zone, ending the 10-play, 80-yard drive with 3:13 still to go. Hansard jumped into Scotty Howard's arms and was carried for 15 yards toward the sideline before being let back down to his feet.

"Ken had taught us that when something doesn't go right, it's all about how you respond," Lockhart said. "BA hadn't had to deal with that. When they were on their heels, Ken could read it and set us up to punch them in the mouth.

"You could see in their eyes walking off the field after that play that they were in shock. Our team was really good at managing adversity and now their players were going to have to see how they responded."

The point-after kick was partially blocked, however, keeping the score knotted at 20-20.

But by that point all the momentum had shifted squarely onto Marion's side, a point that became obvious when Howard stuffed a BA runner for a three-yard loss and on second down Johnson looked right then squared his shoulders to throw to his left, where a receiver waited near the Eagles sideline. But Hansard stepped in front of the curl route to intercept the pass and after breaking one tackle, outran two other Eagles along the home sideline for the go-ahead touchdown with just 1:50 showing on the game clock.

The 5-foot-8, 151-pound Hansard, who had just scored two dramatic TDs in three minutes, was mobbed in the back of the end zone by three teammates, all jumping up and down like little kids opening presents on Christmas morning. Pemberton carried the ball on an inside veer for the two-point conversion that gave Marion a 28-20 lead.

"I remember looking at the clock and worrying there was too much time," Lockhart said. "If there was any team in the state that could score in a hurry and break our hearts, it was those guys."

Believing that his sophomore quarterback's confidence had to be shaken by the pick-six, legendary Eagles coach Carlton Flatt sent in the team's third QB of the game, senior Kyle Holmes for what would be a desperation drive.

Holmes began picking apart the Marion defense, including a connection with Allen Jackson to the Warriors 29. Later, facing a fourth-and-four scenario, Holmes found Harris for a 23-yard touchdown with 48 seconds remaining. But on the two-point try, which would have evened the score once again, Marion defenders Andy Koger and Patrick Moon hit Holmes just as he released the pass, causing the throw to fall short of an open receiver in the end zone and protecting the Warriors' narrow 28-26 lead.

The only hope that remained for BA was to recover the onside kick, and after the ball was batted by two Marion players, it ricochet back into the arms of an Eagles receiver and the Marion faithful suddenly realized that like Dracula and cockroaches, Brentwood Academy refused to die easily.

Holmes completed two quick passes, the second to a diving Jackson on a 16-yard slant at the Marion 27. Without any timeouts remaining, Holmes then threw the ball out of bounds to stop the clock with 22 seconds left and everyone in the stadium rose to their feet as Flatt sent his strong-legged kicker onto the field for a 45-yard field goal attempt that would decide the game's fate.

Young put his foot into the ball and it soared end-over-end through the gray-sky night before falling short, about midway through the end zone.

"From the sideline it looked like their kicker split the uprights until I heard our crowd go nuts and realized that it came up just short," Colquette said. "I looked up at the scoreboard one more time, just to make sure and it said 'Marion 28, Brentwood Academy 26'. All we had to do was run out the clock and go get that gold ball trophy."

Stephens took a knee, setting off bedlam in the stands and on the field as Marion players and coaches rushed out to celebrate becoming the first team in program history to finish 15-0.

As Colquette met Flatt near midfield, the two coaches put their arms around one another and Colquette spoke first.

"Sorry about your quarterback," he said to Flatt. "Y'all have got a helluva team."

"Congratulations, coach," was all the stunned Flatt could muster.

As he turned to look into the camera of one of the Chattanooga TV stations, Colquette threw up his arms and shrugged as if to say, "What just happened?"

"I had something prepared to say to the media if we lost, but I didn't have anything ready for if we won," Colquette gushed. "I'm tongue-tied. I really don't know what to say."

In the distance, the tractor whistle blew long and loud, signifying to the rest of the state that the best team in Tennessee was no longer Brentwood Academy. It was the team from podunk Jasper.

Standing just off the sideline, away from the commotion, TSSAA executive director Ronnie Carter shook his head. All he could offer was one simple sentence, "Biggest upset in the history of the state championship game. Wow!"

"It was really shocking for those of us in the mid-state," said Larry Taft, the former sports editor of the Nashville Tennessean. "BA had become so established and were so dominant and I'm sure they, and the rest of us, didn't think that a place like little ol' Jasper could put together a group that could play with them.

"The rumor at the time was that BA was considering moving up in class to AAA, just to get some competition because they didn't think anybody in AA could stay on the field with them anymore."

Once the purple party had settled down a bit, TSSAA officials began handing out the hardware, beginning with the silver runner-up trophy.

Only two BA players, Chris Holt and Hill slowly trudged toward midfield to accept the trophy. Holt, a 6-1, 260-pound two-way lineman, took it and held it low at his side as he made his way back to the sideline and placed the trophy on the bench.

Eagles coach Carlton Flatt did not meet with the media, which gathered to interview him and his team, but instead walked briskly toward the team bus. Before the game rumors had swirled that the majority of schools in the state were in favor of creating a separate division for private schools, so that public school would no longer have to face them in the playoffs. As Flatt passed TSSAA administrators, he looked up at Carter and, motioning behind him toward Marion's celebration, said, "Tell everybody they better leave us in with the public schools or one of them will have to play that bunch."

Flatt did not realize his team had left the runner-up trophy sitting on the bench where it had been placed by Holt. It was only after Carter instructed school officials that the Eagles had to come claim their unwanted hardware that Flatt sent a team manager back onto the field to retrieve it.

"I didn't know the captains had sat it on the bench," Flatt said later. "Our guys were down and they walked off the field and it wasn't there. It bothered me that they left it behind because everybody made a big deal about it.

"Before we played I had respect for them, but I'm not sure about all of our kids. The lesson we learned was what can happen if you don't take every team you play serious. I'm not making excuses, but things were going our way for a while and then boom, it turned on us and we just got beat."

After taking a job as an assistant at a mid-state program years later, Stewart was at Brentwood Academy for a game and stopped to peek through the glass trophy case, where so many championships are on display.

"I just wanted to see where the trophy from 1992 was," Stewart said. "It took a while to find it because it's hid in the back corner where you can't even read it. You can barely see the top of it, just enough to recognize it's silver, and not gold.

"That was the game that made our kids believe they could beat anybody from then on. A lot of what we accomplished for the next few years was because of the confidence kids in our program got that night."

Marion's offense finished the game with a balanced 144 rushing yards and 148 through the air, and its defense, led by game MVP Jamie Wells, held the Eagles to 30 yards under their season rushing average.

"The truth is we should've lost that game," Gentle said. "It was not evenly matched. At all. If we played 100 times, we would win one. But we won that one when it mattered.

Marion offensive line coach Don Stewart was a master motivator.

"What can't be overlooked is that for all their talent the game just meant more to us. Our whole identity revolves around football. How our parents and grandparents and everybody we know and love feel about themselves is tied to winning that championship.

"We knew those people from Brentwood Academy wanted to win but they didn't need to win. We did and we were willing to sacrifice our bodies and do whatever it took to get it."

As players were loading onto the bus for the spirited ride back home, Colquette was stopped and congratulated by one of his former players who had clearly had a few too many spirits already.

"I mean he was completely soused," Colquette said. "There was no way he was going to make it home without hurting himself or somebody else and I couldn't find anybody to take him so I just put him on the front seat of the bus with me.

"He must've had a heck of a good time before and during the game because he passed out before we left the stadium and slept all the way home until we got back to our field house."

Both Gentle and Lockhart would go on to play at MTSU and Eric Westmoreland, a freshman who was merely a modest contributor on that 1992 team, wound up becoming one of the program's most decorated stars.

But much of the rest of that championship team never again put on pads once their high school career ended. Many of them remained in the community, working in those factories and farms just as Colquette had said, and settling in as husbands and fathers who sit elbow to elbow with neighbors, cheering for the Warriors through the years.

The only framed photo — other than family portraits — resting on Lockhart's work desk is one of himself, along with the other starting linemen and Coach Stewart, taken just before the 1992 title game.

"I'll look at it sometimes and remember so much about that night," Lockhart said. "I can still smell it in the air and feel the butterflies in our stomach. College never could live up to that feeling of playing on Friday nights with the whole community behind you.

"I always think about Ken's speech and how he was right. For a small town like Jasper, most of the guys will stay home and work a job there and never leave. He knew that game was a defining moment in a lot of people's lives. I haven't seen most of those guys in years but when I do there's that bond we'll always have because of what we accomplished."

MARION COUNTY 1992 RESULTS

Sept. 4	South Pittsburg	14-7
Sept. 11	Howard	42-0
Sept. 18	Knox West	47-7
Sept. 25	Bledsoe County	47-0
Oct. 2	Whitwell	24-3
Oct. 9	Grundy County	21-7
Oct. 16	Notre Dame	59-7
Oct. 23	City	7-0
Oct. 30	Tyner	28-14
Nov. 6	Sequatchie County	35-14

Playoffs

Nov. 13	Polk County	46-6
Nov. 20	Livingston Academy	63-6
Nov. 27	South Doyle	29-22
Dec. 4	Knox Powell	7-6

State championship

| Dec. 12 | Brentwood Academy | 28-26 |

1992 Warriors

Players: Eric Westmoreland, Rayburn Prince, Kenny Smith, Donnie Pemberton, Scott Stephens, Jamie Thomas, David Donahue, Travis Houston, Ben Harris, Anthony Martin, Terry Acuff, Jason Rush, Jason Evans, Ryan Bradford, Keith Venable, Rusty Parker, T.J. Gentle, Brandon Raulston, J. Pickett, Lenny Cookston, Jamie Wells, Jason Dykes, Matt Clark, T. Johnson, David Dame, Keith Walden, Chris Webster, Tim Rash, S. Keahey, Kevin Spears, Jason Teague, Patrick Moon, Matt Renfro, Chuck Jones, Cliff Moore, Tim Westmoreland, E. Moore, Adam Billingsley, Cheyney Graham, Mike Canales, Chip Lockhart, Larry Ziegler, Bobby Alder, Davie Graham, Les Thomas, Jacob Dawson, Guy Hansard, Roy Keahey, David West, Lavon Powell, Andy Koger, Scottie Howard, James Keeler, Jamie Muir, Jason Muir, Davis.

Coaches: Ken Colquette, Johnny Grimes, Landon Pickett, Don Stewart, Jerry Tate, Larry Richards, Eddie Reed, Waymon Mosley, Steve Williams.

Chapter 15

1994 – A GAME FOR THE AGES

*"When they look back at a 9-1 season,
they don't ask who the nine were."*

— **General Robert Neyland,
University of Tennessee coach**

It was less than two weeks from the start of the 1994 season and for once Danny Wilson's mind had drifted from football. Rummaging through Walmart's selection of frozen meats, hoping to find a couple of steaks to grill, South Pittsburg's young coach was approached by an older lady, her brown purse dangling by the straps from her forearm.

Wilson smiled and nodded politely at the stranger, rolling his shopping cart to the side to give her room to pass. Before he could return to his suppertime shopping the lady looked directly at him, cleared her throat, and in her Sunday school teacher tone said frankly, "Coach, you boys don't own this valley anymore. I just wanted you to know that."

Stunned, Wilson watched as the gray-haired verbal assassin strolled around the corner and disappeared down the canned goods section.

"She wasn't playing around either," Wilson recalled. "She told me exactly how she felt and then never broke stride. I knew right then that this was going to be a game that a lot of people were going to take seriously."

Both Marion and South Pitt were coming off disappointing finishes the season before — the Pirates losing by two points to Trousdale

County in the semifinals and the Warriors suffering an equally depressing one-point defeat in the quarterfinals.

In the months dividing the end of one season and kickoff of another, headlines from actual daily events seemed far more scandalous than anything the National Enquirer could make up.

Tonya Harding was stripped of a national figure skating championship for her involvement in an attack on rival skater Nancy Kerrigan and even more bizarrely O.J. Simpson led police on a low-speed chase through the freeways of LA, with more than 95 million people tuned in to watch live on TV. Simpson was being sought as a suspect in the murder of his ex-wife and her friend, and the chase would eventually lead police to his Brentwood home, where he surrendered.

In a bizarre publicity stunt, Lisa Marie Presley married Michael Jackson and tragically Nirvana's talented lead singer Kurt Cobain committed suicide.

A strike by Major League Baseball players canceled the season at the halfway point, but much of the entertainment that summer revolved around a pair of movies — Forrest Gump and The Lion King — that would become two of the highest-grossing films of all time.

And of course The Citadel was ordered to admit its first female cadet, prompting a t-shirt that began selling around Charleston that read "The Citadel: home of 1,952 Bulldogs and one bitch".

With the majority of starters back, and a dogged determination to avenge the previous season's shortcomings, the Pirates and Warriors were certain to be a bitch of a different kind to deal with for every team on their schedules. Both teams had reloaded for a shot at redemption, but only if they could survive their season opener, which would amount to an old-fashioned backyard brawl.

Fittingly, in a year with so many surreal storylines, the morning before the game delivered a dose of controversy.

"I pulled up at the school, got out of my truck and something out of the corner of my eye just didn't look right," said Warriors offensive line coach Don Stewart. "I walked over to the field and saw both our goal posts had been pulled up out of the ground. They were laying face down on the field and I thought, 'Whoa, this ain't good.'"

The night before, a group of students from South Pittsburg had snuck through the gate leading to Marion's field, jumped up to swing from the goal posts, bending both face down to the ground.

"When I got to school there were already a bunch of people standing in the parking lot pointing at the field," said Anthony Martin, a junior defensive back for the Warriors. "I felt an instant rage. They had also sprayed the field with weed killer so the grass would die in the shape of a giant 'P'."

Rather than sending the team onto the practice field behind the locker room for their Thursday workout, Marion coaches opted to take full advantage of the opportunity to stoke the fire and scheduled practice on the game field, the limp goal posts at each end a constant source of agitation.

South Pitt's Corey Tipton and Marion's Eric Westmoreland were a pair of all-state runners in 1994.

"I don't think I paid attention in class those last two days," Martin added. "I couldn't wait for the game to start and get after their ass."

If there was any remorse from South Pittsburg's students it wasn't shown in the team's run-through banner, which read "To be a champion you must have goals!" along with a drawing of two bent goal posts on each end.

Marion's cheerleaders had painted a sign meant to get under the skin of every Pirates supporter who had suffered through six straight losses in the series with an equally agitating message: "7 years in a row! We'll see ya at the Clinic Bowl!"

"It was a bunch of people who didn't even play football that had ripped their goal posts out of the ground," said Wesley Stone, a Pirates lineman that season. "Before we all came out on the field their players were yelling at us about how we were going to pay for what we'd done.

We were yelling back 'We didn't touch your goal posts. But quit talking that shit and let's go!'

"I really thought they might be overlooking us before those goal posts got pulled up. They had beaten us several years in a row and we were planning on showing them just how physical we were. But now they were pissed off and as crazy as it sounds that goal post deal got their motor running and kept them motivated all night."

The only thing thicker than the fans spilling out of the Beene Stadium stands to line the track — three rows deep on both sides — were the wooly mosquitos feasting on an all-you-can-eat buffet in the early-September humidity. Fans from neighboring Whitwell, Sequatchie County and North Jackson (Ala.) had opted to play hookey from their teams' games and watch two of the top teams in the state batter and bruise each other.

South Pittsburg senior Perry Hutchins was ranked the nation's No. 18 defensive back by SuperPrep magazine, drawing recruiting visits from the staffs at Tennessee and Notre Dame among others. The 6-foot, 170-pound speedster was just as smooth on offense, where he ran the show as a dual-threat quarterback.

On the first play of the game Hutchins took the snap and darted off Stone's left hip, breaking past the initial wave of Warriors for a 24-yard gain across midfield. But Marion junior safety Eric Westmoreland, who was looking to use the showdown as a showcase that could catapult his name up recruiting boards, caught Hutchins from behind, stripping the ball loose and the Warriors recovered.

"Trick or treat bitches!" Martin yelled toward the Pirates, a long-standing insult by Marion players referring to South Pittsburg's orange and black halloween uniform colors.

"You knew those guys wanted to beat us more than they wanted to breath," Martin would say later. "And that's exactly how bad we wanted to beat them. So every chance you got to take a dig at them, you took it."

The tone was set for what would be repeated throughout the night as both defenses continually snatched away any hope the offenses had of scoring.

"Everybody knew Perry was really fast and elusive," Westmoreland said. "Nobody knew how fast I was. But my instincts made me play faster because I would watch a lot of film and just sort of understand where I needed to be.

"We knew they had a lot of weapons on offense so we had to keep everything in front of us and not ever give up the big play because that's what they thrived off of."

The Pirates did manage to put together what would be their best drive of the night on their second possession. But after picking up two first downs on the legs of Hutchins, they faced a third-and-8 at the Marion 42, an obvious passing situation.

"All week in practice we had worked on stopping their out-routes," Warriors coach Ken Colquette said. "Every single time we ran it in practice Eric would drop off too deep and not get there in time to defend it. I'll bet I screamed, "Damnit Eric!" a hundred times that week.

"But Eric always had a knack for coming up with the big play when the lights were on and the stands were full."

As the Pirates came to the line, Hutchins paused to survey Marion's defense, scanning from the middle of the secondary to the left side to size up how big of a window he would have to throw into. All-state receiver Bradley "Macho" Green set up on the left side of the formation and looked back in at Hutchins, an unspoken connection between the two that they thought no one else would notice.

"We knew before the game that Perry really liked to throw to Macho and that the out-routes were their favorite to throw," Westmoreland said. "Before the snap I glanced over to see where Macho was lining up and then I just read Perry's eyes. As soon as he dropped back there was no doubt in my mind where he was throwing the ball. I went straight toward Macho and got there just in time to jump in front of him."

As Westmoreland bore down on the spot where Green had stopped, Warriors defensive tackle Jason Dykes came crashing through the line to pressure Hutchins, forcing him to throw the pass a second sooner than he wanted. Westmoreland leaped high, stretched out his arms and snagged the pass with both hands while in mid-air.

He landed with the Pirates intended receiver draped over his back. The diminutive Green, reaching over Westmoreland's shoulders in an attempt to knock the ball down, even got his left hand on the burly defender's face mask and used every ounce of his 140-pound body to try and make the tackle.

But Westmoreland regained his balance, reaching back to steady himself before taking off toward the goal line. Neither Hutchins nor Corey Tipton, South Pittsburg's all-state tailback, could catch Westmoreland once he came to full steam and he took the interception back 66 yards for a touchdown with 4:54 to go in the first quarter.

"It happened right in front of me," Wilson said after the game. "I thought about reaching out and tackling him because I was the only one who could have gotten him."

Eric Westmoreland intercepts a pass and returns it for the game's only score.

In another example of how much both defenses would dominate, Pirates linebacker Vincent Banks even blocked the extra point attempt.

Marion drove deep into Pirates territory twice more before halftime, but were turned away both times. The first came when Marcus Banks forced a fumble and later, after the Warriors had reached the South Pittsburg seven, quarterback Josh Dobson was stuffed for a yard loss on fourth-and-goal to keep the halftime score at 6-0.

The final two quarters only saw the defenses get stronger, completely suffocating any offensive momentum as both teams had more plays that went for negative yardage than first downs in the second half and each team punted six times.

But with 2:34 remaining, the Pirates put together one last threat, beginning with a Hutchins to Tipton connection for a 19-yard gain, and followed with a Tipton run over left tackle for six yards. The clock ticked to :56 when Hutchins snuck over for four more yards to the Marion 32.

But three plays netted five yards and on fourth down Hutchins scrambled to his right to avoid pressure before firing a pass downfield that Westmoreland stepped in front of at the 20, ending the threat and sealing the win.

It was the third straight season that the game came down to the final possession, and for just as many years the Warriors had found a way to make a late lead stick.

"We knew coming in that they had a strong defense," a sweat-soaked and wearied Colquette said at midfield after shaking hands with the Pirates staff. "But ours isn't too bad either, and Westmoreland stepped up and made the difference.

"Right now, I'm just tickled to death to get out of here with a win."

It was exactly the performance Westmoreland had wanted — catching the eye of college scouts by opening his junior season with two interceptions — which he returned for 108 yards — forcing one fumble and recovering another to go with nine solo tackles and a pass broken up.

It was the first time South Pittsburg had been shutout in four years and the first time Marion's offense failed to score in six seasons.

South Pittsburg managed only 73 rushing yards and five first downs and Marion finished with 111 yards on the ground and just four first downs. The Warriors had 138 total yards to the Pirates 93 and the defenses combined for five turnovers.

"Westmoreland beat us, plain and simple," Wilson would say later. "He was all over the field and disrupted everything we tried. No matter how much I pored over the film, I still didn't see much of a way to score on that defense. I can't think of a single play in our book that we didn't try on them.

"I'd like to have tied them. Besides for the obvious reasons, but just to see both teams line up 10 yards away from the other's goal line and see who could move against those defenses. The way both were playing, unless somebody kicks a field goal, we're probably still out there trying to decide that thing."

Both teams would breeze through the rest of their schedules to claim state championships — Marion taking the 3A title by averaging a 45-3 margin and South Pittsburg earning the 1A crown by beating the rest of its opponents an average of 44-7.

"That says something about both of our programs that year," Marion's Martin said later. "We blew everybody else out and so did they. That might have been the two best teams in the history of both programs."

The morning after the epic defensive struggle, as he walked toward the first tee for a round of golf, long-time Marion assistant Johnny Grimes was told by a fan walking off the course, "That's the worst two teams I've ever seen either school put on the field."

Grimes chuckled and replied, "Those were two pretty good defenses getting after each other. I think you'll see just how good the rest of the year."

Chapter 16
1994 WARRIORS

"Defense should take the shortest route to the ball and arrive in a bad mood."

— Bowden Wyatt,
former University of Tennessee head coach

Standing in the center of a circle of players — each of them already frothing with anger and pre-game anticipation, anxious to be turned loose — Landon Pickett arched his back and let out a loud yell.

"Dog pound!" he shouted at the top of his voice.

Fifty eight Marion County players, decked out in solid purple uniforms, began bouncing on their toes and answered back with one loud chorus of barks and growls to let Pickett know they were locked in.

Bending over to slide a plastic Halloween dog mask over his face for affect, the Warriors excitable defensive coordinator stood upright and began howling louder, slapping players on the helmet, bouncing up and down then lowering his shoulder to shove them, amping up the intensity. Losing himself in the moment, Pickett head-butted a player's helmet then let out one last alpha-male howl.

As he ripped the mask off, Marion's players saw blood flowing down Pickett's face from a gash in his forehead. The sight of their bloodied coach still bouncing and pumping his fists in the air sent a surge through the entire team like an electric current.

"Oh my God, we were ready to tear somebody's head off right then," said Jason Dykes, a senior defensive tackle on Marion's 1994 team.

At the opposite end of the field, Kingston coach Vic King stared back at the scene and shook his head as the reality of the atmosphere his team was about to step into sank in.

"He told me after the game that he knew as soon as he saw the way our guys were carrying on that it was over," Pickett said later. "He knew right then that they were in trouble."

Marion County had waited a full year for the quarterfinal rematch with Kingston, and while pre-game theatrics weren't needed, Pickett had stirred an emotional feeding frenzy inside the players.

Marion's excitable defensive coordinator Landon Pickett (left) and Ken Colquette confer during the title game.

"I'm a big believer that you've got to play on emotion in high school," Pickett explained. "That was probably the most coachable group I ever had and it didn't take much to get them fired up to play, especially that night.

"Those kids were so tough, in practice and in games, and if you pushed the right buttons they would run through a brick wall for you. They knew what was coming before it happened because they had paid attention when we watched film and all week at practice. I just wanted them to have fun and be aggressive, so I did whatever it took to light their fire."

The season before, looking to defend their state championship, the undefeated Warriors stumbled at Kingston and were upset 7-6. The 15 starters who returned in '94 had played with singular purpose, laying waste to their first 12 opponents to earn a shot at redemption.

As unstoppable as the offense had been — averaging 42 points per game despite throwing it just 74 times all season — it was Marion's defense, feeding off Pickett's fiery style, that was truly special. Through those first dozen games the Warriors starters had surrendered just one touchdown. One single TD in 48 quarters.

"It literally pissed us off if the other team got a first down," said Eric Westmoreland, a junior safety on that team. "We went into every game with the goal of getting a shut out. We had the fewest points scored against us in the whole state, so yeah, we took defense pretty seriously.

"If we didn't give up a special teams touchdown or cheap points off a turnover, we knew nobody was going to drive the field on us."

Pickett's dog pound mantra was born earlier in the season on a road trip to Howard, coming about by accident when, during pregame warmups, he realized he had left his whistle back at the field house and needed a way to get the players attention.

"I started barking at them to get their attention," Pickett said. "They started barking back at me and I told them we were going to get after people like a pack of wild dogs. The kids loved it. It really got them going and set the tone for how we wanted to play."

He had come to Marion from county rival Whitwell two years earlier, taking over the defense for long-time assistant Johnny Grimes. Pickett had played offensive guard and defensive tackle on a tough-as-sandpaper Whitwell team in 1969, then continued his career at Austin Peay. He began his coaching career as an assistant at Marion in the mid-1970s before taking over as head coach at his alma mater for four years, then stepping away from the game to work as an administrator.

But football was in his DNA and he returned to the sideline as Whitwell's defensive coordinator for three seasons before accepting an offer to join an all-star staff in Jasper and helping them win a state title in his first year.

The 50-slant that Warriors head coach Ken Colquette preferred was a perfect fit for Pickett's fast and physical style, which relied more on a blend of quickness and toughness rather than size.

"I liked it when we had a 300-pounder over me," said Dykes, who weighed 210 pounds his senior season. "I knew I was quick enough to get by him before he could move off the ball.

"Coach Pickett was different from Coach Colquette because he brought a lot of energy. He would get just as fired up as us players and we fed off that.

"We were a hungry group in '94 but we really had no idea just how good we could be yet."

Even as good as Marion's coaches were at poor-mouthing, it was hard to convince anybody the Warriors would not be among the best teams in the state after they came through a series of preseason scrimmages that included a tie with Class 5A powerhouse Murfreesboro Riverdale (the eventual 5A state champion that season) as well as a close battle with eventual 4A champion Cleveland.

"It was intimidating when we went to Riverdale, but we always prided ourself on being able to beat anybody, anywhere," said Rayburn Prince, a senior running back and outside linebacker/defensive end that season. At 5-foot-9, 170 pounds, Prince was another Warriors starter motivated by the knowledge that he would be severely undersized against most opponents. "The coaches wanted us to get challenged to see what we had because they knew we could be really good. Plus I think they wanted to have some film where they could point to us getting beat on some plays so they'd have something to gripe about and tell us how much work we still had to do if we were going to be any good.

"They were all really good at playing mind games and getting us to play harder than we thought we could."

GETTING DEFENSIVE

On the day before the season opener Marion players, coaches, students and faculty arrived at school to find someone had vandalized their field. The previous night unidentified South Pittsburg students had snuck onto the field to uproot both goal posts from the ground and paint a giant 'P' on the grass with diesel fuel.

"The coaches made us practice on the game field that afternoon instead of the practice field," Dykes said. "They wanted us to have to look at those goal posts all evening. That motivated us more than anything.

Instead of hurting us, it just pissed us off. We knew who was responsible and we couldn't wait to get to the game."

Once game night arrived, before opening the visitor's locker room door to make their way across the track to the field, Colquette warned the entire team to strap on their helmet and not take them off again until they returned to the field house.

"As soon as that door opened you saw two rows of their people lining the walkway," Dykes recalled. "They immediately started yelling at us, cussing and flipping us off and telling us we were about to get our asses kicked. It was brutal.

"I kept Pepto Bismol in my locker because my stomach was tore up from the nerves. I had chill bumps by the time I got on the field because you could just feel the excitement coming from both sides."

On the Pirates second possession, Dykes shed a blocker and rushed straight toward quarterback Perry Hutchins, getting his hands up to force a hurried throw that sailed high and was intercepted by Westmoreland, who returned it 66 yards for what proved to be the only points of the game.

Marion quarterback Josh Dobson tries to avoid several tacklers.

"Late in the fourth quarter, I came off the field and Coach (Don) Stewart grabbed my arm, looked me in the face and said 'Son, you've just played in the best game you'll ever play in in your life.'," Dykes said. "I was dead-dog tired. It was hard to catch my breath because they were throwing toward our end zone in the final seconds, so you couldn't feel good about it until the game actually ended.

"As the season went on we realized we weren't just the two best teams in the valley, we were two of the best in the whole state. Those two teams could've played with anybody."

Not only would it be the closest game of the season, but the only time an opponent stayed within four touchdowns of Marion the rest of the way.

"With our defense, six points was all we needed," Pickett said.

When Pickett walked onto the field before Marion's week two game against McMinn Central and saw a familiar face among the referee crew, any pregame jitters vanished.

"I had gone to college with one of the officials and he came over during warmups to say how excited they were to watch us play," Pickett said. "I kind of knew then it was going to be a good night for us."

With the refs among those anxious for a show, the Warriors obliged by scoring three first-quarter touchdowns. Marion out-gained the Chargers with 405 rushing yards — 175 from Westmoreland on just six carries — in a 44-3 cakewalk.

"Landon was pissed because we allowed a field goal," Prince said. "I had a chance to block it but I didn't cross my hands, and the ball sailed between them. He let me hear about that when we watched film the next Sunday.

"Our offense knew we would get pulled once we got way ahead, so we had to get used to only getting about two quarters of work."

Marion had 10 straight wins over Bledsoe County, blistering them by a combined 257-6 in the six games prior to their week three meeting. Bledsoe coaches had threatened to not schedule Marion anymore, which factored into the final tally.

"We didn't want to beat them so bad that they dropped us off the schedule because we were already having a tough time finding teams willing to play us," Pickett said. "We put the game away and then tried to just get through it without running it up."

Quarterback Josh Dobson ran for 95 yards and a TD and threw for another 86 yards and two more scores and Prince added 89 yards and a TD.

Although it was the coaches pulling the reigns back, they still unloaded on the team for what they said was a lackluster effort.

"They ripped us after the game and we had a rough week of practice the next week," Prince recalled. "Coach Colquette told us we wouldn't even make the playoffs if we kept that up. He said we had a little potential but we just weren't working hard enough."

When the team bus pulled up at Howard the next Friday, the coaching staff realized they had some field maintenance to help with before the teams could even play.

"They were just starting to line the field off and we knew if we didn't help there was no way the game would start on time," Pickett said with a laugh. "That was a first."

It took longer for the coaches to get the field ready than for the Warriors to put the game away. They scored 35 points in the first quarter, two from Lennie Cookston who also intercepted a pass and kicked five extra points to earn state player of the week honors. Dykes forced a fumble and Anthony Martin intercepted a pass, both setting up first-quarter scores and Prince ran for 70 yards and a pair of TDs early.

"By the second quarter their guys were telling us the game was over so just don't hit them in the knees because they had basketball coming up and didn't want to get hurt," Prince said.

An equally easy win over City High was followed by a home game against Tyner, with first place in the region on the line.

But any hint of drama was snuffed out by Marion's smothering defense, which held its third straight opponent to negative yards in the first half on the way to handing Tyner its worst loss — 61-0 — in the program's 58-year history.

Senior linebacker Jason Muir established himself as the leader on that side of the ball, sacking Rams all-star quarterback Jackie Buttram five times and returning an interception for a touchdown. Buttram, who entered the game as the area's leading passer, completed just two throws for 30 yards and Marion played the second half on cruise control after taking a 45-0 lead by halftime.

"I'm totally shocked," Colquette said as he stared at the scoreboard. "We came out ready to play and I'd have to say that's the sharpest we've looked all year."

Seven Warriors scored and they out-gained the Rams 501-78 in total yards, led by Westmoreland's 154 and three TDs on eight carries and Prince's 107 yards.

"We really don't feature just one back in our offense, but when Eric runs like that without all the dancing, he's the best in the state," Colquette added, delivering a trademark back-handed compliment to his budding star.

"Everybody in the area told us how good we were all weekend," Prince said. "And then we get to the field house that Sunday afternoon

Eric Westmoreland breaks a tackle in the title game.

to watch film and Coach Colquette starts out by saying 'I bet y'all believe what everybody's saying, don't you? Well, after watching the film that's the worst effort we've given all year.'

"He just lit into us and found all kinds of things that he swore would get us beat in the playoffs. Nobody could crush our ego and bring us back down to earth like him."

The shutout streak ended the next week at Sequatchie County when Marion reserves gave up a touchdown with less than a minute left. That didn't overshadow the fact that Sequatchie had been held to minus-14 yards rushing.

"That was a big rivalry for me because I had a lot of relatives that lived in Dunlap," Dykes said. "We would eat dinner at my grandma's every Sunday and there was a lot of trash talk on both sides. After we destroyed them, they couldn't say a whole to me. I had bragging rights."

The next week, after Dobson connected with Anthony Martin on a 73-yard touchdown pass and Westmoreland brought back a punt 63 yards for another score to highlight a first half that saw five Warriors score, Madisonville coaches requested the second half be shortened from 12 to 8-minute quarters to get the game over quicker.

Through their first eight games the Warriors starting unit had yet to give up a touchdown. But Spring Hill snapped the scoreless streak with a first half TD.

"It was a total let-down on our right side," Prince said, recalling the play more than 20 years later as if it had happened just a day earlier. "We slanted the wrong way, I didn't close my gap down and we missed a tackle in the secondary and they broke one for a big play.

"We knew when we showed up to watch film that we were going to be in for it and sure enough, that was the first thing that got brought up. It was a piss-poor effort and what really bothered us was we had let a mediocre team score on us."

The lone first-half miscue aside, Marion again made it look easy with a 49-6 win and capped the regular season with a ho-hum 42-0 win at Grundy County, where Prince and Westmoreland combined for 182 yards and three TDs on just 13 carries.

It took just three offensive plays for the Warriors to announce that their first-round playoff foe, York Institute, was out-classed. On the game's second play, Dobson hit Martin, who turned a short route into a 58-yard touchdown connection and after holding the Dragons to three-and-out, Westmoreland broke loose for a 60-yard scoring sprint.

Marion would scored 22 points in the first five minutes and build a 36-0 lead by halftime as Dobson threw for 119 yards, ran for 97 more and accounted for three TDs.

Not even the flu could slow Marion's playoff run. Despite much of the team feeling puny after a week-long bout with the virus, they recovered in time to make sure round two opponent Rutledge would be just another bug on the windshield as they continued steaming toward the rematch they craved.

Marion scored on five of its first six possessions and again had put the game away by halftime, taking a commanding 37-0 lead with 23 points in the second quarter, while holding the Pioneers to 16 total yards.

"We wanted to send a message back toward Knoxville," Pickett said. "The teams we had coming up the next couple of weeks were from that area and we wanted them to know how good we were."

Prince and Westmoreland, who ran for 145 of his 173 yards in the first half, each scored three touchdowns and the Pioneers managed their only TD with just 26 seconds remaining.

In the locker room after the game, Colquette calmed the celebration by informing the players that Kingston had held off Gatlinburg Pittman by a point. Marion would have its shot at redemption the next Friday.

"I'll tell you this," Colquette concluded, ignoring the fact his team had just hung half a hundred on a playoff foe. "If you play next week like you did tonight your season will be over."

Kingston rolled into Jasper with a matching 12-0 record and a stingy defense of its own, having allowed more than two touchdowns just once all season. The Yellow Jackets averaged scoring four touchdowns per game and earlier in the week King had been quoted in the local paper saying that his team would prove the previous season's outcome was not a fluke.

That quote was clipped, copied and taped to the bulletin board inside Marion's locker room and by Friday had rubbed the Warriors pride pretty raw.

"We would've been ready for that one anyway because of what happened the year before, but seeing their coach's quote, that stirred a hornets nest," Dykes said.

The scoreboard alone hadn't been enough of a challenge to that point and even Pickett's demand of a shutout had become routine, so the Warriors defense decided to set an even more outrageous goal for their quarterfinal showdown.

"The whole defense met before the game and decided we would not allow them to cross the 50 yard line," Prince recalled. "I don't remember ever being as hyped up for a game — not even South Pittsburg or a state game — as I was for that one. We had hoped they would make it back because we knew we'd be waiting on them and we really wanted to make a statement."

No tricks or flashy play calls were needed as Marion simply lined up and pounded Kingston into submission, scoring three times in both halves.

"We're just a bunch of dumb ol' coaches," Colquette said afterward, trying his best to downplay every aspect of the machine he had built. "We're not smart enough to have some real elaborate playbook with a hundred plays in it, and I'm not sure if our kids would be able to grasp it if we did.

"But when we execute we can be pretty doggone tough."

Westmoreland, who had more than 1,000 yards rushing, had been named a Mr. Football finalist earlier in the week and added to that total with 173 yards and three touchdowns, including an 82-yard sprint.

"We've waited for tonight for a year," he said as he watched Kingston's players limp off the field with their heads down. "They never should have beaten us last year, and it was probably one of the most disappointing losses in our history. We proved when we work together, nobody can stop us."

Although Prince was kept out of the end zone for the first time in 11 games, he added 115 yards and helped the defense pitch its seventh shutout. Kingston managed just 37 rushing yards and finished with 95 total yards, losing three interceptions and a fumble.

Even after Kingston salvaged a small portion of pride by crossing midfield, preventing Marion from clicking off its absurd goal, the Warriors had made their statement. As the final seconds ticked off the 42-0 win, Colquette sought out Prince and gave him a bear hug.

"He ran his heart out tonight," Colquette said as his team celebrated around him. "I just wanted him to know how much I, as a coach, appreciated his effort."

In the days that followed Colquette and everyone around Marion's program would come to appreciate and respect Prince's effort and toughness even more.

Early in Marion's semifinal Prince broke through a gap in the middle of the defense and bolted upfield, lowering his shoulder when he reached a Knoxville West linebacker. At impact Prince felt his shoulder dislocate from its socket, but as he landed on his side he felt it pop back into place. A burning sensation down his right arm confirmed he had separated the shoulder and would prevent him from carrying the ball in the second half.

Rayburn Prince sprints for an early touchdown in the title game.

"The pain was terrible," Prince said. "I played on defense until we put it away, but I couldn't carry the ball. I was more worried about whether I would be able to play the next week."

The Rebels, whose surging enrollment forced them to move up to 4A the next fall, struck first with a 51-yard pass after recovering a Marion fumble.

It was the first time all season the Warriors had trailed.

"Let's just say we had a come to Jesus meeting on the sideline after they scored," Pickett recalled.

"We were really upset," said Muir, who earned the 3A Mr. Football Lineman of the Year award the next week.

"When we fell behind, it made all of us so mad," Dykes explained. "After they caught that pass and ran it in we got together on the sideline and said it's time to button our chin straps and get to work."

Despite failing to score in the first quarter for the first time all season, Marion got back on track in the second, beginning with Westmoreland's 72-yard halfback pass to Travis Houston. Prince capped the drive with a two-yard TD, and the Warriors took the lead for good when Martin added the two-point conversion run.

The Rebels managed just 42 total yards after their first-quarter TD, picking up just one yard in the second half. Brad Holden intercepted two passes in the second half, taking one back 28 yards on West's first possession of the third quarter for the TD that put the game away.

"We worried as coaches how we'd react as a team if we ever got behind in a game," Colquette said afterward. "We're not worried anymore."

The biggest worry for the Warriors came the next day when Prince had his shoulder examined by a doctor.

"They started talking about surgery, but I knew I only had one more game in my life," Prince said. "I knew I wasn't going to play in college so the state championship would be my last game ever. And it was the game I had worked my whole life for, so I went to get a second opinion and he said surgery wasn't necessary.

"I went straight to Coach Colquette Sunday and asked 'You're not going to hold me out are you?' He said 'Not if you think you can play'. I just said 'I'm playing.'

"My shoulder still gives me a fit if I roll over on it or sleep on it wrong. But there was no question I was playing in that game."

"WE CAME TO DO WHAT WE'VE DONE TO PEOPLE ALL YEAR"

A cold, steady rain began falling on Nashville early Saturday morning and continued right up into early afternoon as kickoff for the 3A state championship game approached.

Decked out in a purple rain suit, his Marion coach's cap turned around backwards as always, Pickett ignored the cold and damp and began inciting his defensive players as they stretched and tried to ignore the blast of frigid air that swirled around the field.

As the Warriors were completing their warm-ups, Johnny Grimes hurried to the rest of the coaching staff to make an announcement. He had been watching Portland's defense practicing its assignments at the opposite end of the field and noticed a key flaw that had to be attacked early.

"Y'all, they don't have a clue how to defend the veer," Grimes reported. "Their end just runs upfield every time. They don't have a soul on the dive back."

The rest of the staff nodded and tried to hide confident grins.

"I remember how scared their guys looked during warm-ups," Westmoreland said. "You could just tell they were intimidated before the game even started."

Marion won the pregame coin toss and elected to put its tone-setting defense on the field first. With a confident swagger linemen Terry Smith, Jason Saylors, Chris Webster, Jason Dykes, Rayburn Prince, linebackers Jason Muir and Brad Holden and defensive backs Anthony Martin, Travis Houston, Eric Westmoreland and Ben Harris took their place opposite Portland's offense.

Five plays was all it took for two certainties to come into focus — Portland's offense would put up very little resistance against the Warriors attacking defense, and the Panthers were completely clueless on how to defend the option.

Two of the first three plays went for zero or negative yards, including a sack by Webster that sent water splashing into the air when he threw Portland quarterback George Carroll to the rain-soaked turf. Portland's punt attempt was a disaster as the snap sailed high and rolled back to its own nine yard line before finally being tracked down.

On the Warriors first snap they tested Grimes' theory to see if Portland, in fact, had no clue how to defend the dive. Dobson took a step to his right before putting the ball in Prince's gut and watching his running back cross the goal line without getting touched. Sure enough, the Panthers defensive end bolted upfield rather than squeezing the edge and Marion coaches realized their inside veer would do serious damage.

Jason Muir accepts the championship game's defensive MVP plaque.

In a sign of just how well things would go for the Warriors, Martin corralled a bad snap on the extra point attempt, avoided the rush and found Ben Harris in the back of the end zone for the two-point conversion.

It had taken less than two minutes for Marion to take the lead for good and establish the tone for what would follow the rest of the evening.

Portland countered with its second straight three-and-out, followed by another big play from Marion's special teams, this time a 24-yard punt return by Westmoreland to set the offense up near midfield.

Facing a fourth and one, Colquette — who had worried himself into a tizzy before the game over the potential for fumbles in the slick conditions — opted to go for it. As the Warriors got to the line, right guard Jason Saylors and right tackle Adam Baker immediately recognized which play they needed to check into, even before Dobson could make the call.

Turning their heads to look back over their left shoulder at their quarterback, Saylors and Baker yelled, almost in unison, "Josh, 36, 36, 36!!" realizing the dive off the right side would work again for a huge gain. It was a testament to how well Marion's linemen and backs had been taught that they could recognize which play needed to be called as quickly as any coach.

Prince took the handoff and blew through the seam, sprinting 42 yards untouched for the touchdown.

Just halfway through the first quarter and Marion's train whistle was already getting a workout as the Warriors built a commanding 15-0 lead. Meanwhile the gray skies and temperatures hovering just above freezing suddenly felt even more miserable for the shell-shocked Panthers, who were making the program's first title game appearance.

Neither the score nor conditions improved for Portland in the second quarter as Westmoreland capped a 10-play, 80-yard drive with a six-yard scoring run.

Later in the quarter, Dykes — who had two tackles for loss — forced a fumble and Jason Muir pounced on the ball at the Panthers 17, setting up a two-yard TD by Westmoreland three plays later.

In a sure sign that the Panthers were ready to raise the white flag, they gave little effort to recover the bouncing squib kick before Webster jumped on it. Three more plays was all it took for Westmoreland to follow the block of 300-pound offensive lineman Kelvin Spears into the end zone. When Westmoreland scooped up a low snap and tossed the ball to Landon Phillips for another unlikely two-point conversion, the Warriors had officially put the game away before halftime.

One Marion fan, who had made a $100 bet with a Portland fan before the game, made his way to the Panthers side of the field, found the man and announced loudly, "Where's my damn money?!?"

Portland, which had won 11 straight coming into the title game and hadn't lost to an in-state team all season, managed to avoid the shutout with a desperation heave for a 51-yard TD on the final play of the first half. But after Westmoreland broke free for a 63-yard scoring sprint on the third play of the second half, the Warriors began subbing in younger players freely and the soggy celebration began, just as rival South Pittsburg had done after its Class A title the previous night.

"We wanted to come here and do what we've done to people all year – get them out of their game," Pickett said. "This is a great way to go out for 17 seniors and the rest of this bunch.

"Two of the three teams from the county walked off this field as state champions. That's unheard of for a county our size."

Playing through pain, Prince gained much of his 154 yards in the first half before injuring the shoulder again. Westmoreland ran for 151 yards and four TDs to earn Offensive MVP honors.

"Rayburn deserved to win this MVP award as much as I did," Westmoreland said after the game. "I honestly wish they had co-MVP awards. I'll gladly share this one with him."

For the season he finished with 1,300 yards and returned two of his seven interceptions for scores to become a Mr. Football finalist. His slashing running style and Prince's bulldog tenacity were a perfect compliment to one another and in the title game they accounted for 305 of the team's 409 yards and all six TDs.

The pair was also primary in helping break the school scoring record, setting the new mark with 633 points – averaging 42 in the regular season then picking up the pace for 46 in the playoffs.

For a second straight week, Colquette sought out Prince in the closing seconds, wrapping his arms around the gutsy senior.

"He knew how bad my shoulder was hurt so he just said he was proud of how tough I was," Prince said later. "I think he was worried I might be upset that I didn't get MVP but I told him I wasn't worried about that at all. To me, individual awards didn't mean anything compared to winning it all.

"For me it was all about playing with my buddies and accomplishing a goal we had set. That's what I still miss about the game every day."

Muir, who had nine tackles and a fumble recovery, added the Defensive MVP award to his Mr. Football trophy, leading a starting defensive unit that gave up a miserly 22 total points in 15 games.

Marion celebrates yet another title.

"All the way up through the last game our coaches had talked up the other teams so much that we felt like we had to do everything perfect or we couldn't win," Dykes said. "Now when you look back on that team, because the first game was the only time we got challenged all year, it puts the question in your mind of just how good were we?

"The next year's team proved a lot by beating all those bigger schools but I believe we were just as good if not better, so I wish we could've had that chance to prove ourselves too.

"Everything we've ever done after school, whether it was coaching little league or at work or being a family man, we wanted to strive to be the best because that's what playing on that team taught us."

MARION COUNTY 1994 RESULTS

Sept. 2	at South Pittsburg	6-0
Sept. 9	at McMinn Central	44-3
Sept. 16	Bledsoe County	26-0
Sept. 23	at Howard	41-6
Sept. 30	at Phoenix III	56-0
Oct. 7	Tyner	61-0
Oct. 14	at Sequatchie County	42-8

Oct. 21	Madisonville	41-0
Oct. 28	Spring Hill	49-6
Nov. 4	at Grundy County	42-0

Playoffs

Nov. 11	York	49-7
Nov. 18	Rutledge	50-6
Nov. 25	Kingston	42-0
Dec. 2	Knox West	41-7

State championship

| Dec. 10 | Portland (at Vanderbilt) | 43-14 |

1994 Warriors

Players: Eric Westmoreland, Rayburn Prince, Gavin Thomasson, Josh Dobson, Anthony Martin, Chris Coffelt, Avery Pickett, T. Layne, Brandon Graham, Travis Houston, Ben Harris, Wayne Westmoreland, Ryan Bradford, Terry Smith, Joe Butler, Keith Walker, Labron Pickett, James Patrick, Brad Holden, Rusty Parker, Michael Fulfer, Jason Gibson, Lenny Cookston, Landon Phillips, Jason Dykes, Matt Clark, Jason Teague, Roy Simpson, Eric Parker, Jason Saylors, Adam Baker, Chris Webster, Nathan Capps, Stephen Dover, Kelvin Spears, Matt Howard, Kelvin Hill, Brian Pruitt, Chuck Jones, Garrett Sowder, Tim Westmoreland, Cliff Moore, Adam Billingsley, Jason Graham, Mitch Smith, Ben Roberts, Larry Ziegler, Brian Cooper, Nathan Mosley, Les Thomas, Chris Hopkins, Robert Holloway, Josh Cannon, Jeremy Pruitt, Josh Chambers, Jamie Muir, Charley Gilliam, Jason Muir.

Coaches: Ken Colquette, Landon Pickett, Johnny Grimes, Don Stewart, Jerry Tate, Larry Richards, Eddie Reed, Paul Underwood, Randy Munn, Steve Lawson.

Chapter 17
1994 PIRATES

"Carpe diem. Seize the day, boys."
— John Keating, Dead Poets Society

Bone-weary tired and wanting nothing more than to close his eyes for a night of satisfied sleep, Danny Wilson was jolted awake by the insufferable ring of his home phone.

It was the end of a day that had begun before sunrise — really even earlier since he had been too excited to sleep the night before. South Pittsburg's 29-year old second-year head football coach had just guided the program to its first state championship in 25 years and the celebration that followed had been long and loud.

When the Pirates team bus returned home from Nashville on the damp, dark early-December Friday night in 1994, players and coaches exited for the five-block walk through what looked to be an endless line of appreciative fans and well-wishers who braved the cold drizzle to welcome their returning heroes. The team made the trek through the heart of town to their field house and then made plans on where to meet up to keep the party going through the night.

"There were people with tears in their eyes slapping the kids on the back and thanking them," Wilson recalled. "It was something really special and I wanted all our guys to experience that because I knew it would be something we would all remember for the rest of our lives.

"I had promised some of our kids that I would drive them back to Nashville after the parade that night to be with their parents who were staying over so they could watch Jasper play the next day. I don't know what I was thinking."

The day after South Pittsburg had capped its memorable season by claiming the Class 1A championship, rival Marion County was set to try to do the same in the 3A title game. It would be a historic weekend since only twice previously had two teams from the same county won state titles in the same season, and those came from Metropolitan counties Shelby (Memphis) and Knox.

But once he made it back home after a second trip to Nashville, sometime after 2 a.m., the only history Wilson cared about was putting an end to his long day.

Just before he felt himself drifting off, the phone rang and he sprang straight up from under the covers. His first thought at such an ungodly hour was to hope nothing bad had happened during all the celebration that was surely still carrying on around town.

"Hello?" Wilson answered hesitantly.

The Pirates quick-strike offense huddles early in the title game.

He was met by a momentary pause on the other end before a man's raspy voice replied, "You should've beat Jasper!"

Click.

"We had just won the state for the first time since 1969 and it was the wee hours of the morning, but all this guy had on his mind was a game we had lost four months ago to our rival," Wilson said, shaking his head as he retold the story.

Wilson identified with the man's lingering disappointment because the same dislike and jealousy between the two programs now flowed through his veins as well.

"What was sad was, after he hung up, I knew he was right."

FATE DISGUISED AS A PIRATE

It was almost by accident that he began his coaching and teaching career at South Pittsburg. Shortly after graduating from Lipscomb University in 1987, where he had played baseball on scholarship, the confident young coach interviewed for jobs at Northwest Whitfield in Georgia and Montgomery Christian in Alabama, which he felt certain he would choose.

But fate stepped in when the director of education at Lipscomb called Wilson into her office and asked for a favor.

Marcus Banks (66) blocks for Pirates running back Corey Tipton.

"She said she was good friends with the principal at a small school just outside of Chattanooga and had promised she would send someone there to interview for an opening they had," Wilson recalled. "She gave me gas money to go and I stayed with Mr. (James)

Warren, who was the principal, overnight and had my interview with Coach (Don) Grider the next morning.

"They were desperate for a football assistant and head baseball coach but I wasn't so sure at first until we went for the ride."

The ride was Grider asking Wilson to hop in his 1979 Econoline van — which he had customized with orange paint and a black stripe down the side as well as orange and black shag carpet inside — for a drive through town.

"I noticed everybody on the road kept moving out of his way and I thought 'man, they must really respect this guy around here.'," Wilson said. "But then Don turned to me laughing and said, 'I don't see so good, so most of these people that know that are giving me enough room to go around them.'

"That's when I started looking for the seatbelt real quick."

Grider drove Wilson through Sweetens Cove, a narrow, winding road that passed the town's only golf course and is lined by cornfields and farm houses. As Grider steered the van along the backroads he talked to Wilson about the things he believed in — work ethic and how athletics can make a difference in a kid's life.

"As he was talking I realized his core values were exactly what I believed in too," Wilson said. "I knew that's where I belonged so when I got back to Nashville I called my mom and told her I was taking the job in the little town near Chattanooga. That ride changed my life."

For the first 10 years of his professional career Wilson changed not only the lives of many of the kids he coached and taught but the success rate for every sport he was a part of. Regardless of whether he coached baseball, football, girls' basketball, softball, even volleyball, he quickly established himself as a winner. If the school had offered soccer — something the locals referred to sneeringly as "communist kickball" — no doubt Wilson would have developed the Pirates into a contender in that sport too.

In the spring of 1994 he led the girls' basketball team to the sub-state round for the first time in school history and two years later guided the Pirates baseball team to a state title. As of 2018, that remains the only state crown claimed by any school in the county in a sport other than football.

"I was pretty confident when I started my career," said Wilson. "I had pitched and played quarterback all my life, so I was used to being the man. So when Coach Grider retired and told me the head football job was mine if I wanted it, I took it not realizing how big a deal it actually was.

"I was 27 years old, too young to know all the things I didn't know."

In his first season as head coach the '93 Pirates won 11 consecutive games — all by at least 14 points — to reach the semifinals for the first time in seven years. But a heartbreaking two-point loss to eventual state champion Trousdale County had left an empty feeling that could only be filled by winning it all the following fall.

The return of 15 starters had expectations soaring through town higher than they had in a decade.

"We couldn't find anybody willing to scrimmage us that fall," Wilson said. "So I called Bill Price at Soddy-Daisy, but he really didn't want to come since they were a 5A team and we were just a little ol' 1A school.

The Princess Theater marquee wishes the Pirates luck

He finally agreed as long as he could bring his freshmen so they could get some work in too.

"They came down and we proceeded to beat the breaks off them all evening. Bill was madder than a wet hen and his freshmen never got on the field because we were wearing his varsity out.

"We knew right then that we were pretty doggone good."

OUT TO PROVE A POINT

When the Pirates opened the '94 season nobody knew for sure just how doggone good they, or the Marion County team they played that night would be. Months later that question would be answered, but on the first muggy Friday night of September the two rivals stood toe-to-toe trading body blows.

The game might as well have been played in a phone booth since, for the most part, both teams rammed their stable of talented running backs into brick wall defenses that refused to budge. The Warriors returned an interception 66 yards for a score midway through the first quarter and that would be the only points of the game as the teams combined for more negative yardage plays than first downs.

A week later the Pirates took out their offensive frustrations as the all-state duo of quarterback Perry Hutchins and tailback Corey Tipton each ran for two touchdowns in the first quarter, helping build a 41-0 halftime lead over Vonore. The defense picked up where it had left off, setting a school record by holding the Blue Devils to minus-23 total yards for the game.

Another lopsided win followed at 3A Grundy County as Hutchins, Tipton and Tommy Rector combined for 274 yards and six TDs as the Pirates proved they had picked themselves off the deck, put the tough Marion loss behind them and taken care of business with back-to-back wins over outmanned opponents.

But they would be tested again with a trip to top-ranked Greenback, where first place in the region and home-field advantage in the playoffs would be decided. A line of violent thunderstorms that moved through the Knoxville area on Friday forced the game to be pushed back a day and by Saturday afternoon's kickoff the late-summer humidity made the air as thick as southern gravy.

Greenback had eliminated the Pirates from the playoffs three consecutive years in the early 90s and appeared on the verge of dashing their dreams again by taking control before most of the fans had even settled into their seats. The Cherokees had wasted no time in moving for a quick score on their opening drive, then returned a punt 82 yards for a TD that staked them to a 14-0 lead at halftime.

Once South Pittsburg's players slowly shuffled into the visitor's locker room, Wilson let it be known their effort in the first half would not be tolerated. As he stepped through the doorway he snapped a wooden clipboard over his knee, slammed the splintered pieces against a wall and lit into the entire team.

"Gutless!" he shouted, his voice reaching a level that surely came close to peeling the gray paint off the walls. "Absolutely gutless effort by everyone of you!"

Stopping long enough to catch his breath and scan the room at the dejected players — heads dropped and all eyes staring at the floor — he continued to spew venom. "Complete bullshit out there! That's what I saw! It ain't about drawing up different plays, it's about whether or not you want to keep giving no effort and just lay down and take that ass-whippin' they're handing you right now!

"There's some guys in here who need to take the rest of this half and figure out whether or not you're really man enough to do something about it!"

There would be no Xs and Os adjustments or scheme changes. Wilson's point was clear — does this team have enough backbone to fight back against a quality team? With several monstrously talented teams awaiting them in the playoffs, this would be the pivotal moment deciding which direction the season would take.

"I was sitting there and all of a sudden Coach Wilson comes in and just went completely insane," said Wesley Stone, a two-way lineman on the team who later became a Pirates assistant. "I had never seen him so angry. We knew we weren't playing well, especially on offense, but when he went off on us, it woke us up. Really it pissed us off is what it did."

The Pirates wasted no time in answering the challenge to their manhood. On the second half's opening kick-off, South Pittsburg special teams blockers met a wave of charging defenders and put them on the ground, opening a lane for speedy kick returner Bradley "Macho" Green to weave his way around the scattered bodies, then race 87 yards for a momentum-shifting touchdown.

It would be the first of three third-quarter touchdowns by the Pirates, who continued to physically dominate the stunned Cherokees. Tipton ran for 97 yards and two scores and South Pittsburg's defense — led by linebacker Vincent Banks who was in on 12 tackles and knocked down three passes — held Greenback without a first down in the second half.

Don Grider passes the field house keys to Danny Wilson after naming him the Pirates new coach.

"Every time I ran the ball in the third quarter I had tears in my eyes," Tipton said. "I was mad as hell and I was afraid we were going to lose."

Leading 18-14 as the fourth quarter began, Hutchins stepped in front of a pass across the middle and returned the interception 38 yards for a score that gave South Pittsburg a little breathing room. On the next series, Tony Jenkins picked off another Cherokees pass and brought it back 35 yards for the score that salted away a 31-14 win.

"We came alive in the second half," a mellowed Wilson told reporters afterward, not giving a hint of knowing what had inspired his team's second-half flurry. "I thought we showed a lot of heart coming back after being down like that."

It became tougher for the coaching staff to find flaws in their team's play for the rest of the regular season, beginning with an annihilation of county rival Whitwell — never needing more than three plays to score any of their eight touchdowns and giving up just 62 total yards — followed by another blowout win over Midway, where Hutchins threw for 115 yards and three TDs in the first quarter.

"We showed we have a killer instinct finally," Wilson said with a wide grin as he made his way off the field.

The Pirates had developed a swagger, believing no team in their classification could handle them and proving that point by surgically removing the will of every team that set foot on the field against them, usually ending all doubt before halftime.

After helplessly watching six different Pirates score touchdowns, including four in one quarter, Lookout Valley coach Wes Green admitted, "If there's a better team in Class A, I'd hate to see it."

On the heels of Wilson's halftime rant at Greenback, the Pirates would not allow a point to be scored in 23 of the next 26 quarters, outscoring their final seven regular-season opponents 332-20.

"Our offensive philosophy was to be as deliberate as possible, run it at people and wear on them," Wilson explained later. "Defensively we had some guys who had a mean streak and just like to hit. I mean they would light you up and walk back to the huddle smiling about it."

No players embraced the team's reputation for inflicting pain more than brothers Marcus and Vincent Banks, 170-pound heat-seeking missiles who played outside linebacker on the '94 defense that allowed just 1.9 yards per carry.

"God knew it wouldn't be fair if He had made those two guys any bigger," said Marion County all-state athlete Anthony Martin, who played against the Banks brothers. "The hardest I've ever been hit in my life was by Marcus Banks. The second hardest hit I ever took was from Vincent. Those two dudes would absolutely tattoo you."

But while the Banks brothers set the defensive tone and Tipton needed just six games to rush for more than 1,000 yards, it was Hutchins who remained the biggest target for college recruiters. In early November, when the Chattanooga Times released its Elite 11 — the top senior prospects in the state — the Pirates 6-foot, 170-pound safety was on the list at No. 8, good enough to be just two spots behind Jackson Central-Merry linebacker Al Wilson and a rung ahead of Harriman athlete Jermaine Copeland, a pair of future University of Tennessee stars.

Hutchins, who had seven interceptions in the regular season, was being courted by Notre Dame, Tennessee, Miami, North Carolina, Alabama and Clemson. The only question besides which school he would choose was whether he would earn a high enough test score to qualify academically.

"Perry is still the best athlete I've ever coached at any school or any level," Wilson would say years later. "Whatever sport he played, he was the smoothest looking kid out there."

Pirates receiver Bradley "Macho" Green.

Recruiting worries would take a back seat for the time being however as the postseason began and South Pittsburg looked to erase the hurtful memory of the way the previous playoff run had ended.

The first step toward atonement was a continuation of the regular-season domination as Tipton set a single-game school record by running for 349 yards, averaging more than 19 yards per carry, and scoring three times. The offensive line bulldozed Unaka's front seven, clearing the way for another school record as the Pirates rushed for 527 yards in a 54-6 first-round beat-down.

Round two presented much more of a challenge as Donelson Christian Academy scored first, putting the Pirates behind for only the second time all season, and went into halftime trailing by just 12-10. But Tipton scored three times in the second half, finishing with 182 yards and five TDs to advance South Pittsburg to the quarterfinals with a hard-fought 32-10 win.

Pirates quarterback Perry Hutchins breaks free for a big gain.

When Coalfield's players stepped off their bus for the quarterfinal match-up they walked past a large sign outside the visitor's locker room that read, "Welcome to the slaughterhouse". It was a warning that should have been heeded.

The teams had scrimmaged months earlier and had nearly ended that day in an all-out brawl. Even coaches had to be separated and bad blood remained in the moments leading up to kickoff.

Yellow Jackets senior Lester Morgan had earned a reputation for delivering big hits on special teams and had even knocked a couple of opposing players out of games with vicious blows. In the days leading up to the game Pirates coaches made it a priority for the Banks brothers to look up Morgan every chance they got.

"Watch this," long-time assistant Dave Baxter said as he pointed in Morgan's direction just before the opening kickoff. "We're about to tear that kid a new ass all night."

Baxter would later say the Banks brothers were the hardest hitting players he ever coached. With them carrying through on their assignment to de-cleat Morgan every time he got back on his feet, South Pittsburg's special teams continually set up a wall of blockers, allowing Michael McCarver to return two punts for scores and Green to bring back another for a TD on the way to a commanding 35-0 halftime lead.

Green added a 63-yard TD catch, Tipton ran for 158 yards and three scores — including a 96-yard sprint — and the Pirates defense allowed just 54 rushing yards as a Coalfield team that came in boasting an 11-1 record left town chapped after a 63-6 spanking.

Halfway through his post-game locker room speech Wilson set the mood for the coming semifinal round.

"Men, we'll play whoever is put in front of us next week, whether it's BGA or Trousdale. But personally, I'm hoping to go to Hartsville. I think we owe 'em a little payback."

Moments later an assistant informed the team that Trousdale had upset BGA 41-28, provoking Wilson to shove his fist into the air and yell over the commotion, "That's what we wanted! I want to go to their house and take it from them. I've wanted that all year, and so have you. We've got that shot now."

The sting of the previous year's 16-14 loss, when the Pirates had held Trousdale to 49 total yards in the second half but were stopped inches short of converting three fourth down attempts as well as a two-point conversion, had left its mark.

But now the rematch was set and the Pirates would have a chance to put some balm on that wound.

When players met at the field house for Monday's practice, they found reminders taped to each locker — purple cardboard squares with the score of the previous year's game in yellow ink (Trousdale's colors).

"We really didn't need the coaches to do anything to remind us because we had lived with that loss for a year and we were ready to play that game as soon as we walked off the field from beating Coalfield," said two-way lineman Brandon Price.

THE CREEK BANK

The locals in Hartsville call their team's football field 'The Creek Bank' because of its close proximity to Goose Creek. By early December the combination of the frigid air blowing off the nearby water and Trousdale County's tradition, has given countless opponents the cold shoulder.

The Yellow Jackets had already claimed two state championships in the 90s, including the one from the previous season that Pirates supporters felt should have been theirs. Bleachers along both sidelines run the length of the field and when visiting teams step out of their cramped locker room, they're immediately met by Trousdale fans lining both sides of the walkway leading to the field, all ready to remind them what kind of hostile environment they've gotten themselves into.

Wilson instructed his players to keep their eyes forward until they got onto the field. It was a directive easier given than followed once the Pirates stepped out to a greeting much colder than the freezing temperatures.

"You boys came a long way for another ass whippin'!" yelled one Yellow Jackets fan wearing camouflage coveralls.

"We had gotten there about two hours before the game and when we passed one of the banks in town it already showed the temperature was in the 20s," remembered Stone. "By kickoff it was a lot colder than that.

"When we came out for pregame our adrenaline was so high we didn't feel the cold or pay any attention to what their fans were hollering at us. We had the kind of guys who weren't going to be intimidated and if anything, all that did was just get us more ready to kick their ass."

More than 5,000 fans packed the field and, adding to the circus atmosphere, the opening kickoff was delayed while a local television camera crew's helicopter landed in a nearby field.

Much as it had the year before, Trousdale drew first blood with a big-play score when Brandon Gooch returned the game's first punt 82 yards. Tipton answered by capping a long drive with a 39-yard touchdown run, sparking a span of four possessions in which the teams traded scores before South Pittsburg finally got a stop and went up 22-12 at the half.

Back in the prison cell sized visitor's locker room, Wilson began going over halftime instructions when he noticed two TV reporters he didn't recognize huddled in a corner trying to get warm and talking loudly to one another.

"Hey!" Wilson shouted in their direction. "If you ain't wearing a headset or a helmet you need to take your ass back out in the cold!"

This was no time for distractions.

Just before halftime the coaching staff had noticed an option out of the power-I set to the weak side had worked with Hutchins keeping the ball and getting to the edge for several big gains.

"We were just looking for something that would work and that play was next on the list so we just kept running it in the second half," Wilson said later. "They never adjusted to stop it."

Trousdale began the second half driving nearly the length of the field before settling for a 21-yard field goal that cut the lead to 22-15.

Pirates celebrate their first state title in 25 years.

Two plays later the Jackets intercepted a Hutchins pass and drove to the Pirates 15 before stalling and being faced with a fourth-and-4.

The call was for kicker Brandon Sampson to fake the field goal and throw for the tying score, but Hutchins got a measure of payback for his earlier bad throw by picking off the pass in the back of the end zone.

"I was watching for the fake. That's my responsibility," a relieved Hutchins said after the game. "I just saw who he was throwing it to and went to get it."

The Pirates continued to nurse a seven-point lead into the fourth quarter when Gooch, who had scored earlier, dropped a punt and Vincent Banks was there for the recovery.

Two plays later, the diminutive Green — who at 5-7, 140 pounds was as quick as a hiccup — provided a bit of distance on the scoreboard. Using the same look on the option where Hutchins had kept the ball — the play that had given Trousdale fits until their coaches finally adjusted — the Pirates suckered the defense to commit to coming up on Hutchins, who flipped the ball to Green on a reverse.

Green slipped past two Trousdale tacklers before cutting back across the field, where he was knocked off balance from behind before somehow managing to regain his balance just long enough to outrace a pair of defenders 16 yards to the corner of the end zone with just 3:06 remaining. Before he could get back to his feet to celebrate Green was swamped by teammates in a dogpile.

"I felt like there were more than 11 guys out there trying to get their hands on me," Green joked afterward. "I think a few guys came off their sideline and chased me for a while. There was no way I was going down unless somebody wrapped me up good."

Tipton, who ran for 155 yards and had been the big-play threat all season, shook his head and marveled at his tiny teammate's massive play.

"I think somebody must have sneezed real hard and blown him across the goal line," Tipton said with a laugh. "It was real easy to get caught up watching him run and forget to block downfield.

"As little as he is, there should have been somebody who could have knocked him down but that just shows you what heart will do for you."

As he stood in the center of the locker room, arms raised to calm the noisy celebration, Wilson reminded his team that while the 35-23 win was sweet revenge, all it had really done was keep their title hopes alive for one more week.

"Let me make this very clear," Wilson said. "That was not the state championship game tonight. It was just one more rung on the latter we're climbing. We've still got one more to get what we've wanted."

"WE DID IT"

While most everybody else in town had worked themselves into a salty lather worrying over the state championship game, senior lineman Wesley Stone had even more on his plate. His girlfriend at the time, Glenna Hibbs — who would later become his wife and have a family of four boys — was expecting their first baby.

"I was hoping Glenna didn't go into labor during the Trousdale game or the state game," Stone said later. "I worried all week. I told her 'if you go into labor, the game only lasts a couple of hours so by the time you get checked into the hospital, I'll be there after the game.'"

Fortunately the couple's first child had the good sense to wait until after the season before deciding it was time to come into the world.

Danny Wilson won a title in his second year as coach.

The rest of South Pittsburg wasn't willing to wait any longer on the precious prize they were expecting.

"There's really only one thing we've worked for or thought about for more than a year, and that's getting our hands on the gold trophy and bringing it back with us," Hutchins said before the team began its last week of practice to prepare for its match-up with Lake County for the 1A championship.

A crowd of more than 7,000, including many from Jasper who came a day early to support the Pirates before cheering on their Warriors the next day, braved the cold, constant drizzle and swirling icy winds that made Vanderbilt's Dudley Field a bowl of misery.

Hoping to draw a bit of favor from the football gods, South Pittsburg — designated to be the visiting team — wore black pants with its white road jerseys, a similar uniform combination worn by the 1969 title team. But the biggest tip of the cap to their heritage was the bruising style the Pirates played on both sides of the ball that evening.

Pirates linebacker Kevin Case.

In the days leading up to the game, Lake County coach Tim Stallings had heard enough about how physical South Pittsburg was, telling the Nashville Tennessean in its game preview, "We're a power football team. We'll run the ball until somebody stops us. People who have never seen us play don't realize how good we are. We get after folks too."

The Falcons, in their green jerseys and

gold pants, would rely on senior tailback Jewel Flowers, who led the state in rushing with seven games of 200-plus yards, and a stingy defense that hadn't given up more than 14 points in the playoffs.

It was that defense that got the game's initial big play, intercepting Hutchins on the first series of the game. But the Pirates countered when, on third down, Lake County quarterback Michael Crawford was forced to scramble to his right before throwing back across the field, where middle linebacker Michael Grider made a diving interception at midfield.

Not wanting to squander such good field position South Pittsburg refused to put the ball back in the air, instead relying on the experience of its offensive line and the legs of Hutchins and Tipton. Hutchins kept the drive alive with a 15-yard option keeper to convert third and 12, but it was Tipton who carried the ball on eight of the 10 snaps, including a six-yard scoring run off right tackle.

Looking to answer, the Falcons put together an impressive drive before Marcus Banks delivered a wicked hit on Flowers, forcing a fumble that the alert Grider immediately pounced on at the Pirates 33.

But the Pirates failed to capitalize on the second turnover when, on third down, Tipton slipped as he tried to cut back across the field and was stopped short of picking up a first down he likely would have gained had he just continued running straight ahead instead of trying to avoid contact. As he trotted off the field with his head down, Tipton was met on the sideline by an aggravated Wilson.

"Did you bring the right cleats?" Wilson asked.

"Yeah," Tipton managed.

"What about your nuts? Did you bring them?" Wilson fired back. "Quit dancing and run the damn ball!"

The first-half irritation continued for the Pirates, who failed to score again despite starting two drives inside the Falcons 40. Hutchins had a 25-yard scoring run called back for clipping and John Bonner's 29-yard field goal attempt just before halftime was blocked, keeping South Pittsburg's lead at an uneasy 7-0.

The first play of the second half proved just how shaky that lead was when Flowers took the handoff on a counter to the right, zipped past the line and sprinted 75 yards, untouched, for a touchdown, waving at the Lake County crowd from the five yard line until he cross the goal line.

With the game suddenly tied, and starting from its own 20, Wilson gathered his offense around him on the sideline and got straight to the point before sending them onto the field.

"We're just gonna line up and come right at 'em. If we're going to win, it's going to come the same way we've won all year."

What followed was an 11-play drive that chewed up chunks of yardage as well as the clock. On ten of those snaps the Pirates ran the exact same play — 46 — a power run off right tackle with Tipton carrying the ball.

"I kept thinking we might need to change this up and run to the left," Wilson would say later. "We tried it to the left once but only gained about two yards, so we didn't do that again."

The rain and fog that moved back over the field obscured the Nashville skyline outside the stadium and caused the temperature to drop so much that as the Pirates offensive linemen leaned forward in their stance, their breath billowed in huge puffs of smoke from their face masks.

The group continued to surge, pushing the Falcons front seven backward and giving Tipton enough room to choose a hole and do yeoman work.

Although Lake County had enough defensive speed to recover from the initial blocks and prevent Tipton from ripping off one of his customary game-breakers for a while, eventually there was simply too much talent to keep him from breaking free.

And like a pretty girl in a tight sweater, Tipton had the goods to make you notice quickly, and maybe even do a double-take.

On his 10th carry of the drive, Tipton began off right tackle, cut left inside the pursuit before breaking a tackle near the five and outrunning the safety 19 yards to the left corner of the end zone. Growing up competing against older boys Tipton had learned to swivel his hips, cut back at an angle that would avoid contact and most importantly run faster than whoever was chasing him.

"He's one of the prettiest runners you'll see," Wilson praised later. "He has a knack of seeing the field, and no matter which way the defender comes at him, he can shift away and be gone before you know it."

However Lake County, which had two state titles to its program's credit including one in 1985 over the Pirates, fought back and looked to even the score again. The Falcons converted two third downs in moving the ball to the Pirates six before facing fourth and three. A toss sweep to Flowers to the right looked for a moment to be the right call until Vincent Banks side-stepped a blocker and wrapped up the runner by the legs after a gain of just one.

Again Lake County would threaten in the closing minutes, reaching the South Pittsburg 31 before failing to gain an inch on consecutive plays, setting up another fourth down decision. Needing nine yards to keep their hopes alive this time, Crawford dropped back to survey the field, but the pocket around him collapsed quickly as Brandon Chance and Jarrod Cardin combined to knock him off balance before Daniel Berryhill rushed in to finish off the Falcons quarterback, planting him into the turf for a 15-yard loss.

Linebacker Michael Grider had his best game in the championship.

After taking over on downs for a second time in the final quarter — this time with more room to operate — the Pirates ran the ball eight straight times to bleed the clock dry.

On third and one at the Lake County 43, Tipton gained 10 yards, again off right tackle.

From high above the field in the press box, where he was filming the game for South Pittsburg's coaches, Hoodie Dunwoody could no longer contain his excitement.

"All of a sudden it's not as cold up here," he gushed. "Isn't this great? Oh wow!"

Back down on the field, needing one more first down to exhaust the clock, Hutchins faked to Tipton, rolled to his right and gained six yards to the Lake County 20 with just over a minute to go.

Sensing the outcome had finally been decided, Pirates players began waving their arms up and down to the crowd, asking for more noise.

Realizing the Falcons had no more timeouts to stop the clock, Baxter looked down the sideline and said to nobody in particular, "Hey boys, we're the state champions!"

Hutchins made it official by taking a snap with six seconds remaining and kneeling on the ball. The field flooded almost immediately with players from the sideline, cheerleaders and even a few fans who somehow snuck past security to hug sons and nephews on the turf.

"This was smash-mouth football," Stone told a reporter. "We knew if we couldn't run off tackle, we couldn't win. We came right at them."

Besides scoring both touchdowns for the Pirates, Tipton had finished with a a career-high 34 carries for 208 yards, including all but five of the 80 on the drive that gave his team the lead for good and earned offensive MVP honors.

His night's work gave him 2,130 yards for the season, a record that stood for more than a decade, and he would add another 2,000 the following season as a senior.

The Pirates had rolled through the season outscoring opponents by an average of 42-7 and a record six players were named all-state: Tipton, Hutchins, Green, Cardin, Berryhill and Vincent Banks, who was also a Mr. Football finalist.

"We'll celebrate this one and then support Jasper tomorrow," Banks said as he left the field. "It's like one big family in our county except when we play each other. Then it's just like a family feud."

Both Banks brothers and fellow linebacker Michael Grider all finished with five solo tackles and Grider also added an interception and fumble recovery.

"We had a lot of kids step up. But the one who stepped up biggest was Michael Grider," Wilson said. "Our offensive line controlled the line of scrimmage and Corey had a great game, but we won this game with defense."

Pirates running back Corey Tipton cuts back to avoid the defense.

With the giant scoreboard flashing the 14-7 final behind them, South Pittsburg's players and coaches posed for a team picture with the gold ball trophy reflecting the stadium lights shining down. While the rest of the team stood and began making their way toward the warmth of the locker room, Michael Grider remained on one knee, wiping the rain from his face with a white towel.

Baxter stopped to pat the burly senior on the shoulder pads and said, "Hell of a job, son."

"Thank you coach," Grider answered as he looked up smiling.

As Baxter walked away slowly, Grider continued soaking in the moment until a Chattanooga reporter knelt next to him to begin an interview.

"I'm sorry, I'm just too tired to stand up right now," Grider said with a sigh. "Give me a second."

Nodding toward his teammates who had stopped along their sideline to celebrate with the fans, Grider pumped his fist and said simply, "We did it."

SOUTH PITTSBURG 1994 RESULTS

Sept. 2	Marion County	0-6
Sept. 9	at Vonore	48-0
Sept. 16	at Grundy County	48-17
Sept. 24	at Greenback	31-14
Sept. 30	Whitwell	56-0
Oct. 7	Midway	42-0
Oct. 14	at Lookout Valley	50-6
Oct. 21	Boyd-Buchanan	49-0
Oct. 28	Copper Basin	55-0
Nov. 4	at Charleston	49-14

Playoffs

Nov. 11	Unaka	54-6
Nov. 18	DCA	32-10
Nov. 25	Coalfield	63-6
Dec. 2	at Trousdale County	35-23

State championship

| Dec. 9 | Lake County (at Vanderbilt) | 14-7 |

1994 Pirates

Players: Perry Hutchins, John Bonner, Michael McCarver, Pres Holder, Kevin Case, Tony Jenkins, Courtney Gaines, Jason Gomez,

Bradley "Macho" Green, Corey Tipton, Nathaniel Beavers, Michael Daniels, Tommy Rector, Jeremy Scott, Bradley Reed, Tyrone Green, Brandon Chance, Daniel Berryhill, Eric Scott, Jeremy Willis, Vincent Banks, Marcus Banks, David Warren, Will Watkins, Jason Bryan, Brandon Price, Jarrod Cardin, Wesley Stone, Ernie Cagle, Trey Cantrell, William Gray, Brandon Wilkerson, Michael Grider, Paul O'Leary, Roger Mayfield.

Coaches: Danny Wilson, Vic Grider, Dave Baxter, Jon Lovingood.

Chapter 18
1995 WARRIORS

*"Don't talk, just act
Don't say, just show
Don't promise, just prove."*

— **Unknown**

He had made similar drives into small towns on countless other Friday nights; it came with the job of being a college football coach. Steve Caldwell not only understood recruiting was the lifeblood of maintaining a winning program, he actually enjoyed the occasional road trip, seeing it as a chance to get away and watch the game he loved at its purest form.

As Caldwell, a University of Tennessee assistant with a keen eye for spotting high school talent, turned off Interstate 24 and slowly drove into Jasper — storefronts around the courthouse square decorated with spirit signs and purple flags hanging from the polls that lined the roadway leading to the school — he realized his surroundings were different, more unique than many of the other places he had visited.

He was there on a chilly November evening in 1995 to watch Eric Westmoreland, Marion County's gifted senior who seemed to have a knack for always being the best player on the field, regardless of whether he was playing running back, safety or returning kicks.

After parking outside the stadium, Caldwell strolled onto the field to watch warmups, pausing for a moment to shake hands with a couple of Chattanooga sports writers and comment on the atmosphere that had caught his attention.

"I've always heard about this place," Caldwell began. "It sure does have to be intimidating for opposing teams coming through town to see the way everybody makes such a big deal over the team.

"This is what high school football is all about."

BULLIES OF THE VALLEY

Seven points separated Marion County from a legitimate shot at an unheard of run of five consecutive state championships to begin the 1990s. Sandwiched between the Warriors titles in 1990, 92 and 94 were a six-point quarterfinal loss at Rockwood in 1991, when a late drive was stopped near the goal line, and a one-point heartbreaker at Kingston when a two-point conversion attempt failed and another late drive was stopped inside the two.

Otherwise, opposing coaches had likely developed facial tics from staring at film and trying to figure a way to slow the Warriors.

"There were times in those years where we not only didn't think about losing, we were upset if we weren't beating teams by 40 points,"

Josh Dobson tries to break a tackle.

said all-state running back and defensive back Anthony Martin, a senior on the '95 team. "To us we were suppose to be kicking your ass."

Marion's '94 title team had been so unstoppable — outscoring opponents by an average of 38 points and having just one opponent stay within four touchdowns — that the Chattanooga media nicknamed the Warriors "Bullies of the Valley".

The by-product of the program's success was that head coach Ken Colquette couldn't find anyone willing to schedule the Warriors. At least not in their own classification. Needing four non-region games to fill the schedule — rival South Pittsburg was the only team not in a larger classification willing to continue playing Marion — Colquette was forced to put together a brutal run of four state-ranked opponents from larger classifications, and three of those would be on the road.

"It wasn't like I was trying to prove a point at first," Colquette said. "We just didn't have anybody else who would play us. It was either play all those bigger teams or not have a full schedule.

"The biggest worry was getting some of our guys hurt and not being full-strength for the playoffs. But I think our kids took it as a challenge and decided they were going to raise their level."

Although Marion had knocked off nationally ranked Brentwood Academy in the 1992 state championship, there remained skeptics who believed the Warriors were simply beating up on small-school competition. If they could hold their own against the likes of 5A's Soddy-Daisy and Rhea County and 4A foes Baylor and Shelbyville, those doubts would be put to rest and the Jasper juggernaut would be validated.

"I was glad we had bumped up our schedule because most of those schools were from the Chattanooga area and I wanted to play them in front of a big crowd to show how good we were," Westmoreland said. "We had heard people say we couldn't compete with the private schools or the bigger schools and how we would probably finish 5-5 with that schedule.

"We heard all of it. And we just kept working to be ready."

Josh Dobson calls a play at the line.

When the page turned from summer workouts — those dreadful days of lifting weights and seemingly endless sprints — to practicing in pads, the coaching staff knew they had the foundation for something special. But the process would not be easy.

Before the Warriors stepped on the practice field for the first time in early August, Colquette stood in front of them and set the tone for what was to come.

"Are y'all satisfied?" he asked rhetorically. "You can sit back and enjoy last year, but if you do that we'll be done in the playoffs. We've got a chance to do something no other team has done here. We can win back-to-back championships."

Two hours later, as players unbuckled shoulder pads and removed helmets hoping to catch even a hint of a reprieve from the heat as they walked off the practice field, Colquette lagged behind. He paused to slip the towel off his shoulder and wipe sweat from his face before summing up what he had seen.

"We couldn't beat the cheerleaders right now," he said solemnly. "People in town are telling them how good they are and I'm telling them how bad they are. Eventually we'll find out which one of us is right."

CIRCUS COMES TO TOWN

On the last weekend in August, the day after Microsoft released Windows 95, the Warriors opened their season at home against rival South Pittsburg in a game that marked the first time in state history two defending state champions kicked off a season against each other.

The Pirates, who would go on to win 12 games and reach the 1A semifinals, were simply no match for Marion, which raced out to a 28-0 lead and had 230 more rushing yards by halftime.

Westmoreland didn't touch the ball for the first seven minutes, but went 65 yards on his first carry to set up a 1-yard TD. He would finish with an effortless 130 yards on 11 carries, while quarterback Josh Dobson ran for 100 yards, including a 58-yard scoring run on the third play from scrimmage.

"I'm built more like a guard than a quarterback," Dobson joked afterward. "The coaches rag me a lot, so I was thinking 'Please God, just let me score this one time so they will quit ragging me.'"

The Pirates failed to gain a first down until early in the fourth quarter as Marion out-gained them 304-80.

A pedestrian 21-point win over McMinn Central followed, where Westmoreland, Dobson and Terry Smith each ran for more than 100 yards.

Marion's first test against its amped-up schedule came in week three at Baylor, marking the first time since 1939 the teams had met. The opening line in the Chattanooga Times preview story in Friday morning's edition read, "Marion brings its high school football act to the city."

"We had been so good for so long that we had built a following and had a lot of other people in Chattanooga who were finally getting the chance to see us play since we hadn't really played many teams in the city before that night," Westmoreland said. "It was like the circus coming to town. When we walked on the field, there was a huge crowd and I remember seeing people my parents worked with in Chattanooga and my cousins from there waiting to see us.

"You wanted to put on a show and prove that we were as good as advertised."

Westmoreland had scoring runs of 80 and 8 yards, and he and Anthony Martin each had an interception on defense. Martin's came late in the first half when he picked off a pass in the end zone to end a Baylor scoring threat.

For the first time since becoming the starter Dobson, who had attended Baylor briefly before returning to Marion, struggled for much of the first half.

"I think he was trying too hard to beat some of his old buddies," Colquette said later. "He played one of his worst games that night. I told him in the second half I was going to give him one more series to get going before I pulled him."

Although Baylor had managed just two long field goals through three quarters, Marion mistakes kept the Red Raiders within striking distance and with only 1:18 remaining quarterback Kurt Keene, an all-state baseball pitcher, looked to make a play. As Keene scrambled Anthony Martin came up to make the tackle, leaving receiver Chris Whitis wide open and Keene hit him in stride for a 62-yard touchdown pass. Jason Green added the two-point conversion run to tie the game and the overflow crowd at Heywood Stadium prepared for overtime.

"I was afraid to go to the sideline because I knew Coach Colquette would be on me," Martin said after the game. "I messed up on the coverage. I should have stayed man-to-man, but I thought their quarterback crossed the line of scrimmage. I take total blame for that touchdown."

Once he reached the sideline, Martin was met by his coach, who poked his finger into Martin's chest and said, "That one's on you! Now go out there and make up for it."

Marion ran two plays, then called timeout so the coaches could discuss whether to take a knee on third down and play for overtime or try to throw the ball downfield and hope. Dobson had attempted just 74 passes in 15 games the season before, and while he was the ideal option quarterback in the veer, deep throws were not his strength.

"The coaches were talking about just playing for overtime," Westmoreland said. "But all us players wanted to run one more play. Somebody in the huddle said we should try the halfback pass. We had practiced it, but never really ran it before.

"Coach Colquette asked Anthony if he could get open and Anthony nodded, then Coach looked at me and asked if I could make the throw. I looked at Anthony and said 'Just run as fast and as far as you can and I'll throw it.'

Marion County's defense gang tackles a runner.

"Once I got the pitch, I just threw the ball as far as I could in his direction before getting hit. I never saw him catch it."

At the snap Dobson and Westmoreland rolled to their right and Dobson quickly shuffled the pitch into Westmoreland's hands. Martin sprinted along the sideline, never looking back until he had flown past the secondary, and Westmoreland planted his foot in the ground and heaved a spiral as far as he could, connecting with Martin who crossed the goal line with the 65-yard game-winner with just 15 seconds left on the clock.

"When coach called the play I said 'God, please don't let me drop it'," Martin said. "I didn't and I redeemed myself. If I hadn't, I probably would have had to walk home and I probably woulda been sleeping on the couch."

Marion had nearly doubled Baylor in total yards to claim its 18th consecutive win. Beating a state-ranked 4A team that would go on to reach the state quarterfinals also quieted most of the questions about whether the Warriors could play with bigger programs.

"After that win we felt invincible," added Westmoreland, who ran for 142 yards on 12 carries. "We had just beaten a very solid team so it felt like that was the start of a journey toward something great."

The next week Marion clobbered City High 48-0 without attempting a single pass. Westmoreland ran for 227 yards and four TDs as the Warriors out-rushed the Dynamos 423-38.

A steady evening drizzle did nothing to dampen the excitement for Marion's mid-season trip to Soddy-Daisy, a team ranked among the state's best in 5A and led by 230-pound all-state running back Jarvis Smith, who stood just behind Westmoreland among the Chattanooga area's leading rushers.

"Coach Colquette always called me 'five'," Westmoreland said. "All that week in practice leading up to the game he kept saying 'Five, if you can't tackle this guy then you can't play in college. I doubt you can because everybody says he's better than you.'

"I was pretty pissed off about hearing that all week and thinking there were people out there who thought he was better than me. I felt like I was the best player on the field on both sides of the ball and I had to go out and show that."

One of the largest crowds to pack a Hamilton County high school stadium filled every nook and cranny, even overflowing onto the hill that overlooks Soddy-Daisy's field.

"I looked around before kickoff and it looked like ants up on the hillside," Colquette said. "The stands had been full since an hour before the game and there was nowhere for anybody else to stand along the track.

"It was two dang good teams and two really good players about to go at it. If you can't get up for a game in that type atmosphere you better find something else to do."

Bill Price, who had quarterbacked Red Bank to a state championship game in the late 1970s, had returned to Chattanooga and built a Soddy-Daisy program that had never reached the playoffs into not only one of the city's top teams, but also one that could play with anybody in the state. A year earlier Smith had become the Trojans first 1,000-yard rusher and had college coaches drooling over his size and strength as a ballcarrier.

The Trojans' only loss had been by one point at Shelbyville, which was ranked No. 3 in 4A, and Marion brought a 41-game regular-season win streak into the showdown, the first meeting between the two schools in more than 50 years.

Soddy-Daisy scored first, then held Marion on downs and had a chance to put the visitors on their heels. However the Warriors defense got a stop of their own to force a punt.

Gary Partrick, who had been Price's main target during their high school days together at Red Bank, was a Trojans assistant and worried that Marion's special teams speed could take back momentum in a flash. Walking toward Price as the Trojans punt team trotted onto the field, Partrick called out to his friend.

"Bill, punt the ball out of bounds. Don't give Westmoreland a chance to return this punt!"

Price either didn't hear the advice or ignored it and elected to punt the ball deep. Westmoreland drifted back 10 yards as he tracked the flight of the ball, then fielded the kick, juked to the left to let the initial wave of defenders race past him, cut back to his right and sprinted 74 yards for a touchdown that did exactly what Partrick had feared — shifting momentum squarely onto the visitor's sideline despite Marion missing the extra point and still trailing 7-6.

"I didn't think they would actually kick it to us, but I was really glad when I saw the ball coming in my direction," Westmoreland said. "We needed a big play to get things going for us and that's all I was trying to do. All of a sudden our crowd was back into the game and we started to feel pretty good about ourselves."

The good vibes were slowly drained as Soddy-Daisy countered with another touchdown to extend its lead to 14-6, and then, on the fifth play of the second quarter, Dobson limped to the sideline with a badly bruised shoulder. He would not return, leaving the game in the hands of junior backup Gavin Thomasson, whose cousin Shane had led Marion to its first state title in 1990.

"You could tell in the huddle he was scared shitless," Westmoreland said. "Who could blame him? He didn't expect to play and now he was going to have to go the rest of the way against a really good team and with one of the biggest crowds we had ever seen watching.

"I told him no matter what happens, when we run option, just pitch it to me and I'll make a play."

After the Warriors offense stalled, sensing the need for their special teams to make another play, Colquette called for a fake punt and Martin found an opening that gave his team a fresh set of downs. Westmoreland capped the drive with a nine-yard scoring run and Thomasson added the two-point conversion to tie the game. By halftime, Marion had pulled ahead 20-14.

"I was a bundle of nerves until my fourth play," Thomasson said later. "That was how long it took me to figure out they were keying on me and not taking the backs on our outside veer. I knew I would have to take some hits, but I had to make the pitch and let our backs do what they do."

Eric Westmoreland breaks a Baylor tackle.

The Trojans rallied in the third quarter when quarterback Danny Williams hit Smith on a perfectly executed screen pass that converted a third-and-18 into a 32-yard touchdown that tied the game.

"Being who we were and who our coach was, at the end of the day our mindset back then was, who's going to stop us?" Westmoreland said.

Thomasson connected with Martin on a 36-yard pass to the Trojans four, but on the next play the inexperienced quarterback made his first mistake, losing a fumble that cost his team a chance to retake the lead.

But after another defensive stop, Marion's offense turned to Westmoreland late in the third and he delivered with a 38-yard scoring run to put the Warriors back up 26-20.

It appeared as if the back-and-forth would continue as Soddy-Daisy drove to the Marion 25, and Smith rounded the corner on a sweep with nobody between him and the goal line besides Westmoreland coming up from his safety position. With his coach's taunts still in the back of his mind, Westmoreland wrapped up Smith for a short gain and the threat ended when Les Thomas sacked Williams with just over three minutes left.

Needing one first down to run out the clock, Westmoreland stepped out of a foothold at the line on third and five, and broke free for a 39-yard gain with 43 seconds remaining.

During Soddy-Daisy's final timeout, Colquette called Thomasson over to the sideline and demonstrated exactly what he wanted.

"Take the snap, take two steps back, hit a knee and let's get the hell out of here," Colquette instructed.

Westmoreland finished his night's work with 143 yards on 14 carries with three rushing TDs and another on a punt return. He also made 11 solo tackles, while Smith ended with 127 rushing yards and caught a TD pass.

"Everybody wanted to compare Jarvis to Eric," Colquette said afterward. "But, hell, Eric played offense, defense and on kickoffs and punts. Their big kid is a tough runner, but I'll take our guy.

"This was one of the best high school games I've ever been a part of, but it's going to take us all night to get out of here with all these people."

Surrounded by media, Westmoreland answered questions as he got pats on the back from fans of both teams.

"We shouldn't feel like we have to prove anything with three state championships in five years, but people in Chattanooga were still not convinced," Westmoreland said. "They should be by now.

"We've heard a lot of talk about how we don't play anybody. Well, we've come over here and beaten Baylor and now Soddy-Daisy, so I hope this stops all that talk. This team can play with anybody. Classifications don't matter."

A third trip to Chattanooga in four weeks was for a region battle with a Tyner team that was 4-1 and also ranked in the state. Proof that the players and students had embraced the program's new nickname, cheerleaders held up a run-through sign that proclaimed, "We're not just Bullies of the Valley, we're Bullies of the state!"

Martin and Westmoreland ran the Rams ragged, combining for 556 all-purpose yards. Martin, who had played receiver, was moved to running back because of injuries in the Warriors backfield and finished with 172 rushing yards, returned a punt 90 yards for a score, intercepted two passes and recovered a fumble as Marion scored 36 points in the second quarter alone.

"If I had missed the holes out there I would've been blind," Martin joked.

Marion ran for 459 yards and held Tyner to just 82 as Terry Smith, Stephen Dover and Brad Holden all sacked Rams all-city quarterback Jackie Buttram.

Three days after much of the nation had tuned in to the O.J. Simpson verdict — and were stunned to hear him declared not guilty of double homicide — Marion was back home to host 5A Rhea County.

Martin continued to show he was adjusting fine to his new role, rushing for 69 of the team's 75 yards on Marion's opening drive, including a 26-yard touchdown, and had 113 yards by halftime as Marion built a 24-7 lead. Once Rhea County's defense shifted its focus to him, Westmoreland took his turn for a big second half, gaining 100 yards on just eight carries in the final two quarters.

Defensively, Jason Saylors controlled things up front as Marion held the Golden Eagles to just 47 rushing yards.

The Martin and Westmorland show continued the next week as both players again ran for more than 100 yards in a 52-15 shellacking of Sequoyah.

The final test before the playoffs came at Shelbyville, the unbeaten and third-ranked team in 4A. On the Tuesday before the game Westmoreland strained his calf muscle and it was questionable how effective he would be. He spent the rest of the week icing his calf and doing nothing more than light stretching as he hoped to be well enough to somehow help by game night.

By the time the adrenaline started pumping during pregame warmups, Westmoreland assured coaches that he was good to go.

Dobson made his return from the shoulder injury that had sidelined him since the first half at Soddy-Daisy and tossed a short pass to Westmoreland, who took it 54 yards for an early touchdown. Shelbyville's trailing defenders quickly found out that even with a hitch in his giddy-up, Westmoreland was just at another level.

Martin continued a smooth transition to running back with his fourth straight game of more than 100 rushing yards and Marion's defense held Shelbyville to just 50 yards on the ground and also blocked a short field goal attempt.

Eric Westmoreland is off to the races against Soddy-Daisy.

With the game tied at 14 in the final two minutes, Westmoreland broke loose on a 55-yard TD run that wound up being the game-winner after the Warriors forced their second turnover on the Eagles final drive. Despite being iffy before the game, Westmoreland finished with 149 total yards and scored all three Marion touchdowns.

"Shelbyville had athletes all over the field, pretty much at every position," Colquette said. "But they didn't have anybody like No. 5."

Although the starters rested the entire second half of the regular-season finale against Grundy County, Westmoreland put in enough work to finish tied with South Pittsburg tailback Corey Tipton for the state lead in points scored — both with 31 touchdowns and five two-point conversions.

Once the playoffs began, despite the nagging calf injury to Westmoreland and Dobson's sore shoulder, it was clear that the decision to move Martin into the backfield — giving the team two runners with game-breaking speed — was the final piece needed to make Marion's offense virtually unstoppable.

PUTTING ON A SHOW

Lenoir City would not be the typical first-round sacrificial lamb opponent because of all-state running back Travis Adams, who entered the game as one of the state's leading rushers with more than 1,700 yards.

On the second play of the game, the shifty 5-10, 180-pounder lived up to his billing, breaking loose for a 63-yard touchdown run. The Panthers relied almost exclusively on Adams in the first half as Marion struggled to bring him down. He added a 52-yard run off right tackle to put Lenoir City ahead 20-16, their third lead of the first half, and he ended the first half with 17 carries for 217 yards.

Marion countered with a drive just before the half, capped by Westmoreland's six-yard scoring run to edge ahead 24-20 at halftime, but a frustrated Colquette knew he had to get his team's attention and wake them up from their sluggish start.

As players were still filing into the field house, Colquette stood in the doorway between the locker room and coaches office and lit into them.

"If y'all don't want to play another game this year, just keep playing like you did in the first half!" he said, his voice rising louder than usual. "You ain't tackling worth a dime. You're getting your butts whipped and you act like you don't even care.

"Keep it up and you'll watch them walk out of here with your dang season."

Properly motivated and refocused, Marion went right to work in putting the Panthers in their rearview mirror. It took just three plays before Martin busted free for a 48-yard touchdown and, after stuffing Lenoir

City for negative yards on three plays, Lebron Pickett capped another scoring drive with a nine-yard run that allowed the Marion fans to breath a little easier at last.

A 96-yard scoring drive, which chewed up nearly half the fourth quarter and ended with a 22-yard TD run by Westmoreland, was the final statement of a dominant second half.

In shutting out the Panthers over the final two quarters, Marion held Adams to 34 yards on eight second half carries and gave up just 47 total yards. Westmoreland gained yards in bunches, averaging 21 per carry and finishing with 271, while Martin added 130.

"Our guys finally got sick of getting run over and came out to do something about it," a relieved Colquette said afterward.

A second-round visit from Knox Fulton turned into the exact opposite of the previous week's first-half struggle as Marion averaged scoring a touchdown on every fifth play in a 65-8 demolition.

Martin scored the Warriors first two touchdowns, Dobson added the next two, including a 67-yard sprint in the rain, and Westmoreland and Martin then took turns pouring on the points before Fulton finally avoided the shutout. Marion's backfield trio all finished with more than 100 yards and Westmoreland walked off the field having compiled exactly 6,000 career yards. The Warriors out-gained Fulton 502-151 in total yards, and went over the 4,000-yard rushing mark for the season.

It was the most points scored by a Colquette-coached team and was Marion's 38th straight win at home, a streak that dated back to 1990.

The following week the Chattanooga Times released its Elite 11, a list of the top prospects in Tennessee, and Westmoreland — who had 1,946 rushing yards with 34 TDs, plus 78 tackles, three interceptions and two punts returned for TDs at that point — was included.

On the weekend that Disney released Toy Story — the first full-length computer animated feature film — Marion fans all had to find a moving buddy and get comfortable for a nearly four-hour trip to the Virginia border and a quarterfinal match-up at frigid Sullivan North.

Opposing defenses had been forced to pick their poison with both Westmoreland and Martin running wild, and the Golden Raiders chose to focus on gang-tackling Westmoreland, even when he didn't have the ball.

"They were taking away a lot of our regular plays that we usually had success with, but once we adjusted in the second half we started moving the ball in big chunks," Colquette said. "There was one play where we faked to Eric and ran a cross-buck to Anthony and he could have walked in for the touchdown because all 11 tacklers were piling on Eric."

The Raiders' plan worked for a half as they stripped Westmoreland of the ball twice and held a 7-6 advantage at halftime.

Marion opened the second half with a methodical 13-play, 79-yard drive capped by Westmoreland's one-yard dive into the end zone.

Determined to make up for his first-half mistakes, Westmoreland then intercepted a pass on the Raiders first play of the second half, setting up a 10-play drive that ended with Martin's eight-yard scoring run on the final play of the third quarter.

The frustration of having the ball for only one play in the third was compounded early in the fourth when the Raiders had a scoring threat end on Westmoreland's second interception of the half, at the Warriors three yard line.

Marion's offense failed to gain a first down, but facing fourth and four from its nine, as Martin took the snap and noticed every Raiders player peeling back to set up a return, he took off and gained 19 yards on the fake. A late hit moved the ball near midfield.

"I had an agreement with Anthony on punts that if he thought he could get the first down he had the green light to go," Colquette said later. "When he took the snap and took off, I was yelling 'what the hell are you doing?!?'

"Then I saw he had an open lane and I got excited and said 'Go son!' I never intended for him to ever fake one from our own goal line, but since it worked I'll take credit for that call."

The fake eventually resulted in Dobson's short TD run with 5:09 remaining, putting the game away. Dobson, who had just 12 yards at halftime, led the team with 129 as the Warriors gained 215 of their 299 rushing yards in the second half and held Sullivan North to 51 total yards in the deciding final two quarters.

A rematch from their regular-season win over McMinn Central awaited the Warriors in the semifinals. With the chance to return and defend their championship on the line, they jumped on the Chargers from the start and eliminated any thought of drama.

McMinn Central managed just 79 total yards in the first half as Marion took a 28-7 lead into halftime that eventually swelled to 41-7.

The one-two punch of Westmoreland and Martin combined for 341 yards as Marion rolled up 448 rushing yards.

"Our defense was outstanding in the first half but the second half was awful," said Colquette, as he shivered from the icy Gatorade shower his players had given him in the closing seconds. The Chargers had closed the gap to 41-29 in the final minutes before Westmoreland added his third TD of the night to alleviate his coach's concern and assure the Warriors of their fourth trip to the title game in six years.

"I GUESS YOU CAN CALL IT TRADITION"

The 3A championship was nearly a rematch of the previous season, but Humboldt held off Portland 21-20 in the semifinals to give Marion a different opponent to prepare for. The Vikings were led by Mr. Football running back finalist Kelcey Williams and future UT offensive lineman Toby Champion (6-5, 285). They also were coached by John Tucker, who led the state in number of wins at the time.

On a sun-splashed December Saturday afternoon at Vanderbilt's Dudley Field, a Warriors team that began the season having to add four teams from larger classifications because no one else would play them, needed just one more win to cap an incredible run with their second straight title.

Champion dominated the first series, bulldozing his way through the Marion line for a pair of tackles in the backfield. But on their second possession the Warriors — wearing their all-purple home uniforms for the first time in their run of title games — were able to get Westmoreland on the edge, allowing him to break loose for a 54-yard gain before being caught at the Humboldt 26. Five plays later, Westmoreland finished what he started by diving into the end zone from a yard out. The two-point try failed, but after stopping the Vikings on a fourth-and-two at the Warriors 28 midway through the second quarter, Marion made the 6-0 lead hold up going into halftime.

The Vikings opened the second half with a nine-play, 68-yard drive, capped by a six-yard TD run from Williams, and the extra point made it 7-6.

Unable to answer that score, Marion got a huge special teams play from Martin, whose 59-yard punt pinned Humboldt back at its

Anthony Martin stiff arms a defender.

three yard line. Two plays later, senior lineman Terry Smith came crashing through the right side of Humboldt's line to drop running back Maurice Jelks in the end zone for a safety and an 8-7 lead.

Trying to counter punch, Humboldt needed just inches on fourth down to continue a drive into Marion territory but Williams was stuffed for a loss by Warriors linebacker Stephen Dover, who was later named the game's Defensive MVP for making 12 solo tackles and six assists.

On its next series, Humboldt again drove into scoring position, but after a 12-yard run to Marion's 28, Williams was caught from behind and stripped of the ball by Westmoreland.

Having dodged bullets on the last two defensive series, Marion's offense fired a shot of its own. Dobson flipped a late pitch to Westmoreland, who lowered his head to break one tackle, then took off for a momentum-shifting 53-yard TD run. Pickett's two-point conversion run made it a two-score lead at 16-7 with 8:20 to go.

On two previous kickoffs Marion came close to recovering squib kicks, and when it was needed most James Patrick came up with the ball on a short, bouncing kickoff that ricocheted off a Humboldt player. That allowed Marion to use up another four minutes off the clock before Martin ended the drive with a five-yard TD run.

Pickett put the finishing touches on the team's 30th straight win when he picked off a screen pass and took it back 54 yards for the Warriors third score of the fourth quarter.

The cheer began with 36 seconds left on the clock from high above Dudley Field and made its way down, flooding over the field. The familiar chant of "We're number one!" rang from the packed home side, filled with folks proudly wearing their purple and white.

Once the final seconds ticked off the clock, for the fourth time in six years, and second straight season, Marion had claimed the state championship.

"Look at the crowd," Martin said as his teammates celebrated around him. "It looks like the whole town came out and brought all their friends with 'em."

Westmoreland, who accounted for 153 of Marion's 226 rushing total, was named Offensive MVP for a second consecutive year. He was also in on 12 tackles defensively.

"This is the way Marion County is supposed to end its season, every year," he said as he walked off the field waving at a section of fans chanting his name.

He, along with Martin, Dover and center Matt Clark all earned all-state honors. Colquette was later named the Lawrenceburg Quarterback Club's state Coach of the Year and Westmoreland, who averaged 13 yards per carry in finishing with 2,359 yards and 40 TDs, earned state Player of the Year honors to go along with his Mr. Football award.

"If you play in enough big games you'll know how to respond to any situation," Colquette said as his team hoisted yet another gold trophy on the field behind him. "Our kids know how to win. I guess you can call it tradition. You can't teach it. It grows with you.

"I've had a lot of special groups but I knew from the time these guys were playing in junior high that if everybody stuck together it could be the best of all. They proved me right. They've won three state championships and only lost one game in four years. That's kind of hard to argue with."

MARION COUNTY 1995 RESULTS

Aug. 25	South Pittsburg	34-13
Sept. 1	McMinn Central	35-14
Sept. 8	Baylor	20-14
Sept. 15	City	48-0
Sept. 22	Soddy-Daisy	26-20
Sept. 29	Tyner	49-18
Oct. 6	Rhea County	24-13
Oct. 13	Sequoyah	52-15
Oct. 20	Shelbyville	21-14
Oct. 27	Grundy County	46-7

Playoffs

Nov. 3	Lenoir City	45-20
Nov. 10	Knox Fulton	65-8
Nov. 17	Sullivan North	32-7
Nov. 24	McMinn Central	49-29

State championship

| Dec. 2 | Humboldt | 28-7 |

1995 Warriors

Players: Eric Westmoreland, James Bible, Chad Gravitt, Gavin Thomasson, Josh Dobson, Anthony Martin, Avery Pickett, T. Layne, Brandon Graham, Sean McAlister, T. Smith, Wayne Westmoreland, Ben Canales, Terry Smith, Joe Butler, Lebron Pickett, James Patrick, Brad Holden, Rusty Parker, Anthony Holloway, Michael Fulfer, Brian McFalls, Jason Gibson, Josh Weeks, Keith Parker, Matt Clark, Brent Talley, Michael Willis, Joe Dan Gudger, Randy McCallie, Roy Simpson, Eric Parker, Jason Saylors, Buck Holland, Nathan Capps, Stephen Dover, Matt Howard, Kelvin Hill. Brian Pruitt, Chuck Jones, Garrett Sowder, Todd Muirhead, Billy Rankin, Jason Graham, Mitch Smith, Ben Roberts, Larry Ziegler, Brian Cooper, Lamar Campbell, Nathan Mosley, Les Thomas, Chris Hopkins, Robert Holloway, Jackie Howard, Josh Cannon, Brandon Dawson, Charles Gilliam, Bill Roberts, Josh Chambers.

Coaches: Ken Colquette, Landon Pickett, Johnny Grimes, Don Stewart, Jerry Tate, Paul Underwood, Larry Richards, Eddie Reed, Randy Munn, Terry Grimes.

Chapter 19
ERIC WESTMORELAND

"It's how you show up at the showdown that counts."
— Homer Norton

If ever a loss has inspired one player to greatness this was it. Mighty Marion County, coming off its shocking title game upset of nationally ranked Brentwood Academy the season before was cruising toward another state championship in 1993. Eric Westmoreland had shown flashes of his potential as a running back, safety and kick returner, but as a sophomore he didn't yet need to be the focal point of a team loaded with experienced playmakers.

Having won two state titles in three years — and coming within six points of claiming three consecutive championships — the team felt invincible by the start of the '93 season. And that was pretty much how the rest of the state looked at them too.

The Warriors won 11 straight games to begin their run at a title defense, all by at least 15 points, and no opponent scored more than seven points all season. The playoffs were expected to be just another coronation until a stunning 7-6 quarterfinal loss at Kingston on a field that was messier than small-town politics.

"It poured all day and the field was basically just a mud pit," recalled Warriors coach Ken Colquette. "I went back and watched the film and counted about a dozen things that if any one had gone our way we win. We had a touchdown called back on a penalty, lost a fumble as we were going in for a score and had the ball inside the one with less than a minute to go but got jammed up and stopped."

After pausing to think back on the make-up of the team he still believes might be the most talented in program history, Colquette finally added, "We had some jealousy on that team over who would carry the ball more and that wound up costing us. I should've had Eric in the game late, but he was just a sophomore then and I wasn't sure about putting a young kid in that type situation.

"If I knew what kind of knack he would have for coming up big in critical situations I wouldn't have hesitated."

Warriors fans stood in rain-soaked disbelief as the final seconds ticked off the clock, then slowly wandered through the fog back to their cars for the long ride home. The heartbreaking outcome had stung the Warriors unlike any previous loss.

It also served as the white-hot coals that would fuel the ultra competitive Westmoreland to become one of the best high school players the Sequatchie Valley has ever produced.

"I remember me and Kenny Smith walking off the field hugging each other and crying our eyes out," Eric said. "I told him and everybody else who would listen that we would never lose again.

"It was the first time I had experienced walking off a field after a loss and I hated it. Nothing was going to fix that feeling except getting back out there and winning every game. I was determined to do whatever I could to make sure none of us ever had to feel like that again."

A BAD BREAK

As a kid, more than anything else, Eric hated being confined indoors. The only thing he would sit still for was to watch sports on TV. It didn't matter which sport — baseball, football, basketball — once the game ended he would rush outside and try to mimic the moves he had watched his heroes make.

"It was just me with a ball in the back yard," Eric said. "Later on when my brother got older we would play together, but even when it was just me, I was working on spin moves and my stiff arm or how to cut back without slowing down.

"By the time I was in sixth grade I was the only kid they let play up with the junior high team. Nobody ever told me how to run. The coaches trusted what I saw on the field and would just say 'run to daylight.'"

Eric helped the junior high Warriors go undefeated for three straight seasons, but the budding star's varsity career nearly ended before it even began. As an eighth-grader he broke his ankle so badly that the bone grotesquely protruded his sock. Seeing it, he bit down on his mouth piece and tried not to cry as the coaches came jogging onto the field.

Eric Westmoreland breaks free for a long run.

"I happened to be at the game and I remember talking to his mama after it happened," Colquette said. "I didn't think she was going to let him play again. One of her babies had gotten hurt playing football and she was pretty set against him coming back out.

"But he talked her into it, and boy was I ever glad. He had been so good in little league he'd gotten a little cocky, so we decided we'd try to hold him back his freshman year. But the first game he played for the varsity he scored three touchdowns and we knew holding him back would be hard to do."

WORKING TO BE GREAT

Former Notre Dame coach Lou Holtz once announced to his team before off-season workouts began that "No one ever drowned in sweat."

Those words became Eric's personal mantra as he looked for any way possible to find an edge over everyone who would set foot on the field against him. Sitting in class and flipping through a sporting goods magazine, he came across an advertisement for strength shoes that promised to make him run faster and jump higher.

"I knew I had to get a pair," Eric said. "But when I asked my mom to buy them she told me I would have to get a job to earn enough money. Once I finally got them, I wore them every day to work out in or even just around the house.

"I held myself to a higher standard starting that winter before my junior year. This was before people had trainers, so I tried every workout routine I could find that I thought would help me get better."

Once the school year ended, Eric's summer days were hectic. He would spend mornings working his summer job with a heating and air company, then working out in the afternoon at the football field alone before driving — sometimes for hours — to play with his summer-league baseball team in the evening.

"I would be at the field house and he didn't even know I was watching him, but I would check on him every now and then because he would be out there on the field or on the track by himself running in the heat of the day," Colquette said. "I guess it was the only time he had to workout between his job and summer baseball, but he never missed a day.

"He would lift weights by himself then be out there running in those weird looking strength shoes for an hour or so. He would always finish by running a few hundred-yard sprints and then go play baseball somewhere.

"I've had kids who worked hard, but not ones that had his talent and were willing to put it all together. Eric was born with a lot of talent, but that kid worked for everything he became later on. Something in him just drove him to be special, different than everybody else."

The work ethic came naturally, rooted deep in his family's DNA. The oldest of three kids, Eric had seen his mom and dad — Gwen and Wayne — leave at sunrise for the 30-minute commute to work at Wheland Foundary, before returning home just in time to take the kids to whichever sport was in season.

Before cancer took him, his grandad Herschel was another example of working hard to earn what you want. After driving his bus route in the mornings, Herschel would work on his farm until it was time for the afternoon bus route and then back to tend to his cattle and pigs or work in his garden until sundown.

The summer before his breakout junior year Eric lost 15 pounds and stood a solid 6-foot, 190 pounds when his grandad drove the team bus eight miles to the southern end of the county for the season's kickoff at South Pittsburg.

A STAR IS BORN

The defining moment, when his career truly began, arrived just as the sun was setting behind Beene Stadium, which was packed with one of the largest crowds in the rivalry's history to watch two teams with state championship ambitions battle.

On the first play of the game, South Pittsburg quarterback Perry Hutchins, who was also one of the nation's top-rated defensive back prospects, broke loose on a 24-yard run up the middle. But the speedy Hutchins was caught from behind by Eric, who punched the ball loose and forced a momentum-shifting turnover.

It wouldn't even be his biggest play of the quarter.

On South Pittsburg's second possession, Hutchins lofted a spiral toward Bradley "Macho" Green for what looked to be a big-play connection of all-state players. Instead, Eric broke on the route near the home sideline and got to the ball quicker than Cinderella's sisters.

"Everybody was there for that game," Eric remembered. "Not just from around Jasper and South Pittsburg, but from all over the area so I wanted to make a big play.

"We knew what plays they liked to run, and I was just playing centerfield and hoping they would throw it where I could either intercept it or make a big hit. I had to jump to catch it and then try not to go down because I had somebody on my back. I leaned back until I regained my balance, and then I just took off."

After making a leaping interception he managed to shrug off Green, who was draped over his back and even tugging on Eric's face mask from behind as the two landed. After hesitating for just a moment to regain his footing, Eric bolted for the end zone, even outrunning Hutchins for a 66-yard touchdown that wound up being the only points in a game dominated by defense.

Eric Westmoreland steps out of a tackle against Soddy-Daisy.

"That was an incredible catch that Westmoreland made," said Pirates coach Danny Wilson afterward. *"Perry threw it high and I actually though it was going to sail out of bounds, but Westmoreland po-goed up for the pick and made a great play. He's big-time material."*

Eric went on to make nine solo tackles, including several that prevented long gains, forced one fumble and recovered another, broke up one pass that would have gone for a long gain and finished off his heroic night with another interception, this time at the Marion 20 with 15 seconds remaining to ice the victory.

"It's one of the few times that I felt like one guy beat us," said Vic Grider, a Pirates assistant that year. "Very seldom do you feel like one guy beats you but he kept us from scoring two or three touchdowns that night. He dominated the game."

His 108 return yards on the two interceptions were more than South Pittsburg's offense managed all night.

After shaking hands with the rival coaching staff Colquette, who had been hesitant to heap too much praise on the precocious youngster previously, let out a relieved sigh and knew he could no longer keep his true feelings hidden.

"We knew coming in that they had a strong defense," he said. "But ours isn't too bad either, and Westmoreland stepped up and made the difference. We knew to come here and win he'd have to be the one to step up and make the key plays and he did. He could become something special."

Motivated by having Colquette finally, reluctantly celebrate his efforts publicly, Eric spent the rest of his junior season proving just how special he could be. In an offense designed specifically to prevent any one player from standing out, Eric stood out, averaging 11 yards per carry. And he was just as outstanding on defense and special teams, helping the Warriors break the school record for points scored in a season and earning a spot as a Mr. Football finalist.

When the playoffs rolled around Marion cruised through the first two rounds by a combined 99-13, setting up the quarterfinal rematch everyone wearing purple had hoped for.

Kingston came into Jasper unbeaten and having allowed more than two touchdowns to just one opponent. But as the team which had upset Marion the year before, the Yellow Jackets also wore a clear bullseye on their back and it didn't take long for the Warriors to begin hitting the target.

Eric ran for 173 yards and three TDs, including an 82-yard sprint as Marion raced out to a 21-0 halftime lead. By the time the game ended the Warriors defense had forced four fumbles and held a Kingston offense that had averaged four TDs per game to just 37 yards on the ground and fewer than 100 total in the 42-0 thumping.

"We've waited on tonight for a whole year," Eric said as he watched the Kingston players slowly make their way off the field. "They never should have beaten us last year, and it was probably one of the most disappointing losses in our history.

"We proved when we work together, nobody can stop us."

Two weeks later, Eric and the Warriors continued to prove that point. He earned offensive MVP honors after running for 151 yards and four TDs, including a 63-yarder that put the exclamation on the season. Despite giving up more than 8 points for the first time all fall, Marion made claiming a state title look easy, completely out-classing Portland 43-14.

Eric finished the season with more than 1,300 rushing yards despite averaging just eight carries per game and intercepted seven passes, returning two for scores.

His summer work had paid off. He had put himself squarely on the recruiting radar of nearly every college program in the nation.

"IF THERE'S A BETTER PLAYER IN THE STATE, I AIN'T SEEN HIM"

In the months leading up to his senior season a group of teammates had decided to join Eric for his summer workouts. With the schedule Colquette had put together — four state-ranked opponents from larger classifications — the Warriors would need all the help they could muster.

The upgraded slate of games would also give him the chance to prove he was elite at any level. Eric's image — wearing his trademark white breathe-right strip across the bridge of his nose and black cleats — appeared on the front of the sports sections of both Chattanooga newspapers nearly a dozen times, making it tough to find new adjectives to describe just how dominant he was.

Needing just six games to surpass 1,000 rushing yards, he was most impressive against the toughest competition — those state-ranked large-school opponents.

Eric threw for the game-winning score in the closing seconds at Baylor, accounted for all three scores — including the game-winner with just 33 seconds left — at Shelbyville, ran for 129 yards on just eight second-half carries to pull away from Rhea County and in one of the most epic prep performances the Chattanooga area has seen, was a one-man wrecking crew in front of more than 8,000 fans at Soddy-Daisy.

In a match-up of all-state backs, Eric left no doubt who the area's top player was by running for 143 yards and three TDs — including one where he stepped out of a tackle near the line and outran the pursuit 38 yards for what would be the game-winner.

He also brought back a punt 74 yards for a score and made 11 solo tackles, including one that prevented Trojans 230-pound star Jarvis Smith from scoring late. As Smith rounded the corner, nobody stood between him and the goal line besides Eric, who never hesitated in coming up from his free safety spot like he was shot form a cannon to wrap up the burly back.

Eric Westmoreland had a huge game in a playoff win over Powell.

"Coach Colquette had told me all week that if I couldn't tackle Jarvis I wasn't good enough to play at the big-time college level," Eric recalled. "There was no way I was going to miss any tackles. I was going to make sure I proved I was the best player on the field that night."

With the Warriors facing a third-and-five late in the game, Eric put the finishing touches on a spectacular night by breaking loose for a 39-yard run that allowed them to run out the clock on a 26-20 win.

As he made his way off the field, Eric was stopped by an older man wearing a blue and gold Soddy-Daisy cap.

"Son I've been watching football for more than thirty years and you're the best two-way player I've ever seen," the man said, extending his hand to shake Eric's. "As good as you are running the ball, I think you're even better on defense."

Having narrowed the list of schools he would choose from to Alabama, Notre Dame and Tennessee — and with each of those teams recruiting him to play defense — Eric knew his time being a featured runner would be coming to an end soon. He planned to make the most of the few carries he had coming.

He and South Pittsburg tailback Corey Tipton, a childhood buddy, each finished the regular season with 31 touchdowns and five two-point conversions to tie for the lead in points scored across the state and when the Chattanooga Times released its Elite 11 list of state prospects, Eric was among them.

Once the playoffs began he would run for nearly 1,000 yards in five games, including 153 in the championship win over Humboldt, earning offensive MVP honors for a second straight year as Marion defended its title.

"If there's a better player in the state, I ain't seen him," gushed Colquette, no longer reluctant to pile compliments on top of the heap of hardware his star was collecting. "I've been around a lot of great teams and some great players, but Eric ranks right up there with the best I've ever seen at this level."

By finishing the season with 2,359 rushing yards, 40 touchdowns, 93 tackles and five interceptions Eric earned Mr. Football honors and was named the state's Player of the Year for all classifications by the Lawrenceburg Quarterback Club.

For his prep career he accumulated more than 6,000 total yards and 85 touchdowns and was responsible for the game-winning touchdown seven times. He once had a streak of more than 200 carries without a fumble.

"Of all those accomplishments the one I'm most proud of is that I helped us live up to that promise I made walking off the field at Kingston my sophomore year. We never lost another game the rest of my career," said Eric, whose senior class finished 56-1 overall with three state championships.

SOMETHING TO PROVE. AGAIN

Steve Caldwell was in his first year recruiting on the road as an assistant coach at the University of Tennessee when he drew the difficult assignment of determining whether the pride of Jasper was as good as advertised.

On a bitterly cold mid-November night Marion was set to host Lenoir City and star running back Travis Adams, who led the state with more than 1,700 yards, in the first round of the playoffs. Sitting amongst all the Warriors fans, Caldwell watched Eric's every move, taking detailed mental notes on whether the kid could open his hips, turn and run fluidly or if his movements looked stiff. How did he take coaching on the sideline? How did he interact with his teammates? Did he elevate his level of play to match another stud runner?

It didn't take long for each of those questions to be answered, and any lingering doubt over whether or not the Vols should extend a scholarship offer was erased.

Late in the first half, as the hood of his parka obstructed Caldwell's view for a split second, the crowd's reaction told him all he needed to know.

"He's broke another one," he said before rising and beginning to make his way toward the field for a closer look.

Adams showed he was a very talented high school player, but Eric's play on both sides of the ball proved beyond all doubt that he had Southeastern Conference ability. Adams ran for 251 yards, but was held to just 34 in the deciding second half. Meanwhile Eric finished with 271 despite getting just 13 carries because of a pulled calf muscle. His 21-yard per carry average would have been even greater had a 96-yard scoring run not been called back by penalty.

"After I saw him play I couldn't wait to get back and give my report to Coach (Phillip) Fulmer," Caldwell said. "We had been debating over whether or not to take him; the big worry was that he might be an inch or so short and a step slow.

"But that night I saw him, even though he was slowed with the injury, he ran up and down the field and nobody could catch him. So when I got back I told the coaches I could honestly say one thing about Eric — every time he touched the ball he made things happen."

With Alabama and Notre Dame turning up their pursuit, Fulmer used an ace in the hole to get Eric's attention during his official visit to the UT campus. Memphis had been the only school to promise Eric the chance of playing both football and baseball, but during his meeting with Vols coaches, Fulmer extended the same offer.

"I loved baseball and really wanted to play both," said Eric, who was an all-state catcher for the Warriors and even named the area's Player of the Year by the Chattanooga News-Free Press. "Tennessee had just played in the College World Series and had a great program at that time.

"I knew I didn't want to go too far from home, so that ruled out Notre Dame and left me to decide between Alabama and Tennessee. That weekend in Knoxville I hung out with a lot of guys from around the state that I connected with and then when Coach Fulmer said I could play baseball too, that sealed it."

He arrived on UT's campus as an underrated recruit in a freshman class that included defensive linemen Shaun Ellis and Darwin Walker, linebacker Raynoch Thompson and quarterback Tee Martin. And while he would be undersized at linebacker, Vols coaches believed he would grow into the position and made the switch almost immediately.

"Guys on the team would ask me what I was rated in high school and I had to tell them I honestly didn't know," Eric said. "There wasn't a star rating then, so when I got to UT and heard about all these highly-rated guys, all I knew was I was out-playing them in practice.

"I never had a doubt I could play at that level. I wasn't intimidated at all when I got there. The speed was different, but after a couple of weeks I had adjusted."

He had spent most of his football career feeding off the adrenaline rush of proving doubters wrong, but to get on the field against SEC competition he would have to rely on the work ethic he learned from his parents and grandad. Talent alone wouldn't be enough anymore.

"A lot of times you'll have that moment when a freshman gets hit with the reality that they aren't the most talented guy on the field anymore," said Caldwell, a defensive assistant on Fulmer's staff. "But Eric had the smarts to go with his talent and he studied film, listened to the older players and learned quickly what he needed to do.

"Once he got on the field, it didn't take long to figure out what kind of player he was."

By the time the Vols ran onto the field to open the 1996 season against UNLV, Eric had worked his way into a starting role on special teams.

"My first game was one of those experiences you never forget," he said. "You hear the crowd roaring and stomping their feet above you and then you see the band make the giant 'T' and you start getting goose bumps.

"I can't even explain why but a lot of us would get emotional right when we would run out onto the field. You would see guys with tears coming down their face, they were just so excited, so jacked up and all that emotion had to come out somehow."

After calming the butterflies enough to make the tackle on the opening kickoff, continued his knack for big plays later in the game when he scooped up a fumbled kickoff and returned it 23 yards for a touchdown.

Eric Westmoreland helped Tennessee win the 1998 national championship.

One game into his college career — similar to his high school days — he had already proven his point. He could play on the big-time level and wound up being on the field for more snaps than any other freshman in his class. Torn knee ligaments in the fall of 1997 forced him to redshirt and miss the entire season, but by the following spring Eric had rehabbed the injury well enough to be in contention for a starting spot at outside linebacker.

Knowing he needed to concentrate solely on winning that job, he decided to give up baseball, a tough call that paid off when he began the 1998 season starting alongside All-SEC linebackers Al Wilson and Thompson.

He not only started every game in that sophomore season, but finished second on the team with 79 tackles and led the Vols with 11 more for loss.

Late that year he also proved he had already matured into a leader. With both Wilson and Thompson sitting out the game at Vanderbilt with injuries, Eric led the defense with 12 tackles on the same Dudley Field turf where he had helped Marion win three state titles. Late in that game he blasted running back Everett Robinson so hard on a screen pass that the Vandy player's back hit the turf before anything else. Eric stood over the writhing Commodores runner as Vols teammate Chris Ramseur scooped up the ball and returned it for a score.

The next week, with Wilson and Thompson back on the field next to him, it was Eric who helped seal the SEC Championship and punch the Vols ticket to play for a national title. Tennessee had fought back to take a 17-14 lead over stubborn Mississippi State with 6:15 remaining, and one play after the go-ahead touchdown Eric pounced on a fumble at the Bulldogs' 26. On the next snap the Vols put the game away when Tee Martin connected with Cedrick Wilson in the right corner of the end zone — the second TD for Tennessee in 28 seconds.

"Once we got a 10-point lead, as a defense, we knew there was no way we were going to let them come back from that," said Eric, adding that only four of 13 opponents scored more than two TDs against the Vols that season.

One month later the Vols defense forced three turnovers, scored a TD and held Florida State to just 108 rushing yards to help claim the program's first national championship in decades. In his first season as a full-time starter, Eric finished second on the team in tackles.

By the next fall he had come full circle, taking former South Pittsburg rival and incoming freshman linebacker Eddie Moore under his wing.

"People think you're supposed to hate each other coming from those two schools," Moore said with a laugh. "But E-Mo squashed that right off and from day one he made my transition a lot easier. He was older than me so we really hadn't had much interaction but he became like a big brother and tutored me on how to prepare for that level.

"We became family and while we were at Tennessee we had each other's back. But we still have that rivalry back home, that one week out of the year when we don't like each other a whole lot."

By the time he finished his UT career he had helped win two SEC titles, was a team captain as a senior, when he also earned All-SEC honors, and ranked third in program history in tackles for loss, just behind Reggie White and Leonard Little.

He was taken in the third-round of the NFL Draft by the Jacksonville Jaguars and after three injury-plagued seasons, finished his pro career with the Cleveland Browns.

"I was at my parents house when I got drafted and we had a lot of family there to celebrate," said Eric, now a defensive assistant at Baylor. "But one of the best memories I have was all the random people who stopped by just to congratulate us. That's really what makes coming from a small town so cool.

"The kids I work with now never saw me play. They just hear stories. But I always tell them what got me to that level was my work ethic. I was just following what my parents and my grandad taught me."

Chapter 20

MARION'S WHISTLE

"The hammer never complains about the noise."
— Marty Rubin

"The noise was like, well, it was like a thousand vampire cats clawing on Plexiglas - it made their teeth hurt."
— Christopher Moore, *Bite me*

The sound would pierce the fall night air and reverberate throughout the Sequatchie Valley like some sort of alarm clock from hell, jolting everyone in Jasper to life. At ear-splitting volume — think front-row Metallica concert loud — the noise became as synonymous with Marion County football as purple uniforms.

It was compared by the man who was responsible for putting it together as sounding "like a freight train". And like a tornado — which is often described as creating the same ominous sound — the Warriors left a path of destruction in the wake of each new blast.

"It's the sound I most identify with football," said Warriors former all-state defender T.J. Gentle. "A warm breeze blowing across the field, the smell of fresh cut grass and hearing that whistle when we would walk past on our way to the field, it gave all of us a little extra bounce in our step.

"I can close my eyes and imagine seeing the stands packed and hearing the whistle after every big play we made. Hearing it let you know all was right in the world."

Depending on which side of the field you sit on, for more than 40 years — even on road trips — the noise has either been as welcome as Gabriel's trumpet or as annoying as fingernails down a chalkboard for two-plus hours.

"It was kind of like the cavalry blowing their horn as they rode over the hill before battle," said former Warriors coach Ken Colquette. "It really got our kids and fans fired up and ready to play. It's just soooo loud.

"It definitely lets everybody know that the Warriors are in town. I walked right by it one night when they lit that sucker off and I about jumped out of my skin."

Countered former South Pittsburg coach and principal Danny Wilson, "I hate that damn thing. There's absolutely nothing more annoying than hearing that whistle.

"They called us one year when we were hosting them and asked about bringing it to the game. I made it real clear that thing was not allowed anywhere near our school property. They had to park it a few blocks away, but you could still hear it in the distance. It makes our people's skin crawl."

The original whistle came from the first steam engine that ran out of Chattanooga in the 1870s and rolled through Jasper. It weighed about 20 pounds and was powered by a massive air compressor that had to be towed into games by a truck and parked next to the Warriors field house in the corner of the north end zone. Because the rotary air compressor had a constant flow of air, it allowed the whistle to blow as long and often as the controller wanted.

And when Marion got rolling on a Friday night, the controller — and everyone in purple — wanted the whistle to blow real long and real loud. Even more than the flashing scoreboard, the number of times the train whistle blew was the most sure-fire way of telling how well Marion was playing on any given night.

The late Burton Cagle, a native of Grundy County, moved to Jasper in 1948 after a tour of military duty at Pearl Harbor. Although he was not a Marion graduate, Cagle never waivered, saying only "I've been a fan of Marion County football for a long, long time."

So Cagle, who had begun Cagle and Sons towing service, approached Marion County principal Bill Baxter in 1978 about blowing a horn or siren or something to sound off at games when the Warriors did something good.

"Burton asked me if I wanted to make some noise at a football game," Baxter said. "I said sure. And that's how it all got started."

Cagle would let off steam so to speak anytime the Warriors would score or make a big play. And for more than four decades since, with several new engineers in charge, the whistle has remained a fixture at Marion games. A third-down stop? The whistle blows. A long pass completion? The whistle blows. A touchdown? The whistle b-l-o-w-w-w-w-w-s! Hard and long and LOUD!!

Marion's tractor whistle.

"Our fans grew to expect it to be there," Colquette added. "Burton would pull that cord and a horrible sound would come out. That helped a bunch as far as giving us an identity and it's remained the same ever since, no matter who's in control of it.

"It created a lot of hate, and it still makes other team's fans mad. We would always hear about it after the game, about wanting it to shut up."

Cagle pulled the string that ignited the sound for more than a dozen years. Before he passed away, he once said he had been cursed at, had rocks thrown at him and was once threatened with being arrested in Dunlap for noise pollution.

He poured thousands of dollars into the contraption and its upkeep, and admitted before a playoff game in the early 1990s that he got as much of a kick out of pissing off opponents as firing up the Warriors.

"It's the damndest noise you ever heard," Cagle once said between tugs on the rope that let loose each new blast. "They don't like it in South Pittsburg or Dunlap or Whitwell. They don't care for it one bit."

During a meeting of school administrators, coaches and officials before the 1990 state championship game, TSSAA executive director Ronnie Carter asked Colquette if Marion intended to bring "that confounded whistle"? Colquette shot back, "You better believe it!"

"Well," Carter replied, "I guess we'll have to find a place for y'all to park it." And sure enough, a special area was designated near the top level of a parking garage that sits across a small service road from Vanderbilt's stadium. Once the whistle had parked and the first resounding blast was let loose, the large Warriors contingent of fans jumped to their feet and returned a rowdy roar of approval.

In 1984 a group of South Pittsburg teenagers, under cover of darkness, snuck onto Cagle's property and ripped out enough wires and cables to disable it, preventing it from being blown at the game the next night.

"After we lost to them in 1997 we had to walk right by it on our way back to the locker room," recalled Pirates coach Vic Grider. "The guy operating it then just laid down on that thing and it kept blasting the whole time we walked by and even after we got in the locker room. All I remember was thinking how bad I wish I had a stick of dynamite right then.

"The rumor here is it went through about a 10-year period where it rusted shut because they didn't have any reason to blow it. I think they had to buy a can of starter fluid to revive it."

By the mid-1990s, the whistle's reputation for annoyance had spread across the state and most opponents joined South Pittsburg by telling Marion administrators that it would not be allowed on their campus. When the TSSAA moved the site of the state title games to Tennessee Tech, game organizers joined the growing ban on the whistle.

But ever so often, as the team would make its way out of Jasper for a road game, the whistle would join the convoy and as it followed the team bus on the way out of town, the loudest cheer from bystanders lining the street came when the whistle drove past.

"There are just certain things that would calm your nerves or make you feel more ready to get the game going," said Marion's former all-state running back and defensive back Anthony Martin, who helped the Warriors win back-to-back state titles in the mid-1990s. "Hearing the whistle rev up that first time during pregame warmups, that let you know the whole community was behind you.

"Even now, when I'm there to watch them, I'll hear the whistle and get jacked up and want to put on the pads again."

There are countless examples of people crossing from one side to the other through the years, but maybe the biggest act of treason came when Danny Davenport, a 1988 South Pittsburg graduate who helped the Pirates beat Marion his junior and senior seasons, agreed to be in charge of the whistle in the mid-2000s. He even hauled it to away games while his son Wes played for the Warriors.

"I was called a traitor and told several times I needed to have my ass whipped for doing it," Davenport said with a laugh. "When I played, we always knew that if we could shut the whistle up it meant we had a chance to beat Marion County. I used to hate it. If somebody had told me years ago that I'd be blowing it, I'd have thought they were crazy."

When Joey Mathis joined the Marion staff before the 2014 season, he began acclimating himself with the tradition around the program. One of the first things he was introduced to, and adopted as what makes Friday nights special in Jasper, was the whistle.

"When we came running out for our first home game, I noticed it. For sure," Mathis said. "I remember thinking what a cool atmosphere we have and that sound just adds to all the excitement.

"Now, whenever we score or make a big play on defense I find myself listening for it sometimes. You can't help but get a little extra charged up because for a real long time, that's how our folks have known things are going our way."

Chapter 21
EDDIE MOORE

"I'm a fighter. I believe in the eye-for-an-eye business. I got no respect for a man who won't hit back. You kill my dog, you better hide your cat."

— Muhammad Ali

It was nearing midnight when the white Honda Accord made its way along Cedar Avenue, the main artery that runs through the heart of South Pittsburg. The street was deserted and storefronts had long been darkened as Eddie Moore guided his rental car slowly through the town's five traffic lights, each blinking yellow, until he reached his destination.

Turning left into the gravel parking lot he noticed the wrought iron gate leading to the football field was open so he coasted onto the asphalt track that encircled the field, turning the headlights off and rolling to a stop near the home stands. The street lights above each corner of the track cast slivers of milky light like bony fingers reaching out across the field.

Surveying the surroundings outside his windshield, Eddie saw no one else around and exhaled a deep sigh. As he sat alone in his car, a warm spring breeze drifting through his window, he scanned the 100-yard stretch of Bermuda, beginning at the end zone closest to him then slowly moved his eyes the entire length — from goal line to goal line — and his mind wandered back to all the Friday nights he had worn the solid black Pirates uniform under the bright stadium lights.

The ink was barely dry on his first NFL contract when, as the second-round pick of the Dolphins, Eddie decided to return home for a quick visit. The next week he would fly to Miami to begin rookie workouts but now, as he had driven into town, a voice inside led him to make a late-night detour to the empty stadium where his career had begun, and where his life had taken a turn for the better.

"I don't really know why, I just kind of felt led to go there," Eddie said. "I wanted to sit there for a little bit and just kind of think about everything — what I had been through and the next step I was about to take.

"People look at football as a sport, and it is, but a lot of boys have been made into men on that field. A lot of lives changed on that field. So much history happened on that field. A lot of teams came here and found out they're not as good as they thought they were on that field. You literally leave it all out on that field. All your memories, your best plays, your best days are on that field.

"I was one of the ones that a lot of people thought wouldn't make it out or do anything with my life. But because of what happened on that field, and so many people who were pushing me, I did. I sat there for a while kind of lost in my thoughts and then drove home to start the next chapter of my life."

LEARNING TO TRUST

Eddie's earliest memory was waking up to screams from his mother, Tammy Walker. The four-year old boy ran to his parents' doorway and saw his mother sobbing and his father lying motionless in bed, dead from a heart attack he had suffered in his sleep.

"All I knew was my daddy wasn't moving and my mama was crying really loud," Eddie recalled.

The days that followed became a blur but as time passed, in the absence of having a man around the house, Eddie began to take on the responsibility of looking after his family. He became sullen and withdrawn, cocooning himself inside a tough exterior, refusing to allow anyone to reach him. The way he saw it, if you don't trust anyone you can't be hurt.

But it wasn't just his emotions that were calloused hard. Physically he was tougher than a Waffle House steak and during a routine trip to the dentist as a teenager, when a BB pellet was found embedded in his gum Eddie shrugged and told the nurse he had been shot by another kid when he was 10, as if it were no big deal.

It wasn't until his sixth-grade year that he began to open up to an adult outside of his family, making a connection with a young coach and PE teacher. For the first time since his dad had died he began to listen and trust that a man had his best interest at heart.

"Coach (Vic) Grider had this attitude about him, kind of cocky, but I liked it," Eddie said. "This was way before anybody knew I would be good at football, so he was just taking time to talk to me. I needed somebody to act like they cared about me and that's what Coach Grider did.

"He would joke around sometimes but he also made sure I knew he wasn't going to take any crap from a kid. Everything he does is organized and structured and I respected that. He brought that discipline that every kid needs."

Even before he became South Pittsburg's head coach Grider became somewhat of an older brother for Eddie, and the only adult the tough-as-nails teenager would trust, besides his mom. That was until he met Thomas Murphy, an elderly janitor at the elementary school better known simply as Mr. Tim.

One afternoon, as Eddie stood with classmates in the lunch line, Mr. Tim approached and stooped down to tie the boy's shoe.

"Do you like to fish?" Mr. Tim asked.

Unsure of why the stranger was taking an interest in him, all Eddie could manage was a quick, "Yessir."

From that brief introduction, Mr. Tim became an important role model who not only took Eddie fishing on weekends, but also helped find odd jobs — yards to mow, leaves to rake or gardens to tend — to help the kid earn a little pocket money.

"Later on he told me that he had seen me around town and noticed I never really had a grown man around and thought I needed one to teach me a few things," Eddie said. "He had seen me pushing my lawnmower all around town, even one day when I had pushed it a couple of miles from home to mow a yard. He saw something in me and just wanted to help."

One humid afternoon Mr. Tim arranged with his sister for Eddie to rake her yard. But with friends waiting for him at the city park's swimming pool, Eddie rushed through the job haphazardly then hopped on his bike and pedaled quickly to cool off.

"Mr. Tim pulled up at the pool in his truck and called for me to come over to him," Eddie recalled. "He put my bike in the back of his truck and we drove back to his sister's house."

Motioning toward the yard, still scattered with sticks and leaves, Mr. Tim asked Eddie, "does that look like you did a good job?"

All Eddie could do was shrug, not wanting to admit the answer he knew would disappoint Mr. Tim.

"If you're going to do anything you do it right or don't bother doing it at all," he lectured.

That was all it took. Eddie nodded, unloaded his bike and went to find the rake and begin finishing the job the way it should've been done.

"That always stuck with me," Eddie said. "He taught me what work ethic meant and from then on if I was going to do something, no matter what it was, I made sure I tried to do it the best I could."

In the years that followed, once he reached high school, Eddie learned there were plenty of others in his little town willing to look out for his best interest and earn his trust.

THE NIGHT THAT CHANGED HIS LIFE

It was late May, the night before the last day of school and the three friends were walking home from a grocery store when they heard a car approaching behind them. Eddie, and football teammates Charles Beene and Josh Robinson, turned to see the car slow as it got closer and a window lowered.

"Get out of the road you bunch of niggers!" yelled one boy's voice from inside the car. As the word stung the three black teenagers like a slap across the face, they heard another boy inside the car roar with laughter.

The three friends picked up rocks and began firing them at the car as it sped off. Moments later, the car returned, this time approaching at a high rate of speed before sliding to a stop across the street. Three white teenagers, one of them much larger than the others, stepped out of the car, and the larger boy held his arm behind a door to hide what might be in his hand.

"Oh shit, he's got a gun," Eddie said, and the instinct to run jolted through him. But as he and Robinson looked at one another, they realized Beene, at 6-foot-4, 320 pounds, would not be able to move fast enough to get away.

"We couldn't take off and leave big Beene there by himself," Eddie said, remembering the night that changed his life. "So we just stood there and yelled back and forth at those guys. Luckily they just wanted to scare us, so they got back in the car and took off."

Eddie Moore was tough for opponents to catch up with.

The driver, Billy Gray, wasn't shy about being racist and had antagonized Eddie several times before that night. He had been expelled a month before the end of that 1996 school year and seemed content to continue looking for trouble as the summer began.

The next day, the last day of his sophomore year, as Eddie was walking to class, Robinson approached and told him that Gray had snuck into school and was talking with some of his friends in shop class. Eddie detoured from his class and along with Robinson, Beene and some other black friends, walked into the classroom to confront Gray and his buddies.

Eddie grabbed a broom as he approached Gray and whacked him across the shoulder with it, then tossed it to the ground and tackled Gray. As he began to punch and beat on Gray with both fists, Eddie's friends stood guard to make sure none of the white kids jumped into the fight.

"Honestly, it felt good to get that out," Eddie admitted. "He'd been asking for it for a long time and I was just tired of it and figured after I whipped his ass he would leave me alone."

For fighting in school Eddie was given a 10-day suspension, a punishment that would have to carry over into the first two weeks of the next school year, what would be his junior season and also Grider's first year as head coach.

When Eddie appeared in juvenile court several weeks later, Judge Ben Hill ordered him to serve 60 hours of community service and the rest of his suspension from school, ending his ruling by emphatically requesting that Eddie be allowed to continue competing in sports, citing his promising future.

Nothing else was said about the incident as Eddie completed his community service and the rest of his suspension before returning to school and rejoining the football team in time to run for five touchdowns in a 53-point win over cross-county foe Whitwell in the season opener.

The following week word began to spread through town that the Marion County School board would discuss whether Eddie's suspension should be reviewed. On the Monday after the Pirates second game, three days after Eddie had again rushed for more than 100 yards and two more TDs, the tiny meeting room where the county's Board of Education typically met with around a dozen spectators was overflowing. More than 200 people packed the room, forcing some to wedge themselves against the walls and others stood in the hall outside, craning their necks to listen to the proceedings.

At the table, five white board members — three from Jasper, one from Whitwell and one from South Pittsburg — discussed whether the punishment had been too lenient. One of the board members stated that the broom Eddie had used should be considered a weapon, the same as if he had brought a gun or knife to school, and therefore would fall under the state's zero-tolerance policy that would require him to be expelled for one year.

The meeting lasted more than two hours, with much of the time taken up by impassioned arguments on Eddie's behalf, including one from a relative of Gray who said that his cousin had a history of racism and had taunted Eddie on more than one occasion, and that Eddie should not be expelled.

Despite the emotion in the room the board responded with a curt 4-1 decision to expel Eddie for the remainder of the school year. Only Bedford Allison, who represented South Pittsburg on the board, voted against the expulsion.

"At the start of the meeting we stood to pray to a forgiving, loving, understanding God," South Pittsburg principal Chief Miller said afterward. "Then four members of the school board turned around and showed neither forgiveness, love nor understanding for this kid."

Sitting at home with his mom and three sisters watching television, Eddie was clueless there was even a meeting that night to determine his future.

"I had no idea there were people trying to kick me out of school," Eddie said. "Me and my sisters had just finished watching a show on TV and then the news came on and the first thing they said was 'South Pittsburg superstar expelled for the year'. That's how I found out. Everybody looked at me like what's going on? I found out later that night that I couldn't go back to school."

The three month delay before addressing the issue raised a red flag that waved far outside the Pirates football community. The Chattanooga chapter of the NAACP was notified and media from as far away as Huntsville, as well as both newspapers and all three television stations in Chattanooga, began asking whether some board members had decided Eddie was simply too good to continue playing against the schools they represented.

"It seems awfully convenient that they've had three months to make a ruling on this but they wait until a week before a big football game," Monroe Powers, the county's NAACP representative, said the day after

Eddie was expelled. "It sounds ridiculous to anyone who doesn't live in this community, but this whole thing stems from football."

The next morning coaches from two different high schools in Alabama came knocking on Eddie's door, offering to help him and his family move and promising he could be eligible to play immediately. But Eddie's mother was determined to stay and fight and two days later a temporary restraining order was issued by Judge Thomas Graham, a South Pittsburg graduate, allowing her son to return to class.

Two days after being allowed to return, Eddie was back on the football field, carrying the ball 25 times for 120 yards and three TDs, including the game-winner in a six-point win over Grundy County.

The saga finally came to an end the next Monday when, with the glare of the NAACP and the media fixed squarely on the community, a three-person disciplinary committee of the school system voted to overrule Eddie's expulsion, clearing him of the incident for good.

The unbeaten, second-ranked Pirates could now turn their attention to Marion County that week.

"I'M HERE ALL NIGHT"

When the Pirates bus pulled into the parking lot, Eddie and his teammates couldn't help but chuckle at one of the homemade signs, hung from a broomstick that read "Moore Pirates, Moore problems".

"All I could think about all that week was the people who had tried to expel me would be there, cheering against me," Eddie said. "You're easily manipulated at that age and I was very emotional. I was probably too excited. Before the game I had a coke and a fudge round because that was all I could eat with all the nerves. Looking back, that was just stupid."

Eddie's first three carries went for 23 yards and the Pirates needed just four plays to score. But as the adrenaline wore off, Moore came to the sideline complaining of lightheadedness on the team's second possession. Team doctor Rusty Adcock noticed the kid wasn't even sweating, despite the mid-September humidity and the fact that he had played every snap on both sides of the ball for nearly a full quarter.

"He was dehydrated and then he wound up getting so upset about not being in the game that he started to hyperventilate," Adcock said. "We couldn't get his breathing regulated, so we had to call for an ambulance to come to our side of the field and get him to the hospital."

Once Eddie was loaded onto a stretcher the ambulance began making its way around the track toward the stadium's exit. As it passed through the crowd on the home side some Marion fans began to bang on the side of the ambulance, even knocking on the back windows and extending their middle finger at Eddie, who sat with an oxygen mask covering his face.

With their star out of the game the Pirates managed to keep the score tied at halftime, but Marion switched from the veer to the power-I formation, using the Pirates own offense against them, to simply wear on them in the second half and claim the upset.

For the 363 days between that night and the next time the Pirates would step on the field against the Warriors — a whole lousy, God-awful, agonizing year — Eddie and his teammates were tormented by the events before, during and after that brutal loss.

South Pittsburg began the '98 season beating its first three opponents an average of 66-7, but moments after their third lopsided win, Grider didn't even waste time congratulating the team in the locker room before he announced flatly that it was now officially "Jasper week" and time for everyone to begin preparing for that game.

Midway through Tuesday's practice, Grider decided that the team's focus wasn't where it needed to be and blew his whistle, stopping everyone on the field dead in their tracks.

"Y'all are wasting my time and yours half-assing your way through today," Grider barked. "Do you think they're screwing around like this eight miles up the road? Just get off the field! I'm sick of watching this!"

But instead of following their coaches off the field, Eddie called out for his teammates to stay put. For the next 30 minutes players practiced offensive plays, blocking assignments and ran sprints before leaving the practice field.

"It was just us players and the coaches didn't even leave us a ball," Eddie said. "The coaches were just trying to make a point or get our attention because that's probably the only week in all four years there that I don't think there was a single laugh, or giggle or moment where we were goofing off even for a second at practice.

"But when the coaches left, it definitely brought us closer as a team. It was strictly business and we were going to get ourselves ready for that game with or without anybody else."

The sun was beginning to disappear behind the mountain beyond the home stands as the Pirates emerged single-file from their locker room for pregame warm-ups. Over the click, clack, click, clack of cleats walking along the asphalt track, a Marion fan yelled in his direction, "Hey Eddie, you gonna make it through the first half this year?"

Then, as he began to stretch on the field, Eddie heard footsteps jogging up on the grass behind him and turned his head just in time to hear one of Marion's players call out to him, "Which quarter you planning on laying down in tonight, bitch?"

"I just let them say whatever they wanted," Eddie said. "I didn't respond. All of it was just adding fuel to the fire. I had put up with crap like that for a whole year. People saying stuff to me and my teammates and I couldn't wait for the game to start."

As Grider and defensive coordinator Allen Pratt stood near midfield watching both teams finish their warm-ups, they heard Warriors coach Landon Pickett telling his team, "Boys, remember if you hit 'em, they'll quit. Just like last year!"

After warming up the Pirates returned to their locker room to cool off and wait for kickoff. As other players took off their helmets and sipped Gatorade, tugged at their equipment to make sure everything was adjusted to their liking, Eddie sat at his locker, helmet still on, chinstrap still buckled, and tears beginning to roll down his cheeks.

He couldn't control the emotion any longer, and a year's worth of anger, hurt and bitterness began to flow in tiny droplets from his eyes. He didn't even bother to wipe his face.

But as he looked around and saw several teammates, including Beene, staring back at him with tears streaming down their faces, he nodded his head, stood and began walking toward the exit, reaching up to slap the horseshoe over the door before making his way back to the field. The rest of the team followed behind in lock-step.

It remains the only time in his coaching career that Grider did not give a motivational pregame speech. There was no need.

Back on the field, the head referee motioned for both teams' captains to meet for the coin toss and as Eddie walked toward midfield his teammates joined hands, making a long line behind him that stretched across the field, and followed closely behind their captain. As Eddie reached Marion's three captains the rest of the Pirates stopped and did an about-face, turning their backs to their opponents.

"We didn't even want to give them the respect of facing them before the game," said Ronnie Griffith, a halfback and linebacker on that team.

Meanwhile Eddie's glare was locked on the three opponents in solid white uniforms and the purple helmets standing across from him. Each of Marion's players simply looked at the referee instructing them about the coin toss but never looked back at Eddie, who began taunting them.

"Look at me," Eddie said as the official continued his pregame instructions. "You bitches know what's coming but you can't even look at me. You know what's comin' and ain't shit you can do to stop it now."

The same way he had unleashed all his pent-up rage on a racist bully in the shop class, Eddie now was a category-five hurricane of anger waiting to make landfall and wreak as much destruction as his 6-foot, 205-pound body could unleash.

"I have never been more ready to just go out and destroy people in my life," he said.

And on the first series it was clear the most talented player on the field was also on a mission.

The Pirates opened the game driving 60 yards in nine plays – all runs – to the end zone. On his first scoring run Eddie broke free off right tackle and had clear sailing to the end zone, but instead cut back to his left and lowered his shoulder to plow over a Marion defender, sending him flailing backward several yards.

"I'm here all night, bitch!" Moore shouted, making sure whichever opposing player had mocked him during warmups knew his intentions.

"I wanted to hurt as many of them as I could. I wanted to break them," Eddie said. "I wasn't going to avoid any contact. I was letting everything out that I had built up."

For the rest of the night the Pirates offense remained brutally simple, and simply brutal. By halftime they had built a 35-0 lead and when the final seconds mercifully ticked off the clock, Eddie had 201 of the Pirates 420 rushing yards and scored three TDs. They had also held Marion to just 76 yards on 40 runs in the 49-0 dismantling.

"It could've been a lot worse," Eddie said. "That was back when Coach Grider had a little bit of a conscious and he called off the dogs after halftime. He shouldn't have.

"We were showboating the whole game, too, which usually we weren't allowed to do. But that was the only time Coach Grider didn't say anything to us about it. He knew. He loved it as much us players did."

"THAT'S A GROWN-ASS MAN"

The only headlines from the next two games focused on how unstoppable South Pittsburg looked to be. Despite running the power-I, an old-school offense designed to grind it out and beat people up physically, the Pirates were still scoring points like it was a video game. They hung 43 on 3A Sequatchie County, 77 on region foe Greenback and would go on to be highlighted in USA Today as the nation's highest-scoring high school team that year, averaging nearly 55 points over their first 13 games.

But in week seven of the regular season Eddie again became a lightning rod for controversy in an otherwise pedestrian 41-6 thumping of state-ranked Boyd-Buchanan. He and fellow safety Tim Starkey blasted Buccaneers quarterback Jon-David Blair on one run — Starkey going low on the tackle and Moore hitting the ballcarrier around the chest. But as Blair lay on the ground, it was obvious his right arm was badly cut.

By game's end, some Boyd-Buchanan coaches were convinced their star player's arm had been laid open as the result of being cut by a metal object. A call was made to the TSSAA and an official from the state's high school sports governing body arrived at South Pittsburg's field house requesting Eddie's chin strap, which was still stained with Blair's blood.

"They said that Boyd-Buchanan's coaches were accusing me of filing the metal piece on my chin strap into a sharpened point," Eddie recalled. "I was like, 'Are you kidding me?' Who even thinks to do that? Now I was pissed all over again. We knew there was a chance we could play them again in the playoffs, if they got there, and I really wanted them to get there."

The Pirates and Bucs each won their first two playoff games, setting up the rematch Eddie and his teammates had hoped for in the quarterfinals. Just before the game, after the teams had warmed up and returned to their locker rooms, the referees entered South Pittsburg's field house and instructed Eddie and several other Pirates players to hand over their helmets for inspection.

He thought he had buried all that emotion in a deep grave and covered it with dirt for good, but as the officials walked out of the room, for the second time that season, rage began to fuel him.

Eddie Moore breaks away from a Boyd-Buchanan defender.

Boyd-Buchanan and South Pittsburg were the only two Chattanooga-area teams still playing by that late November Friday and every prep football fan in the area — as well as coaches and players from teams across the tri-state — found their way to Beene Stadium, creating an electric atmosphere.

South Pittsburg's cheerleaders even made a point to call out the Bucs by hanging homemade signs from storefront windows reading "Better buckle up!", "Our team's razor sharp!" and even held up a paper run-through sign for the team reading, "We want another stab at you!".

Early in the second quarter, already having built a lead, the bruising runner sliced through the left side of the line, broke through five defenders who missed tackles and was off to the races. Once again Eddie could've simply veered toward the sideline and scored easily, but just as he did against Marion he veered toward Blair, who was sprinting across the field from his safety position, and delivered more of a right cross than a stiff-arm. The blow crumpled Blair to the ground and Eddie regained his stride toward the end zone, slamming the ball to the ground behind him as he scored on the 50-yard run.

"Did y'all see that?" said Baylor School assistant Gary Partrick, who was standing behind the South Pittsburg sideline. "Damn! Eddie Moore just punched that guy in the jaw! That is a grown-ass man on the field, boys."

That run set the tone for another runaway win and it appeared as if there would be no stopping South Pittsburg from finishing their mission of another state title. But a week later, on a frigid field in Hartsville, the Pirates jumped out to a 20-7 second-quarter lead in their semifinal showdown with Trousdale County, looking to again put the game away before halftime. An interception and a fumble were turned into two quick touchdowns by the Yellow Jackets, who also returned the second-half kickoff for a score and Eddie's prep career ended with a stunning upset loss.

"To this day, I've never had a loss to hurt me more than that," Eddie said. "I think more about the plays I didn't make in that game than any of the plays I did make in my career. We were the better team. It hurt even more the next week when we went and watched Trousdale destroy USJ (63-26) for the championship."

"DAMN DUDE, YOU KILLED A MAN"

For all it's success, it had been more than 20 years since South Pittsburg had produced a Division I signee before Eddie came along. By the time his senior season had ended he had Clemson, Ole Miss, Alabama and Tennessee all very interested. Clemson and Ole Miss projected him to play running back, while Alabama and Tennessee considered him to play either strong safety or linebacker.

On Moore's first recruiting trip, just weeks after his prep career had ended, he and Grider were to fly from Chattanooga to Memphis and then drive to Oxford, Mississippi for a weekend visit with the Rebels staff.

"I had never flown before, so I was already nervous," Eddie remembered. "Then the flight was delayed because of a line of thunderstorms moving across the state. We got into this little 20-passenger plane, basically a tin can with two propellers, and that's what we were going to fly across the state in. Through thunderstorms.

"About halfway through the flight you could see lightning flashing outside the window and the plane is bouncing up and down and all over. I look over at Coach Grider because he's flown before and I figure if he's calm then this is just how flights are. But he didn't look too sure himself, so I finally said if we make it back to the ground safely, I'm never doing this again."

During the visit to Ole Miss, Eddie committed to David Cutcliffe, the former Tennessee offensive coordinator who had just been hired as the Rebels coach. Once he returned home, despite Clemson turning up the heat in an attempt to sway him, Eddie remained solidly committed to Ole Miss, thanks largely Cutcliffe's promise to let him play running back and the phone calls he received from Eli Manning, a fellow commitment in that year's Rebels class.

Eddie had even cut ties with Tennessee because he felt the Vols staff had not recruited him as hard as Ole Miss. But two days before national signing day he got news that would change all his plans. As UT assistant Randy Sanders made a late push, Eddie's girlfriend told him she was pregnant and suddenly he realized that playing at Ole Miss would mean living five hours from his baby, but if he chose to take Tennessee's offer, he'd be less than two hours from home.

"I was dead-set on being a Rebel and playing running back," Eddie said. "But there was no way I wanted to be that far away from my daughter. She's the only reason I went to Tennessee, but it turned out to be the best decision for me anyway."

That fall as he tried to acclimate himself to his new surroundings, it was former Marion County rival Eric Westmoreland, by then was an All-SEC linebacker, who became a mentor and helped Eddie prepare to contribute right away.

"I thought that was really cool the way Eric squashed all that high school rivalry stuff and took me under his wing and showed me how to be a college player," Eddie said. "It didn't change how I feel about other people from Jasper, but Eric was a great teammate."

One lesson Eddie paid particularly close attention to was to be ready at a moment's notice for his chance to get on the field. In his first game, while other young players were wide-eyed by the enormity of the moment inside Neyland Stadium and running through the 'T' with more than 105,000 fans cheering their every step, Eddie found a spot on the sideline near Vols special teams coach Pat Washington.

"I was a back-up on special teams but I stood there and when Coach Washington was sending out the kickoff coverage team, one guy was out of place, lolly-gagging around the sideline, so I got sent in in his place," he said. "I ran down and made a play and whoever it was that I went in for, he never got his position back."

Eddie's hustle and willingness to deliver a big hit made him a special teams demon his first two seasons and he went on to start 26 consecutive games at linebacker his junior and senior years, never missing a game during his four-year career.

During his junior year in 2001, Eddie established himself as a leader and eventually was named a team captain. In a game at Arkansas, made sloppy by a downpour that delayed kickoff, he intercepted a pass late and returned it inside the Razorbacks' 20 to set up the game-clinching touchdown. Later that season he secured another road win over stubborn

Kentucky by causing a fumble near midfield, stopping a fourth-quarter drive for what could have been the game-winning score. A shutout win over Vanderbilt followed, setting up a showdown at Florida to decide the SEC East.

The game had been rescheduled after the 9/11 attacks, and in the days leading up to kickoff Eddie's cellphone constantly buzzed with calls and messages from well-wishers back home. "I think everybody in South Pitt had my cell number and it felt like most of them would call to wish me luck all week," he said. "That was always kind of a cool reminder that I had a lot of people watching back home and pulling for me."

The fourth-ranked Vols entered the nationally televised night game as 17.5-point underdogs but wound up knocking off second-ranked Florida, winning at the swamp for the first time since 1971 to earn a spot in the SEC title game. And it was Eddie who delivered the hit that set the tone.

Late in the first half, with Florida trying to mount a drive, quarterback Rex Grossman was flushed from the pocket and lobbed a short pass to receiver Kelvin Kight across the middle of the field. In a hit that was later replayed repeatedly on national highlight shows, just as Kight secured the ball and turned to begin running upfield, Eddie met him with a full head of steam, launching his 226-pound body into the runner for a hit so vicious that Kight was knocked unconscious and would need assistance to stagger off the field. "I wanted to make sure he wouldn't want to catch another pass in the game again so I just unloaded everything I had on him," Eddie said. "I thought I had killed him. I looked down and got scared for a second because his eyes were rolled back and he was kind of shaking. He had bit his tongue and had blood coming out of the side of his mouth. A couple of our guys came over and saw him and were like, 'Damn dude, you killed a man.' "That put an exclamation point for how we were going to play. It said how physical we were going to be all night."

He led the Vols in tackles each of his two years as a starter which, combined with his steady presence off the field, made him not only an

All-SEC choice, but also one of the top NFL prospects on a team that included tight end Jason Witten and receiver Kelly Washington.

At the NFL Combine, while most of his interviews lasted 30-45 minutes, it was one with Tampa Bay coach Jon Gruden that actually stuck out most.

"I had just sat down when Coach Gruden closed the folder in front of him, smiled at me and said 'We know everything we need to know about you Eddie.' Then he asked how Coach Grider was and it hit me that they were good friends and he had already gotten all his info about me from Vic. That was the shortest meeting with any coach I had that week."

Once draft day rolled around Eddie was at his girlfriend's apartment, dozing on the couch when his cell phone rang. The voice on the other end asked if he wanted to be a Miami Dolphin.

"I said I'd love to be a Dolphin," Eddie said. "They told me to wait on the line because they were about to take me, but then my phone lost service and dropped the call. I was freaking out, running around trying to get a signal so they could call back."

On the third special teams series of the Dolphin's first preseason game, a broken foot cost Eddie his entire rookie season. But sitting out a year also allowed him to rest and heal nagging injuries to his shoulder and both knees that he had suffered during his senior year at UT.

When he returned rested and healthy for his second season Eddie quickly realized he belonged at the highest level.

"I was getting up from making a tackle and saw the name on the back of the jersey of the running back," he recalled. "I remember stopping for a second and saying to myself, 'Wow, I just tackled Emmitt Smith.' That's when it hit me that I could play with the best."

EDDIE MOORE WAY

He would spend three years with the Dolphins and one with Denver before Eddie's body finally spoke loud enough — six knee surgeries, two more on his foot and one on his shoulder — for him to realize he had to retire.

"My doctor told me that I wouldn't be able to play with my kids or maybe even walk a flight of stairs if I didn't give it up," Eddie said. "That got my attention.

"I felt like I was always fighting something — critics, people who didn't know me saying negative things about me or even injuries. I never got to appreciate what I accomplished and that's the only regret from my playing days."

But throughout his career, he knew the support from back home meant he was never fighting those battles alone. So throughout his NFL career, and for several years after his retirement, he returned to his hometown just before Christmas to help kids who came from similar backgrounds.

Eddie Moore was a team captain at Tennessee.

The faculty at South Pittsburg would identify as many as 35-40 students who needed help and Eddie would charter a bus to take those kids on a holiday shopping spree that included a stop for lunch, and a gift card to Target, where they could buy anything they wanted.

"I wanted to do something so that kids from my home could experience a couple of things that I never got to as a kid," he said. "First was going to a nice sit-down restaurant. Not a buffet, or a fast food place, but a nice restaurant where they could experience ordering and being waited on. I was 16 before I got to do that.

"Then I wanted them to have the chance to go to a store and buy whatever they wanted or felt like they needed. The amazing thing was how many of those kids would buy something for their mama or a brother or sister. Instead of video games, most of them would buy jackets or socks or clothes or something that they really needed. It felt good when we would pull up back at the school that night and see the kids unloading all the stuff they had bought."

There's a two-block stretch of Cedar Avenue, just in front of the high school, that was dedicated as "Eddie Moore Way". Fittingly, the street bearing his name runs in front of the football stadium where he changed the direction of his future.

"I still drive by there when I come back home, just to make sure they haven't changed the street sign," Eddie said. "I see my name up there and wonder if I've done enough to have that type honor. That's the same street I drove when I came to the stadium that night to sit and think about my life."

Of all the stages of his life — angry kid, Friday night hero, SEC star, professional football player, the one where Eddie finally found peace is as a father and husband, acknowledging his proudest accomplishment is getting to be the father he never had.

And he remains grateful to the point of being overcome with emotion, brushing away tears, when he reflected back on the people who helped him find his way along the path to become the man he is now.

"So many of our kids are starved to see somebody like that who they can relate to," Grider said. "He gives us somebody to use as an example of how to become a success. A lot of our kids identify with the kind of struggle he had in high school, and to see him make it gives them hope.

"It's no secret that we've had other guys who had the same opportunity but failed. A lot of people try to take credit for what he became but that was something inside him. Eddie was just determined to make something of himself and I think he's the best example we've ever had for what our football program is about."

Chapter 22
1999 PIRATES

*"If you want to go fast, go alone.
If you want to go far, go together."*

— **African proverb**

Unseasonably warm for an early-December evening, South Pittsburg's coaches and players had just finished putting the finishing touches to the game plan for the next day's state championship game. As assistants and underclassmen made their way back to the field house, Pirates coach Vic Grider asked the 20 seniors to stay behind for one final meeting.

Gathered together at midfield, with the lights beaming down on Beene Stadium's brown Bermuda, the uncommonly large group of seniors — with an equally uncommon bond — removed their helmets and listened as their coach gave them a peculiar bit of instruction.

"Guys, we love our school and our town, but this is all about you," Grider began, making eye contact with each player. "Do this for yourself. You're the ones who put in the work and you're the ones who should get the rewards."

Since elementary school they had carried the shared burden of expectations. Their mix of talent and temperament had anointed this class a shoe-in as the next in line to add at least one more gold ball to the program's trophy case. Maybe more.

The season before, despite a record-setting offense, the Pirates fell short in the playoffs and the misery of that memory added even more weight onto their shoulders and they came into the season realizing they had just one more shot at living up to their promise.

Pausing to let his words sink in, Grider then got to the real point of the meeting with a group who made up every starting position on both sides of the ball on that 1999 team.

"You guys have trotted off this field so many times after practice for the last four years. Today I want you to walk off. Slowly. Look around at the stands, the field, each other and think about what it all means to you.

"Think about this — 20 or 30 years from now you guys can get together and say you won a state championship. That's special guys. Not many people can do that."

Long after Grider had walked off the field and the underclassmen had left the field house, the seniors continued to linger.

"We hadn't really thought about it until Coach Grider gave us that speech," said Mike Jackson, a receiver, defensive back, all-state kicker and one of the last to pry himself off the field that night. "It had all gone by so fast and all of a sudden none of us wanted it to be over yet.

"But we had work to do the next day, so we eventually had to focus on that instead."

DRIVEN BY THE PAST

It was a year that had already seen President Bill Clinton narrowly avoid impeachment after details of his inappropriate relationship with former White House intern Monica Lewinsky became public and the deadliest high school shooting in U.S. history had taken place at Columbine, Colorado, where two students massacred 12 classmates and one teacher before killing themselves.

Just weeks before the season would begin Lance Armstrong won his first Tour de France, MySpace was introduced to the internet and the animated children's TV series *SpongeBob SquarePants* debuted on Nickelodeon.

But much of the country was beginning to fret over the coming Y2K problem and whether mass chaos would reign when the new century was ushered in.

The conversation about the 1999 Pirates began to heat up long before the temperatures cooled down. The Pirates had led the nation in scoring the year before, highlighted in USA Today for averaging a staggering 51.2 points per game, and won all but one of their first 13 games by at least five touchdowns.

But turnovers and special teams had cost them in a semifinal upset loss at Trousdale County and now, despite having nine starters back on offense and eight back on defense, there was doubt hovering over a team that would have to replace two Mr. Football finalists – two-way lineman Dan Merriman and running back/safety Eddie Moore, who was playing linebacker at the University of Tennessee.

"I had left that field at Trousdale embarrassed," said Pirates defensive coordinator Allen Pratt. "We should've won and I felt like it was my fault. That was the toughest loss I had been associated with and I spent the whole offseason planning how to stop Trousdale because we knew we'd see them again.

Pirates quarterback Tim Starkey looks to pass.

"The group of seniors we had in '99 had been told since Little League that they would be state champions. That's a lot to live up to in a small town, but I knew what kind of effort they would bring so I had to do everything I could to put them in position to get it done."

It was such a talent-laden group that several earned starting positions as freshmen on a 10-win team, a rarity for a program the level of South Pittsburg, and by the end of their four years they would compile a 49-5 overall record.

This was a class that knew how to bring Pirates fans to their feet, and opponents to their knees.

The only question that remained was whether they could clear the final hurdle to join the memorable teams that had preceded them and leave their own legacy.

"We were pretty damn devastated that whole offseason after the Trousdale loss," said Ronnie Griffith, who played halfback and linebacker and was one of those who had been a starter since his freshman year. "I still get sick to my stomach when someone mentions that game. But everybody kept that in the back of our mind and when a game was close, we would think back to what it felt like to lose that game the year before and find a way to win. Nobody wanted to relive that loss."

At 5-foot-8, 140 pounds, Griffith was a part of a group of undersized scrappers who, despite being no bigger than Rock City gnomes, played with a reckless disregard for their own safety. A toughness that made them appear bigger than they actually were.

"We would always have one or two really good players, but the years when we're special it's because of those average guys who are willing to sell themselves out for what we're doing," Grider said. "That's the kind of guys that win championships for you. You remember those 150 pound kids that played like they were 220 and in '99 we had a whole team full of those guys."

During Griffith's junior year he gritted his teeth and played through the pain of what he thought was a pulled muscle in his lower back. But after finally having the lingering injury checked out by a specialist he was told he had broken a bone and was advised not to play football again.

"I walked out of his office and said to hell with that," Griffith recalled. "I didn't tell anybody what the doctor said and never went back to him.

"The pain got pretty bad and there was one practice where it locked up on me and I just fell over, face first. Looking back, it probably wasn't the smartest thing to do."

Ronnie's cousin Michael Griffith was another undersized linebacker at 5-7, 155, while Matt Blansett and Jonathan Haskew played offensive guard and defensive line at 180 pounds, giving up nearly 100 pounds to some opposing linemen.

"There was a nastiness to us and a lot of that was because we weren't real big overall so we felt like we had something to prove, especially me. We played pissed off all the time," said Haskew, who later became an MMA fighter and jiujitsu instructor.

The Pirates starting offensive line had just one player who weighed over 200 pounds, while the defensive line was anchored by Aaron Chambers, a 6-foot-3, 270-pound freak athlete who would become the program's first Mr. Football award winner but was remembered for painting his face and fingernails black before games.

"Pretty much everybody in our group had a screw loose somewhere," Haskew added. "I'm sure we made people nervous because you just never knew if one of us was going to snap. We were all on edge because we had been built up for so long and now we knew people were saying we were going to be a disappointment.

"When we got to spring practice I was so mad that I started fights in practice just about every day. Coach Grider and Coach Pratt came to me and said if I was going to fight every day they weren't going to keep me around. Finally one day Ronnie got in my face and told me to stop acting like a jackass and just play ball.

"We had all played together all our lives so we were like brothers. We could be blunt and would listen to each other more than anybody else."

The frustration that had boiled over from the previous season would finally take a backseat once the season began and the Pirates showed a glimpse of how good they could be during a preseason scrimmage, taking apart a Tyner team that would eventually win its region and advance to the Class 2A quarterfinals. Later in that same scrimmage, having proved their point against Tyner, the Pirates gave a half-hearted effort and lost to a physical Moore County team.

It would be a result that would come back into play months later.

"LET'S FIND OUT IF WE'RE FOR REAL"

An electrical issue postponed the season opener at Marion and because the lights still weren't working by Saturday, the game was played on a sweltering late August afternoon.

With Marion's defense keying on Pirates tailback Sam Pickett — arguably the fastest player in program history, or as Griffith offered, "Sam's half-ass speed was faster than anybody else's full speed" — quarterback Tim Starkey found plenty of room to operate. Starkey, a lanky dual-threat star with a smooth stride, gashed the Warriors for 166 yards, including a 63-yard scoring sprint for the game's first points.

The Warriors closed within a point midway through the second quarter, set up by quarterback Brennan Paris scrambling 58 yards to the Pirates 14, and five plays later Charles Coffey fought his way into the end zone.

South Pittsburg countered just before the half, converting a fourth-and-one at the Warriors 23, and one play later Starkey hit Jackson for the score and an eight-point advantage. Marion opened the second half with a nine-play 70-yard scoring drive, capped by a 29-yard TD run by Paris, who also added the two-point conversion to tie the game.

"Let me tell ya, I was worried when they tied the game because I couldn't tell whether our players would be able to answer that back," Grider said afterward. "But that's what having seniors on the field will do. We came right back down the field on them."

As the drive stalled, Grider yelled "field goal!" down the sideline. But since attempting field goals was such a rare occurrence for South Pittsburg, players returned blank stares, unsure of who should trot onto the field for the attempt.

"Damnit!" Grider shouted. "Extra point!"

And with that command the confusion was cleared up for the special teams unit, which ran onto the field for Jackson's 25-yard field goal that put them back in front, 17-14. They clung to the precarious three-point lead into the fourth quarter before putting together a 14-play, 93-yard drive that put the game away, converting three third downs, including Pickett bursting through the center of the defense for a 26-yard TD with just 3:50 left in the game.

"It's hard to get a read on just how good we can be," Grider offered as the Pirates walked off the field with a win at Marion for the first time in 12 years. "There's more talent on this team than any I've ever been a part of. We've got 20 seniors who are as good athletically as I've ever been around. It's just a matter of us putting it all together."

Back-to-back bashings of Charleston and Grundy County — by a combined 99-14 — preceded a trip to Boyd-Buchanan for a match-up of top-five ranked teams.

The Buccaneers, who had used a balanced pro-style offense to that point, gave South Pittsburg fits by unveiling a wishbone set they hadn't shown all season.

"We felt like we could really catch them off guard if we switched up our offense and gave them something they hadn't seen us run," said Grant Reynolds, Boyd-Buchanan's defensive coordinator that season. "Coach (Robert) Akins was so paranoid that South Pitt would have a spy up on the levee that overlooked our practice field that we moved practice over behind the girls' softball field where nobody could see us.

"With all their weapons, we wanted to control the ball, run the clock as much as we could. We planned to huddle and play keep-away, hoping to frustrate them. We looked at that game as a huge step toward getting to play for a state championship. We knew they were really good and we believed we were too."

Both defenses adjusted to the new wrinkles the offenses had thrown at them and the only points in the first half came on a 27-yard field goal from Jackson.

On the first drive of the second half, Bucs quarterback Jon-David Blair kept the ball on a midline option and turned a fourth-and-inches into a 30-yard touchdown run that put his team ahead.

"Whoever won that game would get to host a likely rematch in the playoffs and we didn't want any part of having to go down there," Reynolds added. "That's a tough place to play. As soon as you come out of that visitor's locker room their people are waiting on the track to yell and cuss at you. My wife is from there so half of them would be my own family screaming at us.

"The Chambers kid scared about half our team to death. They saw the black face paint and fingernails and they came back to the sideline acting like they had seen a demon or something."

The Pirates answered with another gutsy drive, covering 74 yards in nine plays, before Starkey dove in from a yard out for a 9-7 lead.

But the Bucs proved just how salty they were when Blair, who would finish with 192 total yards, took a reverse pitch and sprinted 57 yards for a TD that gave his team a 14-9 lead late in the third quarter, then stuffed the Pirates to get the ball back.

"You have to understand, I came from a trailer park," Haskew said. "We were on food stamps at times, so when we played Boyd I hated them. They were the rich, private school kids who had what I didn't. There was no way in hell I wanted them to take that game from us.

"They were driving the field, just a few yards at a time, barely getting first downs and running the clock and it was like slow torture. I was so pissed off and just trying to hit people as hard as I could to hopefully make them make a mistake or get something good to happen for us."

Midway through the fourth the Bucs were closing in on a score that would put the game out of reach. They had moved Blair — their best athlete — to running back and brought in freshman quarterback Will Healy, who would go on to an all-state career and later become the head coach at Austin Peay, where he turned what was arguably the worst college program in the country into an FCS playoff contender. But as a skinny freshman, Healy was easy prey for the Pirates seniors, who came after him like a pack of wild dogs chasing a wounded deer.

Boyd-Buchanan moved the ball to the Pirates seven yard line before Ronnie Griffith dropped Healy for a four-yard loss and on the next play, with pressure coming off the left edge, Healy rolled to his right and threw back across the middle, where the ball was tipped by Starkey and intercepted by Eric Reames at the goal line. Reames cradled the interception into his gut and bolted toward the opposite end zone, never slowing down despite several players from both teams stopping to look back at officials who were waving their arms.

What would have been a pick-six for Reames was called back by an inadvertent whistle just after he had intercepted the pass. The ball was brought back to the 20 and the Pirates would have to drive the length of the field to earn the win.

Pirates coaches went ballistic on the officials, but to no avail. Even after their first play, Pirates assistant Heath Grider, who was sitting in the visitor's coaching box above the field, was still furious over the call.

"I can't believe that! What a crock!" Grider yelled through his headset, before dragging out his next thoughts. "Bullllshiiiit!"

Needing a big play from someone, and with Boyd-Buchanan's defense creeping up near the line of scrimmage to take away any running lanes, Starkey connected with Reames, who drug his back foot in bounds to make a spectacular catch for a 27-yard gain to the Bucs 30.

"I remember being in the huddle and looking at Haskew and he had blown his nose and had snot hanging from his face but refused to wipe it off," Starkey said. "He was so mad and locked in that he wasn't even thinking about anything but what the next play was. He would just stand there and stare toward Boyd's players and mumble a few cuss words with this crazy look in his eye. We had some crazy dudes on that team, but Jonathan was a next-level psycho."

Immediately after the play, Heath Grider had calmed down and was back to assessing the game in his typical level-headed manner.

"If we score, we need to be thinking about what play we want to run for two," Grider advised the other coaches through his headset. "A three-point lead could be really big because they may have time for a field goal."

Moments later, potential two-point conversion plays were an afterthought as the Pirates faced fourth and three at the Bucs 22. But Ronnie Griffith plowed over left guard, gaining barely enough yardage to earn a fresh set of downs and Heath Grider was again yelling into his headset.

"Tell those guys up front they've got to man up and start knocking some people off the line of scrimmage!"

The Pirates continued their methodical march and on third and goal from the Bucs one, Pickett followed fullback Matt Stone and Griffith off the right side, diving over the line for the go-ahead touchdown, ending the 14-play drive with the 10th straight running play after the big completion to Reames.

"We all knew that was a desperation drive," said Starkey, who also added the two-point conversion pass to Chris Blevins for a 17-14 lead with 1:58 remaining. "That was the drive that told us we could really be something special. That drive was for the game and we had found a way to get it done when it really counted."

But with enough time for an answer of their own, Boyd-Buchanan moved the ball to the Pirates 46 with a minute remaining before Haskew and Blansett combined to sack Healy for an eight-yard loss, and on fourth and 18 Jackson batted down a desperation pass to end the drama.

"That's the second time this year these seniors have faced a gut check and come through like that," Grider said as he exhaled a sigh of relief after his team ran its region win streak to 19. "I mean, after we get the bad break on the interception return, they could have just folded up and died. But they got ticked off and we did what we do best, just power-run the football down the field."

The Pirates followed that nail-biter with a 34-point win over 2A Sequatchie County and then flexed their offensive muscle in a 76-28 blowout over Lookout Valley, where they set a school record with 711 rushing yards. The Yellow Jackets actually led 14-13 after the first quarter but South Pitt answered with 28 points in each of the next two quarters and Pickett's 290 rushing yards led a threesome of backs with more than 100.

The lopsided final did little to ease Grider's irritation over the way the team had started the game and the following Monday he let it be known as he spoke to the team before practice.

"Fellas you should've found out last year what happens when you get in a ballgame that turns into a shootout," he said, scanning the room at a group of confused players who had spent the weekend being told by everyone else in town how good they were.

"If a team like Lookout Valley can rip through us like they did the other night, somewhere down the road we'll be in trouble," Grider continued, his agitation growing. "I'm not sure how ready we are to play at times and I don't understand that. We don't play with a lot of emotion or fire. There's points in the game fellas where we give absolutely no effort at all. I'm going to show you on that film one time when they're punting to us and it's absolutely the sickest display of football that I've ever seen in my life. It's embarrassing.

"I don't know if you all just want this to be over, but I've never been so frustrated."

The second half of the season's schedule had been purposely sprinkled with tough out-of-region competition to prepare the team for its postseason run, beginning with the next week's opponent, two-time defending Division II-A champion Battle Ground Academy.

Grider knew it was time to refocus his players' attention for the playoffs, and after a tough week of practice he wanted to see how focused they were.

"Fellas, I think you want to be a great football team," he said moments before kickoff against BGA. "But wanting to be and doing it are two different things. It's time to prove whether we're for real or just a put-on. No more Lookout Valleys. No more Sequatchie Countys or Grundys. It's for real now. Against real competition.

"Fly to the football like we haven't done all year. Do what we're suppose to do and let's find out if we're for real."

Determined to show their coach they could answer the call, the Pirates defense held BGA to 188 yards of total offense and forced five turnovers, including an interception by Jackson on the first pass attempt that he returned to midfield. Three plays later Pickett turned the corner on a toss sweep for a 21-yard touchdown.

South Pitt's second score was also set up by another defensive turnover when Blansett recovered a fumble at the Wildcats 27. Again the Pirates wasted no time in cashing in, this time Starkey hitting a wide-open Blevins on a 27-yard TD toss across the middle.

Pirates runner Ronnie Griffith avoids a Charleston defender.

That was all the cushion the defense would need, but Reames added a 76-yard punt return for a third-quarter score just to be safe. Starkey ran for 114 yards, threw for 55 and intercepted two passes, while Griffith ran for another 108 in an impressive 21-0 win that showed they were good enough to beat anyone who showed up on their schedule.

"We liked it when we would find out we were playing against a really good team. It challenged us," Griffith said. "If we heard the other team was good, we were like 'Bring them out here and let's put them to the test'."

Copper Basin all-state running back Johnny Dixon was the next in line to test himself against the refocused Pirates. He came into the game having just gone over 1,000 yards for the season the previous week but by the time the game ended — and the Pirates had claimed a 34-0 win — Dixon was battered, bruised and his season total had dropped back under 1,000 yards after being held to minus rushing yards for the game.

"We had pretty much taken turns just teeing off on him all night and our fans were merciless on him," Jackson said. "He looked over at our fans who were lining the fence and wanted to say something back to them but finally decided to just keep his mouth shut and get out of town. Between our defense and our fans, we made his life hell that night."

Filling in for Pickett, Griffith ran for 192 yards, including a 95-yard TD and the Pirates out-rushed the Cougars 331-93. Starkey proved the Pirates could throw the ball if they wanted, completing 7 of 10 passes for 131 yards and three TDs — two to Reames and another to Jackson.

Just days after the New York Yankees swept Atlanta in the World Series for their 25th championship, South Pittsburg stepped on the field against a team nobody knew much about. Courtland (Ala.) had been a late addition to give South Pittsburg a 10-game schedule and the athletic group — led by a 6-foot-8, 310-pound two-way tackle nicknamed "The Big Show" — would go on to win Alabama's Class A state championship later that season.

Late in the game, with the Pirates pulling away for a 40-25 win, Griffith — who admitted to never passing up a chance to antagonize an opponent when the officials weren't looking — couldn't resist taking a cheap shot at The Big Show.

"He had been running his mouth the whole game and I was pretty sick of it. We were down in a pile and I grabbed him by the nuts and started twisting," Griffith said with a laugh. "All of a sudden I feel this huge hand moving up my chest toward my throat and I knew immediately I had screwed up big time.

"Nobody was un-piling so I knew we were going to be laying there longer than I thought and all I could think to do was start screaming 'I'm sorry!' But that big son of a bitch wasn't going anywhere. He was trying to break my Adam's apple and I just kept squeezing his nuts. We both kind of staggered back up and left each other alone after that."

"TIME TO GET TO WORK"

The Pirates closed out the regular season with a routine 56-7 thumping of Whitwell and Sunbright, their first-round playoff opponent, wasn't expected to be much more of a challenge.

When coaches from both teams met to swap film, Sunbright's staff admitted to Grider that their team's season was likely on life support.

The Pirates wasted no time in pulling the plug, scoring three touchdowns in the first six minutes and finishing each of their first nine possessions with a TD in a 76-10 annihilation. Sunbright moved eight and sometimes nine defenders near the line of scrimmage hoping to stop the Pirates run game, but South Pitt's first-half scoring "drives" had covered two plays, three plays, one play and a 71-yard punt return before finally needing two seven-play marches to the end zone.

"The way our offense is set up, a team could put 11 on the line and we would still move the football on the ground," a confident Grider said afterward, sending a warning to anyone else his team would face.

The next week produced more road kill as the Pirates flattened Charleston 52-7. Pickett had already ran for more than 1,000 yards — most of it effortlessly — and was coming off a five-TD game in the first round, all of which made him the target of Charleston's defense. Aside from a 78-yard punt return for a score, when he took two steps to his left, then broke back to the right and outran six trailing defenders down the sideline, Pickett was mostly a decoy as five other teammates scored in building a 45-0 lead at halftime.

"Sam was one of the fastest players I ever played with. At any level," said Eddie Moore, who had graduated the season before and would go on to become an All-SEC linebacker at Tennessee and play in the NFL. "One time in a track meet he ran the 100 meters without starting blocks because he didn't know how to use them. He still won the race, by a lot. He just had an unreal natural gift."

Pickett's speed would be on full display over the final three weeks of the playoffs. His show began in the quarterfinal rematch with Boyd-Buchanan, which would actually be the fourth meeting between the two teams in the past two seasons, with South Pitt already owning two regular-season wins and had ended the Bucs season in the same round the year before.

"Sure there's pressure with games like this," Grider said in the days leading up to the game. "But if pressure comes along with winning then I'll take the pressure because I want to win."

Similar to their first meeting, the Bucs had installed a few wrinkles that gave South Pittsburg fits. This time it was on special teams, where Boyd-Buchanan had noticed a weakness and exploited it by sending the rush right up the middle to block the Pirates first two punts. They recovered both inside the 30, but while South Pittsburg's defense held the first time, Boyd-Buchanan cashed in the second for a touchdown as Blair, who had moved back to quarterback for the game, dove into the end zone from a yard out.

In another similarity to their first meeting, South Pittsburg would answer right back. The 5-9, 150-pound Pickett took an option pitch from Starkey and bolted 64-yards, untouched, for what looked to be the tying touchdown. However, as he was running past the Bucs secondary, Pickett had slowed just long enough to allow Blair to close within a few feet then waved at him and hit a gear that only he had.

"I had warned our guys all week that we could not let Sam get a step on us," Reynolds said. "He had a level of speed that none of our guys had. Really, that nobody we had seen had. When he waved at us, I couldn't believe it. I was standing there thinking 'Did he really just do that?'"

Even as fans behind the Pirates sideline were buzzing over the move, two referees threw flags and the game-tying TD was brought back.

Grider gritted his teeth and began frantically waving Pickett toward him.

"Are you shitting me?!? Sam, what the hell were you thinking?!?!" Grider shouted, palms up as Pickett trotted to the sideline. "Son, that was about stupid! We can't be giving up touchdowns. You stand over here on the sideline by me and cool your ass off for a while!"

For the next several plays Pickett was Grider's shadow, standing behind him and looking away each time his coach looked back over his shoulder to glare and shake his head in frustration.

Griffith moved to tailback and while it took him four plays to cover the ground, he eventually powered his way across the goal line for a three-yard TD that tied the game and helped Pickett escape his coach's doghouse. Having served his penance, Pickett was inserted back into the game just in time to return a punt to the Bucs 12, setting up his eight-yard scoring run off left tackle that gave the Pirates their first lead.

Just before the half another Pirates miscue on a punt attempt set up a 13-yard TD pass from Blair to Rich Thomas and, despite having just 27 yards on the ground and 31 yards of total offense, the Bucs had momentum thanks to special teams.

South Pittsburg looked to take control in the third quarter and on its second possession of the second half, Starkey, who stood out on a team of stars to become a Mr. Football finalist, capped a seven-play drive with a 3-yard scoring run on third and goal. He then intercepted a pass at the Pirates 40, stopping a Bucs drive, and returned it to Boyd-Buchanan's 35. Two plays later, on the second play of the fourth quarter, Pickett broke free for a 20-yard TD and it appeared the game was in hand.

But the Bucs refused to go away, and when Blair connected with Johnny Taylor for a 74-yard TD with 9:55 to go, South Pitt's lead was cut to 28-21.

"We knew Blair was their main guy and that he had a bad ankle coming into the game," said Pirates middle linebacker Matt Stone, who led the team in tackles for two of his three seasons as a starter. "After just about every play, at the bottom of the pile, we were twisting his ankle or punching him or doing whatever we could trying to get him out of the game.

"You'd hear Blair scream in pain in the pile and get up to complain to the refs but we would all put our hands up and say 'I don't know what he's talking about sir.' He had carved our ass up the first time we played, and since we had a bunch of dirty guys on our team, we wanted to get him out of the game."

Boyd-Buchanan continued gaining momentum, recovering a Pirates fumble at midfield and driving to the 19, looking to even the score again. On first down, as Blair sprinted to his left on an option run, Chris Blevins forced a bad pitch that Starkey scooped and returned to the Bucs 44, and four plays later Griffith fought his way in for a 5-yard TD.

Boyd-Buchanan continued to fight back, but when Starkey leaped to make his second interception, the Pirates 35-21 victory was assured.

For the second straight year Boyd-Buchanan had lost only two games in a season, both to the Pirates, including in the quarterfinals.

The Pirates held Boyd-Buchanan to 24 yards on 25 rushing attempts and a Bucs team that had scored 40-plus points six times and allowed more than 20 only twice all season, was out-gained 377-165 in total yards. Pickett finished with a career-high 29 carries for 227 yards and two TDs and Starkey added 82 rushing yards, intercepted two passes and returned a fumble that set up his team's final score.

About 120 miles to the west, Trousdale County whipped previously unbeaten and top-ranked Christ Presbyterian Academy — a team that had not allowed more than 10 points all season — 35-20, to set up the rematch everyone wearing orange and black had hoped for.

Moments after hearing the Trousdale score, Grider paused to reflect back on the feeling he and his team had carried for an entire year.

"Last year's game was as tough a loss as I've ever been associated with," he admitted. "It was probably the best team we've ever had here. But the problem was somebody else was just as good."

A few feet away, leaning back at his desk, Pratt nodded and was already mentally turning the page toward preparing for the team's shot at avenging that hurt.

"Being in the playoffs was taken for granted," Pratt said. "So it was hard to motivate the kids and the fans to get up for these early-round games. But nobody will need help getting motivated this week. It's time to get to work."

One of the adjustments Pratt had already decided on was to be more aggressive in attacking the Yellow Jackets, who had ran their wing-T misdirection plays to near perfection in the previous year's meeting. He installed a blitz called "lightning" in which both Ronnie and Michael Griffith would fire off both edges to take away any outside running lanes and also make life miserable for Trousdale's quarterback in obvious passing situations.

There would be only three days of class before school broke for Thanksgiving, but even those first three days were dedicated to preparing for Friday's game.

"We had several classes where we would turn in our work early, check out and go watch film," Starkey said. "Nobody was thinking about school that week anyway. All us seniors had the same weight on our shoulders and we just wanted to try and figure out a way to stop Trousdale. That game was very personal."

On Thanksgiving morning, as the team finished its final practice of the week before the next night's game, Starkey approached Pratt with one simple question.

"Coach, are we good to go?"

Pratt nodded confidently and answered, "We're a lot better prepared than we were last year."

"You could tell the guys were a little anxious," Pratt would say later. "It was the first time all year I felt like they were nervous before a game. But the biggest difference from the year before was we were at home and we didn't have the fear of them like we had."

Considering the lack of productivity around town on game day, work may as well have been canceled. All the focus was on that night's final hurdle and the thorn in the Pirates side that had prevented them from a state title the year before.

"When we opened the door before the game the first thing we noticed was the cold air hitting us in the face," recalled Jackson of a day when the temperature hovered around freezing and turned much colder once the sun set behind the mountains. "As we stepped out of the locker room there were so many people lining the track that the cops had to move people out of our way. It was like something out of a movie.

"You couldn't see the end of the line of people who were still coming in through the gates and lining the track. The stands were already full. Everybody turned their head to watch us walk out to the field and our fans were yelling and slapping us on the back. That's the closest to feeling like a god that I'll ever experience."

As the players stood in place during warm-ups, Pratt nervously paced between them, stopping occasionally to look one in the eye and light their fuse.

"Look at you," he said, shaking his head in faux disgust. "You're scared. You ain't ready!"

It was a tactic that was rinse-and-repeat simple, but it worked.

"He had a way of making you say to yourself 'By God I'll show you I'm ready'," Haskew said later. "He knew how to motivate most of us and get us so pissed off that we were like a caged animal just waiting to get unleashed."

Fans made a tunnel — a line on each side of the run-through sign — that stretched from one end zone to the other, showing their support as the Pirates ran onto the field. There were no other teams left alive in a 100-mile radius of Chattanooga, making the overflow from the stands four rows deep on the Beene Stadium track. Some stood on tip-toes or even po-goed up every now and then to get a better glimpse of the action on the field.

On Trousdale's second possession, a pass was tipped and intercepted by Starkey at the Jackets 25, and four plays later Pickett scored on a 9-yard run off the right side, breaking a tackle at the three and stretching into the end zone to send the home-side stands into a frenzy.

The teams then traded long scoring drives before Trousdale tried a fake punt, hoping to catch the Pirates flat-footed. Jackson swung momentum back to the Pirates, and maintained the lead, when he batted down the pass.

"I had deja vu about six times in that game because I had watched so much film on them and thought about every situation so much," Jackson said later. "I had even dreamed about the game several times that week leading up to it."

The Yellow Jackets had a shot at tying the game just before halftime, but Ronnie Griffith pressured quarterback Eli Sanders into a hurried throw that Starkey intercepted at the goal line with just 13 seconds left.

"Tim made a great break on the ball and his interception was huge right before the half because we knew Trousdale would come out attacking in the second half," Pratt said afterward. "Having them playing from behind had us in a much better situation than if the game had been tied to start the second half."

The Yellow Jackets did, in fact, open the second half by attacking. It began when Starkey was rocked on an option and lost the ball to a defender. Trousdale quickly drove 55 yards to even the score midway through the third, but on South Pitt's next possession, on a third-and-four, Starkey used a hard snap count — a play Pirates coaches often use in short-yardage situations to draw the defense offsides for a free five yards via penalty — to give his team the needed first down.

On the next snap, Pickett took the handoff and found a hole off right tackle, bolting through the seam for a 51-yard touchdown run that put his team back in front.

True to his plan, Pratt was aggressive and gave his linebackers the zig-zag hand signal that meant "lightning" was being called for. The two Griffiths nodded and like rabid chihuahuas, sprinted toward Sanders at the snap, forcing another errant throw that Starkey intercepted near midfield and returned to the Trousdale 13.

After the offense was held to just four yards in three plays, the Pirates had to settle for a field goal that gave them a 10-point lead and was cause for a sigh of relief as the fourth quarter began.

Starkey repaid Trousdale for the hard hit he had taken earlier by unloading on a receiver to force a fumble that Jackson recovered at the Pirates 16. It was the second time the 6-3, 180-pound Starkey had turned Trousdale away from the goal line by forcing a momentum-shifting turnover. And that play loomed even larger when the Yellow Jackets got the ball back and again threatened to close the gap.

The drive was kept alive when Chambers kicked a Jackets runner while he was on the ground, drawing a 15-yard penalty. For nearly every defensive snap before that play, the mammoth lineman had controlled his side of the field, helping to shut down Trousdale's vaunted running game. But in the heat of the moment he had given the Yellow Jackets new life by losing his temper.

South Pittsburg called a timeout, but before Pratt made it to the huddle, Ronnie Griffith, who had to tip-toe just to look Chambers in the eye, was unloading on his teammate. "Jesus Christ Chambers how stupid are you?!?" Griffith screamed, his high-pitched voice piercing the cold night air. "I swear to God if we lose this game because of some selfish shit like you getting kicked out I am going to kill you! We need you!"

Griffith's tantrum was loud enough to bring an official over, "Hey 40, calm down, son."

Griffith turned and tried to change his tone before replying to the referee. "I'm sorry sir, but that was stupid!"

While he could have waved a meaty arm and swatted Griffith away, Chambers knew he had cost his team and simply shook his head, clearly aggravated at himself and willing to take the butt chewing from his pint-sized teammate.

By the time Pratt arrived to the huddle he had just one question, "Who did it? Who the hell got the flag?"

The players looked down at the ground, none wanting to rat out their behemoth Mr. Football lineman.

Griffith couldn't contain his anger any longer.

"It was Chambers!" he yelled, pointing toward his teammate. "His dumb ass kicked him, coach!"

Moments later the penalty that had kept the drive moving was compounded when Trousdale scored on a wingback option pass that sailed over Pickett's head and cut the Pirates lead to 24-21 with 4:34 to go.

"That touchdown was my fault," Pickett said. "I came up and bit on the option and the receiver blew by me. I was scared to death that was going to cost us the game, so I had to make sure I made up for it."

Earlier in the week Trousdale players had been quoted in their local newspaper saying their speedy running back Dominique Harper would show Pickett who the fastest player in the state was. It was a comment that had been copied and taped to Pickett's locker as motivation.

He got his chance to make up for his mistake, and prove who the fastest player on the field was on the first snap after Trousdale's TD. Pickett took a hand-off, broke two tackles as he burst through a hole off right tackle, then darted outside and outran Harper, who had an angle on him, along the visitor's sideline for a 68-yard touchdown that reclaimed the 10-point cushion.

As Pickett broke free, longtime Pirates supporter Hoodie Dunwoody began bouncing on the balls of his feet and yelled "Go Sam! Oh yeah! Oh my God!!"

On Trousdale's next series, Pratt called "lightning" one more time for good measure on a third down and the pressure off the edge forced an incompletion that allowed the Pirates to take back possession and punch in one final TD for a 37-21 win that set off fireworks exploding in the cold night air and brought Pirates fans streaming onto the field to congratulate their players.

Almost a year to the day after tears of heartache streamed down the faces of everyone wearing orange and black, it was tears of satisfaction that flowed unashamedly after knocking off the two-time defending state champions.

Jonathan Haskew (66) and Michael Griffith (25) make a tackle in the backfield.

"Words can't say what this feels like," a winded Grider said after his team had ran its home winning streak to 28 games and snapped Trousdale 13-game playoff streak. "There's nobody in the state we respect more than their program. To finally be able to knock them off, it means a lot to us."

The Jackets had averaged 363 rushing yards per game but managed only 120 on 43 attempts against the Pirates. Meanwhile Pickett ran wild, finishing with 261 yards on 25 carries and scoring four touchdowns.

"They're a great team," a dejected Sanders offered. "They're tough and they just come straight at you. They got us."

The days leading up to the state championship game were quiet compared to the previous two weeks, and although Moore County had beaten

South Pittsburg in a preseason scrimmage none of the Pirates players actually felt threatened the way they had before the quarters or semifinals.

As the team began to make its way toward Nashville on the Friday morning of the title game, the bus passed the Princess Theater which had the message: "Last one out of town, turn out the lights" across the marquee.

Nearly two hours before the start of the title game a steady rain settled over Nashville, soaking the field for about an hour before the sun finally emerged.

"That's not the kind of omen I wanted before the game," Grider said as he unloaded from the team bus and looked up to check the clearing skies. "I was worried all the way up here that the field would get sloppy and negate our speed factor. Fortunately, it doesn't look like that's going to be the case."

The home team's locker room inside Vanderbilt Stadium was subdued as players locked in mentally and waited for Grider to give them their last-minute instructions before making their way out onto the field.

As Grider walked to the center of the room, he adjusted the brim of his black cap with the power-P logo and looked at each player sitting in front of their lockers. The 20 seniors locked eyes right back on their coach, letting him know they were ready.

"I've told you since the start of the week the best team is right here in this locker room," Grider began. "All we've got to do is go out and play that way. Guys, I'm awful proud of you. You've come a long way, through a lot of pressure. A lot of doubt. I remember how it felt last year when we lost at Trousdale. People doubted you. They didn't think we could get it done. They didn't know we had what it took to get to this football game. Those same people that doubted you then are sitting up there in the stands saying 'I don't know if they can win the thing.' All we've got to do is go shut them up again.

"Show them from snap one that we ain't going nowhere. We're going to play our type of football. Let's go win us a state championship."

"48 SWEEP ON ONE, BREAK!"

On its second possession of the game, after recovering a Moore County fumble, South Pittsburg covered 40 yards in five plays with Pickett taking it the final 26 yards on a toss sweep to the right for the touchdown.

For much of the season the Pirates offense had operated out of the power-I, but against Moore County — which had a size advantage in the middle of the line — they switched to a regular I-formation with Griffith leading the way at fullback and Pickett having more space to find a crease and use his speed for big gains.

When the teams had played in the preseason Grider took note of how well the play worked and on the Pirates first scoring drive it was again obvious the Raiders defense would have trouble getting to the edge in time to stop the play. Grider decided he would repeat the call — 48 sweep went to the right, 49 sweep was to the left — until it stopped gaining huge chunks of yards.

It never did.

"My daddy taught me a long time ago, if they're not stopping something, don't be stupid," Grider said later. "I kept thinking eventually I've got to go to something else, but they never stopped it, so we kept running it."

On its next possession South Pittsburg converted four third downs and a fourth down in driving 61 yards in 13 plays — all runs — taking 5:07 off the clock, and again it was Pickett capping the drive with a one-yard run coming on a toss sweep.

"That's been my favorite play since I was in pee-wees," Pickett said afterward.

Moments later, Pickett added his third score in an unconventional fashion when Raiders punter Matt Weaver dropped the snap, then shanked a 3-yard punt straight up in the air, which Pickett alertly caught and returned 21 yards for a 20-0 halftime lead.

Soon after the Raiders opened the second half with a Brandon Wells 32-yard TD run, Pickett swept around the left side and scooted down the home sideline for a 35-yard touchdown that seemed to break Moore County's spirit.

"It was scary watching him on film all week. But it was even scarier seeing him in person," Raiders coach Bruce Price said afterward. "He's just so fast and runs so hard and tough. We couldn't do anything with him. He's just a great player."

Pickett added scoring runs of 26 and 68 yards, setting a state championship game record with six TD runs and was the easy choice for Offensive MVP after gaining 231 yards, most of which came off the toss sweep running behind Griffith's edge-sealing blocks.

"If there's a better 140 pound player in the state, I'd like to see him," Grider said of Griffith afterward. "He's a 1,000-yard rusher this year who accepted his role as the lead blocker and that's a huge reason we were able to make it look easy."

In the closing minutes, with the Pirates cruising toward a 42-13 win, and knowing this would be the final game for most of the seniors on the field, Pratt began letting players call the defense.

"Vic was raising hell every time Moore County would gain a yard, but I just wanted the kids to enjoy it at the end," Pratt said with a laugh.

Chambers was named Defensive MVP after making 11 tackles, including five for loss and Stone led the way with 12 solo tackles and five assists. Jackson finished with an interception, a fumble recovery and seven total tackles.

He also made good on a state-record 193 extra points during his four-year career, a total that ranked second nationally at the time, and was one of six Pirates to be named All State along with Pickett, Chambers, Starkey, Haskew and Griffith.

Shortly after accepting the championship coach's plaque, Grider presented it to his dad in the stands. Don Grider had been sick from dialysis all week and was unsure whether he could attend the game. But as he sat high above the field and watched his two sons jog off Dudley Field together with the program's first 15-0 season completed, Don Grider smiled wide and said, "Lord, I don't know how to put into words what this feels like. It's definitely one of the happiest days of my life to see my two boys out there win a state championship.

"I'm just so happy for both of them and all the boys."

Nostalgia also hung in the air for four of Don Grider's former players — Donald Blansett, Freddie Blevins, Gary Reames and Johnny Stone — who had helped him win the 1969 title and now had sons win a championship of their own playing for Don's sons.

"They always claimed they were the best team to come through the school, now we can argue the fact of who's the better team," said Matt Blansett. "We always had to live up to the standard they had set and now we finally have."

Moments later, with AC/DC's "Back in Black" blaring at somewhere near jet-engine decibels in the locker room, Vic Grider found a quiet spot to sit and soak in what his team had just accomplished.

Staring at the gold ball trophy resting in his lap, his reflection returned a satisfied smile.

"I'm so happy for those seniors," he said, his voice shaky with emotion. "There was so much pressure on them, so many doubters, especially after last year.

"These guys had four or five games that really challenged them this year, but they met every one of them and that shows the kind of character they have, the kind of men they're going to be. What a special group."

Outside the door from Grider's corner of solitude, still in full uniform and sitting in front of his locker, Haskew thought back to the day before the game when he and his senior teammates had followed their coach's instructions, taking their time before walking off their home field one last time.

"I walked off the field and thought about all the games we've fought and won together," Haskew said, staring straight ahead as if still reflecting back to the moment. "We only lost one game on that field while we were here.

"Looking up at the empty stands, I had never thought about it before, but this was a very special time in my life. In all our lives."

SOUTH PITTSBURG 1999 RESULTS

Aug. 27	at Marion County	24-14
Sept. 3	Charleston	49-0
Sept. 10	Grundy County	50-14
Sept. 17	Boyd-Buchanan	17-14
Sept. 24	Sequatchie County	48-14
Oct. 1	Lookout Valley	76-20
Oct. 8	BGA	21-0
Oct. 15	Copper Basin	34-0
Oct. 22	Courtland, Ala.	40-25
Oct. 29	Whitwell	56-7

Playoffs

Nov. 5	Sunbright	76-10
Nov. 12	Charleston	52-7
Nov. 19	Boyd-Buchanan	35-21
Nov. 26	Trousdale County	37-21

State championship

| Dec. 3 | Moore County | 42-13 |

1999 Pirates

Players: Jared Cash, Tim Starkey, Tristan Chubb, Rashad Tipton, Mike Jackson, Chris Roberts, Sam Pickett, Michael Griffith, Lamar Case, Chris Blevins, Eric Davis, Ronnie Griffith, Matt Stone, Eric Smith, Tim Fallensen, Shaun Gibson, Ben Chambers, Brett Powers, Marcus Horton, Kevin Matthews, Brett Lewis, Jamie Creekmore, Matt Blansett, Shaun Rice, Adam Blevins, Jonathan Haskew, Charles Jett, Dusty Paul, Lonnie

Brooks, Aaron Chambers, Chase Turner, John Bradley Mount, Michael Clay, Matt Church, Eric Reames, Adam Wileman.

Coaches: Vic Grider, Allen Pratt, Heath Grider, Brent Cooper.

Chapter 23
2007 PIRATES

"On my signal, unleash hell."
— **General Maximus**, *Gladiator*

Eight years old and as wide-eyed as a deer in headlights, Robert Robinson stood along the track that lines South Pittsburg's football field, fascinated by the action on the field and the antics from the adults surrounding him whose mood seemed to swing sharply on the outcome of every play.

Several of his friends — kids around the same age who came to games each Friday night — were busy playing a game of their own in a grassy area just beyond the field, but this was Robinson's first time to experience the spectacle of a game at Beene Stadium and he was too mesmerized by the atmosphere to join them.

The spillover of fans from the stands stood shoulder to shoulder, the smell of whiskey and cigar smoke hung in the chilly night air and Robinson was old enough to connect the dots that whatever the Pirates did would directly affect the crowd's response.

Suddenly Sam Pickett, the Pirates jack rabbit of a running back, darted through an opening, cut outside the pursuit and sprinted toward the corner of the end zone where Robinson stood with his uncle. The noise behind him was like a tap on the shoulder, drawing his attention from the field to see the mass of people jumping, yelling and waving their arms above their head to celebrate the touchdown.

"You could hear the noise start to build and then when Sam took off, all of a sudden it sounded like the whole crowd just exploded," Robinson recalled. "It got so loud and I just kind of stood there and looked at the stands and everybody around me and thought 'This is something special.'

"We couldn't afford to go to a lot of games when I was growing up, but after that first experience I was hooked. That night lit something inside of me and all I knew was I wanted to be a part of it and have the chance to make that crowd go crazy like that. You could tell the game meant so much to all those people, basically the whole town.

"The next summer I decided to try out for football for the first time."

Robinson's football career began with the other pudgy kids playing on the offensive and defensive lines. No matter how much he pestered his coaches for the chance to run the ball, the rule in the 11-12 year old league prevented anyone who weighed more than 115 pounds from playing running back, so the 145-pound Robinson continued to work among the other anonymous linemen.

By the time he reached high school there would be no more restrictions and the once chubby kid's athleticism caught his coaches attention.

One of the traits that separates South Pittsburg coach Vic Grider from some of his peers is a willingness to change the team's offensive style based on the differing talent each season. Through his career Grider has utilized the "I" formation, power-I, wing-T and spread and when he saw how fast and agile Robinson was — particularly for his size — Grider knew he had an ideal wing-T fullback.

The switch to the wing-T prior to Robinson's junior year paid off with seven straight wins to open the 2006 season. But in a match-up of unbeaten state-ranked region foes at Finley Stadium, Tennessee Temple humbled the Pirates and three weeks later, in the first round of the playoffs, Gordonsville exposed them in a lopsided loss.

"We had some guys giggling and playing around in the locker room before the game and, looking back on it, we clearly had a long way to go mentally and physically before we were ready to play with the best teams," Robinson said. "We got pushed around by Gordonsville. I won't lie, we folded up, tucked our tails and went home. We got embarrassed and the ones who were serious knew we had to stop being boys and start being men."

The transformation began during a grinding four-month stretch where the workout pace sifted out the ones who weren't as dedicated. Around the same time that Illinois senator Barack Obama announced his candidacy for President and Apple made public its plan for the first iPhone, the Pirates were setting program records almost daily inside their new weight room.

"We knew we had to get a lot stronger as a team so every day in the weight room started being as competitive as a game," said Matt Wayne, a junior who would play on both sides of the line. "We were all breaking lifting records and trying to out-do each other and when spring rolled around, all of a sudden we could tell how much we had changed."

The first day of spring drills, just before the team walked out to the practice field, they got one final reminder of what was expected.

Sitting in front of their lockers and awaiting last-minute instructions, a room that had been alive with loud conversations and laughter fell silent when their head coach emerged from his office and stepped to the front of the room, a wooden plaque tucked under his arm. All eyes

Pirates quarterback Cody Robinson rolls out.

focused on Grider as he held up the region runner-up hardware from the previous season, then slung it across the room. The loud thud broke the silence as it wobbled on impact, slid across the carpet and came to an abrupt stop once it collided with the cinderblock wall.

"Fellas, I don't know how else to put it," Grider began. "We don't play for runner-up at South Pittsburg. We don't brag about second-place trophies around here. I'll just be real blunt, anything less than a championship is a disappointment to me, to this town and should be for you.

"We're on a mission. If you're not here to win a state championship, there's the door."

Seated along the wall nearest the locker room doors, Cody Robinson — who was entering his third season as the team's starting quarterback — took Grider's outburst as a personal challenge.

"That really opened my eyes," Robinson said. "We were already pretty embarrassed by how the season before had ended and we understood that the first round of the playoffs is not the goal around here.

"With the amount of athletic ability we had in the room, there really was no excuse not to be the team that got the program back to a state championship. It was on us to get it done."

Knowing that his talent was matched only by his pride, the coaching staff challenged Robert Robinson during the spring, adding linebacker duties to his role. The biggest of five running backs who had been timed at 4.6 or faster in the 40-yard dash, Robinson had ran for 1,100 yards as a junior, but now would be counted on to bring a physical style to both sides of the ball.

"I spent all summer getting my body ready for all the extra hits I knew I was going to take," Robinson said. "I had to be in the best shape of my life so every day I'd go to the field and run 100-yard gassers and stadium bleachers for hours. (Teammate) Montrell Mitchell was living with me and we put a weight bench in our room and took turns lifting every night. All I did that summer was work out and eat so I could gain weight and muscle."

From the end of his junior season to the beginning of his senior year, Robinson added more than 20 pounds to his 6-foot-2 frame and at 212 pounds would be a Brahma bull for opponents to deal with.

"When you've got a guy like that, everybody knows he's going to be the one who carries us," Cody Robinson said. "We had speed everywhere and more talent than probably any team the program has ever had, but a guy with Rob's size and speed, you're going to get him the ball a lot and watch him do damage."

INSPIRATION FROM LOSS

As the team was finishing spring practice, and just before school would break for the summer, the Grider family, the program and really the entire town suffered a devastating loss as news spread that Don Grider — who had coached his alma mater into a perennial power for nearly 30 years — had passed away due to complications from diabetes.

As the community mourned together, Pirates players gathered at Rogers Funeral Home to show their support for the family.

"To see our two coaches (Vic and younger brother Heath) and their mom so sad really touched something in all of us," Robert Robinson said. "We had always seen Vic as our big, bad, tough coach but then to see him shedding tears, you realized he was just like any of us who would miss somebody we loved if we lost them.

"We talked about it as a team that we wanted to do something to let their family know that their dad would be proud of them and all of us by how we played. It sounds corny, but even as teenagers we suddenly realized we could play for something bigger than any of us.

"We all grew up hearing about those past championships and it had been eight years since the last one so we wanted to wake the town up again and give everybody a reason to feel good."

Later that summer David Hale, a former Pirates all-state guard on the 1969 state championship team who had also been an assistant under Don Grider, met with another former Grider assistant, Dave Baxter.

"I was going to join another staff, but Vic had talked to me and Dave about possibly coming back and helping the Pirates because he thought they had the potential to win another championship," Hale said. "Dave and I met and decided to come back home and help coach again. I told Dave 'We owe it to Don to come back and help his son one more time.' We both loved Don and we love the program, so we just wanted to help the Pirate family."

In a year remembered for huge numbers — Barry Bonds broke Hank Aaron's home run record by hitting his 756th, the Texas Rangers set an MLB record by scoring 30 runs in a single game and both the Dow Jones and multi-state Mega Million lottery jackpot hit all-time highs — the Pirates would put up staggering figures of their own.

Speedster Rashawn Weatherspoon was too much for Trousdale's defense to handle.

It wasn't just that South Pittsburg made it through a schedule dotted with eight ranked opponents undefeated, but the ease in which it did so. The Pirates led all Tennessee teams by averaging 48 points per game — a better average than 33 boys' basketball teams around the state that year and the second-highest in program history.

Thanks to an overabundance of speed — six backs were timed in the 40-yard dash at 4.6 seconds or faster — and power — every starting lineman bench pressed better than 300 pounds — the Pirates would average nearly 19 yards per snap and 41 of their touchdowns were 30-plus yards, including three in the state title game as they beat all 15 opponents by an average of 36 points.

In orange letters on the back of their black helmets the Pirates had placed the letters "DG" to honor the patriarch of the program, and the entire season would be about sending a clear message that one of the state's proudest programs was back among the elite.

"Besides the talent and all the work in the weight room, one of the biggest reasons for us being as good as we were in 2007 was having Dave Baxter come back and coach on the staff," Wayne said. "He gave us a completely different mentality. He told the linemen that it was our job, on both sides of the ball, to move the line of scrimmage.

"We were playing the same teams as the year before, but they were getting a very different group of Pirates than they had seen."

"THEY JUST DO IT ALL VERY WELL"

With nine starters returning to both sides of the ball, expectations were high when the Pirates opened the season at rival Marion County, which was now being coached by former South Pittsburg assistant Troy Boeck.

"We had to get dressed in the gym, then walk across the parking lot and through all their fans along the track to get to the field," Wayne said. "You could feel their glare as we were approaching from the parking lot and by the time we got to the track there were old women, little kids and grown men yelling at us."

South Pittsburg fell behind Marion County briefly in the second quarter before Cody Robinson's pass across the middle on the final play of the half was deflected and ricocheted into Arkeeme McKinney's hands. Once he gained control of the ball, McKinney turned upfield and took the reception in for a 41-yard touchdown that put the Pirates back in front.

A frustrated Robert Robinson jerked his helmet off as he walked into the visitor's locker room and yelled across the room, "What the hell are we doing?"

Grider trailed shortly behind and in a loud, sarcastic voice announced "If this is the kind of season you want, we'll be in a dogfight with this bunch and the rest of the season too. If you're as sick of how we played in the first half as I am we'll go do what we're suppose to."

After mistakes were called out and adjustments were made, South Pittsburg looked like a different team in the second half, scoring four more unanswered touchdowns and rolling up 457 yards to pull away for a 47-19 win.

"Before we started the second half we got together and said we didn't want to give them a chance to blow that train whistle the rest of the night," said Tony Roden, an all-state right guard that season. "We all hated that whistle so keeping it quiet was a great thing for us."

After playing every snap of a humid first half, Robert Robinson gained nearly 150 of his 202 yards in the deciding second half and even led the team with six solo tackles, three more for loss and a sack. As other players left the game with cramps, Robinson never missed a snap.

"He's always been the guy we go to when we need the tough yards on offense," Grider said afterward. "We know we can put the game on his shoulders if we have to. But if we're going to realize our potential as a team, we really need him on defense because he's big and strong enough to take people on inside and has plenty of speed to get to the edge."

The Pirates jumped on Copper Basin the next week with 33 points in the first quarter, led by Rashawn Weatherspoon who had two TD catches and returned an interception 40 yards for another score. As a glimpse into the rest of the season, Cody Robinson's accuracy provided the balance that prevented the Cougars — and every other opponent that followed — from being able to load the box to sell out to stop the run.

"The biggest difference for me as a senior quarterback was knowing what everybody else needed to do and being smart with the football," Cody Robinson said. "I knew where everybody on the field would be and where to put the ball so our athletes could do what they did best — make big plays."

Lookout Valley brought the area's leading rusher — Chas Scruggs — and a state ranking to town for South Pittsburg's home opener. For only the second time in two years, Scruggs was held under 100 yards — finishing with 23 yards on 13 carries — as the Pirates out-gained the Yellow Jackets 412-97 to give Grider the 100th win of his career. Robert Robinson ran for 130 yards and two scores in the first half of another mercy rule win.

"On two of Robinson's touchdowns we hit him in the backfield but he just bounces off and keeps going," Jackets coach Tony Webb said afterward. "They're so physical on both sides of the ball. Nothing they did surprised us; they just do it all very well."

After a ho-hum 49-0 win over David Brainerd — where Josh Dawson's first punt return for a touchdown on a steamy Saturday afternoon was the highlight — perennial 2A playoff power Tyner came to test a Pirates defense that hadn't allowed a score in 14 quarters.

The defense was responsible for the first points of the game when linebacker David Jones blasted Rams runner Tyrell Grayson — cracking his ribs on the hit and forcing a fumble that fellow linebacker Bubba Ramsey scooped and returned 31 yards for a touchdown.

"All I saw in front of me was green field, white lines and a brown football," Ramsey said. "They were a real physical team but I think that let them know we were too. We delivered the hardest hits we had all season and took the hardest hits we had all season. That was two teams that just got after each other."

Pirates safety Terrell Robinson intercepted a pass at the five to stop a Tyner drive, then recovered a fumble at the goal line that ended another threat.

After being held to 43 yards rushing in the first half, the Pirates changed offensive looks by going to the shotgun, which they hadn't shown all season but installed during that week's practice. The Rams had not allowed more than 148 yards to any opponent all season, but the Pirates new formation gave them fits and helped gain 216 yards in the second half alone. Robinson and David Jones combined for 284 yards for the game.

During a third-quarter drive, facing fourth and short near midfield, Grider decided to go for it. As he relayed the call — 34-G, the bread-and-butter power run to Robert Robinson — Cody Robinson delivered an added message to his offense before breaking the huddle.

"We want this more than them!" he said as he scanned the huddle. "They're not better than us. Line, just move them out of the way and let Rob do what he does."

Standing on the right side of his quarterback, the burly fullback took the hand off and found a hole in the middle of the line. With three Tyner defenders chasing him, Robinson raced 52 yards for a score that put the Pirates up 19-7 midway through the quarter.

Tyner fought back to cut the lead to 25-21 and when Robert Robinson fumbled at midfield with just over a minute remaining, the door was open for the Rams to steal the win. With just six seconds remaining, Arkeeme McKinney — who had not played defense all night but came in to replace an injured teammate — delivered a hit to Tyner's Kelvin Johnson that shook the ball loose at the 10 yard line. McKinney, who was laying on the ground, raked the ball into his arms to seal the win.

"I never prayed to help us win a football game because I felt God had more important things to worry about," Roden said. "But I was praying for the Lord to help us win that game. I was on the ground after diving at the quarterback before he threw that last pass, but when I heard the roar from the crowd I knew we had won.

"Later that night in bed I kept waking up because my muscles were so sore and tired, they kept twitching. We got tested by a really good team, we knew after that game we had something special going."

In what could have been a trap game, sandwiched between match-ups with state-ranked Tyner and Boyd-Buchanan, the Pirates made the most of just 29 snaps by scoring five touchdowns of 42 yards or longer in a 49-point win over county rival Whitwell. Rashawn Weatherspoon had three of those long-distance scores and Robert Robinson needed just five carries to amass 117 yards.

The next week, against a stingy defense that had yet to allow more than 83 rushing yards, the Pirates scored more points in the first half than Boyd-Buchanan would allow in every other game that season. Highlighted by a gravity-defying, tackle-slipping 66-yard scoring dash, junior

David Jones ran for 181 yards and South Pittsburg ran for 424 as a team in a physically dominant 47-7 win.

"We knew they were fast," Bucs coach Grant Reynolds said afterward. "But they just physically whipped us. I can't ever remember us being dominated on this field like that."

Despite scoring touchdowns on seven of their 10 possessions the next week against Silverdale Baptist at Finley Stadium, Grider was furious over three turnovers, including Cody Robinson's first and only two interceptions of the season, and two more scores getting called back by penalties.

Silverdale came into the game averaging 403 rushing yards and 40 points but were out-gained 524-147 in total yards in a 52-7 beat-down.

David Jones scores another TD in the title game.

"They've got so many really good players, but Robert Robinson is a man with a football under his arm," Seahawks coach John Allen said.

The following week, their first game as the state's top-ranked team, was more of the same as five players found the end zone and the Pirates scored 62 first-half points against Tennessee Temple.

The video game numbers continued in the regular-season finale as the Pirates scored 58 first-half points against Grace Academy, the last TD coming on an amazing 55-yard run by David Jones in which he broke nine tackles along the way.

The Golden Eagles were held to minus-23 rushing yards and despite the running clock in the second half, surrendered 72 points.

HITTING ANOTHER GEAR

The playoffs began with anything but a typical first round opponent as Trousdale County, a program that had claimed five state championships, came in having allowed more than 14 points just once all season.

During pre-game warmups, Pirates assistant Wesley Stone leaned down and said matter-of-factly into Robert Robinson's earhole, "You like to talk a lot Rob. But if you're really serious about all that talk then you'll make sure we're coming back out here next Friday to play again. I won't believe you're what people think you are until you prove it tonight against this bunch."

Robinson never looked up. He simply nodded, but never took his eyes off Trousdale's players warming up at the opposite end of the field.

On the Pirates first snap Grider called 34-G, just to test the waters and confirm the game would be as physical as he expected.

At impact an audible groan came from the stands on both sides of the field, then a louder roar from the South Pittsburg fans as Robinson plowed over the defender, regained his balance for a few more yards before finally being dragged to the ground.

"Is that all y'all got?!?" Robinson yelled toward the Trousdale defenders as they made their way back to the huddle. "Hey, get ready cause we're comin' again. You boys are going home tonight!"

Robinson put South Pittsburg on the scoreboard first with a 58-yard run but Trousdale, having installed some of the same power plays that Tyner had been able to give the Pirates fits with, wasn't going anywhere and by the second quarter had cut the deficit to 12-10. The momentum was short-lived as Weatherspoon, coming in motion across the formation, took a hand-off and bolted 80-yards, untouched, down the home sideline for a quick-strike score.

Remembering the advice his dad had once given him — keep running a play until the other team stops it — Grider called the same 21 jet sweep that Weatherspoon had taken to the house on the previous possession. This time however, Weatherspoon had to avoid one tackle near the line before turning the corner and using his long stride to again pull away for a 70-yard scoring sprint.

As Weatherspoon got one step ahead of the pursuit, Grider put his finger in the air, already signaling for the extra point, then looked back over his shoulder and yelled toward his team, "Guys they can't stop us!"

"That made us feel like we're the baddest mothers on the planet," Robinson said. "To have your coach sound so confident, we thought we were invincible."

With three TDs of 50-plus yards in the first half, the Pirates piled up 410 rushing yards on a stout defense.

"Rashawn's speed destroyed them with a simple sweep," Cody Robinson said. "On both of those runs their safety had the angle on him but he still blew by them. We had some fast guys on that team, but Rashawn had a different gear that nobody else did."

Trousdale was stubborn and scored early in the third, cutting the lead to 10, then drove to the Pirates 28 before being held on fourth and four early in the fourth. The Yellow Jackets had 20 of the first 25 second-half snaps before South Pittsburg countered with a grind-it-out eight-play, 72-yard drive, capped by Robert Robinson's 15-yard scoring run on fourth-and-one that brought back childhood memories.

"When I crossed the goal line and turned around I saw that same crowd that I remembered from my first game there as an eight-year old," Robinson said. "I almost passed out I got so excited. I could see the energy going through the stands and I remember thinking 'I hope heaven feels this good.'"

He sealed the win with a thunderous tackle on Trousdale's Tacola Seay, and while they were still on the ground, Robinson pressed his facemask into Seay's and said "You know you're going home tonight, don't you?!"

Friendship Christian, which was the previous season's state runner up, swaggered into Beene Stadium in the second round for their first meeting with the Pirates since escaping with a one-point playoff win two years before.

"The quarterbacks, receivers and backs came out for warmups and Coach Heath (Grider) looks at me and says 'Do you feel that?'," Cody Robinson recalled. "I started looking around and had no idea what he meant. Then he said 'It feels like you're about to give them an ass whipping.' I smiled real big and said 'yeah, I think so.'"

By the time both teams were finishing up their warmups, the trash talk from the Commanders side had nothing to do with the game.

"Hey Robinson, did you buy your cleats with your welfare check?" one lineman yelled toward Robert Robinson. ... "Y'all are going back to the projects tonight with a loss." ... "Go smoke them Black & Milds, drink your forties and eat some more government cheese."

"It wasn't just their players," Roden said. "A bunch of their fans standing on the track were yelling at us, calling us poor white trash and ghetto blacks and a whole lot of other stuff that let us know they were looking down on us and didn't think much of our town or our team. I remember thinking 'this is a Christian school?'

Pirates players celebrate around the 2007 trophy.

"They kept talking about how they were going to show us what grown-ass men did on the field. It pissed everybody off so bad that we didn't even want to have to go back to the locker room to cool off. We just wanted to kick it off and get after them right there."

Commanders 5-foot-10, 180-pound senior Jeremy Rickaway, a two-time all-state runner, was touted as the best back in the state, having gained more than 5,500 career yards and scored 80 touchdowns.

Before unleashing his team, Grider wrote Rickaway's number 32 on the chalkboard inside the locker room and drew a circle around it. Through gritted teeth he challenged everyone wearing the solid black uniforms.

"I want to see somebody knocking his dick in the dirt on every snap!" Grider ordered, using the chalk to draw a line slashing through the giant

'32' on the chalkboard. "Put his ass on the ground! Let's find out real quick how tough this bunch is, or if they're just all talk."

On the first play, David Jones ran past the Commanders line and blasted Rickaway in the backfield, sending him stumbling backward. The impact had loosened Rickaway's helmet and as he took it off to adjust the chinstrap, he revealed the blonde tips in his hair.

"Gonna light your ass up all night pretty boy!" Jones yelled, nodding his head at Rickaway, who suddenly had some of the fight taken out of him.

"All that cocky attitude went away real fast and they weren't saying a whole lot after the first half," Robinson said. "They didn't really want to get physical. They were just a put-on."

The Commanders first possession ended with a punt that pinned South Pittsburg back at its one yard line. But on their first play the Pirates made a statement when Robert Robinson took a handoff in his end zone and barreled through a gaping hole off the right side of the line. Mammoth tackle Dominique Garrett had driven his defender completely out of the vicinity of the line and Roden created an alley with a crushing block on Friendship Christian's end, allowing Robinson to hit full stride before angling toward the visitor's sideline then outrunning the secondary for a 99-yard touchdown that sent the home side of the stadium into wild celebration.

"Robert gets a lot of credit for being a bull, but he showed some speed there because he flat ran off and left their whole team," Grider said afterward.

Fulfilling Heath Grider's pregame prediction, Cody Robinson completed six passes, all to Rashawn Weatherspoon, for a school-record 227 yards and four touchdowns as the Pirates scored on six plays of 35 yards or more.

"It was like throwing at practice out there," Cody Robinson said. "I was putting it right on the money and Rashawn was taking off and leaving them every time he got it. Rickaway was their fastest player so they moved him to cover Rashawn. Coach Grider called me over and said 'We're about to make Rickaway look foolish too.' We threw it deep down the sideline and Rashawn just blew by him like he was standing still. They had no answer for Rashawn."

Weatherspoon hauled in scoring passes that covered 65, 59, 48 and 36 yards as the Pirates finished the first half with an even 181 rushing yards and 181 passing to take a 34-7 lead. In scoring more points in the first half than the Commanders had allowed in a game all season, the Pirates had rolled up 362 total yards.

"I've said all season we can throw it if we want to," Grider said. "We just haven't had to, but I felt like we could hurt them with the pass tonight. It was one of those nights where everything I called worked."

For good measure, Weatherspoon also intercepted a pass on defense and caught a two-point conversion pass.

"I just remember their mouth was shut and they kept their head down the whole second half," Roden said.

The run of Region 4 foes continued for a third straight week with Gordonsville — the team that had embarrassed South Pittsburg the year before. Led by all-state quarterback Justin Smith, his region's MVP with nearly 5,000 career yards to his credit, the Tigers had scored at least five touchdowns seven times coming into the rematch.

In the moments leading up to kickoff, Grider walked into the locker room with his hands stuffed deep in his pockets. Once he was convinced all eyes were locked in on him, he held up both hands to reveal gold state championship rings on his fingers, the light above him causing the jewelry to sparkle.

"If you guys want one of these you've got to go through this bunch tonight to get it," he said, keeping his fingers in the air for affect. "Some people will say we owe them payback for last year, but to me they're just the next team that we've got to move out of the way to go get us one of these."

"If there hadn't been doors to let us out of the locker room we would've just knocked a wall down to get out to the field," Wayne said. "All of us wanted to get one of those rings like he had."

But the shine was quickly knocked off those championship dreams when South Pittsburg fumbled the opening kickoff and Gordonsville wasted no time in jumping out to a 6-0 lead on a 27-yard halfback option pass.

"There really wasn't any panic in anybody's eye when we huddled up before going back out on the field," Cody Robinson said. "By that point in the season we were a really confident team, so we knew we just needed to settle down and keep playing and we'd get things turned around."

Sure enough, the Pirates — who were behind for only the second time all season — answered with an 11-play, 66-yard scoring march, capped by Robinson's 1-yard run, then later closed the first half with a 13-play, 80-yard drive, finished by Robinson's 10-yard TD.

After being pushed around by Gordonsville the year before, the Pirates were clearly the aggressor this time around, opening the second half by covering 80-yards in 16 plays — all runs — converting two fourth downs and chewing up 8:30 off the clock to take a 26-6 lead.

A team that had thrived on big-plays all season was now proving it could also sustain a methodical, soul-sucking pace as well. The Tigers had allowed more than 200 rushing yards only once but by halftime had surrendered 229 and the Pirates finished with 396 on 62 bruising carries, led by Robert Robinson's career-high 30 totes for 198 — 111 of which came in the first half — and four TDs.

"We knew they were too sound defensively for us to get a lot of big plays, so it was going to be up to our line to show how much they've matured," Grider said afterward. "Games like this were won all those months ago when our guys got serious in the weight room. That was the difference from a year ago to now."

With Robinson pounding the center of the Gordonsville defense, speedsters David Jones and Montrell Mitchell were getting to the edge for big chunks, combining for another 163.

South Pittsburg held the Tigers to 81 yards on the ground, just the third time they had failed to gain 100 in 13 games.

"Almost 100-percent of that season we played pissed off, but especially for that game," said linebacker Bubba Ramsey. "It was like reclaiming our manhood. I think it surprised them how we just ran it down their throats."

By the time the semifinals rolled around South Pittsburg was the only team in the Chattanooga area left alive in the playoffs which meant the crowd and media attention would be enormous.

Unbeaten Hampton, which had scored 40-plus points nine times to set a program record with 13 wins, made the four-hour drive from the upper reaches of east Tennessee for its third straight trip to the semifinals and first time to face the Pirates.

Earlier in the season the Bulldogs offensive line — led by Steven Roop (6-foot-6, 360-pounds), Mario Phaumba (6-0, 330), Logan Andrews (6-2, 260), and Lucas Teague (5-10, 230) had posed for a picture that appeared on the internet with the caption "Here comes the pain train".

That caption was repeated all week to the Pirates linemen as a challenge. Despite being outweighed up front by an average of 60 pounds, South Pittsburg's wing-T blocking was about angles, where smaller linemen could use their quickness rather than having to block man-to-man up front.

The Hampton fans — who could have driven into eight different states (Georgia, Indiana, Kentucky, North Carolina, Ohio, South Carolina, Virginia and West Virginia) in the time it took them to reach South Pittsburg — began showing up at Beene Stadium three hours before kickoff. Those travel-weary early birds must've began their pilgrimage shortly after breakfast to arrive so early.

The Pirates, who were back in the semifinals after a six-year absence, emerged from the field house nearly an hour before kickoff to find their stands already full and the walkway to the north end zone blocked by four satellite trucks from regional TV stations.

Once the team returned to their locker room for a brief respite to collect their thoughts and their breath — several players were so amped up they looked like they might hyperventilate from excitement — Grider paced along the rows of lockers to gauge the mood of the room.

"Are y'all scared?" he began. "Guys, I'm sick of hearing about how big and strong they are up front. There are people out there right now who say we can't run the ball inside on them. That's bull. Nobody tells us what we can't do. We're South Pittsburg and we do whatever the hell we want to do.

"What do we do here? We play physical, smash-mouth football."

After a long pause, Grider noticed the jittery looks on the faces of his players had been replaced by suddenly confident head nods. Roden clapped his hands, announcing the team was ready to be turned loose.

"Hell yeah!" he said.

"Who are we?" Grider howled.

"SP!" the players shouted back in unison.

"Then let's go show them what Pirate football is all about!"

Hampton mounted a drive to begin the game, but was stopped short on fourth down at the Pirates 25. As Cody Robinson jogged over to meet his coach and get the offense's first play call, Grider said, "Let's see what his big ass is made of. 34-G."

The handoff to Robert Robinson gained nearly 10 yards behind the block of 6-3, 280-pound right tackle Dominique Garrett — running right at the 360-pound Roop.

Robinson immediately popped up from the ground and began shaking his head emphatically.

The Pirates gather to pray together after another big win.

"They ain't got nothin' for us tonight," he announced to the huddle.

For the rest of the night it wasn't so much the weight Garrett moved as the reps that were so impressive. Garrett, who set a school record with a bench press of 425 pounds, continually moved Hampton's mammoth defensive lineman time and again to clear the way for the Pirates' power run game. Out to prove a point, 46 of South Pittsburg's 52 run plays went crashing into the interior of the Bulldogs line, gaining 408 yards.

"Y'all ain't nothing," Garrett said after the Pirates first touchdown run. "You're in the Pitt now boys!"

"We all just stayed low and drove them back, every snap," Garrett would say after the game. "It was all about our technique we'd been taught. We just came off the ball and pushed them back all night.

"We knew all we had to do was clear a little bit of a hole and our backs can do the rest."

Ahead 21-7 and driving toward another score that likely would have put the game away late in the first half, Robert Robinson lost a fumble that was scooped and returned 76 yards for a touchdown that changed the complexion of the game, opening the door for Hampton to remain within striking distance.

"Robert was beating himself up pretty good at halftime but we told him to put that mistake behind him because we needed him to focus on the second half," Cody Robinson said.

Neither team slowed the other in the second half, Hampton answering each of South Pittsburg's scoring drives with one of its own to remain just one score behind and apply pressure on the Pirates offense to maintain the lead.

Early in the fourth quarter, after Hampton converted a third down on another scoring drive, Grider jerked his headset off and yelled toward the field "All we care about is getting the ball and scoring. We look like we could care less about playing defense!"

For a second straight week South Pittsburg was unable to break its trademark long runs, but relied on physical drives — the Pirates averaged 7 yards per snap — to drain the clock and wear on the Bulldogs.

"You could see them getting tired in the second half on defense," said Robert Robinson, who had been named a Mr. Football finalist. "They were a great team. The best team we played all year. I actually expected it to be a lot harder to run inside on them because of their size, but really there were some huge holes and it was just as easy as it has been all year."

David Jones, who caught a 16-yard screen to convert third and 13 on the first drive, ran for 107 yards on just nine carries and scored twice. He also had two devastating blocks on the final scoring drive, which covered 60 yards. Robinson, who finished with 29 carries for 226 yards, scored on a nine-yard run with just 2:29 remaining to make it 42-28 and Weatherspoon intercepted a pass on the next series to put the game away.

"GO LIKE THEY SLAPPED YOUR MAMA IN THE FACE"

Two things happened on the Monday before the 1A state championship game. During the press conference, McKenzie all-state quarterback Derek Carr had raised the ire of South Pittsburg's entire team with his comments, and later that afternoon, when the state's Mr. Football award was announced, Robert Robinson couldn't hide his surprise when he did not win. Irritated as he left the event, Robinson chose his words carefully as he told media he would use the disappointment as motivation when he returned to Murfreesboro to play for a title later that week.

The 6-foot-3 Carr, who was also a Mr. Football finalist and would later play at the University of Tennessee at Martin, had completed 60-percent of his passes for more than 2,200 yards and 21 TDs to that point and led a late scoring drive in a three-point semifinal win.

McKenzie had not lost to a 1A opponent and had won its 13 games by an average of 26 points.

"Our offense hasn't been stopped yet," Carr had announced to state-wide media during the pre-game press conference. "I'm very confident in what we do."

Carr's comments were the talk of the two-hour car ride home for the Pirates contingent, and by the time they got back home they quickly spread word throughout the rest of the team what had been said.

"Oh, it definitely got our attention," Cody Robinson said. "We didn't do a whole lot of trash talking before games, but we sure did once we got on the field and started whipping somebody's ass and our guys were going to put that in the back of their mind for later.

Robert Robinson steps out of a tackle for another touchdown.

"The rest of the week we just prepared like we had for every other game because that's what had worked all year and nobody wanted to go up there and get the silver ball. You don't win the silver ball, you lose and have to take that one. We weren't bringing that one back to town."

When the Pirates filed out of their field house and loaded onto the charter bus on a drizzly game day morning, as has always been the case before championship games, the streets were lined with supporters and well wishers who wanted to give them a proper send-off before following the team to the game.

As the team bus began to roll out of the parking lot Cody Robinson saw his grandfather, Eddie Saylors, standing alone on the sidewalk. Through a smudged bus window, the two made eye contact and Saylors raised his fist and pumped it, as if to say "Go get 'em!"

"That was my extra motivation," Cody Robinson said. "My pawpaw was my best friend and even though his kids had gone to Jasper and he gave me hell about wearing the orange and black, he would always change his work schedule to come watch me play every game.

"That meant a lot to me that he was there."

The light rain that had fallen earlier in the day finally cleared out of the mid-state area as the Pirates completed pre-game warmups on the artificial turf at Middle Tennessee State University's Floyd Stadium. Several players huddled together and pointed out how they believed the sure footing on the turf should make their speed advantage even greater.

Once everyone was back inside the locker room, offensive lineman Brandon Tetter knelt in the center of the room and his teammates circled close around him, each placing a hand on a teammate's shoulder, then bowing their heads to recite the Lord's prayer.

With all heads still bowed, Tetter began a more personal prayer.

"Dear God, give us the strength to not let our town down or Coach Grider down," he said loudly. "We all know what we're playing for. I love all my brothers. Give us strength in Jesus name."

All 42 voices shouted, "Amen!" before each player found a blue metal folding chair to sit in, facing a giant dry erase board at the front of the room.

Defensive coordinator Allen Pratt, who also moonlighted as the school's principal, was the first coach to stand in front of the team and give instructions.

"If I call any blitz and you're going, you've got to go like they slapped your mama in the face," Pratt began. "There's no excuse to take a play off on defense. Go get the guy down. There is no tomorrow.

Prove to him that he don't know what the eastern side of the state is all about."

Extending his arm to hold four fingers above his head, Pratt concluded with, "Get us four stops guys and we'll win this game."

There were no questions. In fact, there was no noise at all. For the next five minutes the room remained as quiet as morning snow before Grider finally stepped to the front of the room and broke the silence.

"There is no magic. No trick plays," he said. "Do what we do, what got us to this point. Intensity guys, right from the start. Hit 'em in the mouth and let 'em know we're here. Let them know early where we're from and what we're all about. It's an all-day fight. It ain't gonna be over in the first five minutes.

"Nobody believes in you more than I do. I am highly confident in this football team. This is as big as it gets in high school football. Lay it all out there and finish what we started."

Despite what Grider had said the game, in fact, would be over in the first five minutes.

A holding penalty on the first play of the game brought back a gashing 15-yard run to the left by David Jones, but on the next snap Montrell Mitchell took a pitch from Cody Robinson and swept around the right side of the line. Robert Robinson laid out a defender on the edge and tight end Chase Robinson drove a linebacker completely off the field before depositing him on the South Pittsburg sideline.

As Mitchell bolted through the gaping hole and hit a sprinter's stride down the seam, he looked up at the giant Jumbotron in the end zone he was headed for. Seeing his image pulling away from the defense, Mitchell began shaking his head emphatically and talking to himself.

"Come on Trell," he said aloud to himself. "Run Trell. Nobody's near you, just run baby!"

Mitchell took the sweep 69 yards, untouched, for a touchdown that announced not even the state championship opponent could muster much competition for the Pirates.

"My dad would stand on the sideline and send dry footballs in during the game," Cody Robinson said. "That was his way of staying on the field so he could be close to me and my brother (Chase). When Montrell took off, my dad took off sprinting right along with him on the sideline. Dad had a football in his left hand and was pointing his finger in the air with his right hand, like he was saying this game's over already.

"Even though that first touchdown was easy, I kept thinking these guys made it to the state game so they had to be pretty good. I was thinking maybe they made a mistake or lined up wrong. Surely we won't beat the hell out of them. But when we got the ball back, I saw that those guys were in deep trouble."

Cody Robinson hit Weatherspoon, who blew past two defenders before reaching up over his right shoulder to reel in the catch and sprint 80 yards for a score on the Pirates next possession.

Barely four minutes into the game and the outcome was all but settled.

Before he had even carried the ball, Robert Robinson made his presence felt with a vicious hit on Carr for a sack. It was the first of five first-half sacks by the Pirates defense and as Carr came off the field after another in the second quarter and was asked where the rush was coming from, he jerked his chinstrap off and blurted out, "I don't know! They're coming from everywhere!"

"We blitzed them to death," Pratt said afterward. "It was the same blitz call but who rushed was based off how McKenzie lined up. We drove them crazy and I was loving it."

After back-to-back big plays had stunned McKenzie, Robert Robinson was turned loose to pound away at what was left of the Rebels pride, eventually scoring on a 19-yard run for a commanding 21-0 lead.

"We jumped on them in a hurry," Grider said afterward. "We came out of the gate ready to play. When we're playing like that, we're awfully tough to do business with."

Just minutes after the third TD, Pirates safety Terrell Robinson added a defensive score when he scooped a fumble and returned it 26 yards. The ego crushing continued with another long drive capped by Robert Robinson's second TD, which made it 34-0 at halftime.

The Pirates had held Carr to 97 passing yards and McKenzie managed just 47 rushing yards as a team. The Rebels, who hadn't been held scoreless in a half all season and had averaged 41 points, failed to score until early in the fourth quarter.

"Once they were on the ropes, we were always taught to keep swinging, never let up," Matt Wayne said. "We showed them what power football is."

Grider's halftime instructions were short and to the point.

"Don't let up," said Grider, who was annoyed that a missed extra point would prevent the second half from beginning with the running clock mercy rule in effect. "We're going to show them what a state championship team looks like."

As the team began making its way from the locker room back to the field, David Hale, an assistant who was a former all-state defensive lineman that played at Vanderbilt and was still as stout as an ox, went in to hug the 280-pound Garrett but was a little too enthused and knocked him off balance before catching him and yelling, "Let's go son!"

A bruising first half had taught Rebels running backs what was waiting for them in the hole, and they began tip-toeing near the line, which only served to allow the Pirates speed to tee off even harder.

With just over seven minutes left in the third quarter, when Robert Robinson stiff-armed a defender into the turf on his way to a 20-yard touchdown, the unthinkable happened in a title game: the mercy rule was in effect.

"Our line was killing them up front so we could drive it on them and break big runs," Cody Robinson said. "And they couldn't cover Rashawn so we knew we could do whatever we wanted. I had no intention of taking it easy on them. I wanted to keep putting it on them because it would be the last game us seniors played together.

"I can't sugarcoat it for them, we absolutely dominated them."

By the time David Jones weaved his way through the defense for a 39-yard touchdown run — lowering his shoulder to plow over one final Rebels defender on the way — there was only one thing left for the Pirates to accomplish. Ahead 52-6 with 8:20 still to go, Grider decided it was time to honor his late father with a tribute play he had worked on with the offense to end each day of practice in the days leading up to the title game.

Rather than attempt a meaningless extra point, Grider called timeout and came to the huddle to go over any lingering questions on the 46 call — the bread and butter play of Don Grider's offensive success.

"He had told us about the play and that he wanted to honor his dad by running it one time," said Bubba Ramsey. "When Coach Grider's dad died, my dad had told me about playing for him and explained the passion he had for the game. That opened my eyes to how much Coach Vic is the spitting image of his dad.

"One day, after we had ran the play a couple of times to end practice, a couple of us looked up and saw Vic walking up the hill to where his dad is buried. It was like he was going up there to let him know we were going to run his play for him in another state championship and all of a sudden that play, something we had never ran before, meant a lot more to us."

The play would require Cody Robinson to turn sideways, allowing the direct snap to go to Montrell Mitchell before Robinson would then try to seal the end with a block that would open the running lane.

"I had noticed before our last touchdown that Coach Grider kept looking up at the scoreboard clock, which he never did," Cody Robinson said. "I knew he was checking the time because he wanted to make sure we got to run that play for his dad.

"Football is a rough game and we were all a bunch of tough guys, but we love our coach and we wanted to make him happy. I just wish we could've scored on it."

Montrell Mitchell yells as he sprints for a TD to open the title game.

In one of the few plays that didn't gash the Rebels all day, Mitchell was stopped short of the goal line on the two-point try, but the outcome of that play really wasn't the point.

"It accomplished exactly what I wanted it to," Grider said afterward. "Just getting to run it in a championship game was good enough because it was our way of honoring my dad."

As the scoreboard clock mercifully hit triple zeroes, Grider raised his right hand into the chilly night air, then glanced skyward for a couple of seconds and pumped his fist.

Several feet away, Coach Hale was bear-hugging everyone in sight, including a TV reporter who looked confused as to why this stranger was squeezing him.

As the team turned toward their crowd and hoisted the gold trophy, Grider reached out to take his daughter's hand and begin making his way off the field.

"Are you excited?" he asked.

Victoria looked up, nodded her head enthusiastically. Her dad smiled and replied, "Me too!"

South Pittsburg averaged better than 11 yards against a McKenzie defense that had held nine opponents to one TD or less, including five shutouts. The Pirates rolled up 528 yards of offense, led by Offensive MVP Robert Robinson's 204 yards and four TDs. David Jones, who finished the season with the quietest 1,100 rushing yards in the area, was named Defensive MVP.

"We knew they had a ton of speed, but we just couldn't corral them," McKenzie coach Wade Comer said afterward. "You have to respond whenever they score, but we just couldn't. When you get behind, the difficult part is stopping them because they're so explosive."

It was the ninth state-ranked opponent the Pirates had beaten, fourth time they beat a team that had claimed its region championship and the 10th time in 15 games they had inflicted the mercy rule. The Pirates also scored touchdowns on 31 of their 38 possessions in the playoffs and punted only twice in their final 11 games.

"When our bus topped the hill coming back into town, all you saw were red and blue lights flashing," said Robert Robinson, who finished his career as the program's single-season rushing leader with 2,439 yards. "The crowd looked like the Cornbread Festival at night. It was packed with all the former players wearing their South Pittsburg hats and jerseys and letterman jackets letting us know we had joined the brotherhood.

"It was like everybody you ever knew in your whole life was lining the streets to support you, and that's when you realized you weren't just playing for yourself, the whole town really was behind you.

"There was no black, no white, no rich, no poor, no difference that night. We were all just South Pittsburg Pirates. You can call me simple but I know where I'm from and I love knowing how big a deal it is to win a state championship for my hometown."

SOUTH PITTSBURG 2007 RESULTS

Aug. 31	at Marion County	47-19
Sept. 7	at Copper Basin	53-0
Sept. 14	Lookout Valley	41-6
Sept. 21	at David Brainerd	49-0
Sept. 28	Tyner	25-21
Oct. 5	Whitwell	56-7
Oct. 12	at Boyd-Buchanan	47-7
Oct. 19	at Silverdale Baptist	52-7
Oct. 26	Tennessee Temple	69-6
Nov. 2	Grace Academy	72-19

Playoffs

Nov. 9	Trousdale County	32-16
Nov. 16	Friendship Christian	49-7
Nov. 23	Gordonsville	33-13
Nov. 30	Hampton	42-28

State championship

| Dec. 6 | McKenzie | 52-20 |

2007 Pirates

Players: Kartrez Bibbs, David Jones, Cody Robinson, Terrell Robinson, Tyrone Robinson, Kevin Davis, Raquis Hale, Travis Millard, Arkeeme

McKinney, Rashawn Weatherspoon, Shane Boles, Robert Robinson, Montrell Mitchell, Rameal Robinson, Blake Mitchell, Jared Dawson, Bubba Ramsey, Jacobi Malveaux, Trey Skyles, Quinten McCamey, Kendall Robinson, Jonathan Blevins, Tony Roden, Brandon Tetter, Reece Stevens, Will Maynor, Matthew Wayne, Cody Wordlaw, Zach Fitzgerald, Keaton Jones, Trevor Barnes, Aubrey Earvin, Tyler Griffith, Dominique Garrett, Jakoby Reynolds, Torrey Chubb, Jordan Wooten, Josh Dawson, Chris Masterson, Corey Adams, Chase Robinson, Jiajuan Fennell.

Coaches: Vic Grider, Allen Pratt, Heath Grider, Glen Smiley, David Hale, Shiloh Edging, Wes Stone.

Chapter 24
2010 PIRATES

"Now these towns, they all know our name
6-gun sound is our claim to fame
I can hear them say, 'Bad company'
And I won't deny
Bad, bad company, 'Til the day I die."

— Bad Company, *Bad Company*

Just before the entrance to the city limits, at the bottom of a wooden sign welcoming visitors, a list proclaims the state championships won by South Pittsburg.

There is no mention of the runner-up teams.

The kids who returned from the 2009 Pirates to make up a determined group the following season knew all too well how quickly an otherwise noteworthy season can become a mere footnote in the program's history. Similar to the anguish felt by past Pirates teams that came up just short — most notably losing the 1986 title on a controversial failed two-point conversion attempt in overtime and the '98 team that led the nation in scoring before shooting itself in the foot in the semifinals — members of the '09 squad had to chew on the sour taste of losing a title they had believed would be theirs.

Led by an incredible array of talent that included future college players Terrell Robinson at quarterback and Jiajuan Fennell at defensive end, as well as all-state athletes Malcolm Jones and Raquis Hale, South Pittsburg scored 40-plus points in 10 of its 14 games and outscored its three playoff opponents by an outrageous 51-6 to reach the '09 title game. But a laundry list of mistakes — penalties, turnovers, missed scoring opportunities — opened the door for heartbreak as Union City drove the length of the field in 12 plays, then kicked a short field goal in the closing seconds to claim a two-point upset.

Unlike their heartbroken predecessors, including the previous year's seniors who walked off the turf at Tennessee Tech University inconsolable, the 2010 Pirates fed off the opportunity to write a different ending to their season.

Pirates quarterback Travis Milland tosses a TD pass against Marion.

"When we were coming back into town after we lost, we saw some guys rolling up a big sign hanging over the roadway outside of the school that had said 'Congratulations!'," said Jakoby Reynolds, a two-way lineman on both the 2009-10 teams. "They had decorated town because everybody thought we would win. Coming back home, everything was dark and it just felt like we had let the whole town down."

The winter months that followed felt a little extra dreary but the hurtful memory also began driving the small but determined group of returners once preseason workouts began.

"The toughest part was it wasn't like we could do anything about it right away," said Josh Wilson, a tight end and defensive end on that team who admitted that, like several other teammates, he was so upset over the loss he did not leave his house until the following week when he returned to school. "We couldn't get rid of that awful feeling until the next season, and even then the only thing that was going to fix it was to get back and win the whole thing."

Wilson, whose dad Danny was the Pirates defensive coordinator, had transferred from Cleveland and had also watched his dad coach at Maryville Heritage previously. "It's a completely different setting here than anywhere I've been," he added. "They're a lot more serious about the all-or-nothing mentality here. Most places, just getting to a championship is a big deal. But not here. That's kind of amazing to me. There have been so many 10-win teams, or teams that won playoff games, but if you lose that last game you're forgotten."

With the loss of so much talent from the previous season, nobody outside the team's inner circle knew what to expect in 2010. Wilson said faith in his teammates never wavered.

"The summer before our senior year my mom asked me what kind of class ring I wanted," Wilson recalled. "I said I didn't need one because I was getting a state championship ring.

"We knew how people were doubting us. We even had guys who had played before us betting against us. They were literally putting money down against us being able to get back and win it."

ROLLER COASTER REGULAR SEASON

The Pirates were dominant in every aspect of their season opener, scoring on a pass, a run, a punt return and an interception return on the way to a 53-14 win over Grundy County. Demetric "Little Man" Johnson's 73-yard punt return and Antonio Chubb's 93-yard touchdown reception from Travis Millard highlighted the first half.

Millard had the unenviable task of taking over for Terrell Robinson, who rewrote the school's passing records before signing to play for the University of Tennessee at Chattanooga. Millard had been an emergency starter the season before at state-ranked Boyd-Buchanan when Robinson had the flu. The game, played in horrible conditions after a line of severe thunderstorms drenched the Chattanooga area, was a nightmare for Millard and had spent the entire offseason regaining his confidence.

"When you live in a small community the pressure to play well is immense and I felt it all summer," Millard said later. "I wasn't ready to be in a game like Boyd-Buchanan the year before and I blew it. Luckily social media wasn't a big deal yet, but I knew there were people doubting me and I had to prove myself to everybody.

"I wasn't going to be better than Terrell, but I just had to do my job because of the talent around me."

When Marion County came to town in week two the plan was to play fast, turn the tempo into a basketball game on grass, and the Pirates got right to it.

"We always chose to take the ball if we won the coin toss because Coach Grider wanted to attack teams and put them on their heels right off the bat," Reynolds said. "We loved that kind of attitude. It always made us feel like we were the aggressors."

South Pittsburg went no-huddle on its first series, and found little resistance on its way to a quick score. For the rest of the first half they scored both lightning quick — two TDs in three plays or less — as well as sustaining a 14-play, 94-yard drive to score.

"We ran 24 counter over and over and over," said Raquis Hale, who ran for 106 yards on his first four carries but sat out much of the rest of the game with cramps. "I was thinking 'How are they not picking up on this? We're calling the same play and just wearing them out with it.'"

After their fourth touchdown of the half, a Marion defender dove into Jake Stone, South Pittsburg's holder on extra points and the team's backup quarterback. The hit also grazed Millard, who doubled as the Pirates kicker, and drew a flag for unnecessary roughness.

It also lit the already centimeters-short fuse on Grider's temper.

"We've got both our quarterbacks exposed on kicks," he yelled into his headset to let the rest of the staff know his intentions. "By God, if they want to pull some cheap shit like that, we won't kick another damn extra point the rest of the night!"

After the ninth play of their final drive of the half, sensing the Warriors were on the ropes, Grider rolled his arm in a circular motion to tell his team he wanted the pace quickened.

"Hurry up! Let's go!" he shouted. "Look at 'em, they're quittin'!"

Two Marion defenders closest to the Pirates sideline looked over at Grider and one, pretending to adjust his face mask, extended his middle finger toward the rival coach's taunts.

"Jakoby!" Grider yelled. "Keep pounding their ass!"

With the tone set, the Pirates scored on their first five possessions as well as a punt return in building a 42-0 halftime lead, despite having two scores called back by penalty.

As Grider burst into the locker room behind his team he announced, "Starters be ready! We ain't taking our foot off their throat for a while! If they could do it to us you better believe they would."

South Pittsburg opened the second half with three more touchdowns, including a 28-yard pass by Millard, and true to his word

Ruquis Hale turns the corner for a long run.

Grider raised his arm and put two fingers in the air to signal they would go for two-points each time.

"They can look in the mirror if they're wondering why we went for two every time," Grider said afterward. "They asked for it, and to be honest it could have been a whole lot worse.

"Going no huddle early and scoring on our first couple of plays let them know what they were in for. From there on we did pretty much what we wanted."

The 64-0 win was South Pittsburg's fifth straight in the series and largest margin since 1953 — the year that caused the rivalry to take a year off because of the threat of violence after a similar blistering.

"That scoreboard is something I will remember for the rest of my life," said Millard, who threw for 182 yards and three TDs and also ran for another. With the weight of having to replace Terrell Robinson, an all-state quarterback who rewrote every program passing record, the performance against the Warriors was the shot in the arm of confidence Millard needed.

"To leave here and know I never lost to Jasper from little league on up and then win like this, that's pretty big," he added. "It was real important to come out and put them down early."

Even without Hale — their top offensive weapon — for most of the game, the Pirates out-gained the Warriors 529-104 in total yards, averaging 11 yards per play.

As the teams met at midfield to shake hands after the game, the exchange between Grider and Warriors coach Troy Boeck was terse, and as Boeck passed he looked at Grider and said, "Nice class."

Believing he had been called an ass by his counterpart, Grider — still very much on edge — stopped in his tracks, turned and yelled back, "What did you say?!?"

With television cameras rolling to catch the moment, the two coaches exchanged more insults before assistants got between them and coaxed them to go their separate ways. One wide-eyed TV reporter, who was new to the area, looked at his cameraman and said excitedly, "Please tell me you got that on tape!"

Long-time WTVC sports anchor Dave Staley slid the camera from his shoulder, shook his head and said, "Oh my God, I thought they were going to start throwing punches!"

A second straight shutout followed as South Pittsburg scored 42 points in the second and third quarters alone, highlighted by Antonio Chubb who scored on a 40-yard interception return, a 66-yard run on a jet sweep and a 31-yard pass from Millard. Reynolds had three tackles for loss and a sack as the Pirates defense allowed 2A Cascade to gain just 125 total yards.

Reynolds, who started on both offensive and defensive lines, loved the physicality of the game so much that he volunteered to play on kickoff coverage as well.

"You need that kid who brings an attitude that he's just going to be tougher than the next guy," Danny Wilson said. "Jakoby ain't backing down from anybody, and that attitude can be contagious."

In one of the most hyped games in years, the top-ranked Pirates hosted 2A's second-ranked Signal Mountain in week four. All three Chattanooga TV stations as well as the Times Free Press treated the matchup like a state championship was on the line, running feature stories each day leading up to game day. Even several statewide media personalities showed up, just to be a part of the atmosphere.

Signal Mountain brought a huge contingent of fans, filling the visitor's stands an hour before kickoff and by the time the two teams emerged from the locker room, the track surrounding the field was lined with people on both sides as well.

"It was like a wall of people on the track, red and black on one side and orange and black on the other," Hale said.

The toughest part would have been for the game to live up to the hype, but that's exactly what happened with six lead changes and a combined 895 yards by the teams. Signal Mountain, which would go on to finish unbeaten and claim the state title in its class by scoring more points than any team in Chattanooga-area history, took the lead for good on quarterback Hogan Whitmire's seven-yard run with 7:59 remaining.

The Pirates countered with a drive deep into Eagles territory, but on a first-down run Millard, who had thrown for 161 yards in the first half and was having by far the best game of his young career, appeared to flip the ball to the ground as he stood up to motion first down with his arm. Signal Mountain defender Donnie Garner pounced on the ball and the referee trailing the play signaled a fumble recovery. Eagles ball.

"I rolled over on my knees to get up and then Garner reached out and jerked the ball and acted like it was a fumble," Millard said later. "I couldn't believe it when the referee said it was their ball. I watched that play over and over and never could understand how they gave them the ball. They were tired and we were gashing them and about to take the lead back with just a couple of minutes left.

"To this day, that call still bothers me more than anything in my whole career."

When Whitmire connected with Reese Phillips to convert a third down, the Eagles were able to run out the clock for a 40-36 win.

"This is the biggest win in our program's history," Whitmire said after throwing for 229 yards and three TDs and running for another score.

Looking to take out their frustration on 4A Central, some of the Pirates let their emotions get the better of them late. South Pittsburg raced out to a 40-0 lead thanks to "Little Man" Johnson scoring on a 30-yard interception return and a 95-yard kickoff return, and the defense allowed just 8 total yards in the first half.

Travis Millard, Raquis Hale and Coltin Blevins during a quiet moment before the title game.

But with under eight minutes remaining, after Central had kicked off following its first touchdown, a frustrated Pounders defender continued shoving a Pirates player after the whistle. Words and a shoving match quickly escalated into a benches-clearing brawl that resulted in five South Pittsburg players and three Central players getting ejected. As coaches from both teams ran onto the field to separate players, some moms of Pirates players took matters into their own hands.

"I was going at it with one of their players when I felt somebody from behind pull me back," Reynolds said. "I turned around, ready to swing because I thought it was another Central player, and saw my mom holding my arm and telling me to get off the field and stop acting stupid. That took the steam out of the fight for me right then."

Reynolds and four teammates had to sit out the next week's game at Whitwell as punishment for the fight, but they were hardly missed. It took just 30 seconds for the Pirates to score their first touchdown, and they were ahead 48-0 by halftime, rolling up 593 yards.

Millard and Josh Parker set a school record with a 99-yard touchdown connection in what became a 64-7 runaway. Parker had ran so hard that he barely made it back to the sideline before puking.

"I didn't want to get caught from behind," he said after finally catching his breath, not realizing he was 10 yards ahead of the pursuit.

Although he had ran for more than 100 yards in the first six games, Hale had yet to have a true breakout performance. That changed when the Pirates took on 2A's sixth-ranked Boyd-Buchanan and he dissected a solid opponent with 251 yards, averaging 18 yards per carry, and scored four TDs.

For the two years he was the Pirates starter — earning all-state honors both seasons — all Hale needed was to get one step ahead of his pursuers and he was a vapor, a memory. Forget it, he was gone.

He would eventually finish with more than 4,000 career rushing yards, but arrived in South Pittsburg only after being ignored by his little league coaches in Jasper.

"I was seven years old when I started, but since I hadn't played before I guess the coaches thought I wouldn't be very good so I just stood on the sideline a lot," Hale recalled. "My mama got mad because I wasn't getting to play so she pulled me out of Jasper and put me in little league in South Pittsburg.

"By the second week they had me running the ball because they saw how fast I was and that's where I played the rest of my career."

Hale's dad, Marcus Reynolds, was an all-region player for the Pirates in the early 90s and is still considered one of the most athletic players to come through the program. South Pittsburg has had bigger and faster backs through the years, but few could match the total package of the 5-foot-10, 175-pound Hale's speed, physicality — especially as a blocker — and vision.

"That's what stood out the most about Raquis," Grider said. "He could see the field so well, and know where the hole would be and where he needed to make a cut to get in the open field. He was about as complete a runner as I've seen come through our program."

Against Boyd-Buchanan, Hale bolted 51 yards for a score on the second play of the game, then added TD runs of 69, 70 and 12 yards to pile up 181 by halftime. Matthew Allen returned an interception 77 yards for a TD and the Pirates out-gained the Bucs 410-198 for their sixth win by the mercy-rule in seven games.

After another tune-up — Millard threw for 198 yards as South Pittsburg scored five times in the second quarter and had a 42-point halftime lead against Lookout Valley — the Pirates traveled to 3A Polk County in week nine.

The Wildcats, led by University of Tennessee baseball signee Jared Allen at quarterback, were in the midst of a 10-win season in which they won their region crown and narrowly lost in the second round of the playoffs.

A group of Pirates players had traveled to watch Polk County lose its season opener and came away unimpressed, believing their speed would prevail. The Wildcats quickly erased that belief, using their considerable size advantage up front to pound South Pittsburg on both sides of the ball. A rain-soaked field also negated the Pirates speed advantage and Polk took advantage of two early turnovers, cashing them in for short TD drives.

Trailing 20-7 in the third quarter, the Pirates were driving to cut into the deficit before Allen intercepted a pass and returned it 68 yards to essentially put the game away. Allen was unstoppable, rushing for 105 yards and a score, throwing for 89 and two more TDs helping administer the worst whipping the Pirates had taken in six years.

The blowout loss exposed plenty of areas of concern and the senior leaders knew if they didn't get better in a hurry, their stay in the playoffs would be short-lived.

"I really believe that game was the turning point for us," Josh Wilson admitted. "We had a close loss to the best team in 2A, in a game we felt like we should've won, so getting our head handed to us really sort of woke us up right before the playoffs. It definitely got our attention."

Looking to make sure they got their teammates' attention, Wilson, Reynolds and Hale called a players-only come-to-Jesus meeting in the locker room before practice the following Monday, where all involved decided the only solution was to put the embarrassing Polk loss behind them and focus solely on finishing strong.

The only thing that soured an easy win in the final game of the regular season was when Wilson injured his right knee and feared he would be lost for the playoffs before they even began. After scooping a fumble, the burly defensive lineman was caught from behind and the weight of the Grace Academy player caused so much stress on his knee that as he landed he felt something pop.

Led by Hale's four first-half TDs the Pirates easily won but there was little celebration as most of the team was more concerned with Wilson's status.

"I had tried to go back in the game but couldn't get down in a stance without my kneecap feeling like it was out of place," Wilson said. "The

Pirates linemen Jakoby Reynolds and Cody Branham lock in mentally.

next day I couldn't bend it so my dad and I drove to see the doctor. I asked dad on the way if he thought I'd be able to play again, but he just said 'I don't know. We need to be prepared for the worst'.

"I cried the whole way."

An MRI showed that Wilson had torn his PCL and his doctor recommended 4-6 weeks to recover. Wilson was determined he would return before the playoffs ended.

HALE STORM

As the playoffs began, a battered and bruised South Pittsburg team got something it needed more than anything — a week off to rest and heal. The Pirates earned a first-round bye and the week off the field couldn't have come at a better time with nearly half their starters hobbled by injury.

Their second-round foe, Moore County, believed it could follow Polk County's bulldozing game plan to pull off the upset. More worrisome for the Pirates were the five starters, including its entire defensive front of Wilson, Reynolds and Matt Hawkins, who were still not healthy enough to play.

Moore County stuck to its methodical plan to play keep-away, eating up as much of the clock as possible on every possession to limit South Pittsburg's offensive touches. But the Pirates' patchwork defensive line stuffed the Raiders and the offense made the most of each snap, averaging 16 yards per play and scoring all seven of its touchdowns in four plays or less.

Hale backed up a promise he had made to his injured teammates to handle things by rushing for 235 yards on just 12 carries, scoring three touchdowns and picking off a pass on defense.

Leading by just one point going into the second quarter, the Pirates scored twice in the final 33 seconds of that period and put four more TDs on the board on plays covering more than 25 yards, including a beautiful 55-yard strike from Millard to Chubb that sent a message that the offense had plenty more weapons than just Hale.

Despite Moore County running 53 more offensive plays, the Pirates still claimed a 49-14 win. But in the days that followed there were actually grumblings from fans over the fact that they felt the score had remained close for too long.

"That's just a byproduct of the monster we've built," Grider said. "Our people were upset because we we didn't put them away fast enough in their minds. If we're not ahead by 40 points at halftime our fans are wondering what's wrong."

The third round brought Gordonsville to town for the 11th playoff meeting between the two programs. South Pittsburg had embarrassed the Tigers the season before, winning by 40 points, but with eight starters back on both sides of the ball, Gordonsville was considered the biggest threat standing in the way of a state title.

The Tigers hadn't lost to a 1A team all season and had scored 40-plus points in six of their last seven games coming into the quarterfinal. Their defense had allowed more than 20 points just once and had held eight opponents to 7 points or less.

"We knew before the game that Gordonsville was really the only team in the state who could play with us," Millard said. "The coaches always talked to us about not looking ahead, but in our eyes that was the state championship game."

South Pittsburg welcomed back all three of their injured linemen, who wrapped braces around their shaky knees and relied on the playoff adrenaline to help block out the pain against a stout opponent.

Despite the memory of the previous season's beat-down the Tigers came in feeling feisty. During pregame warmups Gordonsville players began woofing at the Pirates and eventually the entire team, including several coaches, gathered in a circle and began stomping on the giant orange 'P' painted at midfield.

It was an act of disrespect that South Pittsburg's players couldn't tolerate and almost immediately they rushed together to meet the Tigers. South Pittsburg coaches got between the two teams and ordered their players off the field.

The only player in orange and black who never bothered to confront the taunts was Hale, who remained seated, reaching out to grab the toe of his shoe to stretch and loosen his calf muscle.

"They could say or do whatever they wanted," Hale said. "I knew all that mattered was what was going to happen during those four quarters when the game started.

"Everybody else was pissed but I just let them have their little time to dance because I knew when it was over we would get the last word."

Still angry from the pregame exchange, South Pittsburg played with purpose in the first two quarters, out-gaining the Tigers 262-80 to take a commanding 20-0 lead into halftime.

Pirates receiver Antonio Chubb scores a touchdown in the first half of the title game.

But after successfully executing a fake punt to keep its first drive of the second half alive, Gordonsville quickly seized momentum. The Tigers scored on their opening possession, forced the Pirates to punt and quickly moved back down field for another score to pull within six.

By the end of the third, Gordonsville had ran 22 plays to South Pittsburg's nine and the Pirates were clearly on their heels. The Tigers appeared set on tying the game, or possibly taking the lead, when they drove to the South Pittsburg one early in the final quarer. But on fourth down linebacker Josh Parker met Gordonsville quarterback Chaz Smith in the hole and, despite giving up 25 pounds, stood up him up at the line until several teammates came crashing in for a gang tackle that prevented the score.

Having dodged a howitzer, South Pittsburg rode the wave of emotion from its goal-line stop to retake command. On third and five, Hale used his innate ability to see the entire field to make a huge play. As he cradled the hand-off from Millard, Hale kept his eyes focused downfield on the Tigers linebackers and safeties.

"I always trusted that our line would take care of things up front," Hale said. "So my job was to look past them and see what the second wave of the defense was doing. That's how I would decide which way to run."

As soon as Hale saw the entire flow of the defense making a hard sprint toward his right, to seal off the edge, he stuck his right foot in the ground, quickly cutting behind the pursuit. After juking to make the safety miss on his tackle attempt, Hale had a clear lane down the visitor's sideline for a 94-yard scoring sprint that gave the Pirates a 12-point cushion.

"As I was running, through my left earhole I could hear our fans getting crazy loud and through my right earhole I didn't hear anything except the wind. It was dead silence coming from my right side so I knew I was gone."

Gordonsville countered with a quick scoring drive of its own, cutting the lead to 26-21 midway through the fourth and shifting the burden back on South Pittsburg's offense to answer.

This time, instead of an immediate response, the Pirates used their own methodical march to put the game away. Running behind a front wall of blockers — seniors Cody Wordlaw, Reynolds and Aubrey Earvin, plus juniors Coltin Blevins, Cody Branham and Karrell Hutchins — the Pirates took more than five minutes off the clock to cover 71 yards.

In the weight room Hale could squat 375 pounds, but on the deciding drive he put the entire town's hopes on his shoulders and lifted them. The first eight plays were carries by Hale before Millard dove into the end zone from a yard out.

"When we got the ball I already had in my mind that we were going to just keep handing it to Raquis," Grider said afterward. "We were either going to win it or lose it with him. That offensive line fought up front, and he got behind them and just kept running hard."

Hale finished with a career-high 30 carries for 320 yards.

"Even though I was really tired, I wanted the ball on every snap," Hale said. "Once we got to the goal line and Travis called 14 quarterback keep in the huddle, I was fine with not getting that last carry. I just wanted to score and get the game over."

With a stubborn mid-state headache cleared, all that stood between a shot at a state title was a Coalfield team that had taken advantage of a weak upper-east schedule to reach the semifinals. The biggest concern for South Pittsburg's staff was overconfidence possibly causing players to look past their outmanned opponent.

It was Grider's 43rd birthday and he made sure he got his team's attention, and kept their focus, with an unusual pregame request.

"I don't believe in asking kids for favors," he began, his voice cracking with emotion. "But I love all of you guys and I love this program more than I ever have, so I'm going to ask you for one favor and you have my word I'll never ask for another thing. Give me a shot to win us another gold ball. Just go out there tonight and get us that shot next week."

Inspired to give Grider the only present he had asked for, the Pirates wasted no time in establishing dominance. They scored on all five first-half possessions as well as a 35-yard interception return by Michael Allen to grab a 41-0 halftime lead.

"We were just gashing them on every play," Hale said. "On one play, they finally stopped me for about a three yard gain and one of their guys on top of the pile said 'Not this time.' I just laughed and said 'Please hurry up and get off me so I can finish giving y'all this ass whipping!"

After gaining 201 yards in the first half Hale bolted 92 yards for a TD on his first carry of the third quarter as the Pirates finished with five touchdowns covering more than 30 yards, including an 82-yard run by freshman speedster Jijuan Lankford late in their 54-6 annihilation.

"It was weird because even though we had killed them I was sad as we were walking off because I knew that would be the last time we would get to play together on our field," Josh Wilson said. "It was a very bitter sweet feeling."

"IF WE DON'T WIN THIS GAME THIS WHOLE SEASON WAS A WASTE OF TIME"

As the chartered bus slowly made its way through South Pittsburg's narrow front street on Thursday evening, fireworks exploded in the air and the sidewalks on both sides of Cedar Avenue were lined with well-wishers. For nearly four blocks the Pirates passed through a cheering corridor of folks who had stepped outside their businesses to wave, along with parents, long-time supporters, and several hundred kids from the elementary school.

The send-off was a mere preview of the celebration that would take place if that bus returned with a state championship trophy the next evening.

The police escort — lights flashing and sirens wailing — bypassed the entrance to the interstate that would have been the quicker route taking the team toward Cookeville and instead continued along Highway 72 through Jasper, as ordered by Grider.

"Make sure you crank those sirens loud when we drive through Jasper," Grider had said just before boarding the bus. "I want every one of them bastards to be reminded that we're on our way to win another championship."

After stopping for dinner, the team arrived at their hotel in Cookeville — about 10 minutes from Tennessee Tech University's Tucker Stadium — just after dark. The coaching staff took up all cell phones and ordered lights out by 10 p.m., making it clear that this was a business trip, not play time.

Butterflies the size of buzzards were

Pirates players rush to accept the state championship trophy.

fluttering in Millard's stomach, and the anxiety of what was at stake the next day wouldn't allow him to sleep. Millard, who had silenced the doubters and would finish the season with more than 1,600 passing yards and 23 TDs, finally had to walk to Coach Grider's room for a late-night pep talk.

"My dad and I sat with Coach Grider and I told him I was a nervous wreck," Millard recalled. "Coach Grider was really calm and just told me to keep doing what I had been all season and we would be fine. Just having him tell me that, and acting so calm about it, I went back to my room and went right to sleep. I was ready after that."

At 7 a.m. Friday, game day morning, coaches began knocking on players' doors to wake them for breakfast. Just as Grider reached up to rap on the door to Reynolds' and Wilson's room, a fired up Reynolds swung the door open and said "We're already up in this bitch!"

Grider smirked, nodded and proceeded to the next room.

The lesson that had carried over from the previous year's title game loss still resonated and later that day, when South Pittsburg took the field against top-ranked and unbeaten Jo Byrns, anything less than a fifth championship would relegate the rest of the season's accomplishments irrelevant.

"If we don't win this game, this whole season was a waste of time," Reynolds said before kickoff. "We might as well not have even played at all. It's like working without getting a paycheck.

"We had nothing to show for last season. We did all that work for nothing is how I look at it."

As he watched both teams finish their pregame warmups in the bright early afternoon sunshine, Grider adjusted the dark-shaded glasses over his eyes and admitted he sensed a different attitude from the previous season.

"I think we're going into this game with a pretty big chip on our shoulder," he said. "Honestly, we felt like we let one slip away last year, and the kids and our whole staff have worked really hard to get back here with something to prove.

"It was a pretty sick feeling leaving that field without the gold ball that we felt was ours, so this is our chance to erase some of that feeling."

Jo Byrns came into the game having not allowed more than 14 points all season and beating eight of its 13 opponents by the mercy rule. Leading the way in its old-school I-formation, which averaged 333 rushing yards per game, was 228-pound fullback Johnny Smith, who had paved the way for a pair of tailbacks — Brandon Holt and Frankie Traughber — to rush for more than 1,300 yards each.

But when the Red Devils cheerleaders held up a paper run-through sign that read "Why not us" it certainly didn't feel like an air of confidence circulated along their sideline.

The Pirates quickly proved why it wouldn't be Jo Byrns' day, establishing a punishing ground game from the very start. Hale ripped off 18 yards on his first carry, but the ball was punched loose and the Red Devils recovered at their 17 to momentarily avoid giving up points.

After getting the ball back with a fumble recovery of its own, South Pittsburg drove 48 yards in eight plays, all runs, with Hale lowering his head to burrow across the goal line from a yard out.

By Jo Byrns' second possession the Pirates attacking 3-5 defensive front, with blitzes coming from all angles, began to confuse the Red Devils blockers. Running lanes were quickly filled and Jo Byrns simply did not have the speed to reach the outside and turn the corner for very much positive yardage.

When the Pirates offense returned, Tech's artificial turf may as well have been a track surface as Chubb blew past a defender and Millard lofted a perfect spiral that dropped over his receiver's left shoulder. Chubb, who was five yards past the defender, reached out, bobbled the ball for a step before reeling it in and sprinting 60 yards for South Pittsburg's second score.

Millard had overcome the pregame jitters and risen to the occasion once again, this time proving himself on a large stage by completing 7 of 9 attempts for 149 yards.

Feeling the desperation to get points, Jo Byrns gambled and went for it on fourth and two at the Pirates 40 but Hale batted the pass away. Three plays later he wiggled through a hole on the right side of the line, broke four arm tackles before hitting stride and pulling away from the scrum for a 45-yard scoring run, making it 21-0 with 1:38 to go before halftime.

Chubb preserved the first-half shutout when he intercepted a pass at the Pirates three and a Jo Byrns team that had entered the game plus-27 in turnover margin had the ball taken away three times in the first half.

On the fourth play of the third quarter Hale — who had ran for 127 yards in the first half — burst straight up the middle, again breaking three tackles in the secondary before shaking loose for another 45-yard touchdown run that sucked any remaining drama out of the stadium.

"Raquis just looked like a guy with something to prove," Grider praised. "His feelings were hurt when he wasn't named a Mr. Football finalist. That put a pretty big chip on his shoulder, and he kept it there the whole way through the playoffs."

Against a Jo Byrns' defense that had held all but two of its previous 14 opponents to fewer than 138 rushing yards — holding nine of those below 100 — Hale put on more moves than U-Haul, ending with 228 yards and five TDs to earn Offensive MVP honors.

He ran for 100-plus yards in all 14 games, and gained more than 1,000 yards in the Pirates four playoff games alone — averaging 13 yards per carry and scoring 15 of the team's 23 postseason TDs. He also finished with the program's single-season rushing record of 2,454 yards, breaking Robert Robinson's record by 15 yards in one fewer game.

As he held the championship trophy, the normally reserved Hale admitted that hardware meant more than a Mr. Football plaque would have.

"I wouldn't trade this right here for anything," he said. "It actually made me want to prove myself a lot more to everybody in the state that I'm the best back in 1A.

"I made a promise to a lot of people that I would help make up for us coming up short last year."

Although Chubb had a 64-yard punt return for a score called back by penalty, he set up his team's final TD with an acrobatic catch along the sideline, his fifth reception for 119 yards on the day.

After Hale's final TD run of the day, from seven yards out, Chubb also took a reverse pitch and weaved his way through the Red Devils defense for the two-point conversion that initiated the running clock with 11 minutes still remaining — the Pirates 11th win by the mercy rule for the season.

Millard's dad, Guy, worked with the coaching staff, charting plays for the offense from the sideline. As the final seconds drained from the clock father and son found one another and embraced.

"I knew he had wanted me to succeed more than anybody in my life," Millard said. "People say your life flashes through your mind before you die. Well when I found my dad, in that moment my whole career flashed through my mind. When you're six years old and just starting to play the game and you don't know how to put your pads on, your dad teaches you the game. So to find him and have that moment together, that was one of the best memories I've had in my life."

The program's fifth state title, and second in four years, was secured in grand style when Cody Wordlaw dropped Jo Byrns quarterback Brandon Adkins on the final play, setting off a wild celebration.

Pirates seniors Josh Wilson (30), Josh Parker (42) and Travis Millard (12) hoist the championship hardware.

"I fell to the ground as time ran out and started to cry," Josh Wilson said. "But Riley (Hargis) came over and said 'No! We cried last year, not today! This time we get to celebrate.' After that I jumped up and just enjoyed every second of it."

Watching nearby from the sideline, Josh's dad Danny, the Pirates defensive coordinator who had brought his family back to the little town where his career began in the late 1980s, pumped his fist in the air and soaked in the scene alone for a moment.

"Two years ago Karen and I talked about moving back and one of the things in the back of our mind was believing Josh would get a chance to compete for a state championship," Danny said. "Knowing the tradition of this program and the talent coming up, we wanted him to get to have a shot at this experience right here.

"Looking out there at all those kids he grew up with, and seeing their faces light up like a Christmas tree, that's pretty dang special."

The attack dog of Wilson's disruptive defense, junior inside linebacker Coltin Blevins, was named defensive MVP after making nine tackles and helping the Pirates shut down an offense that had averaged 41 points per game.

"When we got hammered by Polk County a lot of people doubted these kids," Grider said. "That really motived us. Our guys stuck together and came to work every day to get better and now we're taking another gold ball back home where it belongs."

Six of the nine seniors had also been a part of the 2007 state champions, making them the only players in program history to leave with two titles to their credit and a program record 50 career wins. The state's 35-point mercy rule had been introduced during their freshman season and during the four years that followed the Pirates invoked it 39 times, by far the most of any team in the state, including 11 of 16 playoff games.

"They've got great tradition and great speed," Red Devils coach Tom Adkins said afterward. "We knew we were going to have to contain that speed and tackle well. They're fast enough to make you pay, and in a big way."

The program's fifth title also broke the tie with rival Marion County for the most by any school in the Chattanooga area.

Sophomore back-up quarterback Jake Stone became the fourth young man in his family to be part of a championship, joining his grandfather Johnny, who played on the Pirates first title team in 1969, dad Wesley a starter on the '94 championship and assistant coach in 2007 and 2010, and uncle Matt who played linebacker on the '99 champions.

"To have that connection with them is pretty good," Johnny said as he waited for the team to return for the traditional celebratory walk through town. "It's a bigger deal to share it with your sons, and now grandson, than winning one.

"That's what sets South Pittsburg apart. We're unique because we have multiple generations that play for a state championship."

SOUTH PITTSBURG 2010 RESULTS

Aug. 27	Grundy County	53-14
Sept. 3	Marion County	64-0
Sept. 10	at Cascade	49-0
Sept. 17	Signal Mountain	36-40
Sept. 24	Central	40-14
Oct. 1	at Whitwell	64-7
Oct. 8	Boyd-Buchanan	41-6
Oct. 15	at Lookout Valley	61-20
Oct. 22	at Polk County	7-42
Oct. 29	at Grace Academy	58-7

Playoffs

Nov. 12	Moore County	49-14
Nov. 19	Gordonsville	32-21
Nov. 26	Coalfield	54-6

State championship

Dec. 3   Jo Byrns   41-6

2010 Pirates

Players: Matthew Allen, Demetric Johnson, Jake Stone, Jijuan Lankford, Michael Allen, Deuel Jones, Raquis Hale, Travis Millard, Antonio Chubb, Payne Mosley, Kyle Blevins, Jonathan Sellers, Corbin Hale, Caleb Rector, Josh Wilson, Kam Cunningham, Khalil Mitchell, Josh Parker, Riley Hargis, Karrell Hutchins, Coltin Blevins, Alex Collier, Jawan Smith, Cooper Lewis, Stephon Mitchell, Matthew Hawkins, Chandler McBee, Ricky Fehr, Cody Wordlaw, T.J. Havner, Kyle Channin, Cody Branham, Aubrey Earvin, Alex Mosley, Trey Chance, Jakoby Reynolds, Trey Martin, Alex Shiver, John Wells, Anthony Sellers, Jamie Jackson, Shaquille McKinney, Michael Ashburn.

Coaches: Vic Grider, Danny Wilson, Heath Grider, David Hale, Wesley Stone, Tim Starkey, Jim Thomas.

Chapter 25

VIC GRIDER

*"I don't feel I have to take out everybody.
Just my enemies."*

— Michael Corleone, *the Godfather*

In large block letters the 3-foot-by-4-foot metal sign hanging above the double black doors of the main entrance reads "Donald N. Grider Field House". It serves as a reminder to everyone who enters the 5,000-square foot structure — including South Pittsburg's current football coach — that a certain standard was set and is still expected.

When Vic Grider was handed the keys to take the wheel at his alma mater, it was his daddy, Don, who told him flatly, "If you can't get the job done we'll find somebody else who can."

Since taking over the program he's averaged 11 wins and played for five state titles, winning three, and in 2017 surpassed his dad's total of 192 career wins.

But Vic still approaches the job as if he's guarding a priceless family heirloom. After all, the game is so much a part of his family's roots that his full name given to him by Don is Victory, since he was born shortly after a Pirates win.

"I see a lot of his dad in him. Just the way he prepares for games and how much it means to him," said Vic's mother Gaynelle. "Losses eat him up just like they did Don. I don't know if he even realizes how proud Don was that he wanted to follow in his dad's footsteps. Very proud."

When Don Grider passed away in 2007 he was buried on the hill next to the school, a spot he chose for his final resting place because it overlooks the Pirates practice field.

For Vic and his younger brother Heath, an assistant on the staff, it is just another reminder that they're never far from their dad's presence. Or his legacy.

FIGHT LIKE HELL ON EVERY SNAP

All coaches have a unique routine they follow before a game. Some study their play chart, rehearsing in their mind which plays to run in certain situations. Others sit quietly, finding a moment of peace before stepping out into the chaos awaiting on the field.

Vic spends the time just before his pregame speech to the team working himself into a salty lather. Too anxious and geared up to sit, he paces from corner to corner inside his office — searching high and low for any hint of disrespect to help a never ending "us versus them" storyline he can agitate the team with. Once he finds it, he'll light their emotional fuse, then stand back and wait for them to detonate on the field, watching his team's performance draw oohs and aahs and appreciative applause from the crowd like some Fourth of July fireworks show.

Pirates coach Vic Grider unloads on Marion coach Tim Taylor before kickoff.

"You see these emotional speeches in football movies but none of them would get you as fired up and ready to kick somebody's ass as Vic's," said Michael Allen, who played in three state title games as a receiver and defensive back for the Pirates from 2008-11. "There were times where we'd come out of the locker room ready to fight as much as play football because he had us so pissed off at whoever we were playing."

Once before a 2007 playoff showdown with Trousdale County, the mid-state's perennial small-school powerhouse and constant postseason thorn in South Pittsburg's side, Vic had been given a quote printed from a fan's online chat room that sparked an idea. The Pirates were ranked No. 1 in the state at the time and a Trousdale fan had bragged online that "it'll be one and done for number one". He pasted the quote into a mock headline, making it appear as though he'd stumbled across it on the Nashville Tennessean's website.

Holding up the homemade printout, Vic's voice rose, "Guys, the newspaper that covers Trousdale already has the headline made up for tonight's game. Look at this!" As he pointed to his own handiwork he repeated the phony headline "One and done for number one! They've already got tomorrow's story ready for them beating you! I don't know about you, but that pisses me off!"

That season the Pirates had beaten teams by an average of nearly 30 points but the ploy was used to ensure his team was focused on a dangerous opponent awaiting them. Once he had rattled his team's cage Vic sent an angry team onto the field where, as is usually the case, the preparation and talent took over after the emotion wore off and the Pirates rolled to an easy win.

"I'm a big believer in getting them to play on emotion," Vic said. "If you've got the best players on the field, you can get away without playing on emotion. We've got a bunch of little scrappers, guys who have to fight harder than the other guy to have a chance.

"Look at Jasper. They've got about twice our enrollment, more depth than us and more size. But we've beaten them more than they've beaten us and a lot of that is because our kids go into that game knowing they're going to have to fight like hell on every snap. That's the mentality our kids have, so I make sure we feed off that attitude in a big game."

SUPICIOUS MIND

A man who craves winning more than food when he's hungry, Vic is suspicious nearly to the point of paranoia in the days leading up to big games. Particularly for the whole week of the Marion County game. He'll survey the cars lining the practice field, the ones mostly filled with parents, former players and hangers-on making sure the team is getting prepared to their standards. But if there's a vehicle he doesn't recognize, he'll ask players and assistants, "hey, who's that over there in that car?" If nobody knows, he'll send someone from the team to investigate and find out what business the stranger has watching.

But make no mistake, the concern isn't misplaced. In the week leading up to the 2002 game against Marion, the parent of a Warriors player watched South Pittsburg from the hill overlooking the practice field, then drove to Jasper and drew up every formation he had seen on the coach's chalkboard.

Word quickly leaked back to Vic and when the two teams walked onto the field for pregame warmups he was itching for a fight. After informing Warriors coach Tim Taylor that he knew what had happened, Vic lit into his rival, "You're the head coach and you're responsible for what goes on in your program. Y'all are a disgrace!" he yelled, thrusting his index finger toward Taylor as television cameras videoed and newspaper photographers clicked shots of the spat. "It might not be tonight, but by God you'll get what's coming to you!"

It isn't just his players who have bought into Vic's combative mentality. Most of the town's citizens also view themselves as scrappers, unwanted runts from a litter of mutts who've had to develop a junkyard dog's attacking nature, ready to snap and snarl and bite at the first sign of being mistreated.

Vic's outbursts, whether directed at opposing coaches, fans or officials he believes are slighting the team are met only by shouts of approval from those wearing orange and black. And since most of the Pirates fans knew exactly why their coach was erupting on Marion's coach, they egged it on, waving orange and black shakers and shoving their fists into the air.

"Get him Vic!" one woman yelled as she stood on the concrete bleachers.

"Chew his ass!" howled a man standing on the track.

The fuss lasted only a few minutes, but set the tone for yet another brutally physical game to follow that night.

"It didn't end after pregame," Vic said. "Me and the whole team were pretty pissed off the whole game and it showed in how we played."

Although Marion led for much of the first half, the Pirates found a way to answer each touchdown with a score of their own — a 54-yard pass, an 88-yard kickoff return and a 42-yard interception return that set up a short TD run — forcing a halftime tie despite Marion's decided yardage advantage.

Unable to knock out the Pirates in the first half, the second half momentum shifted squarely in favor of South Pittsburg, while Marion was noticeably worn out in giving up a nine-play, 85-yard scoring drive that resulted in the game-winning 37-yard TD run by tailback A.J. Jones.

"I have no doubt the emotion from before the game carried over throughout the whole game and helped us to win," Vic said afterward. "They were a better football team than us. It showed early. They got up on us quick but our kids kept hammering away and we roughed them up pretty good in the second half."

Pirates coach Vic Grider watches his team from the sideline.

As coaches and players shook hands following the game, Grider's only comment to Taylor was 'Y'all got what you deserved.'

"He never said a word," Vic said. "Not before the game when I was losing my mind on him or after it. He just took it, which to be honest was pretty admirable. After the fact, later on, he admitted everything and we've been fine ever since."

SEND A MESSAGE

If Vic had a coaching motto it would likely come from the H.L. Mencken quote, "Every normal man must be tempted, at times, to spit on his hands, hoist the black flag and begin slitting throats."

When his roster is dotted with stout linemen and fleet runners, Vic views the team as an automatic weapon with a full clip, and he's not taking his finger off the trigger.

"Vic's philosophy is that he'll make a statement, send a message, not just for the team he's playing that night but for anybody else on the schedule and for years down the road that they can't beat him," offered Troy Boeck, who worked as a Pirates assistant for several years and later competed against Vic as Marion's head coach. "It's all about intimidation. And I'll give him credit, he's pretty dang good at it. There were times when you could tell the other team had seen the scores and they were beat before they got off their bus."

It's hard to argue with the results on the field or his approval rating in the town. Along with Knoxville-area power Alcoa, South Pittsburg is one of the chief reasons the state implemented a 35-point mercy rule.

In his first game as head coach in 1997, the Pirates smoked Whitwell like a Texas brisket 61-8 and by his second season South Pitt was highlighted by USA Today for being the highest-scoring team in the entire nation — averaging 51.2 points a game, including wins of 75-7, 70-0, 56-6 and 54-0.

So in 2007, the TSSAA adopted the National Federation of High Schools rule that mandated once a team leads by 35 points or more in the second half the game clock will continually run, a move designed to help avoid embarrassing margins.

In short, the rule was implemented to show mercy on outmanned teams because Vic clearly wasn't going to.

In the 10 years after that rule was passed, despite having to play virtually all its non-region games against teams from a larger classification because most 1A teams refuse to schedule the Pirates, Vic's teams have won 60-percent of their games by invoking the mercy rule on opponents.

On their way to winning the 2010 state title the Pirates scored touchdowns on 24 of their 27 offensive possessions in the playoffs. Of those times they failed to score, twice they took a knee to run out the clock and once they had a pass intercepted.

"Vic makes you work a lot harder preparing your own team," explained Grant Reynolds, who coached Boyd-Buchanan to a split of 10 meetings with South Pittsburg before moving on to another program. "Not only will he find your weaknesses and hammer you for them, but he's so good at taking things you think are your own team's strengths and using them against you.

"If you're not ready, he'll embarrass you pretty quick, but I think playing them so many times definitely made our program better. We knew if we could compete with South Pitt we could play with anybody."

Vic Grider instructs his offense during the 2016 Marion game.

Against teams from their own classification the results are the equivalent of killing mice with a shotgun. Even with the running clock, the Pirates have scored 50-plus points 83 times, all of which has made South Pitt, and its coach in particular, the scourge of small schools across the state.

"Most of the coaches you talk to who have to play them don't want to admit it, but when you see the black helmets with the orange 'P' come onto the field, there's a big-time intimidation factor," said Tony Webb, who coached at Lookout Valley, an annual Pirates league opponent, for more than 20 years. "You know immediately you had better buckle it up, because for all the praise they get about being fast, they're one of the most physical teams around, too. They will light you up."

Rather than shy away from it, Vic embraces the fact that the black hat he wears during games is also literally his image among opposing fans, particularly those in Jasper.

"I understand that people don't always like you when you win a lot, and I'm fine with people outside our program not liking me," he said with a casual shrug. "You have to have an air about you. It's almost like a character you play. It kind of lets you know you've built something good because they don't dislike you if you're not winning and aren't a threat to them.

"From the time you get off the bus, you send a message the whole game. Never take the foot off the throttle. I think our people know what they're getting in me. I'm 110-percent South Pittsburg, and I'm going to fight for this team, our players and our community."

That attitude was on full display in 2008 when South Pittsburg traveled to take on a Tyner Academy program that was two classifications larger.

As the team bus came to a stop in front of the visitor's locker room two men in their 50s wearing maroon and gold Tyner ball caps watched as the Pirates unloaded and began to make their way to the locker room. For more than 20 years Tyner has been one of the most successful programs in Chattanooga, and most opposing teams make the short trek from their bus to the visitor's area with their heads down, avoiding eye contact with the strangers they pass out of sheer intimidation.

By stark contrast the Pirates, dressed in solid black warm-ups with the orange 'P' over the left breast, stepped off the bus with a confident swagger, almost like landlords who had come to check on their property. One after the other, each player made his way with head held high and without expression. Some bobbed their heads to the beat of heavy rock or rap music screeching through their headphones, others nodded at the opposing fans lining the sidewalk, unfazed by the environment as they made their way to their lockers

One of the older men lifted his ball cap, readjusted it on top of his head and let out a sigh before turning to the other and admitting, "that's some bad sumbitches right there."

That was the exact aura Vic had worked to create and carry everywhere the Pirates played.

His devotion is never more obvious than when his Pirates play their cross-county rival. In 2010, South Pittsburg was on its way to another championship, while Marion County had hit a down cycle. But there was no pity shown.

After he felt a Marion defender intentionally dove in and delivered a cheap shot at the Pirates holder on extra points, who was also the back-up quarterback, Vic barked into his headset, "We ain't kicking another extra point all night!"

True to his word, the Pirates went for two — and succeeded — after each of their last four touchdowns in a 64-0 thrashing of the visiting Warriors.

After the game, as the two coaching staffs exchanged icy handshakes, Marion's Troy Boeck said as he passed Vic, "Nice class."

Vic misunderstood and thought Boeck had called him an ass and an argument ensued. Moments later, a longtime Marion supporter met Vic as he walked off the field and began to lecture him on running up the score.

Vic loudly interrupted, "Hey, you can take your ass-whippin' eight miles back up the road with the rest of your bunch! Get off our field!"

"Am I disappointed we beat them 64-0? Absolutely not. I loved every minute of it," Vic said afterward.

Later that season, as the Pirates departed for the bus ride to Cookeville to play for the state championship, rather than following the more direct route from I-24 to the Jasper bypass, Vic instructed the driver and town's police cars escorting the team to drive through Jasper with the sirens wailing and lights flashing.

"Just to remind every one of those suckers that while they're sitting in their office or their kids are sitting in class, we're still playing football," said Vic, who has had 16 Mr. Football finalists and 56 all-state players during his time as coach. "We're going to play for a championship and they'll have to watch us. Hell yeah, I remind them that they're not as good as us.

"I know there are people up there who'll go to their grave despising me. That part of it will never go away. That's pretty special."

SEASON OF CHANGE

For all the success, it actually took two years away from the game for both Vic and the South Pittsburg community to realize how much both needed him stalking the Pirates' sideline.

On a bitterly cold November night, moments after all-state running back Demtric "Little Man" Johnson had been stopped inches short of converting a two-point run to leave the Pirates on the short end of a one-point quarterfinal decision at Gordonsville, Vic put his arm around Johnson's waist, consoling the talented senior who had been the main reason that undermanned team had even kept the game close.

"We did everything we could, man. Keep your head up," Vic said to Johnson before stepping away for a few moments of solitude on the sideline as the final seconds ticked off the clock. Taking a deep breath as he looked at the stars hovering above, Vic knew he had likely coached the final game with his alma mater.

One month later he stunned the audience packed into the school's cafeteria for the team's postseason banquet by announcing his retirement. Similar to all of his pregame speeches, Vic had choreographed the speech to ensure his words would be the last thing those in attendance heard.

So as others from his staff stood to acknowledge what he had built, he slipped out a side door and walked quickly to his office, locking the door behind him, where he stayed until it was certain everyone had gone home.

The timing of his resignation coincided with news that he had been contacted by former NFL head coach Jon Gruden to gauge interest in joining a potential staff if the former Super Bowl winning coach came to an agreement to take over the program at the University of Tennessee.

During Grider's years as a football manager at UT in the 1980s he had roomed with Gruden, who was a graduate assistant with the Vols, as well as future sports agent Jimmy Sexton and future UT-Chattanooga athletic director David Blackburn, who were both team managers as well.

Because of their long-time relationship Gruden called to ask Grider about joining his potential staff as the program's liaison to prep coaches around the state. But the talks between Gruden and UT never went much further and Grider admitted that those discussions had nothing to do with his decision to step away from coaching.

"When the playoffs had started that year, there was a night we were watching TV and he said he thought it was time for him to take a break. I burst out and said 'No!'," said Grider's daughter, and only child Victoria, a 2017 SPHS graduate and the living definition of a daddy's girl.

Among the framed photos in Vic's office is one of his entire family after a game, including Victoria as a baby.

Vic Grider's temper flares easily when things don't go his team's way.

Growing up she was allowed to ride home on the team bus after road games and when her dad calls now, a picture of him lifting her into his arms after a game lights up the screen of her cellphone. "He always included me, even though I wasn't the son he always wanted," she continued. "I knew how much he loves coaching and I felt like he was probably giving it up to spend more time with me before I graduated. But it meant more to me to have him be the coach than anything else. All I had ever known was him being our coach and I love being known as Coach Grider's daughter.

"After the last playoff game that year I met him outside the locker room and was crying and begging him not to give up coaching."

No one could've known the turmoil and calamity that would follow.

Of the more than 100 coaches who sent a resume', it was Calhoun (Ga.) defensive coordinator Ricky Ross who was chosen. The 38-year old Ross had helped Calhoun claim eight straight region titles and reach Georgia's Class AA state title game five straight years, winning it once with an upset of nationally-ranked Buford. During one 29-game winning streak over the 2011-12 seasons Calhoun's defense allowed just five opponents to score more than 14 points.

On the day the hiring was announced, Vic, who remained the school's athletic director and was on the search committee that had been formed to find his replacement, seemed at ease with the choice.

"His football knowledge is off the charts," he said. "If there's such a thing as the coaching lottery, we feel like we hit it with Ricky."

But at a meet-and-greet event designed to introduce Ross to the community, it was former long-time assistant Dave Baxter who warned Vic in private, "you messed up. I'm telling you, y'all hired the wrong guy. He's got too many Jasper ties. Wait and see, he'll burn you."

"I just blew it off that day, but as it turned out, like he usually was, Coach Dave was right," Vic said later.

Two months after blowing away the search committee and accepting the offer, before spring practice had even begun, it became obvious that Ross was all hat and no cattle. His agreement to take over the program turned out to be a counterfeit promise and, frustrated that he would have to wait until the end of the semester for a teaching position to come open, Ross decided he no longer wanted the job and late one night, while no one else was around, cleaned out his new office without informing anyone at South Pittsburg that he was leaving.

Word of Ross's departure actually reached Vic and school administrators from a rival coach, so the split became anything but amicable. Ross lobbed a verbal grenade at the school on his way out, telling the media, "The bottom line is we're on different levels as far as commitment."

Vic was infuriated when he heard what Ross had said and didn't hesitate to fire back.

"I think he's completely accurate about us having a difference of opinion in what commitment means. He committed to me, to our school, to 45 kids on the team and to our community. He's right, there was a lack of commitment, but it wasn't on our part."

There was plenty of hand-wringing in the community over what type coach the program could find just weeks before the end of the school year. But barely more than a month after being publicly rejected by their first choice, South Pittsburg's search committee reconvened and named Tim Moore, who had been an all-state lineman for the Pirates in the late 1970s, as only the program's fifth head coach in the last 50 years, but second in less than two months.

Moore brought a calming presence, coming back home after a successful career at Nashville-area private school Battle Ground Academy, where in 15 seasons he helped the Wildcats win three state titles as defensive coordinator, then won two more as head coach.

With Vic and his brother Heath both out of coaching in 2013, it marked the first season since 1961 that South Pittsburg would play without a Grider on the sideline.

Moore's reserved personality was the polar opposite of Vic's intensity. Rarely cursing and never berating officials, he seemed as square as fudge to locals, who seemed to identify more with Vic's volatile persona.

Moore inherited a team stacked with enough talent to overshadow the surly, brooding attitudes that also peppered the roster. The Pirates cruised to the state championship game in Moore's first season by simply riding the wave of talent that included all-state tailback Jajuan Lankford and bruising running back/linebacker Kahlil Mitchell.

The second season saw a significant drop in talent as well as discipline and ultimately in on-field results. The Pirates were hammered in their first two games, and were *thisclose* to opening the season 1-4, but managed to escape the unthinkable — their first loss to county foe Whitwell in more than two decades. Despite that win, the margin only served to highlight darker days on the horizon, and by the time the season ended with a second-round loss at Copper Basin, the Pirates had finished with a pedestrian 6-6 record.

It was clear something had to be done to redirect the downward spiral. The breaking point came less than a month after the season had ended, when Moore made an announcement asking for all boys who planned to play football to meet in the cafeteria. Others on the staff had told Vic and principal Danny Wilson that there was a severe lack of interest from players and that several who would be returning had hinted they might not play. Most of the assistants staff had also decided not to return under Moore.

So when Moore made the all-call to discuss offseason workouts, Vic peeked in and was numbed by what he saw — just 16 boys sat in the cafeteria.

"I walked straight into Danny's office and said 'We've got a major problem'," Vic said. "I couldn't believe it. For a place where football is so important, to only have that many kids interested, we had to do something. I mean, we were looking at not having enough to even field a team. We were basically Lookout Valley."

Vic and Wilson met with Moore and it was agreed that he would no longer be the program's caretaker. The resignation hurt Moore, but the worst the gracious man could admit to on his way out was that "it's always a challenge to step into a home that's already built and try to remodel it to fit you. The bar is set pretty high here."

So for the third time in less than two years the program which had been such a model of stability would begin a search for a new head coach.

BACK TO BUSINESS

Like so many small-town issues, the business of steadying the football program was conducted over a few cold beers in the back room of a local businessman's shop. As one booster popped the top of his first beer he said firmly, "Look, the rest of the valley knows Vic's an asshole, but he's our asshole. So let's find a way to get him to come back and straighten this mess out."

Meanwhile David Hale, who had been a star freshman defensive lineman on Don Grider's first team, later worked on the staff of both Griders for two decades and was looked at as an extended family member, decided it was time to use a more direct approach and said what most in town were already thinking.

Hale walked into Vic's office, closed the door behind him and spoke from his heart.

"Vic, we're like brothers so I'm just going to tell you, man, this program is your family's legacy," Hale said. "Your daddy built this program, but it's hurting now and you're the only one who can fix it. You have to come back and fix it for the school and for the town."

When Hale left the room, Vic felt the lump in his throat and knew what he would do.

Combined, Don and Vic Grider have won more games than any father-son coaches in the history of Tennessee high school football.

Just days after Hale's plea, Vic called for all boys in the school who planned to play football to meet in the cafeteria. Nearly 40 kids sat waiting to meet their new coach when Vic walked in.

"First, nobody here better say a single negative word about Tim Moore," Vic ordered. "He bailed us out when we were in a bind. He's a Pirate and a good man.

"Now, as for the team, you're looking at your new coach and I'm going to be blunt, after last year nobody respects you anymore. Nobody is afraid of you anymore. You don't intimidate anybody anymore. If you want to just be a part of something fun and drag-ass around then go grab a tuba and join the band.

"We're hurting right now but we're not dead. We'll get it fixed but there's only one way I know how to do that. We're about to go to work."

Standing in a back corner of the room, Wilson, the school's principal who had won a state title as head coach and another as the team's defensive coordinator with Vic, nodded.

Vic Grider gets a congratulatory hug from his daughter Victoria after another win.

"There are no words to express how big this is, not just for our football team and our school but for our whole town," Wilson said. "When you talk about the excitement around small town football, that energy feeds the whole community and that's what we're getting back with Vic."

Any thoughts of a smooth transition back were rocked just weeks after Vic returned when he underwent emergency heart bypass surgery and spent 17 days in a local hospital recovering. His blood pressure had sky-rocketed and caused a valve to burst and his surgeon informed him later that 90% of people who have the same complication die from it.

"I went to visit him in the hospital," said former all-state player Eddie Moore. "When I saw him laying there looking really sick, it scared me man. I had only seen him be so strong and I didn't know how to take it. I left the room and sort of just broke down."

Months after Vic had recovered, a Marion supporter approached a neighbor from South Pittsburg and joked, "The most shocking part for everybody in Jasper was finding out Vic actually had a heart."

The procedure did nothing to curb his intense desire to bring back his program's old swagger.

Informed that Marion County had signed a contract with a the same Adidas rep who had outfitted all of South Pittsburg's athletic teams, Vic called the salesman to ask if the rumor was true. Told that it was, he informed the salesman that South Pittsburg would be breaking its contract with him and switching to a different company.

"I told you when we signed the only request I have is that you don't sell to them," Vic told the salesman. "I'll bury that shit in my backyard or burn it before we wear it now! We won't be wearing the same brand as that bunch so you can consider our business together done."

Later that day Vic had an Under Armour salesman in his office, signing a new deal.

"We've always taken a lot of pride in having our own identity. That's a big deal to us," Vic said. "I talked to the kids about it and it was unanimous that none of us wanted any part of looking anything like Jasper."

In his first year back the Pirates won 9 games, scoring 40-plus points seven times — four more than the year before his return — and reached the quarterfinals.

But by that season old nemesis Ricky Ross had also become the head coach at Marion and was living up to the potential South Pittsburg saw in him when he had been hired there years earlier by building the Warriors back into a state title contender.

When Vic took his team to Jasper, there was a clear talent gap and Warriors fans savored their chance to torment him.

As he followed his team off the field, making their way through the Marion fans to reach the visitor's locker room, Vic was hounded unmercifully.

"It was hard for them to say a lot when we were beating their ass, but they were ahead and it was in the air that night up there," Vic recalled. "My main thought was I need to get the hell out of here. I put my head down and just kept walking.

"But I was thinking, 'Just wait. We'll get payback, I promise and when we do I ain't lettin' up. Walking through that crowd that night, that probably made me work harder than ever to get us back. It just reminded me how bad I hate them and will always want to beat them as bad as we can."

Vic filed that memory away and wrote down his vow for vengeance in blood somewhere in the back of his mind, using it to speed up the rebuilding project. The wait for revenge wasn't a long one, as the Pirates upset No. 1-ranked Marion the following season, scoring the game-winning TD on a 28-yard pass with just 11 seconds remaining to send the home side of Beene Stadium into pandemonium.

That highlighted a 12-2 season in which the Pirates won all but the Marion game by the mercy rule and reached the semifinals.

"It's getting back to the way things are suppose to be with him in charge," said Allen Pratt, a former principal and former defensive coordinator at the school. "He's had chances to go coach other places but I don't believe he would be nearly as happy being anywhere else.

"I've heard plenty of people around town say they feel better when they pass the stadium and see his truck parked there, or even just seeing him mowing the field because it lets them know the program they love is in good hands."

GAMEDAY TRIBUTE

It's early morning. There's just enough of a chill in the air to hint that summer is fading and fall has arrived. The misty fog that hung over the surrounding mountains has slowly drifted down through the valley and will soon dissolve away as the sun peeks through.

Vic parks his gray Ford F150 truck on the hill next to the school, pulls a light jacket over his shoulders and crosses the street to the grassy hillside, stepping briskly through the rows of tombstones until he reaches the spot where his father is buried.

It's Friday. Game day. Hours later, as has been the routine for all but two of the past 50-plus years, a Grider will lead another group of eager teenage boys onto the field to chase an entire town's championship dream. But for a few moments, standing alone with just his thoughts, he is no longer the tenaciously driven coach most know him as. For now he is simply a son missing his daddy.

"I talk to him. I just tell him how much I wish he was here to be a part of it," Vic said. "If it's a big game or if it's Jasper week, I'll tell him we're ready to play. It's just my way of letting him know he's still a big part of what we're doing and that we're working hard to keep up what he started.

"I guess I'm just hoping to make him proud."

Chapter 26
KENNEDY GRIFFITH

*"She is clothed with strength and dignity,
and she laughs without fear of the future."*

— Proverbs 31:25

The dusting of snow still covering patches of grass was unusual for early April in east Tennessee, but that isn't what made the day so uncommon that it became forever frozen in the memory of both Mark Griffith and Pam Griffith.

Their oldest daughter Kennedy had complained of pain in her right leg but everyone in the family shrugged it off as growing pains. The old coach in Mark thought maybe it was a pulled muscle.

After all, 12-year old Kennedy was often the definition of a tomboy — swimming, playing soccer, climbing trees, catching crawdads and generally anything that would lead to her coming in the backdoor covered in dirt.

But on the evening of April 6, 2009, after running a mile at school earlier in the day, Kennedy's leg became so badly swollen that Pam believed she had broken it.

She loaded both daughters into the car and made the 30-minute drive to T.C. Thompson Children's Hospital in Chattanooga where several hours passed after the initial X-ray without any information from the emergency room staff.

Finally a team of doctors entered the room and began to explain to Pam that they would need to schedule an immediate appointment at Vanderbilt Medical Center. The X-ray had revealed a 26-centimeter tumor wrapped around her daughter's femur.

Mark, who was just months into his new job as the superintendent of Marion County schools, was on a business trip in Nashville when he got the call from Pam. As he drove back home frantically at midnight he called his mom, his pastor and several friends asking them to pray that what they feared would somehow not be true.

But after a series of further tests at Vanderbilt, three days later the three of them sat together and stared across the desk in disbelief as a doctor confirmed that Kennedy did in fact have osteosarcoma —

one of the rarest forms of childhood cancer that starts in the bones.

Mark and Pam broke down emotionally, unable to speak for several minutes. As they struggled to compose themselves it was Kennedy who spoke first.

"Does this mean I'm going to die?" she asked.

Marion County painted a message of encouragement when Kennedy Griffith returned home.

"No," the doctor replied. "We're going to help you beat this."

"Okay. What do we do next? When can we start?"

On the two-hour drive home, a surreal mix of emotion came in waves over both parents. If either could have taken the diagnosis into their own bodies and spared their daughter they wouldn't have hesitated.

As he drove, Mark's mood swung from confusion and grief to downright anger.

"God, how can you let murderers and rapists and child molesters walk around this earth but you let my baby have cancer?" he thought to himself.

Once again, it was Kennedy who broke the tension and the silence. Sensing what her dad was feeling, she reached across from the passenger seat to put her hand over Mark's.

"Daddy, God has a plan for this," she said with a warm smile.

"I'm her dad," Mark said. "I'm suppose to be strong for her. But I found out real quick that she was a hell of a lot stronger than I'll ever be."

Word quickly spread throughout the Sequatchie Valley of the gritty little girl battling cancer. And like most families that argue and fight and seemingly have nothing in common, when one of their own is in need the entire community comes together to rally behind them.

Rivalries were set aside and the outpouring of support — fundraisers to help the family financially, adding her name to every church's prayer list, wearing her purple "Kennedy the Warrior" wristbands and T-shirts — was immediate and overwhelming.

"I would go visit the other schools in the county and have kids coming up to me asking how she was doing and saying 'Tell Kennedy we're praying for her and that we love her.' And they would raise their arm up to show me they were wearing one of her wristbands," Mark said. "You just don't see kids at South Pittsburg wearing purple. That doesn't ever happen. But those kids were wearing those colors because they wanted to support my baby. It wasn't because I was the superintendent, they just truly cared about her and wanted us to know they supported her.

"I've had my angry moments alone in a room or my car screaming and crying out to the good Lord. But little things like that did a lot to restore my faith. I will never be able to repay what this whole county did for Kennedy and our family."

Hundreds of students, teachers and community leaders from Jasper, South Pittsburg and Whitwell met and formed a human chain that spelled out "Marion County unites 4 Kennedy", with a plane flying overhead so a photographer could capture the moment and share the photo with her family.

Throughout the football season all three of the county's high schools painted her name or a cancer ribbon on their football field for each home game. Requests for strength and healing for Kennedy and her family were added to pre-game prayers in the locker rooms as well as the stands, and even some coaches and players wore the purple wristbands during games.

In a blue-collar area where toughness is the foundation for every aspect of daily life, it was a teenage girl who was demonstrating the courage, resolve and tenacity the football teams have long been admired for.

> *"Our life's journey is about the people who touch us. You beat cancer by how you live, why you live and in the manner in which you live. So live. Fight like hell. And when you get too tired to fight, then lay down and rest and let someone else fight for you."*
>
> — **Former ESPN anchor Stuart Scott during his 2014 Jimmy V Award speech**

Kennedy underwent 40 weeks of chemotherapy to shrink the tumor, enduring each wretched side effect — hair loss, vomiting, weight loss, mouth sores and exhaustion — with an absolute belief that she could overcome it all with a positive outlook.

"Every drop of chemo that went into her body, I was there," said Pam, who had taken a leave of absence from work to remain at Kennedy's side. "We would check in for blood work and to hydrate and then they gave her the highest dosage a human can take.

"It was any parent's worst nightmare. But through it all, Kennedy would make the best of it. Whether it was gossiping with nurses about their relationships or grabbing a video game controller and beating every challenger in Mario Kart and Call of Duty she wasn't going to just lay there and take it. She made friends and tried to be a light to everybody around her."

There were even times when her fierce competition with the disease brought out a uniquely warped sense of humor. As she was being prepared for the operation that would replace her cancerous femur with a cadaver bone, Kennedy watched as the national news reported details of

Michael Jackson's death and joked that she would be receiving the King of Pop's femur and that once she had recovered she would even moonwalk to prove it.

For the next seven months Kennedy worked through extensive rehab and with each clean scan was told it appeared she was in remission.

Pam Griffith met Marion star player Blake Zeman after a game to thank him for his tribute to her daughter.

But when the excruciating pain in her leg returned, Kennedy was taken back to Vanderbilt where doctors determined the cancer had returned and this time was so aggressive that it had spread from her kneecap to her shin and was even moving upward to attack the transplanted bone in her upper leg.

Another agonizing round of chemo was ordered and this time would be followed by the heartbreaking reality that her leg would be amputated.

"Typical Kennedy, she named the little stump that was left 'Bob' and she would try to joke about it," Pam said. "But she really struggled with having her leg taken. They amputated it as high up as they could just to try and be sure they got all of the cancer.

"We were told if it came back it would come back in her lungs."

Once again Kennedy adjusted to her new life and for several months the tests showed no sign of the disease returning.

Driving along I-24 to T.C. Thompson's for another scan, Pam asked Kennedy if she had one wish would it be to not have cancer?

Kennedy thought about the months of chemo, the sickness and pain and replied, "Mom, cancer has taken so much from me, but I'd rather have cancer than watch someone else have to go through it."

An unbeatable opponent

The phone rang as Pam was preparing food for a Fourth of July family cookout. Nearly a year had passed since Kennedy's leg had been amputated and she was excited that not only had she been accepted into Chattanooga's Baylor School but had earned a scholarship to begin attending the prestigious private school in the fall.

But when she answered the call and heard Kennedy's oncologist say there was something from the most recent scan that needed to be discussed, Pam had just one request.

"If it's bad news, please wait until tomorrow to tell me," she said.

After a short pause the doctor replied, "Call me tomorrow."

"I knew right then that the cancer was back and was in her lungs," Pam said. "She got to start school at Baylor and there will never be a student more proud to walk on that campus than her. But she was getting sicker and after doing some research, eventually we decided to fly her to MD Anderson Cancer Center in Houston."

The family was now hoping, against all odds, for a miracle.

Initially her new specialists believed that by removing half of her left lung, they could prolong her life. But after yet another surgery to have more of herself taken away, the conversation between Kennedy and her doctors eventually changed to discussions about quality of life for her.

"I remember every few days you'd hear she was getting better, then more news would come that said she took a turn for the worst," South Pittsburg coach Vic Grider said. "All I could think about was what that family was going through. Every time they would get a glimmer of hope something bad would happen and it would just break your heart for them."

Coming home

In October of 2012, just after her 16th birthday, doctors in Houston broke the news to the family that there was nothing more they could do for Kennedy.

There would be no more hoping for a miracle.

"Her comment was she was tired and wanted to spend whatever time she had left at home," Mark said. "So we came home. We flew into Nashville and started the drive home on I-24. There were people, mostly kids from other schools, standing and waving on every single overpass along the way. When we got to Monteagle Mountain we picked up a police escort with lights flashing and there was also a motorcycle club with dozens of riders who met us and rode with us all the way home.

Marion all-state running back Blake Zeman wore #1 in honor of Kennedy Griffith.

"As we got off the interstate, the road from South Pittsburg to Jasper was lined with people waving and holding signs that said 'Welcome home Kennedy!'"

Peering out of her passenger's window, Kennedy smiled and said, "It feels like I'm a celebrity."

"We knew this was the last time we were coming home with her," Mark added. "Everyone in the family just wanted to appreciate every opportunity to spend with her. Every moment was a memory we were making."

Book of Life

Just before she had returned home from Houston, Kennedy was given a binder with a spiral notepad she used as her journal and to write poems about her feelings and experiences. She called it her "Book of Life" and each entry reflected her unfiltered personality, ranging from honest fear and anxiety to sharp sarcasm.

In July she began a three-month succession of emotionally honest entries.

"I'm so scared," she began. "I'm screaming inside for someone to help me but I won't give up until they make me. If cancer wants to play dirty, I will too.

"They gave me months. I think I'm okay though. It's a weird feeling knowing it'll be over soon.

"Right now, mom, Kolbe and I are actually planning my funeral while watching TV and eating pizza. This is totally what a normal family does.

"I'm glad God gave me the opportunity to touch people around me.

"I'm no longer scared of dying. I'm no longer afraid of cancer. It may kill my earthly body, but God has my soul.

"I hope everyone knows I'm okay when I leave. I want them to think of it as departing, not dying. Like a little vacation.

"I wonder how beautiful heaven will be. I wish I could see it without dying."

She also sketched a picture of an angel with head bowed and chains around both wrists.

"That's how cancer makes me feel," she said.

On the morning of December 18, after the rest of the family had said their goodbyes, Mark and Pam stood on either side of Kennedy's bed holding her hands. They kissed their daughter's cheek and Mark whispered in her ear, "It's ok to go, baby."

"Sometime after that she took her last breath," Mark recalled. "My only request was to have just one more Christmas with her, but that was just selfish on my part.

"She had picked out the place where she wanted to be buried, under a tree with a light on at all times because she didn't like the dark. That's where I start my mornings, a cup of coffee and just me and her having a conversation. I know it's just a gravesite, but there's a sense of comfort there that I don't get anywhere else."

Tributes for the Ultimate Warrior

It was during his breakout sophomore season that Blake Zeman got an idea. When Marion County hosted county rival Whitwell in the third game of the 2012 season, Kennedy had been asked to be in charge of the pre-game coin toss.

She was wheeled to the 50-yard line wearing a purple jersey with a white No. 1 and an ear-to-ear grin.

"She had met some players from the Houston Texans while we were in the hospital there and had even been to the White House for a visit, but I don't know that anything tickled her more than getting to flip the coin before one of Marion's games," Pam said. "She loved the Warriors and knew what a big deal their games are around here."

A couple of weeks later, after hearing the news that Kennedy's condition had worsened, Zeman switched from wearing No. 20 to No. 1 in her honor. The burly 5-foot-9, 225-pound fullback ran for a school-record 337 yards and four touchdowns against Lookout Valley that night.

"Looking down and seeing the number, I would think about her and how lucky we are to be there at that moment," Zeman said. "She had such a positive attitude, no matter what she was facing. Kennedy was the type of person to talk to everybody, to be friends with everyone. She always made everybody around her happy because she had such a great personality.

"I'll always remember how hard she fought until her last breath. She was a very tough person."

The following season, after Kennedy had passed away, Zeman switched to wearing No. 1 for good in memory of his friend and classmate. That fall he led the Chattanooga area in rushing yards (more than 1,800) and tackles in becoming a Mr. Football finalist.

"Everybody was telling me I needed to go see this kid play because he was honoring Kennedy by wearing her jersey number," Pam recalled. "I went to a game and when I saw him run I thought to myself he plays with the same fighting spirit that Kennedy had. Every time he carried the ball he was fighting for every yard, trying not to go down.

"I met him after the game because I wanted to thank him. The first thing he did was hug me and then raise his arm to show me he was still wearing one of her purple wristbands."

When Zeman was given a Player of the Week plaque by WRCB after running for more than 300 yards against Sequatchie County, he presented it to Pam.

"I told him to keep it because he had earned it, but he said it would mean more to him for me to have it," Pam said. "I still have it on my mantle and any time I look at it I always remember what a special young man Blake is.

Kennedy was excited to get to conduct the pregame coin toss at a Marion game.

"There were so many lives that Kennedy touched and so many examples of kids in this area who just wanted to let us know what an inspiration she was. Those are things that still mean so much to us."

Months after she passed away, a group of South Pittsburg students decided the money they had raised for a class trip would be used instead to honor Kennedy's memory. Just outside the school cafeteria a memorial garden was created, including a large stone bench with the engraved message:

"Kennedy Elizabeth Griffith

"The Warrior

"Her strength in the face of adversity touched the hearts of SPHS."

"It wasn't only her toughness, but her overall attitude that exemplified how our communities are about competition," former South Pittsburg principal Danny Wilson said. "She showed that through her resilience. She even said at one time 'that's just how we're raised around here'.

"All of our kids that knew her loved her. It was important to them that they pay respect to her memory."

"And now these three remain: faith, hope and love. But the greatest of these is love."

— I Corinthians 13:13

Three letters. Handwritten and wise beyond her 16 years. At the time she wrote them Kennedy had already accepted her fate, but was inspired by her faith to pen three personal letters to family members, each flowing with the individual characteristics of her favorite Bible verse: I Corinthians 13:13, "And now these three remain – faith, hope and love. But the greatest of these is love."

"She made a list of all the people she wanted to write a letter to and express how she felt about them," Pam explained. "But over the last year of her life she only wrote three and she told me later that was because she could only write them when she felt inspired by God."

FAITH

The first letter she wrote was to her older brother Tyler, Pam's son from her first marriage. At the time Kennedy was initially diagnosed Tyler, who was then in his early 20s, was battling a drug addiction.

In the later stages of her disease, Kennedy had asked to see her brother. She closed her bedroom door and lectured him sternly from the heart.

"Look at me. I have one leg and one lung and I'm fighting tooth and nail just to live. You're trying to kill yourself and I'm fighting to live.

"Get up off your ass and go straighten up and live."

Kennedy's words made such an impact that Tyler left the house and immediately began getting the help he needed to change his life.

When she wrote her first letter, Kennedy spoke in terms of the faith she had that Tyler could now become a rock for the rest of the family.

"While I am gone I want you to take care of the family. Take care of mom, she needs all the help she can get. One day she told me that I was the reason you got clean. I hold that as one reason I'm happy I got sick. Now I expect you to continue like this, clean and happy. Please. I love you so much and I'm sorry I have to leave."

HOPE

During one of her late-night conversations with her mother, Kennedy explained that her cousin, Brent Layne, would soon get married and have a son. Brent had told her that if he ever had a son he would name him Cru after a character from one of his favorite movies.

"I've been talking to God and Brent's going to have a son so I need to write the baby a letter," Kennedy told Pam.

"Nothing represents hope more than a baby," Pam said. "And Kennedy was certain that Brent was going to have a son and she needed to introduce herself to the baby."

A year and a half after Kennedy had past away, Brent and his wife welcomed a son into the family. Pam gave Brent an envelope marked in Kennedy's handwriting "Do not open until baby is born".

South Pittsburg students paid tribute to Kennedy Griffith with a memorial bench outside the school.

The date at the top of the page — July 16, 2011 — told everyone in the room that Kennedy had written her message exactly two years prior to the day of Cru's birth. In it, she promised the baby that she was leaving so that she could be his guardian angel.

"Dear Cru,

"I'm writing this from a long, long time ago, way before your mom had you in her tummy. I know who you are because of your dad. My name is Kennedy and I am your cousin. You see, I'm not with you right now because I went to heaven before you were born. But as an angel, I'm watching over you. Promise. I love you little Cru."

LOVE

The third letter was written to her grandmother, Toni Griffith. In it Kennedy used the word "love" five times in three paragraphs.

"Dear Granny,

"First off, thank you for being the most loving Grandmother I know. I love you very much for that. I love when you would hug me real tight. That always made me feel safe. Don't worry, Jesus will help me get up there. Don't be sad. Take care of mommy and daddy and keep them on track.

"Granny, I love you so much I can't put it into words. You know that feeling you get when you hug me, that is my love for you.

"See you at the Gates,

Your granddaughter."

"You can't tell me God's hand wasn't in those letters," Pam said. "All children are children of God. He put Kennedy on loan to us for 16 years before He needed her back so I don't look at the cancer years, I look at the good times we experienced with her.

"God let us have this amazing child in our lives and I got to be her mama. I couldn't praise God more for that."

Chapter 27

THAT BROCKMAN GUY

"It's always funnier when it happens to somebody else."

— Kent Brockman, *The Simpsons*

In the mid 1990s I was asked to compile the sports pages for The South Pittsburg Hustler and later the Jasper Journal, the newspapers for my hometown area. Because they are small, weekly editions, the writing was basically just summaries of each week's results of the three county schools throughout the school year. It was a fairly easy way to make some extra cash each month but before I agreed I first had to get permission from my boss at the time at the Chattanooga News-Free Press, Roy Exum. Knowing those sections were not competing against the large daily paper I worked for, Roy gave me the go-ahead but with one request.

"Don't use your own name," he advised. "Make up a pen name so there's no confusion and so you don't get in trouble here."

At the time The Simpsons was one of the most popular shows on television, and one of the minor characters was a glib newsman named Kent Brockman. Bang! I had my pen name.

So for about three years I covered sports for both The Hustler and Journal as Kent Brockman.

About a year into writing about local sports under my pseudo identity, only a handful of folks around town seemed to know who the new sports writer covering their local teams was. One night I was approached at halftime of a South Pittsburg football game by the mother of one of the players, who wanted to thank me.

"I just want to tell you how much we appreciate you covering the team for the Chattanooga paper," the lady gushed. "At least you're here for our big games. We never even see that Brockman guy. I don't think he's even from around here because we were talking in the stands and nobody has ever heard of his family."

I smiled politely and said, "Yes ma'am, I've heard he's a real smart aleck, too. If you think y'all don't like him, you should hear what the people in Jasper say about him."

Series History

MARION COUNTY WINS

Year	Score		Year	Score
1925	9-0		1989	25-0
1925	3-0		1990	32-14
1927	13-6		1991	36-13
1928	21-7		1992	14-7
1929	18-6		1993	21-6
1930	12-0		1994	6-0
1931	6-0		1995	34-13
1932	14-0		1997	32-20
1939	19-6		2000	21-7
1940	7-0		2001	25-0
1944	12-0		2004	27-22
1955	42-19		2005	13-12
1959	20-6		2014	48-6
1960	6-0		2015	62-21
1966	7-6			
1968	18-17			

SOUTH PITTSBURG WINS

Year	Score
1924	27-0
1924	19-0
1926	14-0
1933	13-0
1934	32-0
1935	40-0
1936	20-0
1937	12-2
1941	21-0
1942	39-0

Year	Score
1973	7-3
1978	16-0
1979	10-7
1980	7-6
1981	14-7
1982	26-14
1983	49-8
1984	17-10
1985	35-21
1988	34-0

Year	Score		Year	Score
1943	19-0		1999	24-14
1943	13-12		2002	27-20
1946	14-0		2003	56-12
1949	24-13		2006	48-0
1950	13-12		2007	47-19
1951	14-7		2008	48-13
1952	27-6		2009	20-8
1953	69-0		2010	64-0
1956	6-0		2011	46-0
1958	27-6		2012	49-21
1962	12-0		2013	35-17
1963	39-20		2016	24-17
1964	14-7		2017	56-18
1965	28-9			
1967	13-7			
1969	28-22			
1970	40-20			
1971	12-0			
1974	13-7			
1975	12-0			
1976	35-0			
1977	12-7			
1986	14-13			
1987	21-14			
1996	12-0			
1998	49-0			

TIES

Year	Score
1938	7-7
1957	0-0
1961	0-0
1972	0-0

DID NOT PLAY

1945 (because of WWII)
1947, 1948 (South Pittsburg under TSSAA suspension)
1954 fear of violence from 1953 game

Team, Individual Honors

ALL-STATE PLAYERS

South Pittsburg Pirates

Rusty Adcock (1963)
David Hale (1972)
Dewayne Cobb (1974)
Sam Greer (1974)
Bobby Haden (1976)
Tim Moore (1977)
Mack Moore (1980)
David Goff (1985)
Johnny Sisco (1985)
Carl Lehr (1986)
David Wyatt (1986)
Tony Lollis (1987)
Chris Ferrell (1987)
Patrick Pitts (1989)
Clint Smith (1990)
Kevin Mitchell (1993)
Vincent Banks (1994)
Jarrod Cardin (1994)
Daniel Berryhill (1994, 95)
Corey Tipton (1995)
Bradley "Macho" Green (1995)
Roger Dale Mayfield (1996)
Kevin Case (1996)
Eddie Moore (1997, 98)
Dan Merriman (1997)
Tim Starkey (1998, 99)
Sam Pickett (1998, 99)
Mike Jackson (1998, 99)
Aaron Chambers (1999)
Ronnie Griffith (1999)
Jonathan Haskew (1999)
A.J. Jones (2002)
Ben Blevins (2002, 03)
Cody Walker (2003)
Ron Cook (2003)
Josh Echegaray (2003)
Alan Malone (2005)
Antonio Robinson (2005)
Dominique Garrett (2007)
David Jones (2007, 08)
Cody Robinson (2007)
Robert Robinson (2006, 07)
Tony Roden (2007)
Rashawn Weatherspoon (2007)
Trevor Barnes (2008)

Montrell Mitchell (2008)
Tyler Griffith (2009)
Jiajuan Fennell (2009)
Raquis Hale (2009, 10)
Terrell Robinson (2009)
Malcolm Jones (2009)
Jakoby Reynolds (2010)
Coltin Blevins (2011)
Cody Branham (2011)
Antonio Chubb (2011)
Jajuan Lankford (2011, 13)
D.J. Roberson (2011)
Demetric Johnson (2012)
Corbin Hale (2012)
Jake Stone (2012)
Ricky Fehr (2013)
Khalil Mitchell (2013)
Payne Mosley (2013)
Chase Blevins (2015)
Mitch Butner (2016)
Cade Kennemore (2016)
Sawyer Kelley (2016, 17)
Hayden Branham (2017)
Garrett Raulston (2017)

MR. FOOTBALL AWARD WINNERS

Aaron Chambers (1999 Class 1A Lineman of the Year)
David Jones (2008 Class 1A Back of the Year)
Terrell Robinson (2009 Class 1A Back of the Year)
Coltin Blevins (2011 Class 1A Lineman of the Year)
Jajuan Lankford (2013 Class 1A Back of the Year)

MR. FOOTBALL AWARD FINALISTS

Garrett Raulston (2017)
Jajuan Lankford (2011)
Robert Robinson (2007)
Alan Malone (2005)
Tim Starkey (1999)
Eddie Moore (1998)
Dan Merriman (1998)
Kevin Case (1996)
Daniel Berryhill (1995)
Corey Tipton (1995)
Vincent Banks (1994)

State championships: 1969, 1994, 1999, 2007, 2010
State runners-up: 1974, 1985, 1986, 2009, 2011, 2013

TSSAA HALL OF FAME MEMBERS:

Sam Brooks (2009)
Don Grider (2010)

CHATTANOOGA SPORTS HALL OF FAME:

Vic Grider (2018)

Marion County Warriors

ALL STATE PLAYERS

Joe Cash (1955)
Jimmy Daryl Quarles (1956)
Pat Morrison (1962)
Tommy Smith (1965)
Bill Baker (1965)
John David Martin (1967)
Eddie Brown (1969)
Bob Bible (1973)
Jim Fowler (1982)
Dale Solomon (1984)
Stephen Malsey (1984)
Jim Cheaves (1984)
Pumpy Tudors (1985, 86)
Keith Matthews (1985)
Patrick Carmody (1985)
Brian Barton (1989)
Reuben Prince (1990)
Brian Janeway (1990)
Rodney Rankin (1990)
Mark Moreland (1991)
Chip Lockhart (1991, 92)
Jamie Wells (1992)
Davey Graham (1993)
T.J. Gentle (1993)
David Donahue (1993)
Scott Stephens (1993)
Jamie Muir (1994)
Eric Westmoreland (1994, 95)
Anthony Martin (1995)
Matt Clark (1995)
Stephen Dover (1995, 96)
Derrick Springs (2002)
Joe Muir (2008)
Blake Zeman (2014)
Corey Tucker (2014)
Christian Stevens (2014)
Josh Henderson (2015)
Logan Campbell (2015, 16)
Alex Kirkendoll (2014, 15, 16)
Jacob Saylors (2015, 16, 17)
Hunter McClain (2016)
Hunter Zeman (2016)
Ismael Avila (2016)

MR. FOOTBALL AWARD WINNERS:

Jason Muir (Class 3A 1994 Lineman of the Year)
Eric Westmoreland (1995 Class 3A Back of the Year)
Alex Kirkendoll (2016 Class 2A Lineman of the Year)

MR. FOOTBALL AWARD FINALISTS:

Eric Westmoreland (1994)
Stephen Dover (1996)
Derrick Springs (2002)
Blake Zeman (2013, 2014)
Alex Kirkendoll (2015)
Josh Henderson (2015)
Hunter McClain (2016)
Jacob Saylors (2017)
State championships: 1990, 1992, 1994, 1995
State runners-up: 1982, 1984, 2014, 2015, 2016

TSSAA HALL OF FAME MEMBERS:

Bill Baxter (2002)
Johnny Grimes (2013)
Ken Colquette (2014)

TENNESSEE SPORTS HALL OF FAME:

Eddie Brown (2002)

CHATTANOOGA SPORTS HALL OF FAME:

Ken Colquette (2018)

About the Author

Having seen every game in the series since the mid-1970s—first as a student at South Pittsburg, then as a Chattanooga sports writer beginning in 1990—Stephen Hargis brings a unique perspective to Tennessee's most quarrelsome prep football rivalry.

Having covered all but one of the nine state championship seasons by the two programs, Stephen brings each of those title runs to life with a mixture of history and humor. He takes you right into the locker rooms as coaches prepare for each big game, and onto the sidelines to hear the trash-talking between players.

Stephen brings to life the ultra-competitive characters on both sides as he weaves the heartfelt personal stories of coaches, players, and supporters from the community who give the colorful rivalry so much of its energy.

Fresh Ink Group
Independent Publisher

☙

Hardcovers
Softcovers
All Ebook Platforms
Worldwide Distribution

☙

Indie Author Services
Book Development, Editing, Proofing
Graphic/Cover Design
Video/Trailer Production
Website Creation
Social Media Management
Writing Contests
Writers' Blogs
Podcasts

☙

Authors
Editors
Artists
Experts
Professionals

☙

FreshInkGroup.com
Email: info@FreshInkGroup.com
Twitter: @FreshInkGroup
Google+: Fresh Ink Group
Facebook.com/FreshInkGroup
LinkedIn: Fresh Ink Group

Another Great Fresh Ink Group Book

www.ingramcontent.com/pod-product-compliance
Lightning Source LLC
Chambersburg PA
CBHW060932230426

43665CB00015B/1919